SIR WILLIAM GILBERT.

GILBERT AND SULLIVAN

AND THEIR OPERAS

WITH RECOLLECTIONS AND ANECDOTES OF
D'OYLY CARTE & OTHER FAMOUS SAVOYARDS

BY

FRANÇOIS CELLIER &
CUNNINGHAM BRIDGEMAN

WITH 63 PORTRAIT AND OTHER ILLUSTRATIONS
AND 6 FACSIMILE LETTERS

BOSTON
LITTLE, BROWN AND COMPANY
1914

Printed in Great Britain

EDITORIAL PREFACE

EVERY man's mind is a museum, the storehouse of precious memories. Treasures of gold and silver, and some, may be, of baser metal, with here and there a souvenir of sorrow, graven as it were in jet, lie hidden there.

All serve as landmarks of life's journeyings, all bear witness to the vicissitudes of fortune.

Generally it is a private collection. The museum is open to the public neither on week-days nor Sundays. Its contents are of no value or interest whatever to any but the custodian himself, and, perhaps, a few bosom friends associated with him in those silent memories. His old chums are ever pleased to wander at his side through the dim galleries of the past. Pausing before some particular treasure, they re-enact the life-scene which the relic, sere and yellow with age, recalls. And they are gratified.

It is only when one's mind is crowded with reminiscences of men and women and events that have helped to make contemporary history that he is tempted, either voluntarily or by request, to endeavour, as best he may, to catalogue and chronicle facts and incidents touching the lives of famous people and their works.

Only then may he be privileged to open his museum
to the world at large.

It is in such circumstances that the author of the
present volume, with some temerity, as he confesses,
ventures upon the task to which he has been invited.
Adequately to tell the story of " The Savoy " might
tax the skill of pen more expert than his, whose hand
has been trained to wield the conductor's bâton or
whose quill has usually been called into requisition for
the simpler purpose of notating crochets and quavers.
And so, in undertaking that which is to him a labour
of love, the historian would ask indulgent readers not
to look for *literature* in his book, but simply a faithful,
unpretentious record of facts and figures which will
speak for themselves far more eloquently than lies
within his power as recorder.   Many a delightful quip
and merry jest, not borrowed like those of poor Jack
Point from the works of Hugh Ambrose, but of purely
local origin, although not included in the famous
Savoy Classics, have long since become public pro-
perty.   Nevertheless, the fond and faithful Savoyard
who, in the following pages, essays to relate his personal experiences hopes to bring forth from his private
store a few choice specimens of Gilbertian wit and
Sullivanesque humour that shall not be described by
the vulgar as " chestnuts."   But if, perchance, some
anecdote herein related has been told before, will it
not bear retelling ? Is not an excellent " chestnut "
refreshing fruit to all who love to listen to a good yarn
well spun ?

And thus our present author will seek to brighten

his own dull and unaccustomed efforts by echoing the mirthful sound of voices that have so often gladdened the world, but now—are still.

Whilst as *littérateur* he fears to fail, as *raconteur* he hopes to succeed.

Just one more prefatory appeal before our Musical Director starts his overture.

The act of committing to paper reminiscences so inestimably precious to himself must touch a tender chord in the soul of the narrator. Carried away by the bitter-sweet retrospect of thirty years' familiar intercourse with the founders of the Savoy—all now at rest—he may at intervals appear to express his thoughts in what his late friend, Sir William Gilbert, described as Heart-foam.

What then ? If his admiration, his affection for his departed leaders and colleagues blinds him at moments to a due sense of proportion, shall not such emotion he held excusable ?

It is out of the fulness of his heart his mouth will seem to speak.

CONTENTS

PART I

GILBERT AND SULLIVAN

CHAPTER I

INTRODUCTORY

CHAPTER| II

CHAPTER III

CHAPTER IV

CHAPTER V

CHAPTER VI

CHAPTER VII

CONTENTS

CHAPTER VIII

CHAPTER IX

CHAPTER X

CHAPTER XI

CHAPTER XII

CHAPTER XIII

CHAPTER XIV

CHAPTER XV

CHAPTER XVI

CONTENTS

PART II

GILBERT, SULLIVAN, D'OYLY CARTE, AND CELLIER

CHAPTER I

CHAPTER II

CHAPTER III

" THE MIKADO "

CHAPTER IV

CHAPTER V

" RUDDYGORE "

CONTENTS

CHAPTER VI

CHAPTER VII

CHAPTER VIII

CHAPTER IX

CHAPTER X

CHAPTER XI

CHAPTER XII

CHAPTER XIII

CHAPTER XIV

CHAPTER XV

" UTOPIA " (continued)

CHAPTER XVI

b

CHAPTER XVII

" THE BEAUTY STONE "

CHAPTER XVIII

CHAPTER XIX

CHAPTER XX

CHAPTER XXI

THE D'OYLY CARTE TOURING COMPANY

CHAPTER XXII

CONCERNING AMATEURS

CHAPTER XXIII

CHAPTER XXIV

*b**

CHAPTER XXV

CONCLUSION

LIST OF ILLUSTRATIONS

FACSIMILES OF LETTERS

PART I

GILBERT AND SULLIVAN

1

SIR ARTHUR SULLIVAN.

CHAPTER I

INTRODUCTORY

A Triangle—The virtue of three—The Three Musketeers and the Three Savoyards—Brotherhood of the Savoy—Mrs. D'Oyly Carte—Dedication of this book.

IT is a long time since I left school, and now all that I can dimly recollect of Euclid's Elements is that, after much vexation of spirit, they convinced me of the sublime virtues of a *Triangle*.

I will not go so far as to say that I am indebted to the famous Alexandrian Dry-as-dust, who flourished some centuries B.C., for my first introduction to musical instruments, but many a time when I have been seated in the conductor's chair a tinkling sound proceeding from the neighbourhood of the tympani has reminded me of Problem V., that fatal *Pons Asinorum* which I so painfully struggled to cross in the days of my youth.

How thankful I was to arrive at that Q.E.D.! I grieved then to think of the precious hours wasted over that unmelodious Triangle. How much more profitably, I thought, might those hours have been devoted to studying the bassoon or oboe. Once, in cynical mood, I thought of asking Sir Arthur Sullivan whether *he* had ever studied Euclid's Elements at the

3

Chapel Royal or Leipsic Conservatoire, and if he would tell me the concert pitch of an isosceles triangle ; but I refrained. I felt that it was not for me to attempt a jest within the presence-chamber of Gilbert, our Prince of Jesters.

But all such frivolous disquisition aside ; later experience of life has fully confirmed those ancient theorems which so vexed my boyish brain. I have learnt what endless power exists in the conjunction of any three units, be it of men or of sticks.

Perhaps it will be suggested that I should know something about *sticks*, seeing that one sort or another, either of ivory, bone, or painted pinewood (sometimes with an electric star at its point for conduct during dark scenes), has been my constant companion for the greater part of my life. But, for the purpose now in hand, let us hope to find no further occasion to allude to *sticks* of any kind whatever, either on or off the stage.

Laying aside the bâton for a while, let me now, with much temerity, take up the pen and try my 'prentice hand in offering to the public a few personal reminiscences of three famous men of our period : Three Savoyards.

Those of my readers who have made the acquaintance of another Trio renowned in history—to wit, The Three Musketeers—will endorse an argument I here venture to advance concerning those indomitable heroes of Dumas' soul-stirring romance. The argument is that, however brave, clever, and masterful Messieurs Athos, Porthos, and Aramis may have been individually, it was only the conjunction of forces that enabled them to triumph, as it were, super-humanly, over the strange vicissitudes of fortune through which they were for ever cutting their way.

It was because they were THREE—each one relying on, and essential to, the other twain—that these remarkable French *galants* outlived so many anxious chapters of their momentous history and eventually made the fortune of their publishers. But, whilst Dumas' heroes were mere men of fiction, the Three Savoyards whose story we have to tell were men who but a short while since lived and moved among us, won the world's applause and won its laurels.

And they were Englishmen.

Nevertheless, between Dumas' three quarrelsome musketeers and our brilliant triumvirate of peace a parallel may be drawn. Just as in the case of Athos and his comrades, so it was with our Savoyards, William Schwenk Gilbert, Arthur Seymour Sullivan, and Richard D'Oyly Carte ; each was gifted individually with genius that must have carried him to the front under any circumstances. If, however, their brilliant talents had never been combined, the history of the Savoy in its associations with London would have remained nothing more than a tradition of the ancient Chapel Royal which yet stands beside the Thames, sheltered and dwarfed now by the colossal hotel, erected on the site of the Palace of Peter, Duke of Savoy, and founded in the year 1881 mainly on the fortunes derived from the Gilbert and Sullivan operas.

Before bringing to a close this introductory pre-amble, I would respectfully beg the indulgence of my readers if, in the telling of my story, I am led to adopt what may seem to some a too familiar strain in speaking of my honoured and deeply lamented chiefs. Long and very happy years of uninterrupted inter-course with Sir William Gilbert, Sir Arthur Sullivan, and Mr. D'Oyly Carte established among us the intimacy of close friendship. Although in business relationship I was no more nor less to them than their humble and obedient servant, it becomes my just right and privilege to boast that not only in the ordinary social intervals of life, but also during the hours of duty in the theatre, our attitude, one towards the other, was that of brotherhood.

Further—and I am sure every individual man or woman whose good fortune and honour it has been to serve under the banner of the Savoy will endorse the statement—that every one, from Principal to Call-boy, engaged in the theatre was at all times treated by the management as a member of one family, and, with only such slight intermission as is common to every household, a very happy family we were.

.   .   .   .   .

Just a few more words by way of prologue—words indeed which, like the orthodox postscript of a lady's letter, may, perhaps, appear to embrace one of the most important points of this opening epistle.

Whilst in the present volume our main theme must be the lives and works of the author, composer, and manager of the Gilbert and Sullivan Opera Company,

Photo by Ellis & Walery.

MR. R. D'OYLY CARTE.

6]

it must not here remain unrecorded how in the heart of that great enterprise there existed, unseen, a *Dea ex machina*—one feels tempted rather to say, over the destinies of the Savoy there presided a kind, gentle, ever-watchful spirit in the form of a woman— a woman whose wisdom, tact, and energy did more to enhance the fortunes of the Savoy than the greater world can ever realize.

That woman was Mrs. D'Oyly Carte.

In the following pages that lady's cherished name may only intermittently appear, but it is confidently anticipated that the life-work of Helen Le Noir, wife of Richard D'Oyly Carte, may yet form the subject of a separate volume. Than that no prouder or more powerful testimonial to a true woman's worth could be given to the world.

It is only within the last twelve months that death released Mrs. Carte from the managerial post which she had filled so faithfully and with such extraordinary skill and ability since the loss of her husband in 1901.

Upon the tombs of my departed friends and colleagues of the Savoy I humbly lay this poor tribute of my deep affection and regard.

CHAPTER II

AN expert forester will tell the approximate age of an oak by its girth, the number of its branches, and other indications recognized by his craft ; but concerning the acorn from which sprang the tree, whether it had been wind-sown or planted in the forest by some feudal lord of a long-past century is beyond the art and ken of forestry to divine.

In like manner it may be acknowledged that we, whose lives have been closely associated with the upshoot of the combined genius of Gilbert, Sullivan, and D'Oyly Carte, can measure the circumference and number the branches of the mighty tree which beneath their able husbandry took root, grew, and spread until all other trees in England's lyric forest were dwarfed. But who can tell of a surety how and in what circumstances the seed was sown which was in later years to bring forth such endless crop of rich fruit ?

The question has often been put to me—a question which I have never been able with sufficient confidence or authority to answer: "Can you tell us by what accident or stroke of good fortune the three famous Savoyards were brought together?"

This remains a mere matter of surmise, open, at once, to assertion and contradiction. All that we are able to chronicle is as follows:

Some few years before our author joined forces with Arthur Sullivan, the name of W. S. Gilbert had become familiar to play-goers as the writer of certain burlesques and extravaganzas of that ultra-frivolous type popular in "the sixties." Among the best remembered of these ephemeral pieces was "Dulcamara," a burlesque produced at St. James's Theatre in 1866. In 1868 "Robert the Devil" and "La Vivandière" made successive appearance at the Gaiety. These burlesques brought Gilbert into the light of John Hollingshead's sacred lamp, which in those dull, unelectric days burned brightly within the Gaiety Theatre.

Then came a turn in the tide of Gilbert's ambition. In 1870 there commenced a series of new-fashioned plays invented by Gilbert and described by him as "Fairy Comedies."

It was in these masterpieces of piquant wit and mirthful satire that our author took a distinct departure from the threadbare methods of Victorian playwrights—methods which, it must be admitted, Gilbert himself followed in his embryo days. But now he took the magic reins of his remarkable ability firmly in hand, and drove his Pegasus by rapid strides along the road to Fame.

First of the Fairy Comedies came "The Princess" (founded on Tennyson's poem). This was produced at the Olympic Theatre in 1870.

It may here be recalled how "The Princess" was afterwards transformed by its author into the libretto of the Savoy opera "Princess Ida." November of the same year, 1870, witnessed the production of "The Palace of Truth" at the Haymarket Theatre.

In 1871 followed, on the same stage, "Pygmalion and Galatea," considered by some critics to be Gilbert's masterpiece of versed plays without music. Those who witnessed the original production will not have forgotten how Mrs. Kendal, then in the prime of life and fulness of her artistic power, charmed all hearts by her exquisitely winsome impersonation of the statue come to life, whilst her husband's Pygmalion was proclaimed all worthy of such a stately Galatea. Then, too, who shall ever forget J. C. Buckstone as the Art Critic ? The veteran comedian's very senility added point to his unctuous humour. The infirmities of age, including deafness, seemed admirably fitted to the part sustained. The Kendals' and Buckstone's characters in those Fairy Comedies at the Haymarket are, indeed, amongst the most notable in the long gallery of Gilbertian portraits.

Here one is tempted to linger amidst the delightful memories awakened by the passing mention of each famous play bequeathed to us by Sir William Gilbert. One would wish to be able to describe the sentiments that possessed the mind on witnessing the performance of "Sweethearts," a life-sketch as perfect as any the stage has ever given us. This miniature drama, which enjoyed a long run at the Prince of Wales Theatre, Tottenham Court Road, enriched the Gilbertian gallery with yet another famous pair of character portraits, the one that of Marie Wilton (now Lady Bancroft) as Jenny Northcott, the other that of Squire Bancroft as her devoted sweetheart, Harry Spreadbrow.

By the general non-theatrical public Gilbert's brilliant talents were first recognized through the publication in the pages of *Fun*, a weekly periodical, published by Tom Hood, of " Bab Ballads." These diverting conceits literally set the town roaring with laughter and established their author as a wit of the first water. As is well known, more than one of those quaint, topsy-turvy lyrics were afterwards adapted by their author as the foundation of his comic-opera libretti.

Arthur Sullivan, like his gifted confrère, had made a name in the world some time before he became associated with Gilbert. During his school-boy days at St. James's Chapel Royal—to be precise, it was in his thirteenth year, 1855—his first composition was accepted and published by Novello. This was a sacred song entitled, " O Israel." It was written during a holiday spent in Devonshire at the home of a school-chum and fellow-chorister.

As shown on its title-page, this embryo composition was " dedicated to Mrs. Bridgeman of Parkwood, Devon," the mother of Sullivan's school-fellow.

" O Israel," it must be admitted, gave but slight indication of the budding composer's latent genius. But it undoubtedly betrayed the extent to which

Sullivan, at the outset of his career, had become imbued with the spirit of Mendelssohn. Later and more ambitious works proved the young British composer to be a devoted worshipper and disciple of the great German master of melody.

It was whilst a " child " at St. James's Chapel Royal that Arthur Sullivan joined the Royal Academy of Music, and studied harmony and composition under John Goss—at that time organist of the Chapel Royal —and pianoforte under Sterndale Bennett and Arthur O'Leary.

In July 1856 the young student gained the Mendelssohn Scholarship, then for the first time awarded. One of the stipulations of the scholarship was that it should be available only to students of fourteen years and over. Sullivan had only then become eligible. It was a close race between Arthur Sullivan, the youngest, and Joseph Barnby, the oldest of the seventeen competitors for the coveted honour. It was, in fact, a " tie " between the youthful rivals; but, after the ordeal of further examination, Sullivan won the scholarship and was thus enabled to pursue his studies at the Academy under exceptional conditions.

Sullivan's remarkable triumph determined his father, who held the post of bandmaster of the Royal Military College at Sandhurst and a professorship at Kneller Hall, to send Arthur to complete his studies at the Leipsic Conservatoire. Accordingly in the autumn of 1856 he went to Leipsic. Whilst a student at the Conservatoire, Sullivan composed the work which was to establish his footing in the world of music. This was his brilliant orchestral accompaniment to Shakespeare's "Tempest."

The work was performed with great success at a Gewandhaus Concert in Leipsic, in the presence of the most noted Academicals and masters of music in Germany, who discovered in the author of this composition that which hitherto they had held to be inconceivable—an English musician.

With such a "send off" as that accorded him by the Teuton savants, Arthur Sullivan's future was assured. When performed for the first time in England at a Crystal Palace Concert on April 5th, 1862, "The Tempest" created a furore amongst the young composer's compatriots.

There have been, and probably there still remain, connoisseurs who rank Sullivan's "Tempest" music as his *magnum opus*. Be this as it may, it remained to the end of his days Sullivan's pet offspring, possibly because it was his first-born. Charles Dickens, after hearing the "Tempest" music, shook Sullivan's hand with an iron grip and said: "I don't pretend to know much about music, but I do know that I have been listening to a very great work."

Countless reviews, essays, and critical analyses have been from time to time devoted to the subject of Sullivan as a composer. Admirable sketches in outline of the life of our English *maestro* have been published at different periods from the able pens of Mr. Arthur Lawrence and Mr. B. W. Findon ; but it still remains to fill in the outline, a task which might well be undertaken by some writer of eminence.

And now a few words concerning the third of our distinguished Savoyards before the formation of the famous triumvirate.

D'Oyly Carte was the son of Richard Carte, partner in the well-known firm of Rudall and Carte, musical instrument makers of Charing Cross.

A pupil of University College School, Carte at an early age developed a love of music so intense that, at the outset of his career, he thought of adopting it as a profession. Wiser counsels prevailed. Notwithstanding that he possessed a pretty gift for the making of melodies, and had mastered the theories and intricacies of the art, he never seriously sat down to composition.

With that keen judgment and foresight which marked his character through life, he gauged the measure of his musical ability and found it wanting. He lacked the faith sufficient to move the mountains of difficulty which he knew to beset the path of aspiring British musicians. And so he abandoned all ambition to seek distinction in the executive ranks of music, and resolved to woo fortune by more commercial means, yet maintaining close alliance with the art he loved so well.

Thus, somewhere in the late "sixties," D'Oyly Carte started an operatic and concert agency with a small office in Craig's Court, Charing Cross.

It was in that office that his lucky star guided him to appoint as his secretary one who soon became not only an invaluable help-mate, but, as he was always glad to confess, an inspiring guide, philosopher, and

friend through the many vicissitudes of fortune and
momentous issues attending his profession. This was
Miss Cowper-Black, afterwards better known by the
assumed name of Lenoir. This talented lady, Helen
Lenoir, was destined in later days to become D'Oyly
Carte's devoted wife and ever-faithful partner for life.

It can hardly be doubted that Carte would have
made a big score off his own bat on any ground and
against any opposing team. He had set his mind
to it, and meant to carry out his bat. But it is certain
that the brilliant intellect, business acumen, and energy
of Helen Lenoir greatly aided in the making of the
remarkable runs that marked his managerial innings.

Immediate success attended the establishment of
the musical agency. To D'Oyly Carte was entrusted
the management of many important operatic, concert,
and lecture enterprises not only in the United Kingdom
but on the Continent and through the States of America.
The farewell tour of Mario, the great Italian tenor,
was entirely directed by Carte, and many another
brilliant Covent Garden star entrusted his or her
interests to the well-reputed Agency. Added to these,
such distinguished names as Matthew Arnold, Archibald Forbes, Ballantyne (the renowned Sergeant-at-
law of the Victorian era), and Oscar Wilde may be
found in the list of clients entered in the books of
D'Oyly Carte in his secluded bureau at the back of
Craig's Court.

And so it was that Richard D'Oyly Carte, going out
into the field of labour, put his hand to the plough and
never turned back.

It was at that period of his life to which we have been just alluding that Carte was appointed business manager to Kate Santley, at that time sole proprietor of the Royalty Theatre in Dean Street, Soho.

Then followed incidents which, directly or indirectly, pointed to the coming together—or, rather, the binding together—of Gilbert, Sullivan, and D'Oyly Carte.

In order to make this little moving history as consecutive as may be possible and desirable, it is necessary here to part company for a moment from D'Oyly Carte and turn to the subject of our author and composer's first collaborative work. This was a comic opera called " Thespis, or the Gods grown Old," produced by John Hollingshead at the Gaiety Theatre, on December 26th, 1871.

It is, perhaps, only by claiming a certain amount of author's licence. and indulging in a slight stretch of imagination that I am emboldened to include the production of " Thespis " in the category of my personal reminiscences. Yet do I retain a dim recollection of witnessing the piece and being impressed with the freshness and originality of Gilbert's libretto, especially as regards the lyrics, which were, indeed, a treat to read after the vapid, futile jingle of rhymes without reason which had hitherto passed muster in those degenerate days. To all play-goers it was a new " sensation " in musical plays. As for Arthur Sullivan's music, need I say how every number charmed and charmed again ? Little I dreamed in that day how it would be my happy lot a few years later to become closely associated with the work of the author and composer.

"Thespis," I can remember, was a very funny play, with very funny characters, admirably represented by such very funny and clever artists as Johnny Toole, J. G. Taylor, and Nellie Farren, the idol of her day. If I remember rightly, the famous Drury Lane panto-mimics, the Paynes, father and sons, were included in the cast.

But, as I have before confessed, my recollections of the piece are too dim to justify further personal comment on " Thespis " or its exponents.

I have, however, found much interest in perusing some of the critiques of that production and in com-paring the conditions then existing with those that, as I can bear witness, obtained in the Savoy productions by the same author and composer. For instance, let me quote one critic. He says :

" That the grotesque opera was sufficiently re-hearsed cannot be allowed, and to this cause must be ascribed the frequent waits, the dragging effect, and the indisposition to take up points which, recurring so frequently, marred the pleasant effect of Mr. Sulli-van's music and destroyed the pungency of Mr. Gil-bert's humour. . . . We anticipate that prodigious curtailment and further rehearsal will enable us to tell a different tale."

From such observations it is very obvious that Gilbert and Sullivan had not yet come into their own. How different—how astoundingly different is all this

2

from our own experience at the Savoy! As every one can testify, not even the profoundest cynic or hypercritic had occasion to find fault with a Gilbert and Sullivan opera, at least, on the score of unpreparedness. It may, indeed, be justly boasted that, under our author and composer's careful, astute, and determined supervision and control, rehearsals were brought to such a pitch of perfection, the opera so thoroughly cut and dried before offering to the public that seldom, if ever, was it found necessary to "call" the company for "more study" or for any revision of the work. But in 1871 Gilbert had not yet found his footing. Like every other playwright, before or after him, he had to pay for it. He was not permitted to usurp or interfere with the authority of "the producer." Hence the injustice meted out to the hapless author.

Judging further from the press notices, "Thespis" was by no means an unqualified success. We read that—

"The applause was fitful, the laughter scarcely spontaneous, and the curtain fell, not without signs of disapprobation." But the same critic adds : "Such a fate was certainly undeserved, and the verdict of last evening cannot be taken as final."

Then, again, the writer remarks :

"A story so pointed and happy, music so satisfactory and refined, a spectacle so beautiful and artists so clever, deserved a better reward than a curtain falling in silence and an absence of those familiar calls and greetings which are so pleasant."

Another critic endeavours to excuse the apathy of the audience by the fact that it was Boxing Night. It all sounds like damning with faint praise. It seems to show that not even the leading critics proved themselves true prophets and foreseers of what would result from the collaboration of Gilbert and Sullivan. Moreover, it is quite clear that play-goers had not yet been educated up to the standard of the new masters. Hitherto they had been given simpler food for their minds in the shape of rhymed burlesques spiced with soul-wracking puns which made the judicious weep, whilst the musical setting of the *lyrics* (save the mark !) was borrowed from the topical music-hall tunes of the day, with here and there a *bonne-bouche* from grand opera, such as the Soldiers' Chorus from " Faust," with tit-bits from " Trovatore," " Traviata," etc.

I have ventured to wander thus far beyond the special province of these personal reminiscences, thinking it may be interesting and instructive to my readers to compare the first night of " Thespis " (Gilbert and Sullivan's first conjoint work, be it remembered), as viewed through the lorgnettes of the reporters of that day, with those ever-memorable first nights at the Savoy.

It affords a welcome opportunity to recall the remarkable features of a Savoy *première*. The theatre packed from pit to gallery with an audience on the tenter-hooks of pleasurable anticipation. In mental vision we see again, flocking into the stalls, all the most distinguished personages of the day, men and women, famous, not only in theatrical and musical circles, but in the wider world of literature, science, art, law, and the stock exchange. The balcony and upper circles illuminated with stars of only a shade less lustre than those sparkling in the nearer firmament below. We seem to hear again the volley of cheers that greets the appearance of Sir Arthur Sullivan in the conductor's seat, the hush that comes with the first raising of his bâton, the tempest of delight that follows upon the final note of the overture. And then the house settles down in full assurance to enjoy the rich feast of mirth and melody prepared for them.

Then, as the play proceeds, we listen to the repeated chorus of laughter and applause interluded with moments of dense silence, strangely broken by a *frou-frou* rustle, a whish, as the vast audience, greedy to devour every morsel of our author's humour, turns over the pages of the book of words, and then, last of all, the curtain-fall, the loud, spontaneous call for author and composer, and, with them, the third of the trio of proud conquerors.

Not one syllable of a word of disapprobation mars the effect of the reception ; not a unit in that huge assembly worries about a train to catch—the real world is forgotten in the new and brilliantly fanciful regions where they have passed such happy hours. The only whisper of regret is that they have not had enough of such delicious, appetizing fare. Gladly would they remain to hear the opera right through again. And could any one who once spent a " first-night " with Gilbert and Sullivan ever forget the scene ?

As for my humble self, may I be pardoned if I refer to my own sensations on those momentous occasions? Let me confess I felt as nervous as though I were responsible for everything. It was, I suppose, through some natural affinity that the souls of the author and composer seemed to possess my unworthy body. My nerves strained at the proud burthen. But I was never for a moment anxious. For many a day past I had been assisting in the rehearsals: I knew the opera "by heart," and was confident that there could be only one verdict.

And yet, familiar as I had already become with the construction of the work now launching, when from some secluded nook in the auditorium I watched the performance from "the front," the opera was as fresh and delightful to me as it was to any member of the public, listening for the first time to Gilbert's latest masterpiece of wit and humour and Sullivan's newly cut gems of melody. I laughed—aye, and more—sometimes forgetting the unwritten law of managerial etiquette, I joined in the applause. Who could help it?

CHAPTER III

LET us now return to Mr. D'Oyly Carte.

In 1875 Miss Selina Dolaro, a favourite lyric actress
of that period, opened at the Royalty Theatre a season
of opéra-comique with Offenbach's "Perichole," a
light and frothy work which had proved a great success
in Paris. As a "curtain-raiser" a nonsensical hybrid
entertainment rejoicing in the tongue-torturing title
of Cryptochon—no—my memory fails to spell out the
monstrous name, as unpronounceable as any word in
the Welsh dictionary. This first piece did not prove
quite palatable to the gods, who liked to be played
in with more appetizing *hors d'œuvre*. And so Crypto
was taken off, and in its place, through the recommendation of D'Oyly Carte, who was still acting-
manager of the Royalty, "a new and original dramatic
cantata called 'Trial by Jury,' by Mr. Arthur Sullivan
and Mr. W. S. Gilbert," was put on. This, by the way,
was the only occasion I can recollect on which the
composer's name appeared in front of the author's on
the bill of the play.

It may be interesting to relate how "Trial by Jury"

came to be written. It occurred thus. One evening
Mr. Gilbert happened to visit the Royalty Theatre
where Mr. Carte, in course of conversation with him,
casually suggested that he should write a bright little
one-act trifle as a curtain-raiser and that Sullivan
should be invited to set it to music. Gilbert liked the
proposal, and before he left the theatre he told Carte
that an idea had just occurred to him. He proposed
to write something, the foundation of which should be
a breach of promise case, introducing judge, jury,
counsel, plaintiff and defendant, with all the characteristics of a court of law. The suggestion appealed
to Carte, and the result was, in less than a month the
piece was completed and put in rehearsal, and on
Thursday, March 25th, 1875, without the flourish of
even a tin trumpet, " Trial by Jury " was for the first
time presented to the public.

Expert play-goers who had witnessed " Thespis "
at the Gaiety some four years previously doubtless
expected something above the average of front pieces,
but they wondered in their minds what fun could possibly be extracted from such a dry subject as a British
law-court. Probably they came prepared to scoff.
Be this as it may, they remained to praise in no qualified
manner the little surprise packet of sweets prepared
for them by the newly established firm of bon-bon
purveyors, Messrs. Sullivan, Gilbert, and D'Oyly
Carte. Although the press notices that appeared were
far from what is sometimes vulgarly called " gushing,"
the record remains that " Trial by Jury " was received
with uproarious shouts of approbation.

The part of the learned judge, now recognized as an historic stage character, was "created" by the composer's brother, Fred Sullivan, who at once showed himself to be a singing actor of quaint and original humour. In fact, it may be asserted that none of the past masters of Gilbertian jurisprudence who have succeeded Fred Sullivan on the bench has given a more finished and humorous portrait of the love-smitten judge than that of poor Fred Sullivan. His premature death at the very threshold of fame was widely lamented, and by none so deeply as by his devoted brother, who, it may be remembered, composed his pathetic song, "Thou art passing hence, my brother," beside Fred's death-bed.

The original plaintiff was charming Nelly Bromley, an actress of great personal attraction and winsome manner which endeared her to the hearts of all play-goers. The defendant was admirably impersonated by Walter Fisher, the sweet-noted tenor who flourished for too brief a day and vanished into oblivion.

To the present generation the names I have mentioned above are possibly unknown, but to those who, like myself, recollect the production of "Trial by Jury," the leading members of the original cast are numbered amongst pleasant reminiscences.

But we must not omit here to mention how the foreman of the jury—not in the original panel, but only a short while later—was represented by Arthur Penley, who, although the part was a minor one, with never a line to speak or sing save in chorus, made a name for himself by the—shall we call it ?—*originality* of his facial expression and his quaint antics in the jury-box.

It should be recorded that it was D'Oyly Carte who discovered Penley. Where and how he picked him up matters not; it must suffice that Penley proved a pearl of great price, as all the theatre-going world knows.

Sullivan and Gilbert's "dramatic cantata," so unostentatiously brought to light in the little Soho theatre, is now a classic.

In the Savoy bills many a first piece has come, and, after a butterfly's existence of an hour, gone to the scrap-heap; but "Trial by Jury" is a perennial, an everlasting flower, blooming at all seasons and in all places. It remains the stock-piece played in front of the short operas of the D'Oyly Carte Répertoire Company on tour. I have failed to count the number of times I have personally conducted "Trial by Jury," but, if intermittent performances were included, the aggregate would represent an exceedingly lengthy, if not a record, run. Apart from the Savoy and the provincial tour, the popular Dramatic Cantata has formed the leading attraction of nearly every big "Benefit" performance during the past five-and-thirty years, or more.

The earliest, and one of the most notable instances, was that of the Benefit given at Drury Lane Theatre on Thursday morning, March 1st, 1877, in aid of a Testimonial Fund to the respected veteran comedian, Mr. Compton—father of the present well-known actor, Edward Compton, and the favourite actress, Mrs. R. Carton.

The Benefit was under the immediate patronage and presence of H.R.H. the Prince of Wales (afterwards Edward VII.). A programme, remarkable alike for its quantity and quality, was contributed to by all the leading actors and actresses of the day. Seldom, indeed, had such a brilliant galaxy of stars shed their light at the same moment upon any stage as those which irradiated "Trial by Jury."

Under the personal direction of the composer the popular Dramatic Cantata was deemed the *pièce de résistance* of the matinée. Lengthy is the list of distinguished artists whose names appeared in the programme, yet it may not be considered waste of space if I here record them, one and all, in the order given on the original bill of the play, thus :

THE DRAMATIC CANTATA BY ARTHUR SULLIVAN AND
W. S. GILBERT,

TRIAL BY JURY

The Learned Judge . .	MR. GEORGE HONEY
Counsel for the Plaintiff .	. MR. GEORGE FOX
The Defendant . . .	MR. W. H. CUMMINGS
Usher	MR. ARTHUR CECIL

The Jury, etc.—Messrs. Geo. Barrett, J. D. Beveridge, Edgar Bruce, A. Bishop, Furneaux Cook, H. Cox, F. G. Darrell Everill, J. Fernandez, W. H. Fisher, G. Grossmith, Junr., Hallam, F. W. Irish, H. Jackson, Kelleher, G. Loredan, J. Maclean, Marius, A. Matthison, A. Maltby, E. Murray, Howard Paul, H. Paulton, Penley, Harold Power, E. Rosenthal, Royce, J. D. Stoyle, J. Sydney, J. G. Taylor, W. Terriss, W. H. Vernon.

The Plaintiff . .	. MADAME PAULINE RITA

Bridesmaids.—Misses Carlotta Addison, Kate Bishop, Lucy Buckstone, Violet Cameron, Emily Cross, Ella Dietz, Camille Dubois, Kate Field, Emily Fowler, Maria Harris, Nelly Harris, Kathleen Irwin, Fanny Josephs, Fanny Leslie, Kate Phillips, Emma Rita, Rachel Sanger, Florence Terry, Marion Terry, Lottie Venne.

The Orchestra under the direction of MR. ARTHUR SULLIVAN.

Instrumentalists.—Messrs. Amor, Barrett, Betjemann, Boatwright, Brodelet, Buziau, Chipp, Colchester, Earnshaw, G. Lawrence, Gibson, Hann, Harper, Hutchins, Jakeway, Lazarus, Lebon, A. J. Levey, Markland, Matt, Morley, Neuzerling, H. Pheasant, Radcliffe, W. H. Reed, Howard Reynolds, Ellis Roberts, Scuderi, Shepherd, Snewing, Tull, Tyler, Wallace, and White.

Equally memorable, and, perhaps, yet more interesting to present day play-goers, was the great " Nellie Farren Benefit," which took place at Drury Lane Theatre on Thursday, March 17th, 1898, just twenty-one years later than the Compton Benefit.

Never in the annals of the stage was such a wonderful programme provided, such a vast host of talent gathered together as that which assembled at " old Drury " to do homage and pay tribute of affection and sympathy to their sister in distress, to Nellie Farren, the idol of her day, whose brilliant career had been brought to an untimely end by illness and suffering.

Once again did H.R.H. Edward, Prince of Wales, attest his personal interest in the dramatic profession by bestowing his gracious patronage on the benefit performance. But this is not the place to enlarge upon an event the manifold incidents and glories of which will never be forgotten by those who were present. It may, however, be of interest to recite the names of the distinguished artists who crowded into the most popular and unconventional of all courts of law, there to witness " Trial by Jury " from the Gilbertian point of view.

Accordingly let us here place on record an authentic list of the persons who took part in " Trial by Jury " at Nellie Farren's Benefit at Drury Lane, viz. :

The Learned Judge .	MR. RUTLAND BARRINGTON
The Defendant . .	MR. COURTICE POUNDS
Counsel for the Plaintiff . .	MR. ERIC LEWIS
Usher	MR. WALTER PASSMORE
The Associate . . .	MR. W. S. GILBERT
The Associate's Wife . .	LADY BANCROFT
The Plaintiff. . . .	MISS FLORENCE PERRY

(Miss Florence St. John was to have played "The Plaintiff," but, as she was taken seriously ill before the final rehearsal, Miss Florence Perry kindly took up the part at very short notice.)

Bridesmaids.—Miss Phyllis Broughton, Miss Louie Pounds, Miss Nellie Stewart, Miss Jessie Huddleston, Miss Aida Jenoure, Miss Ellis Jeffreys, Miss Sybil Carlisle, Miss Grace Palotte, Miss Violet Robinson, Miss Maud Hobson, Miss Ina Repton, Miss Kate Cutler, Miss Emmie Owen, Miss Maggie May, Miss Ruth Vincent, Miss Beatrice Ferrers.

Jurymen.—Mr. Harry Lytton (Foreman), Mr. Willie Edouin, Mr. Norman Salmond, Mr. John Coates, Mr. E. J. Lonnen, Mr. Richard Green, Mr. W. Louis Bradfield, Mr. Jones Hewson, Mr. W. H. Denny, Mr. W. H. Seymour, Mr. Mark Kinghorne, Mr. Colin Coop,

Mr. J. J. Dallas, Mr. William Elton, Mr. J. Furneaux Cook, Mr. Scott Russell, Mr. Herbert Standing, Mr. Arthur Roberts.

Counsel.—Mr. J. Comyns Carr, Mr. Haddon Chambers, Mr. Sydney Grundy, Mr. Lionel Monckton, Mr. Edward Rose.

Seats on the Bench occupied by Miss Ellen Terry, Miss Mary Moore, Miss Lydia Thompson, Mr. Charles Wyndham.

Seats by Counsel.—Miss Kate Santley, Miss Constance Loseby, Miss Marion Hood, Miss Rose Leclercq, Miss Kate Rorke, Mrs. Dion Boucicault, Miss Carlotta Addison, Miss Fanny Brough, Mdlle Cornelie D'Anka.

Crowd in Court.—Miss Compton, Miss Florence Young, Miss Helena D'Acre, Miss Rosina Brandram, Mrs. H. Leigh, Mrs. F. H. Macklin, Miss Kate Bishop, Miss Maria Davis, Miss Helen Ferrers, Miss Florence Gerrard, Miss Sarah Brooke, Miss Leonora Braham, Miss Irene Vanbrugh, Miss Evelyn Fitzgerald, Miss Beatrice Terry, Miss Nesbitt, Miss Lily Cellier, Miss Louie Henri, Miss Jessie Rose, Miss Daisy Gilpin, Miss Ethel Wilson, Miss Ada Newall, Miss Pattie Reimers, Miss Dorothy Dene, Miss Hetty Dene, Miss Mary C. Mackenzie, Miss Gertrude de Lacy, Miss Valerie de Lacy, Miss Margery Northcote, Miss Millicent Baker, Miss Laurie Ellston, Miss Marguerite Moyse, Miss Ethel Jackson, Miss Lily Twyman, Miss Annie Russell, Mr. Chas. J. Fulton, Mr. Gillie Farquhar, Mr. Nutcombe Gould, Mr. James Erskine, Mr. W. T. Lovell, Mr. Tim Riley, Mr. J. D. Beveridge, Mr. Chas. Sugden, Mr. Dion Boucicault, Mr. Cory James, Mr. Chas. Childerstone, Mr. Joseph Ruff, Mr. Charles Earldon, Mr. Cecil Castle, Mr. Avon Hastings, Mr. Iago Lewys, Mr. Dudley Jepps, Mr. Edwin Bryan, Mr. J. Ivimey, Mr. Leonard Russell.

Conductor .   .   .   . MR. FRANÇOIS CELLIER

Often I have had the honour to conduct an orchestra in the presence of a distinguished assembly upon whom I have been compelled, through the exigencies of my official post, to turn my back, but I may safely assert that never before nor since have I raised the bâton before such a brilliant array of talent and beauty as that which appeared at Nellie Farren's Benefit.

The performance of " Trial by Jury " on this occasion was under the personal direction of the author, who, it will be noted, appeared as " The Associate."

Gilbert, in wig and gown, seemed literally to revel in playing at law. He was delighted at the opportunity afforded him of pointing the keen darts of his satire, in full view of an audience, at the profession which he had adorned for a brief while before abandoning it for the more congenial calling of the stage.

And so, as we have seen, " Trial by Jury," described by one critic of the day as " an unpretentious trifle," and as such treated by the press scribes in general, has proved, comparatively in as great a measure as the more ambitious works of Gilbert and Sullivan, that our gifted author and composer were inspired to write " not for an age, but for all time."

CHAPTER IV

THE triumph of " the unpretentious trifle " was followed by results exceeding anything that its author and composer could have conceived.

The public rose to the new and very *taking* bait provided, and " packed houses " was the order of things at the Royalty Theatre from March to December 1875.

A musical play, absolutely pure and unadulterated English, not only by parentage, but as regards characterization and *mise-en-scène;* was something to rejoice at. Everybody was delighted. The most confirmed *ennuyé* could not fail to be exhilarated by Gilbert's pungent satire. His witticisms became household words. Sullivan's tuneful numbers were carried away to be murdered and mutilated in every drawing-room and every kitchen throughout the length and breadth of town from Bow to Belgravia. The more thoughtful began eagerly asking, " Why cannot we now have English Comic Opera ? With such able and witty librettists as F. C. Burnand, James Albery, and W. S. Gilbert ; with such masters of melody as Arthur Sullivan, Frederic Clay, and Alfred Cellier, to name only the best known, surely the time is come to take up arms against the invasion of French authors and composers, who have held us in subjection for too long a time."

Thus spoke the *cognoscenti* of the musical and dramatic world. But the suggestion was by no means a new and original one to Mr. D'Oyly Carte. The very same idea had been filtering through his mind ever since the production of " Thespis." Long had he been hatching plots for the establishment of English Opera, and the great success of " Trial by Jury" strengthened his resolution.

Eventually, in 1876,. on Carte's sole initiative, the Comedy Opera Company was formed, and to the promoter was entrusted the supreme management and control.

There can be no question that the new manager was counting upon Gilbert and Sullivan as prime factors in the enterprise. At the same time, it was not his intention to limit the répertoire of the Comedy Opera Company to the works of the author and composer of " Trial by Jury." Carte's scheme embraced, notably, those leading musical and dramatic lights whose names appear above.

Accordingly, F. C. Burnand and my brother Alfred were invited to prepare an opera with a view to production when occasion might arise. James Albery and Frederic Clay, whose operetta " Oriana " had been recently produced with success at the Globe Theatre, were also asked to submit an opera. However, as results proved, through one cause or another which it

MR. FRANÇOIS CELLIER.

is unnecessary here to explain, neither of these commissions was carried into effect.

For some time Carte could find no suitable theatre available, but at length he secured a lease of the Opera Comique. It was not the house he would have chosen for his venture, but it was Hobson's choice, and he made the best of it.

Old play-goers will not have forgotten the subterranean theatre that lay hidden away beneath Holywell and Wych Streets, those narrow, emaciated, grubby thoroughfares devoted then, as they had been for a century past, to bookworms.

The Auditorium of the Opera Comique was approached by a long tunnel opening from the Strand, at a point which it is not easy for the inexpert passer-by to-day to identify in that now truly rural-looking waste in Aldwych, the " bank whereon the wild thyme grows " as yet undisturbed by the ruthless builder of shops, hotels, and theatres.

Access to the stage was through a narrow, dingy doorway in Wych Street and thence direct by the straightest and steepest flight of stone stairs it was ever my task to climb. But I was a younger man in those days than I am now, and I should probably have forgotten so unimportant an item as a staircase but for an incident that nearly became tragedy, but fortunately ended in nothing more aggravating to the persons concerned than an action at law. To this incident we may have occasion to refer more particularly in a later chapter.

But whilst we have been here taxing the patience of

3

our readers by showing them over the birthplace of the Gilbert and Sullivan operas, our author and composer have completed and brought to Manager Carte an opera in two acts, entitled, " The Sorcerer."

On the recommendation of Mr. Carte, " The Sorcerer" was, as a matter of course, promptly accepted by the Board of Directors *nem. con.*

Not having been appointed to the executive staff until some time subsequently, I have no personal recollections of occurrences during the initial days of the Comedy Opera Company beyond fragments collected from time to time in the course of conversation with the renowned *Three* who had now banded themselves together to take the town by storm.

I have often listened with great interest whilst they have fought their early battles over again, and it may not be without interest to the younger generations of Savoy camp-followers to contemplate and compare the very different and more difficult conditions attending the preparation for production of " The Sorcerer " compared with those which obtained in connection with Gilbert and Sullivan's later creations.

In the first place, here was a lyric work of a type totally distinct from any the stage had hitherto produced. It was obvious that the lesson which both Gilbert and Sullivan had come to teach would not precisely suit the existing school of actors and singers. There would be too much to unlearn, too much new-fangled form of study to be graciously accepted by the proud and jealous supporters and apostles of ancient histrionic traditions. The Gilbertian methods appeared at once to be only adaptable to novices in the school of acting. Then also, from the musical point of view apart from all technical consideration of Sullivan's music, the composer's latest score was totally unlike that common to the stage at that or any previous period of musical history. It certainly was not suited to the attributes of Grand Opera singers of either the intensely melodramatic or the *colatura* class. To do adequate justice to the aim and intention of both composer and author, beyond all else distinct emphasis and phrasing, clear enunciation of every word, were absolutely essential, seeing that beneath every bar of music there lay concealed humour of such rich, rare, and refined quality as would prove beyond the understanding and ability of the past-masters of musical buffoonery. That they were clever and accomplished actors and singers of their kind none will deny, but they had become too saturated with the obsolescent spirit of Victorian burlesque and extravaganza ever to become capable exponents of a Gilbert and Sullivan opera.

It is very easy to engage and pay a handsome salary to a comedian to paint his nose red in order to make people laugh, and gain a reputation for himself, but to forbid the cleverest clown to decorate his nasal organ —that is where the fun goes out and poor clown finds his occupation gone.

No man, be he actor, singer, penny whistler, ice-cream merchant, or what not, is equal to two reputations.

Neither Gilbert, Sullivan, nor D'Oyly Carte wanted

their comedians to paint their noses red. The new triumvirate had brought about a revolution. They had devised other methods of convulsing the world with laughter. In short, here was a new school founded and to become established, and so, with these conditions staring them in the face, our manager with his author and composer set to work to *cast* "The Sorcerer." They knew exactly the stuff they wanted to make their new patent bricks of, and they commenced prospecting for the right quality of clay wherein to mould the quaint and original creations of "The Sorcerer."

The casting of parts in later operas was comparatively an easy task. Gilbert and Sullivan, having got together and trained to their standard the nucleus of a stage company, were afterwards able to build a part to the model they possessed, instead of, as in the first instance, having to search high and low for the right artist to embody the part designed.

CHAPTER V

To those unversed in the inner workings of the operatic stage it may sometimes be a subject of wonder how it is, when the selection of principal artists takes place, the author and composer do not find their personal views running counter. Such an undesirable situation may occasionally arise, but it is generally so when the collaborators have not learnt to know each other well enough to make it easy to dovetail their respective interests and requirements, each giving and taking for the sake of the *ensemble*.

But as regards Gilbert and Sullivan it may honestly be affirmed that, from first to last, throughout their long association, they seldom found occasion for any serious controversy concerning the suitability of an artist for the part to be assigned.

During the process of building, like wise architects, our author and composer held continued conference over every detail of the structure in hand. From basement to roof every Sullivanesque bar and every Gilbertian bolt was jointly tested and mutually approved, and then, they being of one and the same

refined artistic taste, the style of decorations was
found easy to decide upon. Sullivan, perhaps, held
some advantage as a judge of the requisite *matériel*.
He knew to what extent he could rely upon finding actors and actresses who could at once be
depended upon to speak the lines to the author's
satisfaction, and, at the same time, be able to sing
effectively and at least without actually murdering the
music—in short, be capable of satisfying librettist
and composer alike. Gilbert, on the other hand, confessed to some lurking dread of singers as actors—
especially so of tenors ; but then it was ever his boast
that he did not know a note of music, that he had not
the ear to distinguish " God save the King " from
" Rule Britannia." On this point, however, his
Savoy associates were inclined to accept this as half-
truth, seasoned with a considerable amount of Gilbertian sarcasm. Anyway, our unmusical genius, the
writer of lyrics that compelled melody, was often heard
during rehearsals humming to himself some of the
latest musical numbers. True, he generally jumbled
ballads, bravuras, and patter songs into a strange *pot-
pourri* wonderful to listen to, and in none of his render-
ings was he precise to Sullivan's original key ; nevertheless, it was not always impossible to identify the
tune or tunes intended, and certainly his efforts were
good enough to raise speculation as to the limit of
Gilbert's aural capacity.

This brief digression may, perhaps, help to throw
some light on the question how our author and composer were guided in the selection of their company.

Piloted, then, by D'Oyly Carte, Gilbert and Sullivan exploited other lyric seas beyond that of the "legitimate" stage. At that time there existed none of those excellent, well organized, and drilled Amateur Operatic Societies that now prevail and which have become useful training-schools for the profession. But there was the Royal Academy of Music, from which "voices" were obtainable, and there was strolling about the kingdom a small army of quasi-theatrical entertainers who had won reputations in town-halls, mechanics' institutes, and other such places as might aptly and without disrespect be styled chapels-of-ease to the theatres. It was amongst the ranks of that army that *The Three* made search and eventually enlisted George Grossmith, Mrs. Howard Paul, and Rutland Barrington to fill principal parts in "The Sorcerer."

For leading baritone they appointed Mr. Richard Temple, who had proved his quality as an actor and singer in English opera of the Balfe school. For the tenor rôle they engaged Mr. Bentham, until then known only as a concert singer. The chorus was selected mainly from students of the Royal Academy and from other private sources. It was with more than ordinary interest and curiosity that play-goers anticipated the production of "The Sorcerer," and accordingly, on the opening night, Saturday, November 17th, 1877, all musical London flocked to the Opera Comique. Every one was on the *qui vive* of expectation, but none present on the occasion entertained the idea that they were witnessing the laying of the foundation-stone of an art institution that would in time become the delight of countless hearers and spectators.

The following is the original cast of—

THE SORCERER

Sir Marmaduke Pointdextre . . MR. TEMPLE
  (*An Elderly Baronet*)
Alexis . . . . . . MR. BENTHAM
  (*Of the Grenadier Guards—his Son*)
Dr. Daly . . . . . MR. BARRINGTON
  (*Vicar of Ploverleigh*)
Notary . . . . . . MR. CLIFTON
John Wellington Wells . . MR. GROSSMITH
  (*Of J. W. Wells & Co., Family Sorcerers*)
Lady Sangazure . . . MRS. HOWARD PAUL
  (*A Lady of Ancient Lineage*)
Aline . . . . . . MISS ALICE MAY
  (*Her Daughter—betrothed to Alexis*)
Mrs. Partlet . . . . MISS EVERARD
  (*A Pew-opener*)
Constance . . . . MISS GIULIA WARWICK
  (*Her Daughter*)

Chorus of Villagers

Stage Manager . . . MR. CHARLES HARRIS
Musical Director . . . . MR. G. B. ALLEN

The Scenery by Mr. Beverley.
The Dresses by Mdme Auguste.
The Dances by Mr. D'Auban.

The libretto of " The Sorcerer " was founded on a story which Gilbert had, a year previously, contributed to the Christmas number of *The Graphic*. The story set forth how a benevolently disposed and domestic-

Photo by Elliott & Fry.

MR. GEORGE GROSSMITH.

Photo by Ellis & Walery.

MR. RUTLAND BARRINGTON.

40]

ally happy clergyman, convinced that in marriage lies the secret of human bliss, administered a love-potion to his entire parish with the utmost indiscriminateness. The results did not turn out as anticipated. Everybody became enamoured of the wrong person, and the moral was that the principle of " natural selection," though it may not work with desirable activity, is the safest in the end.

The leading idea of the plot—the love-philtre business—was by no means novel. It had done service again and again in song, story, and play. It was, therefore, a severe tax on the ingenuity of our author to put new life into such old bones. But Gilbert proved equal to the task. His complete mastery of the art of giving to the most incongruous ideas the semblance of reason, his dialogue, rich in droll conceits and keen but playful satire upon men and things, his admirably turned lyrics brimming over with humour and often reaching to heights of pure poetry—in short, Gilbert's quaint original cut of new cloth succeeded in fitting an old garment perfectly to the taste of his clients.

Even if it were within the province of this book, it would be somewhat late in the day to enter into any critical analysis of " The Sorcerer," either as regards the libretto or the music. Nevertheless, readers may like to learn something of what the press and public of the period thought of Gilbert and Sullivan's earlier works, and what promise they gave of things to follow.

A glance through the press notices shows that the only fault the critics could find with the book of " The

Sorcerer" was that indicated above—the staleness of the joke attached to the love elixir, and the ultra-supernatural incidents which, perhaps, tended to make the play difficult of digestion.

Regarding the music let me quote one expert writer :

"Coming to Mr. Sullivan's music, we do not approach, as in opera generally, the be-all and end-all of the work. The ordinary libretto is scarcely more than a peg on which the composer hangs this theme, but here the importance of the playwright is at least as great as that of the musician, which in strictness should ever be the case. None the less do Mr. Sullivan's songs and concerted pieces command attention as the product of a cultivated, musical mind, and it is gratifying to state that ' The Sorcerer' contains some of his best music. For the ballads we do not greatly care. They by no means come up to the composer's usual mark . . . but the musical charm of the opera lies in its concerted pieces—wherever, in point of fact, the composer had a dramatic incident or situation to illustrate."

Touching the acting and singing, the critics, without discovering " talent of the highest order anywhere on the stage," were yet generous enough in their praise to encourage the leading recruits of the new régime, and perfectly to justify the management in having placed their faith in new blood to give life to Gilbert and Sullivan's revolutionary creations.

The ultimate success of " The Sorcerer " may be judged by the fact that its run extended from November 17th, 1877, to May 22nd, 1878, comprising

175 performances—no slight achievement in those days.

" The Sorcerer," on its first production, was preceded by a one-act operetta, " Dora's Dream," written by Arthur Cecil and composed by Alfred Cellier. The characters were played by Miss Giulia Warwick and Mr. Richard Temple. This little piece was, on February 9th, 1878, superseded by "The Spectre Knight," a one-act opera, the libretto by James Albery and the music again by my brother Alfred, who had then succeeded Mr. G. B. Allen as Musical Director of the Opera Comique.

I trust I may be forgiven if, in parenthesis, I here note with pride that the overture to " The Spectre Knight " remains a living work, and, if I may be allowed to add, has proved worthy of the composer of the cantata " Gray's Elegy," and the operas "Dorothy," " Doris," " The Mountebanks," etc.

CHAPTER VI

To find a foundation for the libretto of the next opera to follow " The Sorcerer," Gilbert determined on plagiarizing from his own past work. That is to say, he turned to his " Bab Ballads."

Readers of those irresponsible yet immortal rhymes will not have forgotten—

> ". . . the worthy Captain Reece
> Commanding of the *Mantelpiece* "—

who was so devoted to his crew that there was no conceivable luxury he did not provide for their comfort ; for example :

> " A feather bed had every man,
> Warm slippers and hot-water can,
> Brown Windsor from the Captain's store,
> A valet, too, to every four."

It will be remembered how the Captain's coxswain, William Lee, " the nervous, shy, low-spoken man," made so bold as to suggest to his commanding officer that " it would be most friendly-like" if his (Captain Reece's) daughter, " ten female cousins and a niece, six sisters, and an aunt or two," might be united to the "unmarried members of the crew." Further, how the kind-hearted Captain, in order to oblige, consented to marry his faithful coxswain's widowed mother, who took in his washing.

Here, then, was a comic plot already cut and dried, with ready-made *dramatis personae*. All that remained to adapt the story to the stage was for our author to embody his eccentric characters, add one or two to their number, train them all to sing and dance, and make them the mouthpieces of his playful, up-to-date satire on sundry authorities and institutions of the day.

Gilbert began, then, by renaming the "Mantelpiece" "H.M.S. Pinafore." Captain Reece became Captain Corcoran; William Lee, coxswain, was promoted to the rank of boatswain's mate and given the name of Bill Bobstay; the widowed laundress was transformed into that "plump and pleasing person" to be known henceforth and famed throughout Christendom as "Little Buttercup," the Portsmouth bumboat woman, "the rosiest, the roundest, and the reddest beauty in all Spithead." But the ship's complement was not yet complete. There must be a sailor youth upon whom the conventional love interest should devolve; and so Ralph Rackstraw, a leading A.B., was duly appointed to that billet—whilst, as a foil to the handsome young hero, another able-bodied seaman, a veritable anomaly, was brought to light in the ugly, distorted form of Dick Deadeye, the one *bête noire* of the *Pinafore's* jovial crew.

But the most important addition that Gilbert made to his *dramatis personae* was the Right Hon. Sir Joseph Porter, K.C.B., First Lord of the Admiralty. To this distinguished personage were bequeathed " the sisters and cousins and aunts " who, in the " Bab Ballad," had belonged to Captain Reece.

Thus, by a wave of his magic wand, Gilbert transformed the stanzas of a humorous ballad into a still more excruciatingly funny opera-libretto. To set to music such a strange conglomeration of unreasonable ideas and unrecognizable individuals as those comprised in Gilbert's book was severely to test the ingenuity of any musician. Was it possible that the composer of such profoundly ambitious works as " The Tempest," " The Light of the World," and " The Prodigal Son " could descend from such lofty heights to the depths of flaring frivolity ?

The weird, supernatural atmosphere of " The Sorcerer " was not less calculated to afford inspiration to Sullivan than " Tristan and Iseult " to inspire Wagner, or " Elixir d'Amore " Donizetti.

There are no bounds to supernatural elements. The poet or the musician can give loose rein to his imagination as he rides through Ideal-land and none may call him " Halt ! " But the deck of H.M.S. *Pinafore*, if not governed strictly by the customary discipline of the British man-of-war and manned, as it came to be, by a caricature crew, nevertheless retained some semblance of real life, and so required musical setting in harmony with its environment. But Sullivan had already, notably in " Trial by Jury," proved himself a born humorist, fully capable of entering into the spirit and essence of his colleague's fun.

Such was his versatility that he was able to express in tone-words of equal eloquence the Soliloquy of Shakespeare's Prospero, the grunt of Caliban, the song of Captain Corcoran, or the patter of Sir Joseph Porter.

Moreover, Gilbert's "Pinafore" was essentially English, and Arthur Sullivan's natural tone was English to his last demisemiquaver.

Musical London had learnt all this. The British public now knew what they might reasonably expect from the collaboration of Gilbert and Sullivan. Thus it came to pass that on Saturday, May 25th, 1878, three days after the withdrawal of "The Sorcerer," the doors of the Opera Comique were besieged for many hours by eager play-goers, pushing and praying for seats or at least for standing-room.

One press critic, describing the opening night of " H.M.S. Pinafore," wrote thus :

"Seldom, indeed, have we been in the company of a more joyous audience, more confidently anticipating an evening's amusement than that which filled the Opera Comique in every corner. The expectation was fulfilled completely. Those who believed in the power of Mr. Gilbert to tickle the fancy with quaint suggestions and unexpected forms of humour were more than satisfied, and those who appreciated Mr. Arthur Sullivan's inexhaustible gift of melody were equally gratified. The result, therefore, was ' a hit, a palpable hit '—a success in fact, there could be no mistaking, and which, great as it was on Saturday, will be even more decided when the work has been played a few nights."

The reception accorded Arthur Sullivan on his appearing in the conductor's chair proved, more emphatically than ever before, in what high esteem the English musician was held by his compatriots.

With a view to the record of interesting and authentic data, it is proposed in this volume to republish the cast of each of the Gilbert and Sullivan operas in the chronological order of their production.

The following is the list of the original *dramatis personae* of—

H.M.S. PINAFORE, OR THE LASS THAT LOVED A SAILOR

The Rt. Hon. Sir Joseph Porter, K.C.B.
(*First Lord of the Admiralty*) MR. GEORGE GROSSMITH

Captain Corcoran . . MR. RUTLAND BARRINGTON
(*Commanding H.M.S. " Pinafore "*)

Ralph Rackstraw . . MR. GEORGE POWER
(*Able Seaman*)

Dick Deadeye . . . MR. RICHARD TEMPLE
(*Able Seaman*)

Bill Bobstay . . . . MR. F. CLIFTON
(*Boatswain's Mate*)

Bob Becket . . . . . . MR. DYMOTT
(*Carpenter's Mate*)

Josephine . . . . MISS EMMA HOWSON
(*The Captain's Daughter*)

Hebe . . . . . . MISS JESSIE BOND
(*Sir Joseph's First Cousin*)

Little Buttercup . . . MISS EVERARD
(*A Portsmouth Bumboat Woman*)

In the above company notable new-comers were Mr. (now Sir George) Power, Miss Emma Howson, an

Photo by Ellis & Walery.

MR. RICHARD TEMPLE.

Photo by Stereoscopic Co.

SIR GEORGE POWER.

48]

American soprano whose début was pronounced "a complete success," and Miss Jessie Bond, the delightful soubrette who afterwards became one of the most popular of Savoyards.

George Grossmith, Rutland Barrington, Richard Temple, and Miss Everard reappeared to add fresh laurels to those earned in "The Sorcerer."

Author and composer alike, having taken the measure of their respective capabilities and personal character-istics, had succeeded in fitting each performer to a part which was found to fit like a glove.

The perfect state of preparedness in which "H.M.S. Pinafore" was launched showed Gilbert to be the Master-absolute of stagecraft. From rise to fall of curtain, there was evidence that every situation and grouping, every entrance and exit, had been studied, directed, and drilled to the minutest point.

Gilbert was a clever draughtsman, as witness his delightful thumb-nail illustrations of "Bab Ballads" and "The Songs of a Savoyard"; and so he always designed his own stage-scenes. For the purpose of obtaining a perfectly correct model of a British man-of-war, he, accompanied by Arthur Sullivan, paid a visit to Portsmouth and went on board Nelson's famous old flag-ship, the *Victory*. There, by permis-sion of the naval authorities, he made sketches of every detail of the quarter-deck to the minutest ring, bolt, thole-pin, or halyard. From these sketches he was able to prepare a complete model of the *Pinafore's* deck. With the aid of this model, with varied, coloured blocks to represent principals and chorus, the author,

4

like an experienced general, worked out his plan of
campaign in the retirement of his studio, and so came
to the theatre ready prepared to marshal his company.

Gilbert was by no means a severe martinet, but he
was at all times an extremely strict man of business
in all stage matters. His word was law. He never
for a moment adopted the methods and language of
a bullying taskmaster. Whenever any member of
the company, principal or chorister, either through
carelessness, inattention, or density of intellect, failed
to satisfy him, he vented his displeasure with the keen
shaft of satire which, whilst wounding where it fell,
invariably had the effect of driving home and impress-
ing the intended lesson. It was, in fact, a gilded pill
that our physician administered to his patients, for
his bitterest sarcasm was always wrapped in such rich
humour as to take the nasty taste away.

As an instance of Gilbert's humorous instinct, let
me recall how, during a rehearsal of " Pinafore," when
the piece was revived at the Savoy, our author was
instructing the crew and the visiting sisters, cousins, and
aunts as to their grouping in twos. When they had
paired off one sailor was found with two girls. Gilbert,
impatient at what he thought was some irregularity,
shouted out, " No—no—go back—I said *Twos*."
They went back with the same result, simply because
one male chorister was absent from rehearsal. When,
accordingly, Gilbert discovered he had been too hasty,
he promptly turned the situation into a joke. Addressing the sailor with the two girls he said, " Ah, now I
see ; it is evident you have just come off a long voyage " ;

then, turning to our stage-manager, remarked that if the ship's crew remained incomplete the only thing to do was to employ a press-gang.

Most remarkable was Gilbert's faculty for inventing comic business. He would leave nothing to the initiative care of the comedians. Not only was a "gag" disallowed, being looked upon as profanation, but the slightest sign of clowning was promptly nipped in the bud, and the too daring actor was generally made to look foolish under the lash of the author's sarcasm.

At the same time, Gilbert was never above listening to, and sometimes adopting, a suggestion for some useful "bit of business" which any principal ventured to whisper to him.

This "strict service" method was observed, not only at rehearsal, but was religiously adhered to throughout the run of the piece. The stage-manager was always held responsible, and was required to report to head-quarters any member of the company violating the Gilbertian "articles of war." Most religiously did Mr. Richard Barker carry out his chief's orders. In evidence of the stage-manager's eagle-eyed watchfulness, Miss Julia Gwynne, who had not yet emerged from the chorus, tells a true story. During a performance of the "Pinafore" Barker called her up to him and said: "Gwynne, I saw you laughing!—what have you got to say?" "Really—Mr. Barker," replied Miss Gwynne, "I assure you—you must have been mistaken—I was not laughing—it was only my natural amiable expression that you saw." "Ye-es, I know that amiable expression!" Then, turning to the call-boy, Barker pronounced sentence thus: "Gwynne fined half-crown, for laughing!"

Such was the undeviating discipline that marked D'Oyly Carte's management throughout, and there can be no question that without it the sterling value of the Gilbert and Sullivan operas could never have been so thoroughly tested and proved as it was.

Whilst on the subject of rehearsals, it must not be supposed that an opera was presented to the public precisely in the state in which it was brought to the theatre from the desks of the author and the composer. Far from it. The main hull of the ship, so to speak, was made ready for the launch, but there yet remained the fitting and rigging to render it sea-worthy. Both libretto and music were subjected to scissors and spoke-shave until every rough edge had been removed.

When the opera was placed in rehearsal, after Gilbert had read his book to the assembled company, the teaching of the choral music was first taken in hand. This occupied many days, after which came the principal singers in concert with the chorus. The trial of the solo numbers followed later in order. Then, if any song appeared to the composer to miss fire, Sullivan would never hesitate to rewrite it, and in some instances an entirely new lyric was supplied by Gilbert.

The author invariably attended the music rehearsals, in order to make mental notes of the style and rhythm of the songs and concerted numbers to assist him in the invention of the "stage-business" to accompany each number.

Like his colleague, Arthur Sullivan was most strict and exacting as regards the rendering of his music. There must be nothing slipshod about it. If an individual departed from the vocal score to the point of a demisemiquaver or chose his own *tempo*, the chorus was at once pulled up and the defaulter brought to book. It was sometimes ludicrous to see some nervous chorister, whose ear was not sensitive and whose reading ability was limited, called upon to repeat again and again, as a solo, the note or two upon which he had broken down. It was a trying ordeal, but the desired end was always attained. Thereupon the blushing chorister thanked the smiling composer for having taken such pains to perfect his singing.

Long and trying as were those rehearsals, there was seldom a sign of tedium or impatience on the part of any member of the company. They loved their work, and, whenever Sullivan came to the theatre with a fresh batch of music, every one appeared eager to hear it and hungry for more study. As with the chorus, so with the principals. There were occasions when a singer would, with full assurance of his own perfection, give forth some song hardly recognizable by the composer, whereupon Sullivan would humorously commend the singer on his capital tune and then he would add—" and now, my friend, might I trouble you to try mine ? "

I remember one instance when a tenor, as tenors are wont to do, lingered unconscionably on a high note. Sullivan interrupted him with the remark—

" Yes, that's a fine note—a very fine note—but please do not mistake your voice for my composition."

" How rude ! " I fancy I hear some amateur remark. Yes, but Arthur Sullivan's rudeness was more winsome than many a lesser man's courtesy. His reproach was always so gentle that the most conceited, self-opinionated artist could not but accept it with good grace.

Photo by Russell & Sons.

MISS JESSIE BOND.

Photo by Elliott & Fry.

MISS LEONORA BRAHAM.

CHAPTER VII·

IN what I have written on the subject of stage re-hearsals I may have somewhat anticipated my own personal reminiscences in their proper chronological sequence.   But, it may be said, the managerial methods of procedure, the "orders of the day" which governed the early productions at the Opera Comique, continued in force to the end of the history of the Savoy.   Accordingly it may not appear premature to have offered in an early chapter some description of Gilbert and Sullivan opera-rehearsals which, in their main features, were, from first to last, all alike.

It was in July 1878, whilst " H.M.S. Pinafore" was in full sail on its prosperous voyage, that I was appointed, on the nomination of Arthur Sullivan, to succeed Alfred Cellier as Musical Director of the Opera Comique, my brother having, for the time being, vacated the post to join Sullivan in conducting a season of Promenade Concerts at Covent Garden

Opera-house, and subsequently to accompany D'Oyly Carte to America.

In the summer of 1879 " H.M.S. Pinafore " found itself in troubled waters.   Affairs at the Opera Comique took a very unhappy turn.   The Agreement originally entered into between the Comedy Opera Company and Mr. D'Oyly Carte as manager and lessee of the theatre terminated on July 31st, when Carte, having arranged to carry on the concern on his own sole account, secured a renewal of the sub-lease from the Earl of Dunraven, the lessee of the Opera Comique, his lordship's agent and holder of the Lord Chamberlain's licence being Mr. Richard Barker, who, at the time, held the post of stage manager under D'Oyly Carte.   This departure created a serious *casus belli* on the part of the Directors of the Comedy Opera Company.

Mr. Carte had recently gone to America, and, by consent of the Company, had appointed Mr. Michael Gunn, by a power of attorney, to act as his substitute in the management of the theatre.

In Carte's absence the Directors, on the ground of dissatisfaction with Gunn's management, passed a resolution dismissing him.   A notice was also posted in the theatre stating that Mr. D'Oyly Carte was no longer manager, and on July 21st, 1879, a motion was heard in the Chancery Division of the High Court of Justice to restrain Mr. Michael Gunn from retaining possession of the Opera Comique Theatre and from receiving the moneys of the Company and otherwise interfering with their management of the theatre.

The motion failed, and Mr. Gunn continued to act as Mr. Carte's *locum tenens*. Following this judgment, a few evenings later, on Thursday, July 31st, the date on which the company's tenure of the theatre expired, the 374th representation of " H.M.S. Pinafore " was disturbed by a disgraceful incident. As the performance of the opera was drawing to a close a cry of " Fire ! " was raised by some one in the flies, followed by scuffling and tumult. Several of the performers were alarmed, and the feeling of insecurity rapidly spread through the audience, who began hurriedly to leave the theatre.

My brother Alfred, who happened on that night to be deputizing for me in the conductor's chair, turned round to the occupants of the stalls and assured them there was no cause for alarm, and begged them to remain seated. But the uproar behind the scenes was so great that it was impossible to continue the performance ; so the band was stopped, and then George Grossmith, with commendable presence of mind, appeared before the curtain and announced that a determined attempt had been made by a large gang of roughs, acting under the inspiration of the Directors, to stop the performance and seize the scenery and properties. Grossmith's remarks, though scarcely audible above the din of riot and disorder, had the effect of restoring confidence in the auditorium. Behind the curtain the battle continued to rage furiously. The gallant crew of " H.M.S. Pinafore," assisted by loyal stage hands, soon proved too much for the enemy, and the invaders were quickly driven off the premises. During the engagement several of the First Lord's sisters and cousins and aunts had fallen in a swoon, but " Little Buttercup," the stout-built Portsmouth bumboat woman, distinguished herself greatly in " repelling boarders." Chief amongst numerous casualties were the foreman fireman, who had been severely bruised and trodden underfoot, and Mr. Richard Barker, who was thrown violently down the steep flight of stone steps before referred to. With the aid of a strong force of police, order was at length completely restored and the programme brought to a peaceful conclusion with the operetta " After All."

As a result of this fracas the Directors of the Comedy Opera Company were summoned to appear at Bow Street Police Court to answer a charge of assaulting Mr. Richard Barker and creating a disturbance at the Opera Comique Theatre. In the end D'Oyly Carte and Barker won the day and their actions at law, and after Gilbert, Sullivan, and Carte had issued a manifesto, making known to the public all the facts of the case, the whole lamentable affair was soon forgotten.

Seeing that the Directors of the Comedy Opera Company had put down only £500 each and drew £500 weekly, the vanquished party had not done badly over their deal in Gilbert and Sullivan operas.

And now to turn to more agreeable reminiscences. Under the new régime of Carte's sole management, " H.M.S. Pinafore " continued its successful course. Our worthy chief, accompanied by Gilbert and Sullivan, had gone to the United States with the special object of countermining the plots of American pirates who had been guilty of privateering the " Pinafore " and who would be ready, if no preventive measures were adopted, to steal in the same flagrant manner the next Gilbert and Sullivan opera produced.

Such was the lawless state of affairs existing previous to the passing of the International Copyright Act that, so far as regards stage-plays, there was no distinction recognized betwixt *meum* and *tuum*. But there was, certainly, a vast distinction between " H.M.S. Pinafore " of England and the American pirate ship sailing under its false title and colours. In order to make this fact quite evident, our author, composer, and manager staged the piece for a week's run in New York on the orthodox lines of the Opera Comique production. After that week the pirates happily found but poor market for their contraband version of the " Pinafore." With the further view of protecting their interests by securing American copyright, the Triumvirate produced in New York the new opera which they had got ready for their next venture in London. This was " The Pirates of Penzance, or the Slave of Duty." A simultaneous representation of the piece was given in England on December 31st, 1879, at the Bijou Theatre, Paignton, Devon. Thus the copyright in both the United Kingdom and America was secured.

In the meantime, at the Opera Comique, " H.M.S. Pinafore " continued to sail along briskly before the favouring gales of public applause, and in due course logged the 500th performance.

Familiarity, instead of staling, seemed to add to the popularity of the piece. Hackneyed as its tunes became, they ceased not to arrest and delight the public ear.

To Gilbert's play might have been applied the remark of the novice theatre-goer who declared he liked " Hamlet " chiefly because it contained so many quotations. For instance, the phrase " What never ? —Hardly ever "—became a British proverb more familiar to all sorts and conditions of men and women than the Prince of Denmark's famous " To be, or not to be."

The jingo jingle—

> " In spite of all temptations
> To belong to other nations,
> He remains an Englishman "—

may be declared to have rivalled in popularity, for the time being, the National Anthem.

The success of " H.M.S. Pinafore " having proved an established fact, it entered the mind of Richard Barker that a performance of the opera by a company of children might prove attractive. The title " Pinafore " may, probably, have first inspired this novel idea. Be this as it may, the suggestion met with the hearty approval of Gilbert, Sullivan, and D'Oyly Carte, and with their full sanction Barker made search for available juvenile talent, and eventually succeeded in forming a full company to man the " Pinafore," and selecting a bevy of charming little ladies all under the age of sixteen to represent the " sisters, cousins, and aunts."

Under a sullen, frowning exterior, Richard Barker

hid a very kind heart. By some "grown-ups," until they came to know him, he was looked upon as a harsh, bullying task-master, but in truth he was by nature as by name a Barker—not a biter. The little ones learnt, by the instinct of youth, the true disposition of "Uncle Dick," and under his strict discipline became willing and happy pupils of a tutor whose love of children was one of his chief characteristics.

It was raw and rough material to work upon ; at the same time, since none of the juvenile corps could boast of any stage experience, there was nothing for them to unlearn.

As a matter of course, the vocal score had to be re-orchestrated throughout to suit the vocal capabilities of the youthful singers. This interesting task was entrusted to my hands, and, as it was necessary that I should be in close and constant touch with Mr. Barker during the rehearsals, Arthur Sullivan very kindly placed his London residence at my disposal whilst he was absent in America.

As may readily be imagined, it was no child's-play to transpose the key of every song to fit each individual child's voice ; the choruses necessitated entire rearrangement, especially of the string parts, and in the unaccompanied numbers orchestral accompaniment had to be substituted for the support of male voices. Nevertheless, despite all difficulties, the labour involved was far from uncongenial, and, I would add, was more than recompensed by the generous commendation of the composer and the compliments of the critics.

The production of the children's "Pinafore" took place at the Opera Comique on the afternoon of Tuesday, December 16th, 1879, and, after running concurrently with the evening performances by the adult company until February 20th, continued to hold the boards until March 20th, when it was withdrawn in order to clear the stage for the final rehearsals and production of the new opera, "The Pirates of Penzance."

Gilbert, Sullivan, and D'Oyly Carte, having returned to England in time to witness the performance, were so delighted with the children that they advised the members of the elder company to go and take lessons from their junior rivals.

Those of my readers who witnessed the children's performance of "H.M.S. Pinafore" will, I am sure, share with me the very delightful memories I cherish of that remarkable exhibition of youthful talent. To others who were not equally privileged it may be interesting to learn what the press and public thought of the performance. To enable them to do so, I cannot do better than quote the words of a leading critic, written after the first production. Thus some knowledge may be gained of the triumph achieved by Richard Barker and his clever little crew.

"Delighted as we were with the extraordinary display of talent we witnessed on the occasion of the rehearsal of the children's 'Pinafore,' at the Opera Comique, our admiration was even increased when we saw the actual performance on Tuesday last. We have no hesitation in describing it as the most marvellous juvenile performance ever seen in the metropolis. So well have these children been taught, and so thoroughly do they comprehend their characters, that it becomes a source of the keenest enjoyment to the spectator to follow their wonderfully attractive performance. Many well-known members of the theatrical world who saw them at the rehearsal declared it to be the most remarkable performance they have ever attended, and one and all expressed the utmost astonishment at the marvellous talents of the children. It was not merely that one or two were possessed of unusual gifts; the entire performance was complete, finished, correct, and diverting in the extreme. Anything more whimsically comic than the Dick Deadeye of Master William Phillips could not be easily imagined. But Master Pickering, as the First Lord, was quite as funny in his way, and the Captain of Master Harry Grattan was absolutely first-rate. Other parts were equally well filled by the young gentlemen, and the young ladies were in no respect inferior. For example, the little Buttercup of Miss Effie Mason completely took the house by storm. The little lady was admirably made up, and was as excellent in her singing as in her acting. Nothing could be better, either, than the manner in which the difficult text was delivered. Every word was clear and distinct, and, what rendered the representation more amusing than all, was the original conceptions of several of the characters. This gave the performance a freshness and individuality of the rarest kind. The choruses were sung with great precision, and it was delightful to listen to the clear, bell-like voices. The greatest praise is due to Mr. R. Barker, under whose superintendence the children's ' Pinafore' was produced. He taught the youthful artistes all their stage business, and has spared no pains in order to make the *ensemble* as perfect as possible ; in teaching the little ones their music, Mr. François Cellier has been singularly successful.   Finally, we may again declare that it is impossible to praise too highly the children's ' Pinafore ' at the Opera Comique."

The following is the cast of the children's " Pinafore" :

CAST OF CHILDREN'S PINAFORE, 1879

Sir Joseph Porter .	MASTER EDWARD PICKERING
Captain Corcoran .	. MASTER HARRY GRATTAN
Ralph Rackstraw .	MASTER HARRY EVERSFIELD
Dick Deadeye . .	MASTER WILLIAM PHILLIPS
Boatswain's mate .	. MASTER EDWARD WALSH
Carpenter's mate .	. MASTER CHARLES BECKER
Josephine	MISS EMILIE GRATTAN
Hebe	MISS LOUISA GILBERT
Buttercup	MISS ETTIE MASON

With the paying off of the juvenile crew, " H.M.S. Pinafore" was put out of commission and laid up in reserve ; but, unlike her prototypes, the old wooden walls of England, the " Pinafore" was not condemned as obsolete.   The day would come when the gallant " three-decker" would be recommissioned for another cruise.   And now, just five and thirty years after her launch, " H.M.S. Pinafore" is as sea-worthy as ever, and bids fair to rival in longevity her parent ship, the old *Victory*, from which she was modelled.

CHAPTER VIII

As mentioned in the last preceding chapter, the first
production in public of " The Pirates of Penzance, or
The Slave of Duty," took place at the Fifth Avenue
Theatre, New York, on New Year's Eve, 1879, a copyright performance being given at Paignton as nearly
simultaneously as difference in longitude allowed.

In America the new opera had been received with
extraordinary favour. Popular as " H.M.S. Pinafore " had been across the Atlantic, " The Pirates
of Penzance " was declared on all hands to be even
more attractive, both in its quaintness and originality
of subject and in its melodious flow of music. The
piece had, in fact, become the rage of the United
States.

The performance of the work at Paignton having
been merely to preserve the legal rights in this country,
not more than fifty persons had been privileged to
witness that tentative presentation, so that next to
nothing was known about " The Pirates " at the time
when the opera came to be introduced to the British
public at the Opera Comique Theatre on the evening
of Saturday, April 3rd, 1880. Consequently the eager-

5

ness of Londoners to be present at the *première* was intense.

In " Trial by Jury " Gilbert had chosen the Law as the object of his playful satire ; in " The Sorcerer " the parsons were caricatured in the person of the sentimental Doctor of Divinity.   Then came " H.M.S. Pinafore," to be made the vehicle of good-humoured laughter at the expense of the British Navy and its ruler-in-chief, the First Lord of the Admiralty.   And now our author turned the search-light of his brilliant satire upon our Army and not less upon our gallant guardians in blue, the Police.   Here was another huge, practical joke to be perpetrated.   Most happily, neither the military authorities nor those of Scotland Yard found cause of offence in being held up to playful ridicule that incited no semblance of scorn. " In Queen Victoria's name," they accepted the unintended affront in the same spirit of amiability as that shown under similar conditions by the dignitaries of the Law, the Church, and the Navy.

Gilbert's darts were sometimes as exceedingly keen-pointed as they were irresistible ; but they were never poisoned by any venom of bitterness, and, since no distinguished personage ever found the jester's cap to fit him, nobody was ever the worse for a dose of Gilbert's strange concoction of knock-me-down pick-me-ups.

With the experience gained by familiarity with Gilbert and Sullivan's previous operas, critics and amateurs alike had been by this time fully educated up to the new school of humour.   All were now more readily able to appreciate the essence of the fun of our two humorists. The consequence was that the applause on the opening night of "The Pirates of Penzance" was more spontaneous than on any previous occasion.

The Press, now quite assured that Gilbert and Sullivan had come to stay, and were more than likely to achieve yet further conquests, became less reserved and more generous in their critical reviews. With the general public it was a matter of individual opinion which of the two was the more amusing piece, "Pinafore" or "The Pirates"; but the general verdict of the experts was that the last was the best production of Gilbert and Sullivan and D'Oyly Carte.

It is true that amongst the *dramatis personae* of the new opera were found characters that bore a certain family likeness to others to whom we had been introduced in "H.M.S. Pinafore." Notably a striking resemblance was discovered between Sir Joseph Porter, K.C.B., the First Lord of the Admiralty, and Major-General Stanley. Beyond question the similarity was intensified by the individuality of George Grossmith, the impersonator of both those characters in turn. Again, Ralph Rackstraw, A.B., of "H.M.S. Pinafore," and Frederic, the pirate 'prentice, were found to be as like in features as twin brothers; whilst Little Buttercup and Ruth, the piratical maid of all work, bore strong evidence of the same parentage. But what cared anybody? They were all such delightful companions that no one for a moment spurned them because of their near relationship to former equally delightful people,

As regards the book, Gilbert had excelled his previous efforts in the drollery of his conception.

For parodying, as he alone of all contemporary humorists could do, in his own masterly way, the extravagances and mock heroics of melodrama of the Tom Cook type, Gilbert had hit on an idea, rich and ripe in possibilities of mirth, and of these he availed himself to the full.

Your recognized and responsible critic possesses, or, anyway, is supposed to possess, the gift of prophecy. He can distinguish, as a rule, fixed stars from satellites and can—sometimes correctly—foretell the fate of the author, not only as regards his work under review, but what promise he gives of lasting success.

In the light of after events, one finds it a particularly interesting occupation to " turn up " old press cuttings—sere and yellow columns pasted in a guardbook, now tumbling to bits, and therein to read what " the malignant deities," as Pope called the critics, had to say after each successive Gilbert and Sullivan production. One will come now and then across some note of observation which is calculated to throw some doubt on the infallibility of press prognostication. For instance, I find one critic—a most worthy and distinguished judge of the stage—remarking :

" A question arises *how soon* these types of character, and also Mr. Gilbert's set form of humour, *will be worked out.*. True, the machinery by which Mr. Gilbert produces laughter is capable of very varied application. The whole world with all that it contains lies before him, to be topsy-turvied at pleasure ; and he need but avoid restriction to a limited range of character in order, it may be, to keep fast hold upon public regard. In what his humour consists everybody knows. One of the most prolific sources of laughter is the unexpected association of incongruous ideas, and Mr. Gilbert draws upon it in a manner peculiar to himself. As a rule, humour of this kind is self-conscious, not to say rollicking. Those concerned in it have, so to speak, put on the livery and taken the wages of Nonsense. But the drollery of Mr. Gilbert's characters is the more mirth-provoking for the gravity and apparent good faith with which they do and say the wildest, and, as regards probability, most outrageous things. Our author carries us into what looks like real life, to show its realism under the influence of pure phantasy, and it is the juxtaposition of ordinary people and things with motives, speech, and action, possible only on the assumption that the world has turned upside down, which excites so keen a sense of the ludicrous. *At present all this is fresh, and we should make much of it.* More, we should encourage it, because it gives pleasure of the finest and most legitimate kind. There is nothing in Mr. Gilbert's libretti to shock the most sensitive nature, and their success demonstrates what, at one time, seemed hardly credible—that, outside its music, a comic opera need not appeal to anything save a perception of harmless and healthy fun."

All this is unquestionably legitimate criticism, clever and admirable. None but the most captious could take exception to it. Yet does it not seem to indicate that the reviewer entertained, as yet, but scant faith in the lasting quality of Gilbert's extravaganzas ? Does not his argument suggest the ephemerality of such eccentric humour ?

Be this as it may, I, for one, find in such doubt-raising disquisition and retrospective reading much to interest. And, after all, it might be asked, who in the theatrical and musical world could have foretold that, in this year of grace, 1914, the Gilbert and Sullivan operas would be drawing as crowded houses as they did in Victorian days ? But it is a fact, and, it may be added, " The Pirates of Penzance " is at the present day as popular as any of the glorious series.

Having thus far recalled to mind some of the expert opinions expressed regarding Gilbert's libretto, let us now turn again to our press cuttings to discover what they had to say concerning Sullivan's share of the opera.

We find the critics unanimous in extolling the music in terms of praise beyond any they had yielded before.

For example :

" Mr. Sullivan has carried out more completely than ever his original and fanciful idea of caricaturing grand opera. The result is that we have music worthy in its artistic qualities to rank with some of the best efforts of the greatest composers, while it has a piquant freshness and buoyancy such as no other modern musician has equalled. Our English Auber has given us melodies as novel in rhythm as the French composer, while there is a geniality in them more welcome even than the glitter and crisp accent of the Gallic school. . . . Many of the musical numbers are absolutely perfect examples of what such music should be."

Another critic writes:

" Mr. Sullivan's share of the work has not been less well done than that of his clever colleague. Indeed, from a musical point of view ' The Pirates of Penzance ' is a distinct improvement upon both ' Trial by Jury ' and ' The Pinafore.' There is scarcely a dull bar in it, while every number not only pleases by its adaptedness to the theme and situation, but presents features upon which the connoisseur who is not content with ear-tickling melodies can dwell with satisfaction.

" It is hard to say whether Mr. Sullivan's humorous or sentimental music carries off the palm in this case. The composer has entered thoroughly into the spirit of the dramatist—so thoroughly that the result of their joint labours is as though it were the product of only one mind. With the utmost flexibility Mr. Sullivan follows the turnings and windings of Mr. Gilbert's eccentric fancy, and it can never be said that the one is not as funny or as pathetic as the other.

" It will surprise us greatly if ' The Pirates of Penzance ' be not strictly recognized as the most brilliant specimen of the combined efforts to which we already owe ' The Sorcerer ' and ' H.M.S. Pinafore.' The subject of the present opera enables both author and composer to give greater breadth to their efforts."

Such words echoed from the past assist us in realizing what measure of encouragement was meted out to our author and composer as they passed each successive milestone on the high road to fame.

CHAPTER IX

Now perhaps it may interest some to learn how it
came to pass that the copyright performance of " The
Pirates of Penzance " was given in such an insignificant,
out-of-the-world locality as a seaside village in South
Devon.   This was simply owing to the fact that
Mr. D'Oyly Carte's touring company happened at the
time to be playing " H.M.S. Pinafore " at Torquay, to
which town Paignton is closely adjacent.   The Paignton playhouse, although but a mere bandbox as to
size, was by no means the ordinary fit-up barn common
to small country towns.   The Bijou Theatre was,
indeed, the pride and hobby of a local magnate, Mr.
William Dendy, a man of wealth and great artistic
taste.

The stage appointments and accessories were of
an up-to-date character, the auditorium was luxuri-
ously furnished, and its walls were hung with a fine
collection of pictures.   The Bijou was, in brief, worthy
of its title, and so not unworthy the historic fame it
was destined to attain as the birthplace of the renowned
" Pirates of Penzance."

The following copy of the original play-bill of the opera may be acceptable as a curiosity. Here it is *in extenso* :

ROYAL BIJOU THEATRE, PAIGNTON

Tuesday, December 30, 1879

For one day only, at two o'clock, an entirely new and original opera by Messrs. W. S. GILBERT and ARTHUR SULLIVAN, entitled :

THE PIRATES OF PENZANCE, OR LOVE AND DUTY

Being its first production in any country

Major-General . . .	MR. R. MANSFIELD
The Pirate King	MR. FEDERICI
Frederic	MR. CADWALLADER
(*A Pirate*)	
Samuel	MR. LACKNOR
James	MR. LE HAY
(*Pirates*)	
Sergeant of Police . . .	MR. BILLINGTON
Mabel	MISS PETRELLI
Edith	MISS MAY
Isabel	MISS K. NEVILLE
Kate	MISS MONMOUTH
Ruth	MISS FANNY HARRISON

SCENE.—ACT 1.—A Cavern by the sea-shore.
ACT 2.—A ruined Chapel by moonlight.

Doors open at half-past one. Commence at two.
Sofa Stalls, 3s., Second Seats, 2s., Area, 1s., Gallery, 6d.
Tickets to be had at the Gerston Hotel.

Conductor	MR. RALPH HORNER
Acting Manager . . .	MR. HERBERT BROOK

Most notable amongst the above names is that of Mr. Fred Billington, who may thus rightly claim to have created the part of the famous Sergeant of Police, although that character must ever remain associated in the mind of Londoners with the name of Rutland Barrington.

Fred Billington is to-day the doyen of actors in Gilbert and Sullivan operas. For thirty-five years his talents have been faithfully devoted to the service of his old friends, Mr. and Mrs. D'Oyly Carte. His appearances at the Savoy Theatre have been brief and intermittent, because, as the years have rolled on, the comedian has so deeply ingratiated himself into the hearts of play-goers through the length and breadth of the United Kingdom that without the name of Fred Billington on the bills no D'Oyly Carte touring company has been considered fully complete and welcome anywhere. His portly frame, his dry, unctuous humour, and clear and incisive diction, have transformed the popular actor into a veritable Gilbertian creation, as it were. Veteran as he now is, Fred Billington to the present day retains to a remarkable degree all those individual attributes that have made him so popular in the wider theatrical world that lies beyond the inner walls of London.

The list of Paignton performers of " The Pirates " included Mr. Richard Mansfield, an admirable singing comedian, who, after serving for a while and obtaining honours under the D'Oyly Carte management, quitted England for America. In the States Dick Mansfield became an established favourite, and his death, which occurred a few years ago, was lamented by a large number of friends and professional colleagues on both sides of the Atlantic.

Another to whom a note of remembrance may here be given was Mr. Federici, the first impersonator of the Pirate King, and one of the best baritone singers and actors among past Savoyards. Poor Federici's tragic death whilst appearing as "Mephistopheles" in Australia will not have been forgotten by any to whom his name was once familiar in the theatrical world.

Mr. John Le Hay will be remembered in association with the Savoy Theatre as an occasional recruit in the Gilbert and Sullivan ranks. In later years his talents have been distributed over various theatrical fields, and have earned for him in London and the provinces a wide measure of popularity both as actor and entertainer.

Touching for a moment the American production of "The Pirates of Penzance," it may be unnecessary here to do more than place on record the original cast of principals who presented the opera at the—

FIFTH AVENUE THEATRE, NEW YORK

December 31st, 1879

Major-General Stanley . . .	MR. J. H. RYLEY
The Pirate King	MR. BROCOLINI
Samuel	MR. FURNEAUX COOK
(*His lieutenant*)	
Frederic	MR. HUGH TALBOT
(*The pirate apprentice*)	

Sergeant of Police	.	.	.	MR. F. CLIFTON	
Mabel	.	.	.	MISS BLANCHE ROOSEVELT	
Edith	.	.	.	.	MISS JESSIE BOND
Kate	.	.	.	.	MISS ROSINA BRANDRAM
Isabel	.	.	.	.	MISS BILLIE BARLOW
(General Stanley's daughters)					
Ruth	.	.	.	.	MISS ALICE BARNETT
(Pirate maid of all work)					

With one or two exceptions the artists included in this cast had been brought from England by D'Oyly Carte. Specially noteworthy are the names of Jessie Bond, Rosina Brandram, and Alice Barnett, all of whom, after a very successful season in America, returned home further to establish their reputations as leading lights of the Savoy.

The opera was rehearsed and produced in New York under the personal supervision of author and composer. Sullivan conducted on the opening night, after which the musical direction was left in the hands of my brother Alfred.

Arthur Sullivan had an amusing story to tell of his experience in association with American bandsmen. These gentlemen were all under the strict control of a musical trade union. A scale of charges was laid down for every kind of instrumentalist according to the nature and degree of his professional engagement. For example, a member of a Grand Opera orchestra must demand higher pay than one who was engaged for ordinary lyric work, such as Musical Comedy, and so on, down to the humblest class of musical entertainment. Accordingly, when the announcement went forth that the opening performance of "The Pirates of Penzance" would be conducted by Mr. Sullivan, and the manager of the theatre had taken pains to impress upon his orchestra the greatness of the honour that would be theirs of playing under the bâton of England's most famous composer, the bandsmen showed their appreciation of such distinction by demanding from the management increased salaries on the Grand Opera scale. There seemed likely to be "ructions." Whereupon, Arthur Sullivan, with characteristic tact and *sang froid*, addressed the men in modest terms. Disclaiming any title to the exalted honours they would thrust upon him, he protested that, on the contrary, he should esteem it a high privilege to conduct such a fine body of instrumentalists. At the same time, rather than become the cause of any dispute or trouble among them, he was prepared to cable home to England for his own orchestra, which he had specially selected for the forthcoming Leeds Festival. He hoped, however, that such a course might be avoided. The Americans promptly took the gentle hint, and agreed not to charge extra for the honour of being conducted by Mr. Arthur Sullivan.

Before leaving the subject of our Savoyards in America, let me venture to relate a little story, for the authenticity of which I cannot vouch

A certain American impresario, whose patriotism excelled his judgment, suggested to Gilbert that, while "H.M.S. Pinafore" had decidedly caught on in New York, he guessed that they could heap up a bigger pile of dollars if an American version of the piece were prepared.

"Say now, Mr. Gilbert," said our American friend, " all *you've* got to do is first to change H.M.S. to U.S.S., pull down the British ensign and hoist the Stars and Stripes, and anchor your ship off Jersey Beach.   Then in the place of your First Lord of Admiralty introduce *our* Navy Boss.   All the rewriting required would be some new words to Bill Bobstay's song—just let him remain an Amer'can instead of an Englishman.   Now ain't that a cute notion, sir ? "

Gilbert, pulling at his moustache, replied : " Well —yes—perhaps your suggestion is a good one ; but I see some difficulties in carrying it out.   In the first place, I am afraid I am not sufficiently versed in your vernacular to translate my original English words. The best I could do would be something like this improvisation :

> " He is Ameri-can.
>   Tho' he himself has said it,
>   'Tis not much to his credit
>   That he is Ameri-can—
>   For he might have been a Dutchman,
>   An Irish, Scotch, or such man,
>   Or perhaps an Englishman.
>   But, in spite of hanky-panky,
>   He remains a true-born Yankee,
>   A cute Ameri-can."

The New York impresario was delighted—vowed it would save the situation and set New York ablaze.

Mr. Gilbert replied that, after two minutes' careful

consideration, he didn't think it would do at all. He was afraid that such words might disturb the friendly relations existing between the United States of America and the United Kingdom of Great Britain and Ireland.

"Besides, my friend," Gilbert added, "you must remember *I* remain an Englishman. No, sir, as long as 'H.M.S. Pinafore' holds afloat she must keep the Union Jack flying."

"Quite appreciate your patriotic sentiments, Mr. Gilbert," replied the American, "but say—ain't it c'rect that 'Pinafore' was translated into German?"

"Quite correct—and played in Germany, but under its Teutonic name 'Amor am Bord' it was not easy for any one to imagine that the ship had been *taken from the English*."

This sounds like a Transatlantic fairy-tale. But it is repeated here for what it is worth.

Having seen their "Pirates" safely established in America, our author and composer, with D'Oyly Carte, returned to London and set to work on rehearsals of the opera there. For the third time Gilbert had created parts specially fitted to the peculiar talents and characteristics of the three popular favourites, Grossmith, Barrington, and Temple. George Power was re-engaged for the leading tenor rôle, and for prima-donna a new soprano had been unearthed in the person of Miss Marion Hood, a young lady whose début was to prove one of the most brilliantly successful ever witnessed under the D'Oyly Carte régime. The music allotted to the part of Mabel in the "Pirates of Penzance" is not only some of the daintiest, most graceful, and florid of any Sullivan wrote for light opera, but is the most exacting to the vocal powers and capabilities of the singer, notably Mabel's first song " Poor Wandering One," with its difficult staccato passages, and again in the delightful duet with Frederic in the second act, " O leave me not to pine alone and desolate." Marion Hood, however, proved equal to all requirements, and her triumph was considered by press and public to be one of the notable features of the new opera.

In the small part of Edith, Miss Julia Gwynne, promoted from the chorus, made a favourable impression by her bright acting and fascinating personality. Close following the young artiste's success in " The Pirates " came two important offers of engagement. The first was a professional one, which Miss Gwynne accepted, from Mr. and Mrs. Bancroft to appear in comedy under their management at the Haymarket Theatre. This proved in every way a success ; but it was not so permanent or eventful as the other engagement of a matrimonial kind which culminated in Julia Gwynne becoming the partner for life of Mr. George Edwardes, our future theatrical Kaiser. Mr. Edwardes was at that time acting-manager to Mr. D'Oyly Carte, an office which he continued to hold at the Savoy for some years before joining Mr. John Hollingshead in the management of the Gaiety. Julia Gwynne was a general favourite with all her "playmates" at the Opera Comique ; she was, indeed, looked upon as the life and soul of our company.

Another lady member of the original " Pirates of

MR. GEORGE EDWARDES.
First Acting Manager of Savoy.

MISS JULIA GWYNNE.
Mrs. George Edwardes.

Penzance " crew was that gifted artiste, Miss Emily
Cross. Owing to the sudden illness of Miss Everard,
who had been cast for the character of Ruth, the
piratical maid of all work, the part was undertaken
by Miss Cross at twenty-four hours' notice. This was
a remarkable instance of quick study. Such a task
as that set Miss Cross could have been successfully
fulfilled by none but an actress of great experience
and consummate ability. Miss Cross's success was
as marked as it was richly deserved.

An amusing incident occurred during rehearsal.
In Act II., where the Major-General and his daughter
Mabel are captured by the pirates, Frederic, who is
supposed to have appeared on the scene, neglected
his cue and was off the stage; accordingly, when Mabel
sang—

> " Frederic, save us,"

Gilbert stood sponsor for the absent tenor, and, adopting his own tune, gave forth—

> " I'd sing if I could, but I am not able."

The Pirates, unchecked, sang :

> " He would if he could, but he is not able."

Sullivan observed that it might be worse ; but, on his
part, he thought the character of Frederic wanted *power*.
Then, turning to the dilatory actor, added, "and strict
tempo, if you please, Mr. Power."

And now to bring to a close our comments on " The
6

Pirates of Penzance," which ran for 363 nights at the Opera Comique, we give hereunder the list of the principals who presented the piece at the—

OPERA COMIQUE

Saturday, April 3rd, 1880

Major-General Stanley . .	MR. GEORGE GROSSMITH
The Pirate King . . .	MR. R. TEMPLE
Samuel . . .	MR. GEORGE TEMPLE
(His lieutenant)	
Frederic . . .	MR. GEORGE POWER
(The pirate apprentice)	
Sergeant of Police . .	MR. RUTLAND BARRINGTON
Mabel	MISS MARION HOOD
(General Stanley's daughter)	
Edith	MISS JULIA GWYNNE
Kate	MISS LILIAN LA RUE
Isabel	MISS NEVA BOND
Ruth	MISS EMILY CROSS
(A pirate maid of all work)	

Photo by Elliott & Fry. MISS MARION HOOD.

Photo by Elliott & Fry. MISS KATE CHARD.

82]

CHAPTER X

NEARLY three and a half years had now passed since
the production of " The Sorcerer." Three Gilbert
and Sullivan operas had been brought to light and
passed to glory. " The Sorcerer " had numbered
175 performances ; " H.M.S. Pinafore " (including
the children's version) 700 ; and " The Pirates of
Penzance " 363 ; in all, 1,238 performances. Throughout the whole period the tide of prosperity had never
ceased to flow. Fortune had been wooed and won
beyond the most flattering dreams.

The lease of the Opera Comique was soon to
expire, but, instead of seeking its renewal, D'Oyly
Carte, ever shrewd and adventurous, determined on
a more ambitious scheme. He would build his own
theatre. It should be one specially suited to the requirements of the new school of comic opera, in the
exploiting and founding of which he had himself been
the prime mover and business factor. And so the
astute manager, confining his own counsel to his colleagues, Gilbert and Sullivan, sat down carefully to

consider figures and to map out plans for his new play-house. Then he began to search for a suitable site.

Meanwhile, the fourth opera was placed in rehearsal. Society for a few seasons past had been suffering from an epidemic of hybrid aestheticism. Under the apostleship of Oscar Wilde, " a passion for a lily " had over-mastered the conventional Englishman's love of the rose. Everybody and everything wore a pewtery grey, " greenery-yallery " complexion. Bright reds, scarlets, crimsons, and blues which had, before that period, helped to dissipate the murk and fog of town were now condemned as heresies against high art. The adherents to primitive colours and natural attitudes were looked upon as Philistines and excommunicated from society. Few survivors of that bilious, unbrawny age, would dare in these days to confess ever having yielded to the craze of the early eighties, for sorely were those preposterous, ape-like beings smitten, hip and thigh, by the scourge of ridicule.

First of the Philistines to take up arms against the mock aestheticism was our old friend *Punch*. Burnand and Du Maurier by their memorable caricatures " Postlethwaite Maudle," and the "Cimabue Browns," led the attack in the London Charivari. These first awakened town to the absurdity of the new-fangled fashion set by the Oscar Wilde tribe. At the little Prince of Wales Theatre in Tottenham Court Road, Burnand, in his comedy, " The Colonel," further lashed out with the whip of scorn. But it was not likely that Gilbert would let such a scope for justifiable satire

escape his attention. Although his idea of a skit on
the aesthetic craze may have been anticipated by his
rival humorist, Gilbert, in the earliest days of the
epidemic, had set to work to dispense a bolus for the
cure of the evil. As a matter of fact, made clear at
the time, " Patience " was written in November 1880.
This was before the production of "The Colonel."
The success of " The Pirates of Penzance " had, however, precluded the earlier production of the aesthetic
opera, and it was not until April 23rd, 1881, that
"Patience, or Bunthorne's Bride," was presented to
the impatient public at the Opera Comique Theatre
by the following *dramatis personae* :

Colonel Calverley	Mr. Richard Temple
Major Murgatroyd	Mr. Frank Thornton
Lieut. the Duke of Dunstable	Mr. Durward Lely
(*Officers of Dragoon Guards*)	
Reginald Bunthorne	Mr. George Grossmith
(*A fleshly poet*)	
Archibald Grosvenor	Mr. Rutland Barrington
(*An idyllic poet*)	
Mr. Bunthorne's Solicitor	Mr. G. Bowley
Chorus of Officers of Dragoon Guards	
The Lady Angela	Miss Jessie Bond
The Lady Saphir	Miss Julia Gwynne
The Lady Ella	Miss M. Fortescue
The Lady Jane	Miss Alice Barnett
(*Rapturous Maidens*)	
Patience	Miss Leonora Braham
(*A Dairymaid*) .	
Chorus of Rapturous Maidens.	

The cast of the opera, as will be seen, comprised

many of the old-established favourites. To their
number were now added some notable recruits, viz. :
Mr. Durward Lely, Mr. Frank Thornton, Miss Alice
Barnett, and last, not least, Miss Leonora Braham.
Each one and all of these artistes proved worthy of
their calling to the Gilbert and Sullivan colours, and
failed not later to win great popularity at the Savoy.

Among my reminiscences, none is more amusing
to my own mind, to-day, than the recollection of the
rehearsals of " Patience." It will be easy for any one
to imagine the spirit of mirth and fun that pervaded
the company while Gilbert drilled each individual to
assume the eccentric " goose-step," and the stained-
glass attitude of mediaeval art, and taught them to
speak in the ultra-rapturous accents of the poetaster.
The " business " was all so novel and so excruciatingly
funny that the most sedate and strict stage discip-
linarian could not but hold his ribs with laughter.
Particularly ludicrous was the coaching of the Duke,
Colonel, and Major for their Trio and dance, after
these gallant officers of Horse Guards have transformed themselves into aesthetic idiots in order to make
a lasting impression on the young ladies of their choice.
Nothing more comical was ever witnessed at stage-
rehearsal than the initiation of the three proud soldiers
into the mysterious antics of the " Inner Brotherhood."

It is only just to mention here that, in the drilling
and fantastic dance-teaching of the company, Gilbert
was greatly assisted by Mr. John D'Auban, that clever
master of the terpsichorean art whose services were
called into requisition at the rehearsal of many of the

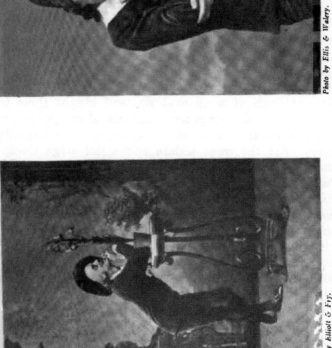

Photo by Elliott & Fry.

MR. FRANK THORNTON.

Photo by Ellis & Walery.

MR. JONES HEWSON.

Gilbert and Sullivan operas. Would that I had jotted down at the time the many amusing episodes and verbal quips of both our author and composer that accompanied the "Patience" rehearsals. I should not have failed to take notes had I dreamed in those days how it would ever fall to my lot to offer the public my personal reminiscences.

As a matter of course, an enormous crowd assembled for the first night of the new opera. Many *quidnuncs* came prepared to be disappointed. Some thought they had been satiated with aesthetic fare. They doubted whether even Gilbert might not fail to extract new fun out of the already much-discussed subject.

There are no play-goers in the world more appreciative or lavish in their praise, when they get precisely what they want, than the British. But they are not always easy to please. They are fastidious and they are fickle. They will follow like a flock of sheep when the bell-wether leads them to new pastures. The playwright they idolize to-day as a god they are ready to pull down to-morrow if haply he fails for a moment to fulfil early promise. Perhaps it is hardly just to speak in these caustic terms of play-goers as a body. Such remarks must be taken to apply more directly to the cynical, quasi-critical, *blasé* individuals, of whom there are too many, who, " fed up " with their own self-conceit, come to the theatre with a jaded palate and no appetite, ready to damn with faint praise, if not utterly to scorn, the new work which the poor author has devoted months upon months of anxious labour to provide.

The composer stands in the same condemnation and equally at the mercy of these senseless croakers. If, perchance, he be found to have, quite unconsciously, repeated so much as a phrase even of his own music, down they pounce on him either with a charge of plagiarism or with a lack of originality.

Is it, then, to be wondered at that success on the British stage is so difficult to achieve ?

Like every other author and composer, Gilbert and Sullivan had to elbow their way through the crowd of obstructionists who seem to take positive offence that quaint wit and humour beyond their own dull minds to understand is attracting crowds to the theatre. Accordingly, although Gilbert and Sullivan had long passed the Rubicon, amongst the vast audience that packed the Opera Comique for the *première* of " Patience " there were doubtless many of these would-be wreckers. But their croaking was drowned by the thunders of applause that accompanied the opera from rise to fall of curtain.

Gilbert and Sullivan had scored another brilliant, instantaneous success. Moreover, they had, on this occasion, done something more than amuse the people ; they had provided an object-lesson which would prove useful as an antidote to the poison that was enervating society.

" Postlethwaite " and " Maudle " had done much to check the aesthetic impostors, but " Bunthorne, the fleshly poet," and " Grosvenor, the idyllic poet," now came to discomfit and utterly rout the preposterous mountebanks and false disciples of high art.

The shaft of Gilbert's ridicule was not launched against pure aesthetic taste, which was, undoubtedly, tending to raise and refine the tone of modern society, but, in opposing the sham affectation and folly then rife, our author struck home with relentless force and vigour.

Sullivan on his part, as usual, entered thoroughly into the spirit of Gilbert's mood. The audience, listening as attentively to every bar of the music as to every witty word of the libretto, discovered how the composer had made every instrument in the orchestra seem to poke fun and ridicule at the objects of their satire.

Seated as I was, night after night, week following week, in the conductor's chair, literally saturated with the opera, some new point of Sullivan's jocularity was constantly awakened in my mind for the first time. I might fill pages with a description of my own personal impressions, but, since these must have been shared by all understanders of music, I refrain from alluding to more than one or two of the multitude of instances of the composer's remarkable power of imagination.

For example, by what tone device could Bunthorne's timorous confession of being a sham be more aptly expressed than by the recitative accompanying the words?—

> " Am I alone,
>   And unobserved ? I am.
> Then let me own—
>   I'm an aesthetic sham !

This air severe
    Is but a mere
        Veneer !
This cynic smile
    Is but a wile
        Of guile !
This costume chaste
    Is but good taste
        Misplaced !

" A languid love of lilies does *not* blight me !
Lank limbs and haggard cheeks do *not* delight me !
    I do *not* care for dirty greens
        By any means ;
    I do *not* long for all one sees
        That's Japanese.
    I am not fond of uttering platitudes
        In stained-glass attitudes.
In short, my mediævalism's affectation
Born of a morbid love for admiration ! "

The chant-like tone of that recitative afforded
striking contrast and emphasis to Bunthorne's
following song, the simple melody of which was
elaborated and enriched by its delightful orchestration.
Daintiest of dainty numbers to linger on the ear is the
duet between Patience and Grosvenor :

" Prithee pretty maiden, prithee tell me true,"

with its plaintive, old-world, madrigal style about it
which reminds the hearer of tunes popular a century
ago, and captivates present-day audiences more, perhaps, than any other throughout the " Patience "
score.

Then, again, among the most popular songs of the

Photo by W. H. Downey.

MISS EMILY CROSS.

Photo by Ellis & Walery.

MISS ROSINA BRANDRAM.

opera, one in which Sullivan displayed his subtle humour is Lady Jane's Recitative and Song, which opens the second Act.

> " Sad is that woman's lot, who, year by year,
> Sees, one by one, her beauties disappear ;
> When Time, grown weary of her heart-drawn sighs,
> Impatiently begins to ' dim her eyes.' "

Gilbert's words, a mixture of pure poetry and chaff, set to Sullivan's music as solemn as an oratorio by Handel, produce an amazing effect upon an audience, and succeed in dispersing the qualms of those who are disposed to call Gilbert rude in causing a lady to make fun of her own physical deformity.

But from a purely musical point of view I would extol, beyond all other numbers in the opera, the sestette—

> " I hear the soft note of the echoing voice "—

which occurs in the Finale of Act I.

Here the composer gives a remarkable exhibition of his genius for adapting music to the occasion.   Moreover, it was a striking instance of Gilbert's appreciation of his colleague's music.

In order to give the best effect to the sestette, it was sung by principals and chorus without the slightest movement or action on the stage.   In other words, precisely as it might be rendered on a concert platform, except that Gilbert took special pains as regards the picturesque and most effective grouping of the company.

No more beautiful setting of beautiful words was ever heard in comic opera. Would that it were practicable to enrich this volume with a copy *in extenso* of that exquisite composition; but it must suffice to adorn a page with the poem that inspired Arthur Sullivan to the loftiest height of melody.

The stage direction reads thus: "*Angela, Saphir,* and *Ella* take *Colonel, Duke,* and *Major* down, while girls gaze fondly at other officers."

And these are Gilbert's words:

> " I hear the soft note of the echoing voice
> Of an old, old love, long dead—
> It whispers my sorrowing heart ' Rejoice '—
> For the last sad tear is shed—
> The pain that is all but a pleasure we'll change
> For the pleasure that's all but vain,
> And never, oh never, this heart will range
> From that old, old love again."

CHAPTER XI

Building of the Savoy—Testing fire-extinguishers—" Star-Harden Grenades "—D'Oyly Carte's address to the public.

AFTER much difficulty and prolonged search, D'Oyly Carte succeeded in procuring a suitable site for his new theatre. It was a very rough, sloping patch of ground situated close by the Thames Embankment, within the precincts of the ancient Savoy and adjacent to the Chapel Royal. The approach from the Strand was down the precipitous Beaufort Street, the most fragrant thoroughfare in all London, for on its east side stood the establishment of Rimmel's, the famous perfumers.

Remembrance of the odour of Ess. Bouquet and of patchouli, which in those days impregnated Society, is somewhat acidulated by the recollection of other less delectable scents that came wafted from Burgess's noted fish-sauce shop, which flourished a few yards farther eastward in the Strand.

Such reflections on scents and sauces must be taken as reminiscences whispered " aside." They had nothing whatever to do with D'Oyly Carte's selection of a site. To the ordinary mind's purview, there appeared little attractive in that wild and rugged waste-plot to tempt one to build a home of pleasure upon

93

it. But our far-seeing manager recognized advantages in the situation. So dogged was Carte's energy and determination that, the greater the difficulty that faced him, the greater pleasure he found in the task of making rough ways smooth.

The wild and flowery acres of Aldwych which to-day offer themselves to the prospective builder were not, unfortunately, available to Mr. Carte. The Opera Comique was then occupying part of that ground. It yet remained the home of Gilbert and Sullivan's creations, pending the completion of their new play-house. And so it was to the unkempt wilderness of the ancient Savoy that Carte was driven with his plans and designs, his bricks and mortar.

With such promptness and despatch was the work of building carried out that, within the space of a few months, the Savoy Theatre was completed and ready for occupation.

Among my readers may be some who remember a little incident that occurred during the process of raising the Savoy Theatre. A trifling incident, yet, I think, not without sufficient interest to recall.

In order to test the efficacy of a new patent fire-extinguisher called the "Star-Harden Grenade," an exhibition of its capabilities was given on a plot of waste ground on which now stands the Savoy Hotel. Among the select company of guests present was H.R.H. the Duke of Edinburgh, who was much interested in the experiments.

A wooden building, saturated with tar, was set fire to. When it blazed, a number of the grenades—globular glass bottles resembling liqueur flagons—were hurled and broken against the burning boards, with the result that floods of magic lotion burst out upon and immediately extinguished the flames. The experiment was so successful that D'Oyly Carte added the Star-Harden Grenades. to the number of novelties he intended introducing for the first time in any theatre.

I have not forgotten how the proprietors of the patent made me a timely present of a case of the grenades, and thus enabled me personally further to test their value in private by extinguishing a fire which very shortly afterwards broke out in my home.

On the eve of the opening of the Savoy Theatre a select number of friends, critics, managers, and others interested in theatres were invited by Mr. Carte to inspect the house. Loud were the pæans of praise poured upon the head of the proud manager by all present.

As a true and authentic record in detail of the manifold pomps and glories of the new theatre, we cannot do better than reproduce here Mr. D'Oyly Carte's inaugural address.

TO THE PUBLIC

" LADIES AND GENTLEMEN,—I beg leave to lay before you some details of a new theatre, which I have caused to be built with the intention of devoting it to the representation of the operas of Messrs. W. S. Gilbert and Arthur Sullivan, with whose joint productions I have, up to now, had the advantage of being associated.

" The Savoy Theatre is placed between the Strand

and the Victoria Embankment, on a plot of land of which I have purchased the freehold, and is built on a spot possessing many associations of historic interest, being close to the Savoy Chapel and in the 'precinct of the Savoy,' where stood formerly the Savoy Palace, once inhabited by John of Gaunt and the Dukes of Lancaster, and made memorable in the Wars of the Roses. On the Savoy Manor there was formerly a theatre. I have used the ancient name as an appropriate title for the present one.

" The new theatre has been erected from the designs and under the superintendence of Mr. C. J. Phipps, F.S.A., who has probably more experience in the building of such places than any architect of past or present times, having put up, I believe, altogether thirty-three or thirty-four theatres.

" The façade of the theatre towards the Embankment, and that in Beaufort Buildings, are of red brick and Portland stone. The theatre is large and commodious, but little smaller than the Gaiety, and will seat 1,292 persons.

" I think I may claim to have carried out some improvements deserving special notice. The most important of these are in the lighting and decoration.

" From the time, now some years since, that the first electric lights in lamps were exhibited outside the Paris Opera-house, I have been convinced that electric light in some form is the light of the future for use in theatres, not to go further. The peculiar steely blue colour and the flicker which are inevitable in all systems of 'arc' lights, however, make them unsuitable for use in any but very large buildings. The invention of the 'incandescent lamp' has now paved the way for the application of electricity to lighting houses, and consequently theatres.

"The 'arc' light is simply a continuous electric spark, and is nearly the colour of lightning. The incandescent light is produced by heating a filament of carbon to a white heat, and is much the colour of gas—a little clearer. Thanks to an ingenious method of 'shunting' it, the current is easily controllable, and the lights can be raised or lowered at will. There are several extremely good incandescent lamps, but I finally decided to adopt that of Mr. J. W. Swan, the well-known inventor, of Newcastle-on-Tyne. The enterprise of Messrs. Siemens Bros. & Co. has enabled me to try the experiment of exhibiting this light in my theatre. About 1,200 lights are used, and the power to generate a sufficient current for these is obtained from large steam-engines, giving about 120 horse-power, placed on some open land near the theatre. The new light is not only used in the audience part of the theatre, but on the stage, for footlights, side and top lights, etc., and (not of the least importance for the comfort of the performers) in the dressing-rooms —in fact, in every part of the house. This is the first time that it has been attempted to light any public building entirely by electricity. What is being done is an experiment, and may succeed or fail. It is not possible, until the application of the accumulator or secondary battery—the reserve store of electric power —becomes practicable, to guarantee absolutely against any break-down of the electric light. To provide against such a contingency, gas is laid on throughout the building, and the 'pilot' light of the central sun-burner will always be kept alight, so that in case of accident the theatre can be flooded with gas-light in a few seconds. The greatest drawbacks to the enjoyment of the theatrical performances are, undoubtedly, the foul air and heat which pervade all theatres. As every one knows, each gas-burner consumes as much

7

oxygen as many people, and causes great heat besides. The incandescent lamps consume *no* oxygen, and cause no perceptible heat. If the experiment of electric lighting succeeds, there can be no question of the enormous advantages to be gained in purity of air and coolness—advantages the value of which it is hardly possible to over-estimate.

" The decorations of this theatre are by Messrs. Collinson & Lock.

" I venture to think that, with some few exceptions, the interiors of most theatres hitherto built have been conceived with little, if any, artistic purpose, and generally executed with little completeness, and in a more or less garish manner. Without adopting either the styles known as ' Queen Anne ' and ' Early English,' or entering upon the so-called ' æsthetic ' manner, a result has now been produced which I feel sure will be appreciated by all persons of taste. Paintings of cherubim, muses, angels, and mythological deities have been discarded, and the ornament consists entirely of delicate plaster modelling, designed in the manner of the Italian Renaissance. The main colour-tones are white, pale yellow, and gold—gold used only for backgrounds or in large masses, and not—following what may be called, for want of a worse name, the Gingerbread School of Decorative Art—for gilding relief-work or mouldings. The back walls of the boxes and the corridors are in two tones of Venetian red. No painted act-drop is used, but a curtain of creamy satin, quilted, having a fringe at the bottom and a valance of embroidery of the character of Spanish work, keeps up the consistency of the colour-scheme. This curtain is arranged to drape from the centre. The stalls are covered with blue plush of an inky hue, and the balcony seats are of stamped velvet of the same tint, while the curtains of the boxes are of yellowish silk, brocaded with a pattern of decorative flowers in broken colour.

"To turn to a very different subject. I believe a fertile source of annoyance to the public to be the demanding or expecting of fees and gratuities by attendants. This system will, therefore, be discontinued. Programmes will be furnished and wraps and umbrellas taken charge of gratuitously. The attendants will be paid fair wages, and any attendant detected in accepting money from visitors will be instantly dismissed. I trust that the public will co-operate with me to support this reform (which already works so well at the Gaiety Theatre) by not tempting the attendants by the offer of gratuities. The showing-in of visitors and selling programmes will, therefore, not be sublet to a contractor, who has to pay the manager a high rental, to recoup which he is obliged to extract by his *employés* all he can get out of the public; nor will the refreshment saloons be sublet, but they will be under the supervision of a salaried manager, and the most careful attention will be given to procuring everything of the very best quality.

"The theatre will be opened under my management on Monday next, October 10th, and I have the satisfaction to be able to announce that the opening piece will be Messrs. W. S. Gilbert and Arthur Sullivan's opera 'Patience,' which, produced at the Opera Comique on April 23rd, is still running with a success beyond any precedent.

"The piece is mounted afresh with new scenery, costumes, and increased chorus. It is being again rehearsed under the personal direction of the author and composer, and on the opening night the opera will be conducted by the composer.

"I am, ladies and gentlemen, your obedient servant,

"R. D'OYLY CARTE."

BEAUFORT HOUSE, STRAND,
October 6th, 1881.

CHAPTER XII

EVER memorable in the annals of the theatrical world
will be the opening of the Savoy Theatre on Monday,
October 10th, 1881.

Apart from the reflection that this was to be the
future home of the Gilbert and Sullivan operas, the
various reforms and innovations introduced by D'Oyly
Carte, notably the installation of electric light, became
the talk of the town.

Men of the old school to whom progress spelt de-
secration shrugged their shoulders at the pioneer's new-
fangled notions. They prophesied all sorts of evils.
The " incandescent lamps," they said—not knowing
what they talked about—" will never do." Not only
would they cast a ghostly glare upon the stage and
auditorium, but they would be playing all manner of
uncanny tricks to upset the performances. As for the
quixotic idea of charging nothing for programmes and
cloak-rooms, and not sub-letting the refreshment
saloons at a high rental, as was the established custom,
what could be more suicidal ? How did the manager

expect to raise revenue? It was eccentricity of the maddest type, and must eventually bring about financial ruin. Thus spoke the conservative savants. But the prophets were put utterly to shame.

The first-night assemblage was prompt to recognize and acclaim Carte's liberal policy. Never before had an auditorium been more densely packed! never before had an audience sat so comfortably in an atmosphere free from the fœtid heat of gaslight. True, the incandescent lamps were now and then inclined to be troublesome, causing a certain amount of momentary anxiety. The electric light in its infancy betrayed some weakness in its power. But this, perhaps, was nothing more than the nervousness common to a first appearance in any theatre; moreover, the inherent brightness of the fairy lamps was now called upon to enhance the lustre of the distinguished personages who filled the boxes, stalls, and circles on this brilliant occasion. On the whole, then, the début of the "Incandescents" was a great success.

Mr. Carte, conscious of the difficulties besetting his plucky experiment, issued a notice in advance, saying that it had been impossible to complete all the arrangements necessary for the perfect lighting of the auditorium and stage by electric power, but that in a few days all difficulties would be overcome and the first steps would have been taken in a method of lighting which would probably become useful ere long, owing to its many advantages. Thereafter the incandescent lamps were seldom known to fail. Yet I recollect how, on the occasion of the first visit to the Savoy of the Prince of

Wales (afterwards Edward VII), the lights displayed a very republican spirit by going out and leaving our royal guest, not in absolute darkness, but in the obscurity of the gas sun-burner.

Gilbert, having inquired into the cause of the breakdown, was informed by the engineer in charge that it was "the bearins' 'ad got 'eated"; whereupon Gilbert propounded a riddle: "Why," he added, "is the electric light like one of my old sows?" "Because they both 'eats their own bearins.'"[1]

With reference to the other reform above alluded to, great was the satisfaction expressed in all parts of the house when, in place of the cheap and common playbill for which, hitherto, a charge of sixpence had been imposed, an artistic programme beautifully designed in colour by Miss Alice Havers was presented to every one, "free, gratis, and for nothing"; it was amusing to observe the varying expressions of surprise and gratification of men who, after following the custom of tendering a silver coin in payment, were politely informed by the attendant that there was "no charge." To some minds this concession had the effect of making the half-guinea stall appear cheap. The reform of the refreshments was no less welcome; in place of the poisonous concoction of fusil-oil, excellent whiskey was provided, and pure coffee took the

[1] Whilst recording the first installation of electric lighting in a theatre, it is interesting to reflect how the Greeks and our ancestors were satisfied with daylight for their dramatic performances. Then came a period of tallow candles and oil-floats. These, in the year 1765, sufficed to illuminate Garrick. In 1817 gas-light was first introduced at Covent Garden Theatre.

place of the customary chicory—and all at a reasonable tariff.

It was under such auspices and agreeable circumstances as those I have endeavoured to outline that "Patience," transplanted from the Opera Comique, was welcomed to her new abode by a host of fervent admirers. Probably every person present on that opening night had already witnessed the opera; but now, surrounded by such improved conditions of comfort, all had come to renew acquaintance with Gilbert and Sullivan's latest work with anticipation of increased pleasure. Unprecedented was the éclat, and when Sullivan's form appeared in the conductor's rostrum, silhouetted against the rich amber satin curtains, the thunders of applause were such as to put to severe test the walls and roof of the new building. It may be recorded that the house shook for the first time, yet held firm to withstand the many equally severe, and ever-welcome earthquake shocks that were to become familiar at every Savoy *première*.

The improvements behind the curtain were as marked as those found in the front of the house.

The stage, considerably larger than that of the Opera Comique, afforded scope for extending and elaborating the groups of the " love-sick maidens " and heavy dragoons of " Patience."

Brand-new scenery had been painted with special regard to the exigencies of electric lighting. Scenic artists alone can appreciate how greatly the new system of stage illumination revolutionized the colour-tones. The incandescent rays enabled them to produce a closer copy of natural daylight than had ever been possible with gas-jets. Accordingly the "Patience" scenes, notably the lovely Forest Glade, revealed qualities far excelling in beauty those in which the opera had been mounted at the old house. The scenery reflected the highest credit on Mr. Hawes Craven, the clever artist, who for many years remained associated with the D'Oyly Carte management.

Thus "Patience" in the full tide of popularity was transplanted in a day from the Opera Comique to the Savoy, reappearing in all the glory of new costumes to enter upon a new lease of life. The only notable change in the company was the substitution of Mr. Walter Brown for Mr. Richard Temple, who remained at the Opera Comique, the sole management of which had been taken over by Richard Barker for the production of Fred Clay's opera, "Princess Toto."

A more brilliant audience than that which attended the opening night of the Savoy has seldom been seen in any theatre other than Covent Garden Opera-house.

"Patience" continued its successful course until November 22nd, 1882. The opera had enjoyed a run of 408 performances, and greatly enriched the coffers of the proud Triumvirate. The powers of "The Three" showed no signs of exhaustion. Prosperity, indeed, seemed to yield fresh inspiration to their united genius, which possessed what Coleridge described as "the faculty of growth."

Gilbert's unrivalled humour and Sullivan's precious gift of melody flourished beneath the sunshine of public approbation, while Carte's master-hand had steered the ship with its rich argosy of pleasure and profit on its prosperous voyage across calm seas, and the Savoy Theatre was now the Mecca of all pilgrims of the play.

Pausing thus to take stock, as it were, it may not be out of place on this page to pay well-deserved praise to the orchestra over which it was my privilege to preside.

Like the stage-company, the instrumentalists, from playing so long together, had ripened into a full, rich, homogeneous band. Men more closely allied together in friendly brotherhood, more loyal to their manager and to their conductor, were never found in a theatre. One and all took personal interest in the welfare of the operas, thus serving to make their musical director's burthen of responsibility light and his task at all times a pleasant one. The effervescent spirit of Sullivan's music had the effect of converting the most staid and solemn member of the orchestra into a humorist. Bassoon, clown of the orchestra, became, forsooth, a first-class comedian, raising, on occasion, a round of laughter from the audience.

Our band, be it said, was always in the picture : even so when a leading character in " The Gondoliers " described them as "sordid persons, who require to be paid in advance."

This rather rude affront was accepted by the orchestra with stoical unconcern. Had it been taken seriously, the heir to the throne of Barataria, with his own " delicately modulated instrument," might have found himself drummed off the stage by the indignant musicians below. But we had learnt our Gilbert by this time. We knew that, like most satirists and cynics, our gifted author sometimes inadvertently allowed his wit to outrun discretion, causing him occasionally, yet very seldom, to err an inch from the canons of good taste. Besides, did not every one know that a fiddler, in truth, is no more sordid nor grasping than the most hungry histrion who struts the boards from Friday to Friday, patiently awaiting the dawn of Treasury Day? And so no one was one whit the worse.

Personally, however, I have always thought the ungracious thrust at that harmless, but necessary body —the band—one of the least funny of Gilbert's witticisms; but then, of course, I may be prejudiced.

It might have been imagined that with the withdrawal of " Patience "—mock æstheticism having received its quietus—the subject was obsolete and done with for ever. A satire launched specifically against the craze and crank of a period could hardly be expected to interest the people of future generations ! Yet what have we seen ? Not only a successful revival of the opera at the Savoy in 1900, but also to the present day " Patience " is found as attractive as it was at the time when Bunthorne and Grosvenor were recognized as prototypes of men and women actually living and gracelessly moving in our midst. In fact, Gilbert and Sullivan's æsthetic opera continues as popular on tour as any of the famous series. I have heard it questioned, would " Patience " have lived but for the music ? That remains a matter of opinion.

CHAPTER XIII

CONTINUING in chronological order the progress of
what we may now term the Savoy Operas, we come to
"Iolanthe, or The Peer and the Peri," which first
saw the footlights on Saturday, November 25th,
1882.

People wondered what phase of contemporary life,
what particular class of the community would next
become the victims of Gilbert's humour. The doings
and undoings, the uses and abuses of the House of
Lords, were just then a subject of bitter controversy.
Peers were out of season and unpopular, at least with
the people. The Parliament Act had not then been
even drafted, and so " Down with the Lords ! " was the
cry of the hour.

What wonder, then, that our author chose a theme
for his libretto that might please all parties of the
State ? The peers should be brought on the stage to
speak for themselves, make their own apologies, and
endeavour to persuade their detractors that they were

not as black as they were painted, that "high rank involves no shame," that—

> " Hearts just as pure and fair
> May beat in Belgrave Square
> As in the lowly air
>   Of Seven Dials " ;

that even a Lord Chancellor is as susceptible to the tender passion as the most amorous plebeian of the slums, be he "either a little Liberal or else a little Conservative." And what more fascinating or persuasive mouthpieces for his saccharine satire could our king of jesters have invented than a bevy of beautiful Peris ? What elfish tricks would they not play upon our hereditary peers ? Far better this than the vulgar abuse of mere mortals. In brief, what better peg whereon to hang Gilbertian squibs and crackers could be conceived ?

But it was only a Gilbert who could dare tackle so ticklish a subject without fear of offence. Need it be recorded how our author used his materials with such masterly tact and broadness of mind that the most sensitive duke, marquis, or earl could never find a coronet to fit his own noble head, amongst the brilliant assortment displayed on the Savoy stage. Probably those members of the Upper House who never came to see "Iolanthe" were in a large minority. The majority who did come were delighted and surprised to find into what a glorious and harmless figure of fun a Legislative Lord could be transmogrified by a past-master of caricature.

The first night of "Iolanthe" marked another
triumph for D'Oyly Carte's management.

All the familiar features of a Gilbert and Sullivan
première were in evidence, only more so than ever.
The house, packed with an enormous audience, comprised a mixed assortment of patricians and plebeians.
Every shade of politics was represented, but, unlike
the assemblies in the greater play-house in Westminster,
here there was no spirit of controversy. Every Act
was passed without a division.   M.P.'s—Unionist and
Radical, Home Ruler and Socialist—alike hailed the
appearance of the composer with far greater and more
spontaneous rapture than any with which they greet
the rising of a distinguished Front-bench orator.
Sullivan's music soothed the angry breasts of poli-
ticians.   And how those senators roared their ribs
to aching pitch as they listened, whilst the Sentry
poured forth his views and sentiments regarding the
modus operandi of the House of Commons, thus :

> " When in that House M.P.'s divide,
>   If they've a brain or cerebellum, too,
>   They've got to leave that brain outside,
>   And vote just as their leaders tell 'em to.
>   And then the prospect of a lot
>   Of dull M.P.'s in close proximity,
>   All thinking for themselves, is what
>   No man can face with equanimity."

Once again a greedy appetite for Gilbert's " words "
was proved by the *frou-frou* swish of book-leaves
turned over. Every pungent point of satire and
ridicule was the signal for a volley of laughter.   Every

song was redemanded, everybody who had done anything to help the play was called before the curtain, and, in short, Gilbert and Sullivan had again captured the town.

One incident attending the first night of " Iolanthe," remembered by all who were present, is worth recalling here. Conspicuous in the centre of the stalls was the well-known form of Captain (afterwards Sir Eyre Massey) Shaw, the renowned and popular Chief of the Fire Brigade. To him the Fairy Queen, with arms outstretched across the footlights, appealed in tuneful serenade :

> " On fire that glows
> With heat intense
> I turn the hose
> Of common sense,
> And out it goes
> At small expense.
> We must maintain
> Our fairy law ;
> That is the main
> On which to draw—
> In that we gain
> A Captain Shaw !
>
> " O Captain Shaw,
> Type of true love kept under !
> Could thy Brigade
> With cold cascade
> Quench my great love ?—I wonder ! "

Spectacularly " Iolanthe " excelled any of the preceding operas.   For the first time on any stage electric lamps were adopted as ornaments by the *dramatis personae*. And so when the classically draped Peris tripped on, each irradiated by a fairy-star in her hair, and another at the point of her wand, the novel effect caused a subdued murmur of wonder and applause to spread through the auditorium. Emden's scenery, especially that of the second act, depicting Palace Yard and the Houses of Parliament, was pronounced a masterpiece of scenic art.

In this connection we may mention the interesting fact that, in the second act set of " Iolanthe," sky-borders were discarded for the first time on any stage either in London or on the Continent.

For the benefit of the uninitiated, it may be well to explain that sky-borders are those flat lengths of painted cloth, which, stretched overhead across the stage from left to right, form, as it were, the upper frame-work of the picture. They are intended to assist perspective; but sometimes the effect is not only to narrow the view, but, worse, to destroy the illusion of the scene. It certainly does not add to picturesque beauty when we observe square yards of canvas once coloured cerulean blue to harmonize with the black-cloth firmament, but now sere and yellow with age, their edges frayed and torn by the rough usage of the scene-shifters, flapping ungracefully in the breeze that blows perpetually on every stage. They look more like giant scarecrows hung on lofty trees than parts of the scenic artist's design. It will be easy, then, to understand how the doing away with sky-borders was one of the most notable improvements

adopted by the Savoy management. To the galleryites the innovation was specially acceptable, since it
enabled them to command a full perspective view of
the Westminster scene, even to the summit of the
Victoria Tower.

Seldom had any more brilliant spectacle been witnessed in a theatre than the Procession of Peers in
their full canonicals of coronets and robes, absolutely
correct to the gilt strawberry-leaves of high-born Duke
or the white satin rosette of belted Earl.

To the trumpet-bray and sounding brasses of the
Grenadier Guards Band entered these—

> " Noble peers of highest station,
> Paragons of legislation,
> Pillars of the British nation ! "

So thunderous was the applause, so emphatic the
demand for an encore that one wondered whether the
audience would have sufficient lung-power left where-
with to welcome the Lord Chancellor following close
upon the heels of the noble cortège. But we were not
long left in doubt. George Grossmith's appearance
was hailed with such a volley of cheers as to necessitate
a rest of many bars before the Lord Chancellor was
permitted to introduce himself in the quaintly dry
patter song :

> " The Law is the true embodiment
> Of everything that's excellent."

Never was an oration from the " woolsack " listened
to with such profound attention mingled with dis-

Photo by Elliott & Fry.

Photo by Elliott & Fry.

respectful laughter half-suppressed, as that which greeted the Lord Chancellor on this memorable occasion.

Incidentally let me here recall how at the Dress Rehearsal, whilst watching the Procession of Peers, Gilbert remarked to me : " Some of our American friends who will be seeing ' Iolanthe ' in New York tomorrow will probably imagine that British lords are to be seen walking about our streets garbed in this fashion." Whether or not Gilbert's suggestion was extravagant we have no evidence to show. One fact, however, may be hinted at—after the production of " Iolanthe," the demand for eligible earls by American heiresses certainly seemed to increase.

An amusing incident occurred during the rehearsals of " Iolanthe." Gilbert took D'Auban aside and whispered certain instructions to the dancing-master. The author then approached Alice Barnett, the Fairy Queen—" Now, Miss Barnett," said Gilbert, " if you are ready, Mr. D'Auban will teach you a few dance-steps which we wish you to introduce in your part." " Oh, thank you, Mr. Gilbert," replied the actress. D'Auban then, taking the stage, executed some marvellous gyrations which none but a past-master of the terpsichorean art could possibly attempt. Miss Barnett stared aghast and then exclaimed, " Oh—really—Mr. Gilbert—I—I don't think—in fact, I'm sure I could never learn that." Readers who may recollect the Fairy Queen's *extra*-ordinary form and stature will appreciate Gilbert's practical joke, which, needless to say, caused a roar of laughter on the stage.

8

By the way, it may be worth mentioning that the first presentation of " Iolanthe " in America was intended to synchronize as nearly as possible with that in London ; but, owing to difference in longitudinal time, the curtain rose in New York some five hours later than did ours. Accordingly, through the courtesy of the Atlantic Cable authorities, D'Oyly Carte was enabled to send a message across the seas describing the enthusiastic reception of the opera at the Savoy. This message, transcribed, was issued to the American play-goers as they were entering the theatre for the first performance of " Iolanthe " ; thus their appetite for the feast was agreeably whetted.

Before leaving the subject of " Iolanthe's " peers, it may be remarked how the illustration of the manners and customs of the British peerage provided an object-lesson to the gallery-boys. One may not gravely assert that any increased reverence for blue blood was instilled into the minds of the *hoi polloi* who came to the Savoy, not in battalions, but in single columns ; yet the expression common to the vulgar herd—" We'r are you a'shovin' to, as if you was a bloomin' Lord ? " was heard more than once as the crowd elbowed their way through the cheap exit doors at the end of the performance.

The only notable addition to the front ranks of Savoyards taking part in " Iolanthe " was Mr. Charles Manners, since become distinguished in the musical world as a plucky and successful pioneer in the cause of English Opera.

Manners gave an admirable impersonation of the

Photo by Ellis & Walery.

MR. CHARLES MANNERS.

Photo by Ellis & Walery.

MR. COURTICE POUNDS.

stolid Grenadier Guardsman, Private Willis, his fine bass voice doing full justice to the famous Sentry's Song, whilst his acting emphasized the drollery of the character and situation.

The following is the complete cast of the original "Iolanthe" company at the Savoy Theatre :

The Lord Chancellor . .	Mr. George Grossmith
Earl of Mountararat .	Mr. Rutland Barrington
Earl of Tolloller . .	Mr. Durward Lely
Private Willis . . .	Mr. Charles Manners
Strephon	Mr. R. Temple
Queen of the Fairies .	Miss Alice Barnett
Iolanthe	Miss Jessie Bond
Celia	Miss Fortescue
Leila	Miss Julia Gwynne
Fleta	Miss Sybil Grey
Phyllis	Miss Leonora Braham

Chorus of Dukes, Marquises, Earls, Viscounts, Barons, and Fairies

Musical Director . . . Mr. François Cellier

Act I.—*An Arcadian Landscape*

Act II.—*Palace Yard, Westminster*

Date.—*Between* 1700 *and* 1882

Turning once again to our press cuttings, we find the critics were all but unanimous in profuse praise of the new opera. But there was one remarkable exception—a very negative report (it could not conscientiously be called criticism), which, read by the light of to-day, is so amusing in its depreciatory remarks on "Iolanthe," so rare as an expert's review, that I

cannot refrain from republishing it word for word. If
the writer of this precious damnatory article has been,
unhappily, spared to the journalistic world till now,
I trust he will fully appreciate the attention I very
humbly and gratuitously venture to direct towards
his far-seeing judgment.

This is what he wrote :

"I was present at the *fourth* representation of
'Iolanthe' [what a pity he was not invited to the
first !], and, though it was impossible not to be struck
with the startling ingenuity of many of the phrases, the
performance as a whole left me profoundly depressed !
melancholy ! miserable ! [oh ! shade of Jacques !]
The dirge-like music,—sacred harmonics gone wrong
—dragged and grated even upon my unmusical ear.
Where is this topsy-turvydom, this musical and
dramatic turning of ideas wrong side out, to end ?
Sitting at the play, constantly consulting my watch,
longing, hoping that the piece might come to an end
and that I for one [possibly the only one] might be
released from imprisonment in a narrow stall, I
amused myself with considering and endeavouring to
analyse Mr. Gilbert's methods."

This very captious critic then proceeds to pour
forth his venom against Gilbert and Sullivan alike.

"Gilbert," he says, "starts primarily with the
object of bringing Truth and Love and Friendship
into contempt, just as we are taught the devil does.
Mr. Gilbert tries to prove that there is no such thing
as virtue, but that we are all lying, selfish, vain, and
unworthy. In the Gilbertian world there are no
martyrs, no patriots, and no lovers."

Photo by Elliott & Fry.

MR. DURWARD LELY.

Photo by Ellis & Walery.

MR. ROBERT EVETT.

After several paragraphs equally eloquent of a perverted mind, he concludes with the confession that—

" Rather than take a stall at the Savoy [the question arises, was or was not the gentleman on the Press List ?] it would pay me better to stand at the corner of a street and watch the coarse humours of the same class, of a Punch and Judy show—as a moral lesson I prefer Punch and Judy to ' Iolanthe.' "

What are we to say to such " criticism " ? When we disclose the fact that it came from the dramatic and musical critic of a leading sporting periodical, it may strike one that the prophetic scribe might better have confined his talents to supplying Turf Tips to punters, instead of pronouncing a favourite like " Iolanthe " to be a certain non-stayer—seeing that our critic was inwardly convinced that the opera would never run.

I wonder whether, if living, he has moderated his views of Gilbert and Sullivan, since their works, including " Iolanthe," have survived to be accepted by an intelligent public as veritable classics.

CHAPTER XIV

To analyse and define the psychological subtlety of a poet's mind is beyond the reasoning power of the present writer. An ordinary man's thoughts are generally restricted to the consideration of what has been or what is. The mists of the future are impenetrable to his limited imagination. He marvels how it is given to any of his fellow mortals to view the " will be " beyond his own narrow span of life. He wonders how the poet can compose epic verse, descriptive of incidents and events of generations to come, minutely etching the characteristics of people yet unborn. And then, when it all comes true, how miraculous it appears to the view of the platitudinarian !

Yet, after all, when we come to reflect how Solomon of old declared there was nothing new under the sun— even in his early epoch—is there so much cause for astonishment that Shakespeare was able, in the sixteenth century, to picture the actions and revolutions, the fashions and the follies or the wiser idiosyncrasies of men—and women too—of this the twentieth century? The poet was conscious that whatever *is* has been before and will be again.

"What then?" you ask.

Well, then, the question is, if you and I possessed the intuition of Solomon, or Shakespeare, might we not be denied the privilege we now enjoy of sometimes finding something that seems like new—even in the works of Mr. G. Bernard Shaw, or the doctrine of the Futurists? Happily, perhaps, for us, our mental visage is not so keen.

Such is the spasmodic whiff of mock philosophy that passes across the surface of one's mind on approaching the subject of "Princess Ida," a play whose main theme was woman's attitude towards man from a topsy-turvy point of view. Our observations may appear somewhat involved, but the idea we would convey is in brief that, whilst there were no Suffragettes in Queen Victoria's reign—or, if there were, they were wisely latent, certainly they were not militant—yet did not Tennyson seriously, and, after him, Gilbert, facetiously propound the doctrine that was eventually to resolve itself into the present-day cry, "Votes for Women"?

Just fourteen years before the Savoy production of "Princess Ida" (January 5th, 1884), the Olympic Theatre, then under the management of Mr. W. H. Liston, witnessed the performance of "The Princess; a whimsical parody (being a respectful perversion of Mr. Tennyson's poem), by W. S. Gilbert." This was in the days when the rhymed, punning burlesques of

Planché, Brough, Byron, Burnand, and other clever playwrights, still flourished. It became Gilbert's ambition to reform and raise the tone of musical plays, to put an end to the ultra-frivolous stuff and nonsense, some of which, Gilbert admitted in an address to the public, had come from his own unbridled pen. He believed the public taste to be ripe for entertainment of a higher class. And so our author turned to Tennyson, and borrowed the characters and theme of the laureate's delightful poem. The outcome was a clever, playful parody in blank verse, relieved by a few light lyrics set to popular tunes from grand operas by Donizetti, Verdi, Rossini, and other famous composers, to whom, by the way, no fees were payable.

Gilbert's first edition of "The Princess" failed to make much impression, chiefly because, as we have previously argued, the public had not yet been educated up to the Gilbertian standard of humour, which was more refined and elegant than any they had been accustomed to.

So the Olympic "Princess" was consigned to the lumber-room of plays that have failed, there to rest and rust for a dozen years and more, forgotten and despised.

But Gilbert's faith in the true worth of his adopted daughter remained unshaken. "The Princess" had been condemned in 1870 ; but condemned by an ignorant and misguided jury on the evidence of false witnesses. Her illustrious Highness, and the authors of her being, had hardly met with poetic justice in the measure of her presentation. For instance, her music

—second-hand grand-operatic music—had not been found in harmony with her peculiar court and surroundings. Further, her supporters may not have been trained to speak in blank verse to the academical standard of Girton or Castle Adamant. But Gilbert believed that his fascinating, yet eccentric heroine, if brought to new trial before the more enlightened tribunal of a later generation, might upset the former verdict. In this confidence the author was readily supported by Sullivan and D'Oyly Carte. Consequently the despised one of the Olympic Gods was reclaimed from obscurity, to be reclothed in costly raiments of " academic silks, in hue the lilac with a silken hood to each."

To the " Princess Ida " Gilbert gave new songs to sing—songs with words not unworthy the author of—

> " Sweet and low, sweet and low,
> Wind of the western sea "—

and Gilbert's lyrics were set to music as enchanting to the ear as any that had been given to the world by Sullivan.

The result more than justified the venture. Far more indeed. " Princess Ida " was welcomed with open arms by the Savoyards. The Press pronounced the new opera to be a success as complete as any in which the brilliant author and gifted composer had been associated. The public, rising to the occasion, once more metaphorically hoisted the conquering Trio, Gilbert, Sullivan, and D'Oyly Carte, shoulder high, and carried them triumphant round the town.

In two notable respects " Princess Ida " marked a departure from the author's usual methods. First, the opera was in three acts instead of two; second, it was written in blank verse. Of the quality of the verse it may be possible to judge by the following true anecdote.

A play-goer from Yorkshire, after seeing " Princess Ida," was asked what he thought of the piece. " Well," he replied, " I do like t' music well enow; 't be bang up to date and full o' tunes I can whistle; but t' words sounds *too much like Shakespeare* for t' likes o' me to understand."

This reminds me of another story told concerning an old lady in a Midland town, who, after a visit to " H.M.S. Pinafore," declared it to be, in her estimation, the next best play to " Hamlet " she had ever seen. " First," she remarked, " it's so full of sayings I've heard before—it seemed like an old friend, you see. And it's all so breezy, too; it brings a sniff of the briny ocean right away into this stuffy inland town. And then that ship—it's so life-like that I couldn't help wondering if any of those sisters and cousins and aunts ever felt sea-sick whilst acting on board. But what I couldn't understand about ' H.M.S. Pinafore ' was *that third act.* How all the ship's crew and the young ladies and all come to find themselves in a law-court, dancing and singing and flirting with the judge —a man, I could have sworn, was the First Lord of the Admiralty in Acts I. and II., I never could make out that ending to the ' Pinafore.' "

But the wonder is why no one explained to the dear

old soul that what she took to be the third act of the opera was, in fact, " Trial by Jury," which was played as an afterpiece to " H.M.S. Pinafore."

Our Yorkshire friend's judgment of the music was by no means too flattering. In " Princess Ida " Arthur Sullivan gave us of his best—songs full of grace, fancy, delicious melody, and, as ever, brimming over with rich humour ; choral and orchestral passages as novel, quaint, and picturesque as any the master's mind had ever conceived.

As regards the material " production," nothing that care, liberal expenditure, and consummate taste could do was left undone by D'Oyly Carte. The staging of " Princess Ida, or Castle Adamant," as the opera was entitled, marked the last phase of perfection. The costumes were as gorgeous in effect as they were rich in texture, exquisite in colour and design. The " girl graduates," as they appeared on the Savoy stage, must truly have been living realities of Tennyson's ideals.

The costly silver-gilt armour, specially designed and manufactured in Paris by the famed firm of Le Grange et Cie., excelled in brilliancy anything of the sort ever seen at Drury Lane.

The scenic sets, those of Acts I. and III. by Emden, that of Act II. by Hawes Craven, were masterpieces of those distinguished artists. In short, no previous opera by Gilbert and Sullivan had involved such vast outlay and been so sumptuously placed upon the stage as " Princess Ida."

But, despite the skill and care of the stage-management, one slight mishap occurred. Through some miscalculation of the master-carpenter, the "stage-well" into which "Princess Ida" descends from behind a flowery bank was of insufficient depth; consequently the gallery-gods were regaled with a gratuitous view of Miss Leonora Braham floundering on a feather mattress spread to receive her.

The brilliant *première* of "Princess Ida" was, unknown to the audience, dimmed by the shadow of a very regrettable incident. When Sullivan arrived at the theatre I noticed that he was looking haggard and depressed. I inquired the reason. "Oh, nothing particular," he replied; "I've had rather bad news—but I'll tell you all about it later." It was not until the end of the opera, when Sir Arthur had taken his call before the curtain, that he told me how, on his way to the theatre, on opening an evening paper, he had read that the ——— Bank, in which the bulk of his money was deposited, had stopped payment. His loss was very heavy, and that he was able to conduct the opera that night was evidence of his indomitable pluck and self-abnegation.

In those minds which judge a stage-work on the main standpoint of artistic merit, without reference to the degree of popularity it may achieve, "Princess Ida" strengthened faith in the ability of our author and composer to produce together a work of more serious import, one that should come under the category of Grand Opera. It was a consummation devoutly to be wished by all who professed an interest in British music; whether such hope was to be realized or disappointed remained then in the lap of the gods.

The following is the original cast of characters who, at the Savoy Theatre on Saturday, January 5th, 1884, presented—

PRINCESS IDA, OR CASTLE ADAMANT

King Hildebrand . .	MR. RUTLAND BARRINGTON
Hilarion (*His Son*) . . .	. MR. H. BRACEY
Cyril } (*Hilarion's Friends*)	. MR. DURWARD LELY
Florian }	. MR. CHAS. RYLEY
King Gama . . .	MR. GEORGE GROSSMITH
Arac . .	MR. RICHARD TEMPLE
Guron } (*His Sons*)	. MR. WARWICK GRAY
Scynthius } . . .	. . MR. LUGG
Princess Ida . .	MISS LEONORA BRAHAM
(*Gama's Daughter*)	
Lady Blanche	MISS BRANDRAM
(*Professor of Abstract Science*)	
Lady Psyche . . .	MISS KATE CHARD
(*Professor of Humanities*)	
Melissa	MISS JESSIE BOND
(*Lady Blanche's Daughter*)	
Sacharissa	MISS SYBIL GREY
Chloe	MISS HEATHCOTE
Ada	MISS LILIAN CARR
(*Girl Graduates*)	

Soldiers, Courtiers, " Girl Graduates," " Daughters of the Plough," etc.

It is not for me to offer any critical remarks about the performance. To express personal opinion on any individual actor or actress would appear impertinent. Yet I cannot refrain from placing on record the excellent impression made by Miss Leonora Braham in the title-rôle. Miss Braham's rendering of the by no means easy songs, and her admirable delivery of the famous speech addressing the "Women of Adamant, fair Neophytes"—I number among my pleasant reminiscences. Mr. Henry Bracey, whose impersonation of Prince Hilarion will be favourably remembered by Savoy patrons, has, for many years past, held the post of Business Manager to the late Mr. J. C. Williamson, the well-known Antipodean *impresario*, who, until his death a year ago, leased the Australasian "rights" in the Gilbert and Sullivan operas.

To conclude these notes and reflections on "Princess Ida," I cannot do better than quote a few remarks from an able critical review which appeared in *The Times* after the first performance of the opera :

"Whatever may be thought of the abstract value of Messrs. Gilbert and Sullivan's work, it has the great merit of putting every one in a good temper. It was pleasant to watch the audience on Saturday. The occupants of stalls and boxes, including many musicians and literary men of note, the dress circle, and even the unruly ' gods ' in the gallery, were equally delighted, and expressed their delight after the manner of their kind. To a poet and a musician who can achieve this by morally harmless and artistically legitimate means it would be unjust to judge the burst of applause which at the end of the piece brought Mr. Gilbert and Sir Arthur Sullivan and Mr. D'Oyly Carte, the energetic manager of the Savoy Theatre, before the curtain. To play the stern critic in such circumstances, one would require the temper of the philanthropic King Gama of the play."

CHAPTER XV

LIKE unto the stars, first nights at a West-end London theatre differ, one from another, in glory. Yet, in general aspect and incident there is, as a rule, no marked distinction between them.

If the play to be produced is by a popular author, with popular artists to support it, a spirit of confidence pervades the house. The audience awaits curtain-rise with the calm solemnity of a special jury, yet happy in the anticipation of a " feast of reason and a flow of soul." They hope for the best. If, on the other hand, a new dramatist is to be introduced to them, a certain degree of apathy and indifference subdues the excitement of the occasion. People speculate whether or not they will " spot a winner." Past experience guides them to lay odds against the desired issue.

Theatrical " first-nighters " are professional play-goers ; each individual is a living encyclopædia of the drama. Every one of them has been a student of the stage since his or her first visit to a theatre, and now, gathered together, they constitute a body of amateur experts, unpaid critics responsible to no editor nor censor for the opinions they form of their own free and unfettered judgment. And these, unquestionably, are the surest prophets, the most reliable arbiters of the fate of all plays. Every " first-nighter " knows every other one, though the great crowd of witnesses may be ever so cosmopolitan. And so, when, after patiently awaiting admission for many a weary hour, they at length gain their seats, they pass the interval pending the performance in their orthodox manner—the men of sober mien peruse the latest edition of the evening paper ; the women turn over the leaves of a novelette, or, more industriously, ply the knitting-needle ; whilst more restless, youthful idlers engage in verbal platoon firing with blank cartridge of chaff and repartee. Anon the galleryites watch the dilatory, dawdling entry of the " upper classes " to the stalls and boxes. Everybody who is anybody is known to them. Recognizing in turn each distinguished personage, statesman or diplomat, hero or poet, millionaire or stock-broker, peer or pet actress, they welcome each respectively in such a manner as betrays their sentiments of esteem or otherwise. Such is a brief outline sketch of an ordinary London *première* ; but a Savoy " first-night," it may be said, used, in the old days, to be a thing of itself. The occasion was marked by features distinct from any obtaining elsewhere.

Our faithful patrons and camp-followers formed a corps, more or less independent of the general army of play-goers. They might be described as Territorials. They liked to call themselves " Savoyards." These never came prepared to scoff; they were too well assured that they would remain to praise the fare which their generous host, Mr. D'Oyly Carte, had caused to be provided for their delectation by those renowned *Escoffiers* of the lyric kitchen—Gilbert and Sullivan.

Here may fittingly be recalled another notable experiment tried by D'Oyly Carte in the early days of his Savoy régime. This was the institution of the Queue System for the benefit of play-goers awaiting admission to the unreserved parts of the theatre. Once again Carte's judgment was called into question by the wise-heads who were over-faithful to past traditions. "The public," they vowed, "will never stand being marshalled and driven like a flock of sheep into their pens." Wrong again were those unreasoning prophets.

The crowd of pittites and gallery-gods assembled in the early hours of the eventful day, and, extending down the steep of Beaufort Buildings to the theatre doors, readily accepted the new regulation, fell into the ranks of the queue, and realized its advantages. Instead of the old order of " might *versus* right," with its rough and rude push and crush, the new rule was " first come first served." The experiment proved so successful that the system was forthwith adopted by every theatrical manager. Humble patrons of the Savoy will ever gratefully remember how, through the kind consideration of Mrs. D'Oyly Carte, on the occasion of first-nights, the weary crowd was refreshed by the management with tea and cake, before the performance began. It was a gracious act that did much to add to the growing popularity of the Carte manage-

9

ment and to increase the number of avowed Savoy
champions and apostles.

There was no " rag, tag, and bobtail " attached to a
Savoy crowd. If, perchance, there were present any
claqueurs of the rowdy class they were never in evi-
dence. The refining influence of Gilbert's wit and
Sullivan's convincing music sufficed to tame the wildest
Hooligan from Shoreditch and the East, and to compel
every man and woman entering the sanctum of the
Savoy to put on company manners.

The people, packed in close order in the gallery, resembled a huge, well-dressed concert choir, not only in
the formation of their ranks, tier above tier, but in
the manner of their behaviour. As soon as they had
settled in their places, instead of reading books and
newspapers, our accomplished " gods " delighted the
house with a gratuitous recital of every favourite chorus
or part-song from the Gilbert and Sullivan répertoire.
A self-appointed conductor stationed in the centre of
the front row was readily accepted, and, responsive to
his beat, the amateur choir rendered in excellent tone
and *tempo* not only the breezy and easy tunes of
" Pinafore," but also such choice and delicate *morceaux*
as " Hail, Poetry ! " the unaccompanied chorus from
" The Pirates of Penzance," and the more exacting
sestette, " I hear the soft voice," from " Patience."

The improvised prefatory concerts—which, by the
way, I am just reminded, were not confined to the
gallery, but were contributed to, in turn, by the *Pit*
choir, became such an important item of a Savoy
première that they had the effect of attracting the early

attendance of the élite in the stalls and circles. Doubtless, the vocal ability of these *première* choristers was attributable to the fact that they comprised a large number of members of suburban amateur societies to whom the Savoy tunes were as familiar as the National Anthem, " Rule Britannia," or "Hymns, Ancient and Modern."

So interesting and attractive was the performance taking place "in front" that our author and composer, with some of the principals, forgetting for a moment the responsible parts they were themselves about to play, listened from behind the curtain and joined in the applause that followed each chorus.

Reference to this incident reawakens reminiscences of the attitude of every one, the disposition of everything pertaining to the stage and the orchestra on these eventful occasions.

Whilst in front of the house under the able control, courtesy, and tact of our Acting-manager, Mr. George Edwardes, all went with the smoothness and decorum of a private "At Home," behind the curtain everything was marked by the quiet discipline of a regimental camp or the deck of a battle-ship. Every man was ready at his post, every rope was coiled, every scene-baton was adjusted, every incandescent lamp tested—all was taut and trim and ship-shape. Of all " the hands" behind the scenes the call-boy alone betrayed nervous anxiety—"Shrimp," as he was familiarly called, was ubiquitous, literally "all over the shop." Like all his colleagues, "Shrimp" was impressed with the importance of the occasion. He appeared to entertain the idea that every lorgnette in the wide world was now being focussed on the Savoy stage, and so he, for one, was resolved to do his level best to make the show a success. How far his efforts succeeded he himself, looking back across the years, can contemplate with supreme satisfaction.

Turning now to more important factors in the scene, to wit, our manager, author, and composer, I trust that the idle gossip I dare to convey touching their demeanour on first nights may not disturb their now resting and no longer anxious souls. When I recall their restlessness and half-veiled anxiety on these momentous nights I cannot forbear to smile.

First, I seem to see again D'Oyly Carte with all the calm concern and forethought of a wise Commander-in-Chief long before the doors are opened, beginning his rounds of the theatre; I watch him peeping into every corner and crevice of the house as though he should discover some lurking evil that might jeopardize his venture. Inwardly satisfied that everything necessary to success has been done, and well done, our chief bestows placid smiles upon every faithful servant or attaché whom he meets. Now and again he pops his head in at the door of my room—"Everything all right, François?" Without awaiting my assurance that all is well in my department, he is off again to pursue another tour of inspection. :

Meanwhile Arthur Sullivan arrives; I had left him half an hour ago after a quiet dinner together. But now he enters muffled against the night air. "Good evening, François; bitter cold outside." I help him

off with his overcoat.   He hangs it on a peg, warms his
hands at my stove, before enticing them into a pair of
white kids ; he lights a cigarette, adjusts his monocle,
and peeps into the special *Evening Standard* ; the
next moment he asks me to give him a lift on with his
overcoat.   This done, he lights another cigarette and
remarks, "Just going for a stroll round—shan't be
long."   He mounts the stairs to the stage-door,
where he exchanges a cheery word with Manton, our
worthy Cerberus.   Two minutes later he reappears
in my room and goes through the same process of dis-
robing, etc.   This accomplished, he asks me to accompany him to the band-room.   Here he cracks humorous
jokes which vastly amuse the gentlemen of the orchestra
—placing them at perfect ease.

Thus the *maestro* was wont to kill the half-hour
preceding his appearance in the conductor's chair.

Gilbert's nervous devices for concealing nervousness
were very similar to those of his colleagues.

With nonchalant air, our author paces the stage.
With his hands deep in his pockets, he inspects the
set scene, occasionally passing a joke to the master-
carpenter.   Proceeding thence to the corridors, he
knocks at the door of the *prima donna's* dressing-room
and asks, "All right, my dear ? "   The lady, in reply,
shouts excitedly, "Oh—is that you, Mr. Gilbert ?—I
wanted to ask you if you would mind if I——"

"My dear girl—do just whatever you like—*I* don't
mind—the rehearsals are all over, and I am now at your
mercy."

Gilbert then passes along to have a word or two with

Grossmith and Barrington. After this he disappears
through the stage-door to enjoy a quiet stroll on the
Victoria Embankment.

This relation brings to mind a story Gilbert used to
tell against himself concerning his experience on the
first night of "Gretchen," one of his early plays produced at the Olympic in 1879.

Suffering from an acute attack of nervous debility,
as he termed it, the author felt it impossible to remain
within the theatre. Accordingly, he spent the evening
patrolling up and down the Strand, wandering through
Covent Garden and Drury Lane. He continued his
peregrinations until he thought it was about time to
return to the Olympic to take his call before the curtain.
Arriving at the theatre, he discovered the last fragments of the audience dispersing from the doors.
Whereupon he addressed an outside official to whom
he was unknown. "Is the play over?" he timidly
inquired. "Over!" exclaimed the man, "I should
rather say it *was* over—over and done for. *Never see'd
such a frost in all my born days.*"

Gilbert thanked his lucky stars that he had absented
himself from such a débâcle—our author, be it observed,
was not accustomed to *frosts*.

CHAPTER XVI

WE have now arrived at October 1884, just nine years after the production, at the Gaiety Theatre, of "Thespis," the first joint work of Gilbert and Sullivan.

Here the reader, having "sat out" a rough recital of seven operas under my very erratic literary conduct, may be glad to indulge in a few bars' rest.

Let us then quit for a short while the Savoy Theatre, where a revival of "The Sorcerer" is in rehearsal to succeed "Princess Ida." Those who have followed the many triumphs of our famous Savoyards may be inquisitive to learn something, be it ever so little, concerning their private lives, and the manner in which our author and composer filled in the gaps of leisure during the lengthy runs of their operas.

Neither Gilbert nor Sullivan was ever an idler. Each, according to his own individual taste or hobby, was able to enjoy to his heart's content the pleasures of life which are the fruits of successful effort. But they never grew weary of work. Ambition was not satiated by the luxury of attainment. Gilbert and Sullivan had other fields to conquer beyond the walls of the Savoy. And so, whilst the people were nightly crowding to the theatre in holiday mood to revel in the feast of mirth and melody, the men who had provided the repast were busy with brain and pen preparing, it might be, yet more substantial if not more tempting fare.

There seems to be much nonsense talked about what Gilbert and Sullivan might have done with the talents they possessed. One might just as wisely question why man, having learnt to fly, is content to remain a citizen of the earth, when, if he liked, he could soar away beyond the clouds to dwell in the higher and brighter realms that are supposed to be located there. There are people—some cynics, some malcontents, and some noodles ; all professing more or less admiration of their gifted compatriots—people who never cease lamenting that neither Gilbert nor Sullivan aimed high enough ; that they were satisfied to continue potting at low-flying follies, mere town-sparrows, whilst, with their skill, they might have brought to earth the Golden Eagles of Parnassus to be stuffed and placed in the British Museum.

These quidnuncs argue among themselves the causes why our two great artists never soared to loftier planes of art. " Was it shallowness of soul or congested ambition ? " they ask. " Or was their motive-power too purely mercenary and sordid ? "

Such inquisitors might be reminded that Sheridan, and, perhaps, even Shakespeare, were guilty of writing " pot-boilers " sometimes, and that Beethoven did not continue composing Symphonies until he found a demand for them. The great *maestro* was not above composing a valse or a polka at a very low figure when occasion offered.

If such a cause has to be tried in public, the present writer, although he holds no brief for the defence, firmly believes that wise counsel's opinion would find that, if any persons suffered through the default of Gilbert and Sullivan, they were the indicted parties themselves.

And what a multitude of witnesses might be called to testify that no two Englishmen, ever before or since, worked so hard and helped so much to make merry the lives of their fellow countrymen and women as the author and composer of the Savoy Operas !

But, after all has been said or suggested, did not both Gilbert and Sullivan, each in his way, sometimes aim higher than simply to hit the bull's-eye of popular taste ?

Gilbert may not have been another Sheridan ; Sullivan may have failed to reach the empyrean heights gained by Beethoven. True ! yet will not their names be handed down to posterity, to be cherished and honoured from generation to generation by all the English-speaking race ?

Of course, we should all have been proud if Sir William had bequeathed us a dramatic work to be placed in the category of " The School for Scandal." Still, although he scarcely succeeded in serious play-writing of classic degree, Gilbert gave us "Sweethearts," and "Pygmalion and Galatea," "Tragedy and Comedy," and, may we not add, "The Yeomen of the Guard"? —for these alone we should be grateful.

Equally, of course, we, as a nation, would have been prouder than ever had Sir Arthur, with some stupendous *magnum opus* of musical art, succeeded in eclipsing Beethoven's "Choral Symphony"; but most of us are perfectly content to have been given "The Tempest" music, the "In Memoriam" overture, and "The Golden Legend," to say nothing of the thousand-and-one lesser gems that have enriched our music libraries.

Here our thoughts must be allowed to digress from the main route of these reminiscences to dedicate a page or two specially to my old friend Arthur Sullivan, not only in the character of composer, but also in that of charming companion.

My earliest association, of a professional character, with Sullivan was in the year 1867, when he was organist of St. Peter's Church, Cranley Gardens, the vicar being the Rev. Francis Byng (now the Earl of Strafford), Chaplain to the Speaker. For a brief period I acted as Sullivan's deputy. It was arranged that I should receive a telegram on Saturday evening whenever he required my services on the following day. The consequence was that a telegram reached me punctually on *every* Saturday eve, until eventually I took it as a matter of course that I was wanted at the church, and so never failed to attend. Sullivan would pop in occasionally for part of the morning service, and then beat a retreat through the vestry door. The choir were always on the *qui vive* for the appearance in the organ-loft of their young curly-headed "chief," who at all times made his presence felt in their midst. I was often reminded of this incident in after-years at the Savoy. The effect produced on the stage company when, during the performance of an opera, the composer's form suddenly appeared at the wings, was similar to that felt by St. Peter's Choir of old. The whisper passed through the ranks of the chorus, "Look out: the Boss is here." Sir Arthur's shining monocle certainly possessed the magic power of transforming apathy into enthusiasm.

My deputizing at St. Peter's Church came to an abrupt termination. A telegram from Sullivan asking me to play at a wedding having miscarried, I was *non est inventus* at the appointed time. Whereupon the reverend Vicar simply remarked, "Exit Mr. François Cellier."

It was not until twelve years later that I touched an organ again, so that it was not without some trepidation that I accepted the post of organist at a Surbiton Church. Meeting Sullivan shortly after my first Sunday on duty, I was asked, "Well, how did you get on?" I told him that the morning performance had been a not very smooth rehearsal, but that I was all right at night.

Sullivan then related how he had once had a similar experience. After having given the organ a long rest, he was asked to play at a nobleman's private chapel in the country. "And how did *you* get on?" I inquired. Sullivan replied, " The psalms completely flummox'd me. I had not the presence of mind to change the stops all through—it was a double chant with strange ' pointing '—I was so overcome with nervousness that my fingers became glued to the key-board—I could not remove them. The result was that the choir *went running about the city*, whilst I sat *grinning like a dog*, after the fashion of David and his enemies as recorded in Psalm lix."

Such are some of my earlier reminiscences dated back several years before I was appointed Musical Director of the Opera Comique.

Sir Arthur Sullivan, as is well known, remained to the end of his days a bachelor. His domestic joys and cares were centred on his aged mother, to whom he was deeply devoted. For a few years after the death of her husband, Mrs. Sullivan shared with her widowed daughter-in-law (Mrs. Fred Sullivan) and her children a quaint old Georgian mansion named Northumberland House, in Fulham. Here Arthur delighted to spend his Sundays as often as he could escape from his relentless pursuers. The quiet hours passed in that old-world homestead, free from the turmoil of the theatre and concert-hall, away from the pomp and circumstance and the irksome idolatry of Society, were to Sullivan the happiest of his life.

Arthur Sullivan has been described by one of his biographers as " a disciple of the beautiful." No worthier monograph could be applied! Loyal and tried citizen of London as he was, in the country he sought and found his loftiest inspiration. Accordingly

much of the spring and summer time was spent at
his delightful riverside home at Walton-on-Thames.
From the whispering trees, the sighing evening zephyrs
and the song-birds ; from the ripple of the stream, the
plash of oars in the water, and the merry laughter of
holiday-makers, he gathered fresh stores of melody,
and, weaving them into Nature's wondrous concord of
sweet sounds, created, it might be, a majestic chorus
or graceful dance, a plaintive ballad, or dreamy
lullaby.

> " As effortless as woodland nooks
> Send violets up and paint them blue,"

so did Sullivan's genius send forth flowers of melody
fragrant and everlasting.

I have known other species of composers, musicians
varying in degree of what is sometimes mis-called
genius ; mortals who are prone to boast that they
seek inspiration in day-dreams (judging from their
produce it might be imagined that they had been
inspired rather by night-mares).

" In order to compose *divinely*," say these æsthetic
dreamers, " it is necessary to lose one's material self
in a trance." Read what my friend Bridgeman has
to say on this subject.

" I remember once meeting a specimen of those
spirit-compelled musical Futurists in a secluded spot
on the north coast of Devon. In the twilight of a
lovely summer's evening I observed a form standing
erect on a cliff overhanging the Bristol Channel. At
first I took it to be a sign-post, for an arm was pointing

horizontally across the purple main. On approaching nearer I discovered *it* to be nothing more nor less than a man—a poet-musician, one whom I had casually met in the musical circles of London, and whose acquaintance I might now claim.

" Addressing him by name, I extended my hand in greeting. For a moment he did not stir : he was under a spell. At length, with a sigh, in a voice which groaned with emotion, he appealed to me thus : ' Friend, pray do not disturb me—I am composing— I am in the throes of a sea-symphony.' Of course I was too polite to continue the conversation, but I felt very tempted to inquire whether it was a Symphony in C or an ode to the mud of the Bristol Channel that was so monopolizing his mental faculties."

The poor fellow, I understand, long since passed beyond the veil without bequeathing to the world that work which he dreamed would be immortal, or leaving behind him even his name and address in *Who's Who*.

Nevertheless he was, so I've been told, a man of more than common musical ability, which, rightly directed, might have brought him to the front. Unfortunately, he had fallen a victim to the mock æsthetic craze of the " Patience " period !

Arthur Sullivan was a composer of a very different type. It was my privilege to be his frequent companion during his composing moods, but if I wanted to speak to him I was never afraid of frightening away the spirit of inspiration. Undoubtedly he, being of poetic temperament, found a dim religious light helpful to the composition of a sacred cantata ; a quiet woodland nook might attune his lyre to a love-song, or an infant's cradle might evoke a lullaby ; but Arthur never, so far as I know, found it necessary to seek the seclusion of the cloisters or the woods or the nursery for the purpose he had in hand.

Sullivan was a reincarnated Orpheus. Music was to him the breath of life, not the painful spasm of congested lungs. His disposition was so perpetually brimming over with sympathetic humour that he would take delight in discovering subjects for facetious music in most unmusical sounds ; such, for instance, as the monotonous notes of the cuckoo, the bray of a donkey, the cry of an "old clo'" man, or the puff and pulsation of a heavy railway train rumbling its way up a steep incline. He preferred to laugh and learn lessons from a broken-keyed hurdy-gurdy, rather than rain anathemas on the poor Italian organ-grinder.

Sullivan's soul was so imbued with the joy of living that it might well be wondered how he could ever divert his thoughts to the musical setting of sacred subjects. In this respect, without question, he owed much to the associations of his boyhood.

At the Chapel Royal his mind was, to use a vulgar phrase, "fed up" with hymns and chants, anthems and ancient madrigals, which, morning, noon, and night, constituted the chief mental food of "the children" of St. James's. Reference to the Chapel Royal reminds me, by the way, of a joke attributable to Sullivan. It is a story which one might well blush to relate ; but, being of that kind, it is all the more likely to amuse.

During the Litany one of "the children" standing

next to Arthur in the choir substituted for the proper words of the Prayer-book the following very irreverent impromptu : " That little girl coming up the aisle makes-my-mouth-water." To which Arthur responded : " Hold your tongue or you'll be hung, that is the Bish-op's-daughter."

It is very wrong, we know, to tell tales out of school, yet we all do it on occasion. The Rev. Thomas Helmore, our much-respected pastor and master, has passed away far out of hearing, and so nobody who might be concerned in this exposure of past peccadilloes will suffer for our gossip.

Cavillers are inclined to aver that Sullivan's sacred music was, at times, too secular ; whilst, *vice versâ*, his opera-tunes were occasionally too sacred in character. Alas, in this connection, we cannot forget that representative of a sporting journal to whom we have directed attention in an earlier chapter, that remarkable critic who described the music of Iolanthe as " sacred harmonics gone wrong." Well, one cannot hold oneself responsible for another man's aural instincts.

Again : honest and devout lovers of music with a keen ear for time, but without any atom of technical knowledge of the musical art, oftentimes remark, " Oh—I've heard *that* somewhere before ! " " Very likely, sir, you may have, but is it not equally possible that you have heard it from the voice of Nature from whence the notes were borrowed ? "

Let it not be supposed that friendship and intense admiration blind us to any imperfections perceived by others less prejudiced in the work of our composer.

Sullivan was not above suspicion of having stolen a bar or two, here and there, from another musician. He himself was ever the first to plead guilty to such soft impeachment. But, it may be asked, is it a more unpardonable offence to paraphrase a musical theme than to parody a proverb ? Surely the composer of " Princess Ida," when he played an occasional joke at the expense of Handel, was guilty of no greater fraud than the author who "respectfully" perverted Tennyson. On one occasion, when accused of having plagiarized Molloy's " Love's sweet Song " in his " When a Maiden marries " in " The Gondoliers," Sullivan replied : " My good friend, as a matter of fact, I don't happen ever to have heard the song you mention, but if I had you must please remember that *Molloy and I had only seven notes to work on between us*." A propos this subject, let me call on Cunningham Bridgeman to give an instance of Arthur Sullivan's aptness to appropriate a musical subject that had appealed to his ear, and of his readiness to confess to having done so.

" Being a very old friend of Sullivan's, I was privileged to lunch with him on Sundays. This was more particularly during a period when his mother was ' keeping house ' for him in Victoria Street, Westminster. On one occasion, faithful to my one particular virtue, arriving at the flat in punctual time, I was, as usual, heartily welcomed by Mrs. Sullivan, who made haste to inform me that Arthur might be a little late in returning from a call he had to pay, but that he had left word that I was to be sure to stay

10

and lunch. My kind hostess, always bubbling over
with loving pride of her gifted son, once again, *pour
passer le temps*, invited me to inspect the collection of
valued treasures, comprising presentation gifts in
gold, souvenirs in silver, and other such choice and
interesting knick-knacks as are generally to be found in
the home of a celebrity. Lying in its open case upon
the grand piano was a violin. I was about to handle
it when the dear old lady exclaimed, in accents of
alarm, ' Oh please, please don't touch that! You will
never guess who that violin belongs to! ' Of course,
although I could not fail to notice a ducal coronet and
monogram on the case, I would not, for all the world,
venture to guess the owner's name. In a confidential
whisper Mrs. Sullivan informed me that it was the
Duke of Edinburgh's fiddle ; that His Royal Highness
had been having a run through some duets with ' dear
Arthur ' last evening, and would probably be round
again to-night.

" It was a delightful object-lesson in maternal pride
to watch the countenance of Arthur Sullivan's fond
mother as she let me into this profound state secret.

" But to come to the main point and purport of my
story. The moment Sullivan arrived and saw that I
was present, without waiting even to remove his overcoat, he went straight to the piano, saying, ' What d'you
think of this for a tune, Bridgeman ? ' To my amaze-
ment I recognized the refrain of a very unacademical
ditty called ' Impecuniosity ' which, a year or two ago,
I had perpetrated and disposed of to the great lion
comique, G. H. Macdermott, who sang it as a duet
with Herbert Campbell in the Drury Lane Pantomime,
scoring, so I was assured, a big success. ' Where on
earth did you pick up that ? ' I asked Sullivan.
' Well, the fact is, I've just come from the organ-loft
of a church in Forest Hill where an old friend and

pupil of mine does duty. By way of a "Voluntary," the organist played this. Never having heard it before, and the theme appealing to me, I asked my friend what it was and he told me *it was a comic song* by a man called Bridgeman—I wondered if you could be the culprit, and now—you stand confessed. Well, old friend, *don't be surprised or angry if you hear something very like it in my next opera.*'

"On the first night of the next opera, which was 'The Mikado,' I eagerly listened to each succeeding musical number, hoping to catch the refrain of *my* song—inwardly resolved that, should it occur, I should insist upon my name appearing as joint composer of 'The Mikado.' Alas, for my vaulting ambition—disappointment was my reward ; the subject of 'Impecuniosity' was omitted, or, anyway, it was so disguised in orchestration that I failed to identify my progeny. Such an opportunity of achieving fame never occurred to me again."

The above is Cunningham Bridgeman's reminiscence —not mine—still, whilst we are impertinently debating as to the originality of our composer, the anecdote quoted may serve as an illustration of Sullivan's unblushing candour. Yet Arthur Sullivan, with all his unconcern regarding minor responsibilities, was by no means insensible to the dictum of honest criticism. No man whose bread and butter is dependent upon public suffrage was ever more anxious to learn the judgment and verdict of the press. It was amusing to witness his impatience to read the notices which appeared in the papers the morning following the production of a new work. Praise was, naturally, pleasant and grateful to him; but, if ever he had just cause to complain of harsh or unjust critical remarks, he simply smiled serenely and treated the matter with apparent indifference, accepting the " slings and arrows of outrageous " scribes as placidly as Gulliver endured the teasings of the Lilliputians.

CHAPTER XVII

Sir Arthur Sullivan in private life—Alone with the composer—His
leading characteristics—Society's idol—Sullivan's visit to the
Riviera—His entourage—Work and recreation in the sunny
South—Sullivan's pets—Parrot stories—Arthur Sullivan knighted.

THERE is no memory I cherish more dearly than that
associated with the days spent alone with Arthur
Sullivan away from the turmoil of the town and the
petty cares and vexations of the theatre. To all who
knew him as intimately as I did, the place left vacant
by his death is one that can never be filled. Sir Arthur
was truly one of Nature's proudest handiworks.
Success and the flattery of the world left unsullied his
natural disposition, the key-note of which was modesty
—modesty of that pure kind that strengthens and beau-
tifies true merit. If one was ever found ready to pick
a quarrel with him, with one soft word spoken in season
he turned away all thought of anger.

> " Through every pulse his music stole
> And held sublime communion with the soul."

During the many years I had the honour of assisting
in the production of and conducting the Savoy operas,
I do not remember ever hearing a harsh word from Sir
Arthur Sullivan. His wonderful tact steered him

through all the shoals of dispute and controversy, which with most men would have provoked enmity. His every suggestion came with such grace and courtesy as to still all idle argument.

One of the most remarkable gifts possessed by Sullivan was his retentive memory. He could play through on the pianoforte overtures and the most intricate concerted numbers of a new opera of which he had not, as yet, scored a single note, and at the same time he carried in his mind the complete orchestration of his work.

Another striking attribute was the care he took in getting the effect he desired. This characteristic is shown in the following letter which he wrote me whilst on a visit to the South of France. It was concerning a song in the opera " Haddon Hall," written by Sydney Grundy.

"¡DEAR FRANK.—Herewith the song for Dorothy.

" Directions for use

" Take Dorcas and Oswald off the stage at the end of ' Rice or Rue,' and, Dorothy being left alone, begin the recitative, she reading the letter to herself, and go on to the end of song. I am writing to Grundy to suggest that, after her song, the Puritan should come on, and cut the scene with Manners altogether—ballad, duet, and dialogue. This will be in exact accordance with what I have always desired.

" Now about song. Recit. *ad lib.* and at the chord of E major—*lento*.

" Song. Light and delicate—two in a bar, exactly the same time as the Peers' March in *Iolanthe* (two

Dear Frank.

I am glad you are getting on so well, & that the music comes out lightly. There are one or two little points to call your attention to in the Finale.

1. I have made the following change.

That is half a bar sooner

though it is in the same.

2. at letter Y.

& instead of a for key, consequent upon change of harmony preceding

crotchets instead of minims, of course) ; this is still
the same beat—two in a bar, the three quavers being
equal to the two quavers previously. The *cada* I want
a little quicker ; not much, but just a little faster than
the waltz measure. Get the accompaniment delicate—
good accent and *colla voce*. If my ' forties' swamp the
voice make them mezzo fortes, of course. I send this
to-day so that you may work at it with Miss Hill.
The score will follow to-morrow ; I can't get it off by
post, although it is done. Give it to Baird at once, and
get it all rehearsed and on the stage by Saturday if
you can, or else Monday. When you receive the score
just wire me as follows : 'Sullivan, Roquebrune,
France. All right.—François.'

" Yours ever,
" A. S."

Society idolized Sir Arthur Sullivan, not so much for
his world-fame as for the charm of his personality.
Welcome at Court, Sir Arthur was ever a polished and
gallant courtier ; but, if truth be told, far greater were
the pleasures he found amongst the small coterie of
boon companions, men after his own heart, whom he
delighted to meet either at his club or in his own
rooms for a rubber at whist or a round of poker.
Sullivan was a man of whom it might, with reverence,
be said, he minded not high things but condescended
to men of low estate.

Like most men of artistic temperament, our "chief"
possessed in no lean measure the gambling instinct.
The excitement of speculation unquestionably acts
as a sedative to the brain-fever that will attack the
over-wrought organ of Imagination. A game of chance

restores the poet's mind to a sense of material things.
Costly, then, as such recreation will sometimes prove,
the player, provided his motive is not primarily lust
for "filthy lucre," finds in *le jeu* an efficacious nerve-
tonic. So it was with Sullivan. There was nothing
he enjoyed more than a visit to the Riviera. Thither
he went season after season, or whenever he was engaged on any special work of composition. Nowhere
else could he find such rich streams of inspiration as
beside the blue waters of the Mediterranean, and
many of his finest creations owned Nice or Mentone as
their birthplace. Oftentimes during his sojourns in
the Sunny South he would send me a wire urging me
to come down and join him. His usual pretext was
that he desired to confer with me on certain points
of the new Savoy opera upon which he was engaged;
but, *entre nous*, I had sometimes reason to suspect that
it was mainly a kindly excuse on his part to afford me
a holiday that prompted his invitation. Delightful
indeed were those holidays to me. Not that I mean
for a moment to imply that there was no business combined with pleasure during these visits to the South.
It was, honestly, not all play and no work; but in a
retrospect of those happy days I find it difficult to
determine which were the most enjoyable hours, those
devoted to the preliminary business of the new Savoy
opera, when the *maestro*, in the peaceful seclusion of
his sunny villa-residence gave me directions regarding
his "intention," with minute instructions touching the
intricacies of his score, or those later hours of the day
when together we sought brief relaxation at the tables

of Monte Carlo. Which of the two distinct *pastimes* proved, eventually, the more remunerative need not be discussed in this place. I am quite sure our readers will not be too inquisitive on such an extraneous point.

Jesting apart, and above all other considerations, it is good now to reflect how those seasons spent in the glorious climate of the Mediterranean served not only to quicken Sullivan's mental faculties, but also to renew the physical strength of a constitution which, never too robust, was slowly but too surely declining.

Sir Arthur's *entourage*, on his visits to the Riviera, as indeed on all his wanderings from home, consisted of Louis, his faithful valet ; Clotilde, his devoted house-keeper ; "Tommy," his collie friend, and Polly, his pet parrot. The last, it might almost be said, played the part of court jester, for Pretty Polly possessed an endless store of humour, doubtless through infection due to many years' close intercourse with her witty friend and master.

Parrot stories, like fish tales, are as a rule boresome. They generally bear too strong a family likeness to be interesting to anybody but the narrator himself. But Sullivan's "Polly" was such an exceedingly accomplished and original "wit" that some of her quaint jests may be worth immortalizing in this book.

On introducing a guest Sullivan would ask his pet to tell her name. "Polly, of course," was the prompt reply. Then, to emphasize it, she started spelling it— "P-O-O-O——" *ad lib*. until her master bade her begin again. After hesitating a moment, she recommenced:

"P-O-O-O-O———," ending it up with, "Oh, go to school, Polly I "

Clotilde, the housekeeper, who had a great affection for Polly, was always proud to exhibit the bird's accomplishments.   One day, she asked her pet to show Monsieur Cellier how much she loved Clotilde.   The good matron, placing her lips close to the cage, said, " Polly, kiss her Clotilde"—to which the reply, accompanied by a satirical screech, was " Ha-ha ! Clotilde kiss her Louis ! "   Clotilde lifted her apron to her face and fled the room.

Polly naturally had a good ear for music, and when asked if she could " whistle all the airs from that infernal nonsense ' Pinafore' ? "—would give an excellent imitation of Little Buttercup's song.   Sullivan remarked that " It might not be a perfect rendering of the music, but it was certainly quite as good as Gilbert's attempts."

One day Sullivan, in private conference with me with reference to Savoy affairs, said, " Ah, by the way, Gilbert tells me that so-and-so happened at the theatre last night."   I found reason to reply, " Gilbert ought not to have said that."   " Of course not," was the opinion volunteered by Polly.

Sir Frederick Gore Ouseley, lunching with Sullivan, told his confrère that he had brought with him the score of his latest work—a commemoration ode— remarking, " My dear Arthur, I think you will say I use the harp in a most novel fashion."   " Really ! " responded Sullivan, " *do you play it with a bow?* " Polly, who was, as usual, listening intently, screeched out " Bow-o—" continuing with a scream of mock-laughter. Sullivan threw his serviette at his pet, whilst Ouseley laughed almost as loudly as the parrot.

Thus, it will be seen, Polly was very observant, and as inquisitive as Paul Pry. Whenever she was not talking she was listening intently—with head twisted to right or left, she appeared to be making mental notes of the current conversation. Great, then, was Polly's concern when, one day, she heard people addressing Sullivan as "Sir Arthur." She couldn't understand it at all. Was it a compliment she should applaud or an insult she should resent? But when it was explained to her that her friend had been Knighted by the Queen, her ladyship exclaimed with a kind of chuckle, "Oh, all right!—Go home!"

If Sullivan's pet could only recount the tales she heard during the long years of their companionship, they alone would suffice to fill a bulky and probably a not uninteresting volume.

It was in May 1883, on the occasion of the opening of the Royal College of Music, that Dr. Arthur Sullivan, in company with Dr. Alexander Mackenzie and Dr. George Grove, received the honour of knighthood at the hands of H.R.H. the Prince of Wales (afterwards Edward VII) on behalf of Queen Victoria. Seldom has the bestowal of like distinction met with such universal approbation and pleasure, never was knighthood more richly deserved for deeds well done in the cause of English art.

CHAPTER XVIII

" PRINCESS IDA," having enjoyed a run of 246 performances, was withdrawn from the Savoy stage on October 9th, 1884. The new opera upon which Gilbert and Sullivan were engaged not being ripe for production, Mr. Carte decided on trying a revival of " The Sorcerer."

Having regard to the fact that " The Sorcerer " had proved the least successful of the series of operas hitherto produced (at the Opera Comique it had run for 175 nights only)—it was a bold experiment to offer it to the public as a *réchauffé*. The wisdom of such policy was much debated. But seven years had passed since the original production, and our astute manager was of opinion that the public had, in the interim, been educated up to an appreciation of Gilbert and Sullivan. D'Oyly Carte knew the British public, and felt confident that an appetite for the new humour, which, in the beginning, was caviare to ordinary play-goers, had ere this been acquired, and that it was now in great demand by a more enlightened generation.

Accordingly, on October 11th, 1884, "The Sorcerer," very slightly revised, was reproduced at the Savoy theatre with the following cast :

Sir Marmaduke Pointdextre	MR. R. TEMPLE
Alexis	MR. DURWARD LELY
Dr. Daly	MR. BARRINGTON
Notary	MR. LUGG
John Wellington Wells	MR. GROSSMITH
Lady Sangazure	MISS BRANDRAM
Aline	MISS L. BRAHAM
Mrs. Partlet	MISS ADA DORÉE
Constance	MISS JESSIE BOND

The soundness of D'Oyly Carte's judgment was once again fully established. The enthusiasm on the first night of the revival far exceeded that which greeted the original production. Points of humour that once fell flat upon an apathetic audience now went home with spontaneous effect. The jest which had beforetime appeared too deep for the ordinary mind to fathom was recognized alike in stalls, pit, and gallery. It was, forsooth, a remarkable reaction.

Probably no one in the theatre was more surprised than the author and composer. They found themselves striking a balance in their favour when they thought they had overdrawn from the bank of public praise as far as touched "The Sorcerer" account. Possibly Gilbert and Sullivan and Carte, too, began to imagine themselves wiser in 1884 than they had been in 1877, or, rather, that they had lived and laboured before their time. More probably they marvelled within themselves that it should have taken seven years for their subtle humour to soak into the brain-cells of an intelligent public.

That the delayed triumph of " The Sorcerer " could not be attributable to a more able representation than that first given was obvious, seeing that, with one or two notable exceptions, the leading parts were again entrusted to the original exponents, viz. George Grossmith, Rutland Barrington, and Richard Temple. Grossmith's " John Wellington Wells " had not grown a day older or staler or less mercurial in seven years. Richard Temple sang and acted as well as, but not better than, he did of old.   Barrington's "Vicar" was a faithful replica of his own admirable caricature of a country parson, and, if this clever comedian's tunefulness had not exactly improved with age, the imperturbability of his demeanour had so greatly developed with experience, that any lapse from absolute musical perfection came by courtesy to be regarded as something like a virtue.   The rendering of Dr. Daly's famous ballad, " Time was when Love and I were well acquainted," may perhaps, to highly critical ears have seemed to fall somewhat short of the absolute standards of pitch, yet who in the world cared one whit for that, when acting and gesture were simply irresistibly diverting and consummately good ?

It may be added that the humour of Barrington's vocal methods was intensified by the discovery that the actor had failed to maintain that high proficiency as a performer on the flageolet which, after much arduous study, he had acquired in 1877.   Then he had succeeded in mastering the stave or two incidental to his own accompaniment of the song, " I'm engaged to So-and-so " ; but now, in 1884, the singer and the reed instrument were no longer on speaking terms. They were, in truth, at very striking variance. But this was a detail which in no way affected the success of Dr. Daly redivivus.

I sincerely trust that Rutland Barrington, who was ever as ready to appreciate another man's joke as he was to perpetrate his own, will not deem me unkind to include in my reminiscences such amusing and perfectly well-meant reflections on his peculiar artistic idiosyncrasies. Barrington and I, throughout the long course of our association, were always good friends and loyal colleagues. At the same time I am bound to confess that, on strictly musical problems, we were not always precisely of like opinion. As a rule, it was simply a question of Key, but there were occasions when more important arguments arose between us.

For instance, in 1909 he and I were guilty of indulging in a small and playful paper war. The *casus belli* was Barrington's public criticism of the Savoy orchestra, and also the views he had expressed regarding the expediency and right of accepting or declining encores.

Vigorous was the fire we directed against each other, but, as our cartridges were blank and our disposition void of intent to wound, neither of us suffered from the duel. Perhaps, also, neither of us succeeded in convincing the other of mistaken judgment.

The subject of our controversy being one of more

than personal concern, with all apologies to friend
Barrington, I venture to reprint an article which
appeared at the time in the *Westminster Gazette:*

"TOO MUCH ORCHESTRA!"

Mr. Cellier answers Mr. Barrington

" The breezy utterances of Mr. Rutland Barrington
on encores and orchestras the other night before the
Old Playgoers' Club have given rise to a good deal of
controversy.

" ' Whoever Mr. Rutland Barrington was aiming at
in his speech,' said Mr. François Cellier, the musical
director of the Savoy, to a *Westminster* representative,
' I am quite certain it was not me.   Sir Arthur Sullivan
was a perfect master of the situation.'

" ' Mr. Barrington suggests that the orchestra should
be as a lifeboat to the singer, and not a foaming wave
to drown him ? '

" ' I quite appreciate the metaphor,' Mr. Cellier
replied with a smile ; ' and it is scarcely necessary to
remind Mr. Barrington that Sir Arthur Sullivan was
often a good deal more than a lifeboat to him !   Indeed, in one particular phrase in " Patience" Sir Arthur
put in a strenuous note for the sole purpose of saving
Mr. Barrington from falling overboard !

" ' So far as the drowning of the singer is concerned,
that tragedy may come about from three causes, either
together or separately—bad scoring, bad orchestra,
and bad singing ; but as a rule this difficulty is removed
during rehearsal.'

" With respect to Mr. Barrington's remark as to
whether the singer or the conductor should determine

the question of taking the encores, Mr. Cellier pointed out that, so far as the Savoy was concerned, the matter was settled by the management.

" ' Mrs. D'Oyly Carte,' he said, ' has received many letters complaining of encores, and they have been stopped because it was found that the enthusiasm of the people in the pit and gallery led to the annoyance of the occupants of the stalls.

" ' Many things in relation to encores would probably surprise the public if they were generally known. In " The Yeomen of the Guard," for instance, we always have a passionate demand for a repetition, which I avoid with the utmost care. All lovers of this opera will remember the quartette towards the end " When a lover goes a-wooing "—a very sad number for Phoebe and Jack Point. The latter retires in distress at the loss of Elsie, and Phoebe is left on the stage to mourn the loss of Fairfax. Not only have Fairfax and Elsie to change too quickly to allow of the encore being taken, but Sir Arthur Sullivan expressly desired that a repetition should not be given, on the ground that the dramatic effect would be utterly spoiled. And that is why we always turn a deaf ear to the clamour of the audience for a second performance of that quartette.'

" A stout defence of the orchestra against the charge of over-strenuousness was made by Mr. F. Orcherton, the secretary of the Orchestral Association, who was himself in the Savoy orchestra for fifteen years.

" ' You will never in any other orchestral performances get such pianissimos as are to be heard at the Savoy,' he said. ' The question of volume is entirely a matter for the conductor.' "

But now to return to our reminiscences of " The Sorcerer's " revival. The new-comers, Durward Lely

II

as Alexis, Rosina Brandram as Lady Sangazure, and Leonora Braham as Aline, each by admirable performance undoubtedly helped to lift the opera. They all maintained the reputation they had already earned as popular Savoyards. But in general acting and singing ensemble the company, it cannot be said, differed materially from the original.

No more could the superior mounting of the opera, made possible by the greater capacity and modern equipments of the Savoy stage, have accounted for the increased favour extended to " The Sorcerer " by the audience. No ! it was simply and purely that Gilbert and Sullivan had come to be understood by the playgoing public, and that our brilliant author and composer were now looked upon as the Castor and Pollux of the lyric heavens, shining down in the full glory of their magnitude through the theatrical firmament. Twin-stars as they were in the brilliancy of their natural wit and humour, it might be imagined that Gilbert and Sullivan, like their mythological prototypes, had been hatched from one egg brought forth by a goddess.

As an after-piece to " The Sorcerer," " Trial by Jury" was revived, and, like the larger work, was welcomed back with enthusiastic applause. Rutland Barrington's Judge was as excellent a caricature portrait as was his Vicar. Durward Lely's singing in the part of the Defendant had been enough to win a favourable verdict of a less irresponsible jury, and the judgment of a less amorous judge, whilst Miss Florence Dysart, who as the Plaintiff now made her début at the

Savoy, charmed all hearts, not only in " The Court," but throughout the auditorium.

These, the first revivals of Gilbert and Sullivan's earliest works, are more particularly memorable as the initial evidence of the perennial attributes of the Savoy operas. It was at least proved that " The Sorcerer " and " Trial by Jury " were far from moribund when withdrawn from the stage after their first runs.

The revival of " The Sorcerer " in America furnished a still more remarkable proof of the altered taste of play-goers. When first produced in the States the opera had been condemned as an utter failure ; when reproduced a few years later its success equalled that achieved in England.

INTERLUDE

Tuesday, Jan. 6th, 1914.

IT is with great sorrow I have to record the death of my friend and collaborator, François Cellier, who passed away at his home in Surbiton last night.

For many weeks he had been in a weak but, seemingly, not precarious state of health. His sufferings were at times so acute that it was only by sheer pluck that he summoned up energy to assist me in the compilation of his personal reminiscences. But, despite excruciating pain, he retained his mental vigour almost to the end; at intervals he was able to dictate a cheery anecdote or happy memory, and generally to guide my pen in describing his experiences of *Thirty Years at the Savoy*. Gradually, however, the pages of the past grew dim in his mind; the light was failing; life was slowly ebbing, and the mirthful stories he was wont to tell and with which it was hoped to brighten this volume he had no longer strength to relate.

So now the task of completing these memoirs devolves upon myself alone.

When, at the outset, Cellier invited me to collaborate with him on a book of the Savoy, I gladly accepted the compliment his confidence implied. I felt sure that the labour involved would be pleasant, seeing that it would embrace many happy memories of a common interest. For, although my name is not widely known in connection with the Savoy, I claim to be one of the oldest and closest surviving associates and camp-followers of the D'Oyly Carte Army Corps. I can boast of having witnessed the original productions of every Gilbert and Sullivan opera, including that of "Trial by Jury" at the Royalty Theatre in 1875, right down to what may be called the interregnum at the Savoy in 1901, when Mr. Carte let the theatre to Mr. William Greet, who then continued the run of the Hood-Sullivan and German Opera, "The Emerald Isle." I have enjoyed the personal acquaintance of leading Savoyards with very few exceptions, and, further, I have served as acting-manager of a D'Oyly Carte Touring Company. Thus I am in an advantageous position to speak of the Savoy and Savoyards in general, and, perhaps, of Sir Arthur Sullivan in particular ; for, as intimated in an early chapter of the present book, I knew the composer long before he met the future part-ner of his fame, Sir William Gilbert.

Arthur Sullivan and I met first when he was a "child" of the Chapel Royal, and I only just escaping from the nursery in my parents' home in Devon, and it was there and then he composed his first song, and dedicated it to my mother.

Such are the credentials I offer whilst venturing to continue these memoirs of the Savoy.

.   .   .   .   .

On Friday, February 9th, 1914, François Arsène Cellier was laid to rest in Brookwood Cemetery. As a

token of respect to the memory of the old Chapel
Royal boy, the funeral service was conducted by Canon
Edgar Sheppard, Chaplain to the King, and Sub-dean
of the Royal Chapels.

.   .   .   .   .

> " Is life a boon ?
>   If so, it must befal
>   That Death, whene'er he call,
>   Must call too soon."

CUNNINGHAM BRIDGEMAN.

PART II

GILBERT, SULLIVAN, D'OYLY CARTE, AND CELLIER

REMINISCENCES OF THE SAVOY

By Cunningham Bridgeman

Photo by Ellis & Walery.

MR. CUNNINGHAM BRIDGEMAN.

CHAPTER I

FRANÇOIS CELLIER

ON the stage it sometimes happens—happily not often —that a sudden attack of illness incapacitates an actor from continuing his performance. In such event an understudy takes his place to the end of the play. It is a trying ordeal for the understudy, yet he is pleased and proud of the opportunity afforded him to air his ability. There have been previous occasions, too, when, death having claimed an author or composer ere the fulfilment of the work he was pursuing, its completion has been entrusted to another's hand. One memorable instance occurred when Edward German undertook the task of finishing the musical score of Basil Hood's Savoy Opera, "The Emerald Isle," which Sir Arthur Sullivan, at his death, had left incomplete —and here, let it be said, right well did German carry out his difficult and most delicate task.

But the circumstances surrounding the compilation of the present book are, I think, unique. Here was a famous Savoyard who, having essayed to prepare a volume of reminiscences of his departed colleagues, is taken from the scene at a moment when his story was but half told. The singer is called away to the silent land, there to rejoin the friends of whose deeds he had been singing songs of praise. Can the refrain be taken up in precisely the same key and in perfect harmony with the opening chords? All that can be hoped for from the understudy is that he shall do his best to attune his mind to that of the principal whose rôle he is called upon to take.

François Cellier has been, as it were, promoted from the post of authorship to take the prouder place of fourth hero of the life-romance which he, himself, had attempted to relate. Another may speak of him as he never could have spoken of himself. For Frank, as his familiars used to call him, was not one to " stir it and stump it and blow his own trumpet." I, who knew him well and greatly esteemed him, can testify that a more unostentatious man never lived. In these few personal notes I intend to speak of my friend as I found him, without adding to or detracting from his true merits.

His only enemy in the world, if he had one, was himself. He was not, I think, his own best friend, seeing that Cellier was possessed of talents which he was too well content to hide beneath the bushel of his obligations to the Savoy. This was the excuse he was wont to make for not turning to account his own latent musical ability. It might almost be said that his good fortune was his misfortune. Yet it need not have been so had he not made the Savoy his world. That his post of Musical Director was a very responsible, and, at times, arduous one may not be gainsaid, yet, during the long and continuous runs of the Savoy operas, he was not without leisure, there were hours and opportunities of which he might, had he so willed, have advantageously availed himself. But if Frank Cellier was a Savoyard of Savoyards, he was, at the same time, a chief amongst Bohemians. There was no recreation so pleasurable to him as to foregather with kindred spirits, hour after hour, to recount, as he alone could, stories spiced with wit and humour. In his prime, Cellier was an acknowledged king of raconteurs.

As a conductor of light opera, François Cellier was, generally, accepted as the beau-idéal. To quote the words of "Lancelot," the esteemed musical critic of the *Referee*:

"Mr. Cellier was connected with the D'Oyly Carte Opera Company, directing performances of the Gilbert and Sullivan operas, at home and abroad, for over thirty-five years, during which time he maintained the high standard set up by the librettist and composer with whom his life was so closely identified. It was while fulfilling these duties that Mr. Cellier gained the esteem of musicians by the finish of the performances under his direction and by his quiet and unostentatious manner."

It should be added that Cellier obtained the faculty possessed by few conductors of controlling not only his orchestra and the stage company, but also the audience. If he thought an encore unreasonable or inconsiderate, he had only to shake his uplifted hand, when, lo ! as if by wireless telegraphy, the signal was read, the meaning interpreted, and the loudest shouts promptly subsided.

Cellier's love of music was, seemingly, confined to
the compositions of Arthur Sullivan and his brother
Alfred. With· the natural predilection of blood relationship, he esteemed the composer of " Dorothy "
and Gray's " Elegy " as *facile princeps* among contemporary English composers.   Frank often argued
that, given the same conditions, and, especially, an
equally worthy librettist, his brother would never have
played, as it were, second fiddle to Sullivan in the
overture to Fame and Fortune.   Be this as it may,
it is incontrovertible that the Cellier brothers, each
alike gifted with the genius of melody, were lacking
in ambition and aptitude to work out their own salva-
tion.   Alfred, it has often been told, was so egregiously
inert that, on critical occasions, such as happened when
he was composing the music to Gilbert's " Mountebanks," he had to be locked in a room and not set free
until he had finished the required score.   Frank, his
younger brother, was naturally of the same disposition.
In witness, let me give personal evidence.

Mrs. D'Oyly Carte having accepted an unpretentious
one-act piece of mine, called " Bob," commissioned
Frank Cellier to write the music without delay, as she
wished to place it on the programme on the touring
Répertoire Company.   Despite entreaties, protesta-
tions, and threats from Mrs. Carte and myself, it was
months before his score of six musical numbers was
handed to the management.   The music of " Bob,"
like that of other small pieces written by Mr. Frank
Desprez and by Mr. Harry Greenbank and produced
at the Savoy, was exceedingly graceful, pretty, and

melodious, indicating that the composer might be capable of bigger things if only he would sit down and work. " Bob " proved so successful that Mrs. Carte commissioned Cellier and myself to collaborate on another " first piece."

I lost no time and prepared a libretto. With typed copy I hastened to Cellier. He appeared much pleased with it, in fact he said it was vastly superior to " Bob." " Very well, Frank," said I ; " you remember it is a fortnight to-day since you asked me to write a book ! Now, there are only seven lyrics to set ; will you let Mrs. Carte have the music a fortnight hence ? "

Mrs. Cellier, who was present, smiled—a questioning smile ! She knew, as I did, Frank's vagaries. Nevertheless, within the fortnight Cellier had composed every number, and much to my delight played them through to me. But—he had not put his compositions down on paper.

Some weeks later, Mrs. Carte wrote to me asking if I could not induce Cellier to let her have the music, as she wished to produce the piece. But, since I could not lock my colleague in a room until he finished his task, we could never get the score, and so, alas ! the little piece could not be produced. Mrs. Carte thereupon revived " Trial by Jury " as a first piece. " Buncombe's Benefit," as my trifle was called, was shelved, whilst Cellier's seven charming songs were, for all I know to the contrary, buried with the composer. Such is the eccentricity of genius ! Thus it will be understood how I have ventured to suggest that my old friend's self was his worst enemy.

Like his brother Alfred, who composed music to Gray's "Elegy," François "wasted his fragrance on the desert air." He took but the vaguest interest in either drama or music apart from the Gilbert and Sullivan operas. One day I begged him to come with me to hear Glück's "Orpheus," which, produced and played by Madame Marie Brema, was drawing all musical London to matinées at the Savoy. I had attended the performance several times and felt sure that Cellier would enjoy it as much as I had done. He promised to join me, but, much to my disappointment, he did not enter his stall until just as Orpheus was beginning the glorious "Che Faro." He was sufficiently pleased to remain to the end of the Act. He then left me, saying he had to meet some one for a moment in the Savoy Hotel, but would return in good time for Act II. But he never came back. When afterwards we met, Frank apologized and explained how, in the first instance, he could not tear himself away from a congenial party of story-telling friends, and that afterwards, on entering the hotel, he was again beset by friends—that he had been telling everybody all about "Orpheus," how much he had enjoyed it, and advising them all not on any account to miss such a treat. It was always the same; if once a group of convivial acquaintances got hold of Frank Cellier, they would never let him go until they had extracted from him just one more anecdote.

Mr. Joseph Ivimey, the well-known musical director of the Strolling Players' Orchestra, and an old friend of the Cellier family, tells some amusing tales concerning Frank.

" He gave me my first lesson in conducting," says Ivimey. " I was rehearsing some amateurs in ' Trial by Jury,' which was to be performed in Surbiton, with full orchestral accompaniment. Never having conducted, I asked Cellier to give me a few hints. Frank sat himself at a piano saying, ' Now, take the stick and conduct me—whilst I play " Trial by Jury." ' Before I had beat many bars he stopped. ' My good friend, *I* am conducting *you*, and if I followed your beat Sullivan would never know his own music.' That was a hint I have never forgotten—but," said Ivimey continuing, " here's a real good story about our poor old friend. One summer Cellier and his family were spending their holidays at Folkestone, and I formed one of their party. On a fine August morning Frank suggested that he and I should make a day's excursion across Channel ' just for the sake of a blow,' he said. Arrived in Boulogne, we repaired to the Casino, where we indulged in a mild game of *Petits Chevaux*. At length, returning to the pier, we saw our boat a mile out of harbour. What were we to do ? After much debate we determined upon a visit to Paris. So Cellier wrote out a telegram to his wife in Folkestone: ' Lost boat—going on to Paris—home to-morrow.' At the same time he prepared a wire to an hotel proprietor whom he knew in Paris, engaging two rooms. These telegrams he entrusted to a commissionaire to despatch. On arriving at the Hôtel de Bade we found that our rooms were reserved, but Monsieur l'hôtelier, handing

Cellier the telegram he had received, remarked that he could not interpret it all. Following the order for rooms were these words: ' Could not send Folkestone message—you gave me bad five-franc piece.' The consequence was, poor Mrs. Cellier was kept in terrible suspense until we turned up at Folkestone the following night.''

Mr. Ivimey's description of his day in Paris with François Cellier, with no clothes but those they stood in, would form an interesting brochure; but, as our pages are limited, I may not here tell more of their adventures. Let it suffice that Mr. Ivimey vows that, although he did not know a word of French, he never had such a delightful experience as during those few hours spent in the gay city.

No cheerier or more intellectual holiday companion than Frank Cellier could one desire. His charm of manner, combined with infinite tact, ingratiated him into the hearts of strangers, just as his humour and *bonhomie* endeared him to his numberless friends who deeply lament his loss.

Frank Cellier left a widow, three daughters, and a son François (familiarly " Jack "), who adopted the stage as a profession. After having served his apprenticeship under the ægis of Mr. Edward Terry, young François entered into a partnership, at first commercial and afterwards matrimonial, with Miss Glossop Harris (daughter of Sir Augustus Harris). Together they manage a Shakespearean Touring Company, which in due time has achieved high reputation throughout the provinces. Without hesitation I may affirm that, next to Sir Johnston Forbes Robertson's, young Cellier's Hamlet is the finest I have ever seen. His exposition of Shakespearean text, rendered in a rich, melodious voice, is most convincing, and a treat to listen to. If I am not much mistaken, François Cellier, *fils*, will, when the chance comes, be found in the front rank of English actors.

Cellier's second daughter, Marguerite, is also on the stage and fast gaining popularity. At the time of her father's death Miss Cellier was appearing as leading lady in an English dramatic company touring the United States.

There can be little doubt that the strenuous labour attached to a musical directorship on tour was too much for the veteran conductor. Not only did it tell on his physical constitution, but the ungrateful task of rehearsing a full répertoire of operas, week after week, with local orchestras of varying quality, grated on his sensitive nerves. He held on as long as strength permitted, but it was too long. Nature at length asserted its sway, and the worn-out conductor was compelled to resign his bâton to a younger man.

CHAPTER II

THE unqualified success that had attended the children's performance of " H.M.S. Pinafore " at the Opera Comique in 1879 induced Mr. Carte to arrange a similar juvenile production of " The Pirates of Penzance," to take place at the Savoy for a series of Christmastide matinées.

To Richard Barker was again entrusted the stage-drilling of the miniature company, whilst François Cellier was a second time appointed music and singing master to the little people.

Obedient to call, no fewer than 400 boys and girls, of all sorts and sizes, mustered at the stage-door on the appointed day in November. From that morning onward until the production of the piece on Boxing Day 1884, or, in fact, to the end of the holidays, neither Barker nor Cellier had an hour they could call their own. Their first task was to select from that swarm of youthful histrionic aspirants twenty young ladies and twenty-five young gentlemen who could not only sing but speak. As regards their acting qualifications, that was a secondary consideration. Mr. Barker would see to that ! When, in his later and lazier period of life, Cellier looked back upon those auditions, he

marvelled how he could have summoned up the patience
and energy to listen for hours on end to the vocal
attempts of those four hundred untutored juveniles.
Yet, at the time, there was so much of the serio-comic
element in those trials of voices that the tedium of
the task was vastly relieved.

Notwithstanding the fact that it had been advertised that no girl or boy above the age of sixteen
need apply, it was easy to discover, on close inspection,
that a small percentage of the assembly, especially
amongst the young ladies, had arrived at years of
discretion ; at any rate, they were well out of their
teens.   These, after severe cross-examination, were the
first to be politely weeded out.   Then the concert began.

Each candidate was requested, in turn, to sing a scale.
Some did not know what a scale was.   That did not
matter.   If the voice showed promise of fertility,
master or miss was asked to sing a verse of a song—
any song he or she knew.   As a rule, the song chosen
was one of the latest music-hall ditties—such, for
instance, as " Two lovely black eyes," which was much
in vogue at that time.

There were comparatively few amongst the competitors who had been taught a note of music, but,
generally, they displayed remarkably keen ears for
tune and time, whilst the voices were sweet enough to
justify their parents and guardians in offering the
services of their children.   There were, of course, a
certain number who came of musical and dramatic
stock.   These were ready to render a grand-operatic
aria, or to recite Shakespeare by the yard.   They con-

sidered themselves born actors or actresses. It was from this rank that the final selections were made.

It was pathetic to witness the anxiety of each little candidate to learn the verdict after trial; the smiles of the accepted ones, the tears of the rejected.

Very few of the warblers betrayed nervousness. They had been accustomed to face an audience in the Theatre Royal Back Parlour. The glare of the footlights might, perhaps, dazzle them at first; but there was little cause to anticipate that they would suffer from stage-fright—a complaint that more generally attacks experienced artistes who become self-conscious that the issue of their performance means success or failure, not only to themselves individually, but to all concerned in the stage-production.

The auditions lasted for a week, or more, at the end of which time the gallant 400 had been reduced to 100, then further, it might be, to 60. From these were chosen the principals, and from the residue the chorus of 45. All that then remained for Barker and Cellier to do was to transform the young people into singing actors and actresses.

Fortunately, Cellier had had, before his theatrical days, considerable experience in teaching children music, so that the means and methods were no insuperable problems for him to solve. The intelligence of the little people was most remarkable, added to which they one and all entered upon their studies with splendid keenness, patient attention, and untiring energy. The very thought of appearing in public, and at the Savoy too, of all places, was to them a

dream of immeasurable glory. The boys had all
played at policemen before in their gardens or play-
grounds, but now they would be " real life-like Bobbies,
just like Mr. Rutland Barrington " ; and some of them
were to be bloodthirsty pirates, only with stupidly
tender hearts. Oh, what a spree they were going to
have, these holidays—and—just fancy!—going to be
paid for it ! Wasn't it all enough to incite the boys
to do their best ? " As to *the spree*," thought Barker,
" I'll see to that ! "

The little girls, in less demonstrative fashion, betrayed
becoming pride in their new and responsible vocation.
Probably they had all, at some time or other, heard
of Madame Patti—" Patti had been next to nobody
when she was a child. Why shouldn't we become
stars of equal magnitude ? As for Leonora Braham,
and Jessie Bond, Rosina Brandram, and other popular
Savoy ladies, we have seen them often ; but we are
not going to try and copy them—they are all splendid
actresses and singers, of course, but then "—argued the
juvenile ladies—" they are not so young as we are,
and people like young—very young persons on the
stage if they are not *too* precocious—*we* don't intend
to be at all precocious "—" No," thought Dick
Barker—" not if I know it ! "

Naturally there were several well-meaning people
who once again must direct their pince-nez towards
the Savoy stage. They took exception to these performances, fearing that the children's education would
be neglected, and that they would be first over-worked,
and then spoilt by adulation. The minds of these

worthy people were, however, very soon set at ease, when it became known that Mr. D'Oyly Carte and his kind-hearted and ever-thoughtful managerial help-mate, Miss Helen Le Noir, were making the welfare and good conduct of the little company the object of their special care. The Board of Education were more than satisfied that every child would not only be well looked after, but would also reap great benefit by the tuition and discipline that would attend their pro-fessional engagements at the Savoy Theatre.

Without pausing to gossip about the rehearsals which, by the way, it was my privilege occasionally to witness, let me now recall the cast of principals who appeared in the children's " Pirates of Penzance " on the afternoon of Boxing Day, 1884.

General Stanley	. .	MASTER EDWARD PERCY
Pirate King	. .	MASTER STEPHEN ADESON
Samuel	. .	MASTER WILLIAM PICKERING
Frederic	. .	MASTER HENRY TEBBUTT
Police-Sergeant	. .	MASTER CHARLES ADESON
Mabel	. . . .	MISS ELSIE JOEL
Ruth	. . .	MISS GEORGIE ESMOND

It would be a pleasure to record the names of all those five-and-forty other children of the Company, seeing that they, one and all, won butterfly fame during that Christmas-time of 1884. But I should be sorry to provoke, as I might by so doing, the jealousy of elder Savoyards—those who for many succeeding years have done yeoman's service in the Chorus of the Gilbert and Sullivan operas.

Thirty years have passed by since the juvenile

" Pirates" captured London. Those of the crew who
have survived have reached the prime of life, and,
may be, become proud parents of equally clever mites
of humanity. Some have continued to pursue the
theatrical career they started so auspiciously; but
the majority have been swallowed up in the vortex
of London and been reduced to nobodies in particular.

Recalling to mind that bright and merry crowd
who gladdened us all by their sweet singing and
winsome acting, some of us may instinctively feel a
pang of regret that those delightful children should
ever have been forced to grow up into men and women
of every-day life.

But some of us say the same about kittens :

> " Kittie, Kittie !
> What a pity—
> What a dreadful pity that
> You, who are so pert and pretty,
> Should become a nasty cat ! "

By way of a testimonial to the success of the children's opera, I cannot do better than reprint an
extract from a notice of the first performance which
appeared in the *Daily Telegraph*. If I am not much
mistaken, it came from the pen of the late Clement
Scott.

" It was not mere training, parroting or imitation
—they did not talk their lines as if they had been
drilled—the meaning of the words went home to
every individual in the audience solely through the
intelligence of the performer. Let the truth be told

—when before has any one ever understood a Gilbertian opera, without a book to guide them ? A rustle of leaves has shown how slavishly the printed words have been followed. But yesterday afternoon not one in a couple of hundred had a book, or even wanted a book, for the very good reason that the first principles of elocution had been conveyed to the baby performers. Delighted, indeed, must Sir Arthur Sullivan have been to hear his charming music interpreted with such skill —which is one thing—and such taste—which is quite another thing. The rarest thing in the world is it to get a boy with one of those pure, piercing, and heavenly boy's voices ever to sing with expression and feeling. We hear them in cathedral ' quires and places where they sing.' We compare them to the angels without a soul. The long cathedral aisles, the mystery of the place, the devotional attitude of those about them persuade us that there is a heart in a boy's soprano voice. As a rule it is illusion—*Vox et praeterea nihil.*"

After the Christmas holidays the children " Pirates " were sent on tour, and in all the leading provincial towns were welcomed with unbounded enthusiasm.

Among Cellier's reminiscences of the Savoy none was to him more pleasant than that of his association with the infant crew of " H.M.S. Pinafore " and " The Pirates of Penzance."

CHAPTER III

" THE MIKADO "

False prophets—A foreign subject—Japanese village at Knightsbridge
—Queen Victoria's gift to Emperor of Japan—English society
becomes Japanesey—Gilbert discovers new material—The author
originates his leading *dramatis personae*—No character taken from
Japanese history—No Samurais introduced and why—A Japanese
dancer and a Geisha engaged to coach the Savoy Company—
Savoyards transformed into Japs—Amusing rehearsals—" The
Three Little Maids " excel as students—Costumes and accessories
—Cast of " The Mikado "—The critics—*Punch's* view of " The
Mikado "—George Grossmith's " understandings "—Success of
" The Mikado " in London and New York—Sullivan entertains
Prince of Wales at dinner—H.R.H. listens to performance of the
opera through telephone.

AFTER a run of 150 performances, " The Sorcerer "
expired, or, rather let us say, retired to rest for a
while on March 12th, 1885. Two nights later " The
Mikado " came to light.

After the production of " Princess Ida," a rumour
had got about that Gilbert and Sullivan's next venture
would be an opera of a different type, less extravagant,
more psychologically subtle and serious, and, at the
same time, quite as humorous as any of the past
series. " It is to be," said the prophet, " a real,
genuine, English comic opera, no topsy-turvy precious
nonsense this time." Like every man who talks *à*

travers son chapeau, the foreteller was somewhat out of his reckoning.   One marvels at the fabulous number of falsehoods bred daily by Busybody out of Imagination !   And to what end ? Simply, it may be supposed, to provide " copy " for hungry journalists.

Gilbert and Sullivan, it might be assumed, knew better than anybody else what style of work best suited them conjointly or separately. If they had discovered that their united strength lay in serious opera, they would, doubtless, have turned their attention to such rather than risk continuing to harp on the same strings that had hitherto pleased the public ear, but which might in time become monotonous and tedious.   " The Mikado " marked some departure from both the Gilbertian and Sullivanesque methods, in so far as it was not another facetious skit on the follies and foibles of the author's compatriots, and that the music was not so redolent of Old England.   But the good wine needed no label to tell its vintage.   Its bouquet was sufficient.

Only Gilbert and Sullivan could have written and composed " The Mikado."   Gilbert, having determined to leave his own country alone for a while, sought elsewhere for a subject suitable to his peculiar humour. A trifling accident inspired him with an idea.   One day an old Japanese sword which, for years, had been hanging on the wall of his study, fell from its place.   This incident directed his attention to Japan.   Just at that time a company of Japanese had arrived in England and set up a little village of their own in Knightsbridge. Beneath the shadow of the Cavalry Barracks the quaint

little people squatted and stalked, proud and uncon-
scious of the contrast between their own diminutive
forms and those of the Royal Horse Guards across the
road. By their strange arts and devices and manner
of life, these chosen representatives of a remote race
soon attracted all London. Society hastened to be
Japanned, just as a few years ago Society had been
æstheticized. The Lily, after a brief reign, had been
deposed ; it was now the turn of the Chrysanthemum
to usurp the rightful throne of the English Rose.

As all the world knows—although nowadays it is
difficult to realize the fact—the last decades of the
nineteenth century marked the full awakening of Japan.
In 1857 the Queen of England had sent the Emperor
a present of a warship, following which the Emperor
had graciously yielded assent to his subjects visiting
England for the purpose of studying Western civilization. But it was not until the native colony was
formed at Knightsbridge that the Japanese and the
English began to know each other. Hitherto comparative strangers, the former had now come across the
seas to cement more firmly the friendship which
Queen Victoria's gift had done so much to promote.
Our visitors came to learn our manners and customs.
They little imagined how ready we should be to take
lessons from them. The most imitative people of the
universe soon found us imitating them. It was not
because we desired to bestow upon our guests " the
sincerest form of flattery " ; it was, rather, because
English Society delights in the New : especially if
the new be old, very old ; the older the better, so long

as some one has made it famous somewhere at some time. Because it was new to London, Society was charmed to adopt even a celestial mode. Our Japanese friends were surprised, and, naturally, gratified. They were still more flattered when they learnt that they had inspired England's most distinguished librettist with the basis of an opera, an opera that was destined to become the most popular of the Savoy series.

For the material of his play Gilbert had not to journey to Yokohama or Tokyo. He found all he wanted in Knightsbridge, within a mile of his own home in South Kensington. But our author had to face many difficulties in the development of his novel notion of preparing a Japanese play for the English stage.

To begin with, one of the most essential qualifications of Savoy actors and actresses was that of physical grace ; the poise of each limb, the elegant sway and easy motion of the figure, the noble dignity of action which distinguishes the English stage. All this had to be undone again, only more so than had been necessary in the case of Bunthorne, Grosvenor, and their followers in the play of " Patience." Every proud, upright, and lithesome Savoyard would have to be transformed into the semblance of a Jap who, to our Western eyes, was not the ideal of perfect grace and loveliness.

But Gilbert soon found a way out of that difficulty. Here were living models, real Japanese ready to hand. They should teach the ladies and gentlemen of the Savoy how to walk and dance, how to sit down and how to express their every emotion by the evolutions of the fan. Confident, then, in his ability to overcome all obstacles, our author applied his mind to the subject of Japan, read up the ancient history of the nation and, finding therein much from which to extract humour, soon conceived a plot and story.

It must not, however, be supposed that Gilbert discovered the originals of any of his *dramatis personae* in the chronicles of the times of Jimmu Tenno, first Emperor of Japan, or his descendants. " Pooh Bah " —that worthy who comprehended within his own person a complete cabinet of ministers, together with other important offices—Pooh Bah, it will be remembered, traced his ancestry back to a " protoplasmal primordial atomic globule " ; consequently, no Japanese gentleman of rank, however sensitive, could imagine himself or his progenitors to have been made the subject of the English author's satire. Likewise neither Koko, the Lord High Executioner, nor Nanki-Poo disguised as a second trombone, could possibly be identified with persons associated with Old Japan. Figuratively, all these notabilities may have been portrayed on lacquer-trays, screens, plates, or vases, but none of them had ever lived in the flesh before they came to life at the Savoy Theatre.

As regards Gilbert's portrait of a Mikado, having carefully studied the outline history of Japanese civilization, I have failed to discover any sovereign potentate, from the Emperor Jimmu, founder of the Empire, down to the present dynasty, or Meiji Period, who could by the greatest stretch of imagination be taken as the prototype of that Mikado to whom we were presented in the Town of Titipu, that sublime personage and true philanthropist who assured us that "a more humane Mikado never did in Japan exist." Nevertheless, it will not have been forgotten how, on the occasion of the last revival of the opera at the Savoy, the play was temporarily banned on the ground that it was likely to give offence to our friends and allies.

One of the first observations made by Sullivan after reading the libretto in the rough, was that he was rather surprised to find that the author had not made use of any of the distinctive class titles of Old Japan, such as, for instance, "The Shoguns." Gilbert's reply was: "My dear fellow, I agree with you. Some of those names were very funny; in fact, so ear-tickling as to invite excruciating rhymes. But when I found that the aristocracy of Old Japan were called "Samurais" —I paused. Supposing I wanted to introduce the Samurais in verse, the obvious rhyme might have seriously offended those good gentlemen who worship their ancestors. Moreover, the rhyme would certainly have shocked a Savoy audience, unless your music had drowned the expression in the usual theatrical way— Tympani fortissimo, I think you call it."

"Ah!" said Sullivan, "I see your point."

Through the courtesy of the directors of the Knightsbridge Village, a Japanese male dancer and a Japanese tea-girl were permitted to give their services to the Savoy management. To their invaluable aid in coaching the company it was mainly due that our actors

and actresses became, after a few rehearsals, so very
Japanny. The Japanese dancer was a fairly accomplished linguist. The little gentleman artist was far
too polite and refined to need any of the rude and
hasty vernacular common to the impatient British
stage-manager of the old school. For polished
adjectives or suitable pronouns he would turn to the
author, or, it might be, to Mr. John D'Auban, who was,
as usual, engaged to arrange the incidental dances.

The Geisha, or Tea-girl, was a charming and very
able instructress, although she knew only two words
of English—" Sixpence, please," that being the price of
a cup of tea as served by her at Knightsbridge. To her
was committed the task of teaching our ladies Japanese
deportment, how to walk or run or dance in tiny steps
with toes turned in, as gracefully as possible ; how to
spread and snap the fan either in wrath, delight, or
homage, and how to giggle behind it. The Geisha also
taught them the art of " make-up," touching the
features, the eyes, and the hair. Thus to the minutest
detail the Savoyards were made to look like " the real
thing." Our Japanese friends often expressed the
wish that they could become as English in appearance
as their pupils had become Japanesey. Somebody
suggested they should try a course of training under
Richard Barker, who could work wonders. Had not
he succeeded in making little children assume the attitude and bearing of adults ? If anybody could transform a " celestial " into an " occidental," Dick Barker
was the man. But I don't think the experiment was
ever tried.

It was extremely amusing and interesting to witness the stage rehearsals, to note the gradual conversion of the English to the Japanese. One was sometimes inclined to wonder if the Savoyards would retain sufficient native instinct adequately to study the English music.

As usual, the ladies proved more apt pupils than the men. Most apt of all, perhaps, were the " Three little Maids from School," who fell into their stride (if such a term can be applied to the mincing step of the East) with remarkable readiness, footing their measures as though to the manner born.

One of the most important features of " The Mikado " production was the costumes. Most of the ladies' dresses came from the ateliers of Messrs. Liberty & Co., and were, of course, of pure Japanese fabric. The gentlemen's dresses were designed by Mr. C. Wilhelm from Japanese authorities. But some of the dresses worn by the principals were genuine and original Japanese ones of ancient date ; that in which Miss Rosina Brandram appeared as " Katisha " was about two hundred years old. The magnificent gold-embroidered robe and petticoat of the Mikado was a faithful replica of the ancient official costume of the Japanese monarch ; the strange-looking curled bag at the top of his head was intended to enclose the pig-tail. His face, too, was fashioned after the manner of the former Mikados, the natural eyebrows being shaved off and huge false ones painted on his forehead.

The hideous masks worn by the Banner-bearers were also precise copies of those which used to adorn the

Mikado's Body-guard. They were intended to frighten the foe. Some antique armour had been purchased and brought from Japan, but it was found impossible to use it, as it was too small for any man above four feet five inches, yet, strange to say, it was so heavy that the strongest and most muscular man amongst the Savoyards would have found it difficult to pace across the stage with it on.

Mystery was always D'Oyly Carte's managerial policy. And a wise policy it was, as I shall endeavour to explain later on.

Accordingly, to no one outside the managerial inner circle were made known the constructive lines of the vessel then on the stocks. Japan was scented, but not until the moment of the launch was the name of " The Mikado" whispered. It was as profound a cabinet secret as that which surrounds the building of a new class of cruiser in one of His Majesty's Dockyards.

And so it came to pass that on March 14th, 1885, in the presence of the usual crowded and distinguished company, which included T.R.H. The Duke and Duchess of Edinburgh, " The Mikado, or The Town of Titipu," was presented for the first time by the following cast :

The Mikado of Japan . . . MR. R. TEMPLE
Nanki-Poo . . . . . MR. DURWARD LELY
    (*His Son, disguised as a wander-*
    ing minstrel, and in love with
    Yum-Yum)
Ko-Ko . . . . MR. GEORGE GROSSMITH
    (*Lord High Executioner of Titipu*)

13

Pooh-Bah . . . MR. RUTLAND BARRINGTON
  (*Lord High Everything Else*)
Go-to . . . . . MR. R. CUMMINGS
Pish-Tush . . . MR. FREDERICK BOVILL
  (*A Noble Lord*)
Yum-Yum . . . MISS LEONORA BRAHAM
Pitti-Sing . . . . MISS JESSIE BOND
Peep-Bo . . . . . MISS SYBIL GREY
  (*Three Sisters ; Wards of Ko-Ko*)
Katisha . . . . MISS ROSINA BRANDRAM
  (*An elderly Lady, in love with Nanki-Poo*)
Chorus of School-girls, Nobles, Guards, and Coolies

ACT I.—*Court-yard of Ko-Ko's
  official residence*   } HAWES CRAVEN
ACT II.—*Ko-Ko's Garden*

The leading critics were, generally, loud in their praise of the new opera; but, as usual, some of the praise was qualified. One expert thought "The Mikado " the best of the series of Savoy operas, another declared it to be not up to the mark of " The Pinafore," or " The Pirates," or " Iolanthe "—or—well, any other. It was a matter of opinion then, as it has remained ever since. Our greatly revered friend *Punch,* who was seldom anything if not humorous, did not always seem to take kindly to the Gilbertian school. Perhaps the clever, conservative " Chief of the London Charivari" was too old-fashioned fully to appreciate the " new humour." *Punch* seldom descended to serious dramatic or musical criticism. It was not the policy of his paper. Why should he bore his merry-minded readers more than he could help doing ? Being himself the oldest established merchant in Funniments and Witticisms known to the world, and, withal, the very pattern of polished style and refined views of life, *Punch* would never besmudge a column of his brilliant periodical by *damning* anything or anybody, like any ordinary press critic.   But, as regards the Savoy operas, even though he might not like them quite so well as he did the old burlesques of the 'sixties, *Punch* could not very well ignore what most of his worthy contemporaries were belauding.   The dear old hunchback was never exactly bitter, only a wee bit playfully caustic at times.   He seemed to enjoy pouting his lips at Gilbert and spluttering, " Poo, poo to you ! "—just as a jealous schoolboy who thinks himself clever behaves towards another schoolboy in a higher class, who has proved himself to be more clever.

We are reminded of this playful satire whilst re-perusing a full-page notice of " The Mikado," which appeared in *The London Charivari* after the first production of the opera.

Punch, or his representative " Before the curtain," starts by devoting a column to theorizing on the acknowledged fact that Gilbert and Sullivan at the Savoy produced their pieces under conditions which few other authors or composers have had the luck to meet with ; that they (Gilbert and Sullivan) were their own managers, that the theatre was practically theirs, that they selected their own company of artistes and, in short, that they did just whatever they liked—all of which theory suggests that, given equally favourable conditions, any other authors or composers could have commanded as great success as the lucky collaborators of the Savoy.

But, may not the same argument apply to every line of life ?   The man who is clever enough and possessed of sufficient self-confidence and business acumen can, provided he brings the right ware to market, make his own conditions.   Gilbert and Sullivan, aided by D'Oyly Carte, made their own beds, and that they proved beds of roses they had chiefly, if not only, themselves to thank.

Then, *Punch*, after explaining to his own satisfaction, or mortification, how the author and composer of " The Mikado " had always had " greatness thrust upon them," proceeds to note the chief point of humour which he had found in the new opera.   This was when George Grossmith, who, throughout the first Act, had been hiding his " understandings " beneath Ko-Ko's petti-coats, suddenly, in Act II., gave a kick up and showed a pair of white-stockinged legs under the Japanese dress.

" It was an inspiration," said the facetious *Punch*. " Forthwith the house felt a strong sense of relief. It had got what it wanted, it had found out accidentally what it had really missed, and at the first glimpse of George Grossmith's legs there arose a shout of long-pent-up laughter.   George took the hint ; he too had found out where the fault lay, and now he was so pleased at the discovery that he couldn't give them too much of a good thing . . . from that time to the end of the piece there wasn't a dull minute."

A very amusing and instructive dramatic criticism !

I dare say such a notice was the means of inducing many
Punchers, and footballers too, probably, to go to the
Savoy to see George Grossmith kick up his legs.   At
the same time one can hardly dare say that it was
Ko-Ko's comic spindle-shanks that accounted for
" The Mikado" running without a stop for 672 days.
But there ! we all know it was only a well-meaning,
friendly attempt on dear old Punch's part to *out-wit*
Gilbert, and it is only because of the brilliancy of the
humour that I have ventured thus lengthily to refer to
the famous chief of Fun-mongers.

Other leading critics, as I have already acknowledged,
were generally more kind if less amusing.   In fact, the
London Press could not have given Gilbert and Sullivan's latest opera a warmer or more hearty send-off.

Not only throughout the provinces, but also in
America and in Germany, to both which countries
D'Oyly Carte sent complete companies, " The Mikado's " triumph was equal to that achieved in London
notwithstanding the absence of George Grossmith
and his legs.   Is it not therefore safe to aver that the
success of " The Mikado " owed no more to Ko-Ko's
"shrunk shanks " than to Katisha's " left shoulder-
blade," that was " a miracle of loveliness which people
came miles to see ? "

During the run of "The Mikado " an interesting
incident of a private nature occurred in connection with
that opera. Sir Arthur Sullivan entertained the
Prince of Wales (afterwards Edward VII.), to dinner
one Sunday, when, to amuse His Royal Highness, a
private performance of the opera was given at the

Savoy; and this, by means of the telephone, was conveyed distinctly to Sir Arthur's private residence. And when the Prince, in a speech, thanked the company for their efforts, his words were heard on the stage of the Savoy Theatre.

CHAPTER IV

THE secrecy of the Savoy management, alluded to incidentally in a preceding chapter, became ever more and more the text for facetious comment on the introduction of each succeeding opera. And so, when " The Mikado's " reign drew to a close, inquisitiveness ran rampant through the town. Every irresponsible scribbler of theatrical topics strove to ferret out the plot, the title, and everything else that might possibly forestall the production of the new piece. Each scribe worked with the zeal and stratagem of a war correspondent eager to be the first to despatch the latest news from the front.

The smallest scrap of intelligence that leaked out, or was supposed to have been confided to some favoured member of the fourth estate, was pounced upon by the reporters as greedily as hungry sparrows flock down upon a crust of bread, each striving to peck and carry away a morsel to retail further afield.

The preliminary press paragraphs which preluded the launch of the opera, then on the stocks, afforded vast amusement, to say nothing of enlightenment, to all behind the mysterious curtain of the Savoy. And what bold and cheap advertisement! what need to expend capital on "displayed advertisements" at a guinea or more the inch per diem in all the leading newspapers, when every interested person in the world already knew all about the new Gilbert and Sullivan opera to be produced on a date foretold by the "Zadkiels" and "Old Moores" in their theatrical calendars? And it was all such good fun too; and it hurt nobody a whit either before or behind the scenes. One or two samples of the fusillade of satirical squibs that appeared may be worth quoting. For instance, the usually staid and sober *Pall Mall Gazette* devoted half a column more or less to a clever illustrated skit headed thus:

"SCENE AT THE SAVOY

"Time—Midnight"

Here followed a cartoon representing Sullivan and Gilbert disguised as conspirators striking melodramatic attitudes on the Savoy stage, whilst, peeping timidly from behind a piano, appeared the head of D'Oyly Carte. Beneath this came the following dialogue:

Sir Arthur Sullivan : So that's settled—the name of our new opera shall be——
Mr. Gilbert : Hush! we are observed.

Sir Arthur Sullivan : Allegro, crescendo ! Tempo
di valse ! who's it ?
Mr. Gilbert : 'Tis the cat : She may have heard all—
let us dissemble.

> *(They dissemble, and mysterious paragraphs
> giving the wrong cognomen of their opera
> appear in the papers.)*

" The audience attendant upon ' The Mikado' are at
last beginning to thin, and Messrs. Gilbert and Sullivan
are rehearsing their new piece with much assiduity.
The rehearsals commence at 12.30 and are seldom over,
we believe, before 5 a.m. The greatest secrecy prevails.
No outsider's presence is allowed in any part of the
theatre. If but a chink be open in the door in pit,
boxes, or gallery a warning shout is raised until that
door is closed ; when the performers have occasion
to accost one another during rehearsal, they do so as
A. B. and C. So great is the fear of piracy that even
the actors themselves do not know the name of the
play, nor the names of the characters they are severally
engaged to represent."—*Theatrical Paragraph,* " *Pall
Mall Gazette.*"

What amount of truth was contained in the paragraph may be gathered from the following letter
which Mr. Gilbert thought fit to send in reply :

" *To the Editor of the ' Pall Mall Gazette'*

"THE SAVOY CONSPIRATORS

" SIR,
" You are pleased to make merry with what
is supposed to be an exaggerated anxiety on the part
of Sir Arthur Sullivan and myself, lest the details of
the opera now in rehearsal at the Savoy should become

prematurely known to the public. So little has this consideration troubled us that we invited to the reading of the piece which took place three weeks before the first rehearsal no fewer than forty-four ladies and gentlemen of the chorus, who are in no way concerned with the dialogue, besides a dozen personal friends. We have declined to accede to several requests which have been made to us to allow the details of the plot of the piece to be published in newspapers ; and in acting thus we believe we have taken no unusual course. It is not customary for dramatic authors in this or any other country to publish their plots eight weeks before the production of their piece. You say that so great is the fear of piracy that even the actors themselves do not know the name of the play, nor the names of the characters they are severally engaged to represent. The name of the play is at present unknown to myself, and I shall be much obliged to any one who will tell it to me. But the cast is as follows :

Robin Oakapple . . .	MR. G. GROSSMITH
Richard	MR. DURWARD LELY
(*His Foster Brother*)	
Sir Despard	MR. BARRINGTON
Sir Roderic	MR. R. TEMPLE
Old Adam	MR. RUDOLPH LEWIS
Rose Maybud . . .	MISS LEONORA BRAHAM
Mad Margaret	MISS JESSIE BOND
Zorah	MISS FINDLAY

ACT I.—*A Seaport Village*
ACT II.—*A Baronial Hall*
DATE—1810

" I am, sir,
     " Your obedient servant,
                    " W. S. GILBERT."

Another wag contributed to a satirical weekly thus :

HEARD IN THE STALLS

" Heard the name of the new piece by Sullivan and Gilbert ? "

" Why, it's——"

" H's-sh ! "

" I was only going to say it's ——"

" H-s'sh ! You mustn't."

" I was only going to say that it's not known to the author——"

" Oh !——"

Which was nearer the truth than the report of the *Pall Mall Gazette*.

Then Mr. Gilbert had to endure the torture of a press interview. After severe cross-examination our author was driven to plead justification for denying the public, whose servants he and his colleagues were, the privilege of knowing, in advance, full details of their new work yet to be produced. Mr. Gilbert's evidence, as reported, so fully explains the cause of the managerial secrecy, that it may be instructive to quote from The Interview—published in the *Evening News*, a few days before the production of the new opera.

THEATRICAL PIRATES

" No," said Mr. W. S. Gilbert, " no one knows the name, the plot, the dialogue, nor anything else connected with my new piece to be produced next Saturday, and therefore all ' information ' given in connection with it must be mere conjecture."

" I suppose you have had plenty of inquiries about it ? "

" Any number, I assure you. There is scarcely a paper either in London or out of it that has not sought some kind of intelligence from me about the nature of the production ; but, of course, I cannot give it. Why should I ? Such a thing is unheard of."

" Not quite unheard of, Mr. Gilbert. Many theatrical managers and dramatic authors have been very pleased to have the opportunity of getting their pieces well commented upon before production. You see, the public take an exceptional interest in your pieces."

" I am sure I am very much obliged to the public, and to you for saying so ; but you see it would be most prejudicial to the interests of my colleagues, Sir Arthur Sullivan and Mr. D'Oyly Carte, as well as to myself, to let any information leak out."

" How so ? I don't quite understand."

" Why, I am surrounded at this moment by a lot of hungry American newspaper reporters who would snap up any little item of news concerning our new production, and at once cable it over to their journals, and, were we not very discreet, the whole thing would find itself over there in a short time and we should be defrauded of our copyright——"

" Has such a thing ever happened to you before ? "

" Most certainly it has. It occurred with ' The Mikado.' An American pirate, bit by bit, obtained an imitation of the piece, and when he discovered that the costumes were to be Japanese he sent to Messrs. ——" (mentioning a well-known firm), " and ordered facsimiles—or as near them as possible—of all our costumes."

" What did you do then ? "

" I had to go to Messrs. —— and tell them that, if

they supplied these costumes, I should withdraw all the custom of the Savoy Theatre, and I had to buy up all that were made."

" Did this put an end to the affair ? "

" As far as Messrs. —— were concerned only, but the American pirate referred to then went over to Paris and tried it on again there, and again I had to buy up all the Japanese costumes that were to be found. I cannot tell you the amount of trouble and expense we have been put to by this kind of thing."

" I suppose you had often to invoke the aid of the law ? "

" Very frequently indeed. I should think we must have been concerned in about fifteen or twenty actions. Is that not so, Carte ? " said Mr. Gilbert, addressing the manager of the Savoy Theatre.

"A great deal more than that," replied Mr. Carte. " If you say between forty and fifty you will be nearer the mark."

" Then I suppose none of the actors and actresses themselves are permitted to know anything more than is absolutely necessary ? "

" Not a word ; and I can assure you that even the costumes they will wear are not known to them until the last moment."

"When will your new piece be produced in America ? "

" In about three weeks' time after it is produced here. The last time we sent a company out to America it was with ' The Mikado,' and we were compelled to exercise the utmost secrecy. The company were taken down in a special train from London to Liverpool, from thence transported in a special tender on board the steamer, and were sent down into their cabins at once and strictly forbidden to hold

converse with any one until the steamer was well on
its way."

"Was all this necessary ? "

"Absolutely. Even Mr. Carte was obliged to take
his berth in an assumed name, and, thanks to the strict
vigilance he kept over everybody and everything, not
a soul knew of the company's departure until days
afterwards."

"I suppose you got the best of some one by all this
stratagem ? "

"Oh, yes. There was, as usual, a pirate over the
water, preparing to bring out his version of ' The
Mikado,' and, indeed, he had advertised its production
for the Saturday following the Sunday or Monday
that our company arrived.

"Of course our unexpected appearance completely
upset his plans. His production being billed for the
Saturday, however, we advertised that we would
produce ours on the Friday previous. He then again
changed his to the Thursday, upon which ours was
announced for the Wednesday, and it was actually
produced on that night and met with a brilliant
success."

Such was the state of dramatic affairs five-and-
twenty years ago. Can it be wondered at that D'Oyly
Carte veiled his managerial concerns in mystery ?

The first individual outside the official circle of the
Savoy entrusted with any of the secrets of the new
opera was the late Dr. Louis Engel, the distinguished
musical critic of *The World*, in which journal the
following interesting preliminary notice appeared just
ten days before the production of the piece on
Thursday :

"With regard to Sullivan's music I may perhaps be able to say a little more—inasmuch as I asked him to let me see the orchestral score. As he is just now working at it, and would not send it to me, I acted like Mahomet, and went to the score. When I arrived, there sat Arthur and Tommy hard at work. Arthur remained setting and scoring, but Tommy jumped up and nearly embraced me. What Tommy? Tommy is Arthur Sullivan's faithful friend and critic —one of those impartial friends who are not given to praising blindly everything you do ; and so I must say there is an air in the new opera which Tommy disapproves to such an extent that, when he hears it sung, played, or even whistled, his disapproval is at once uttered in a loud bark, or even a prolonged howl, for Tommy is a creature as far superior to vile flatterers or envious gossipers as a collie dog can be to men. Having shaken hands with Tommy and his master, I was installed in one of those oriental arm-chairs before a large table, and, before I could say a word, a slight pressure inundated the room with electric light in all colours and I began reading.

"There is no overture. Perhaps there will be though. That the piece is in reality a caricature on the old-fashioned melodrama, with the virtuous peasant girl, the wicked baronet, etc., you may take for granted. I am not allowed to say what the surprise will be, but I will tell you that the wicked baronet *has* to be wicked, in consequence of a curse which compels him to commit a crime every day or—to die. Now Grossmith, the mild baronet, refuses the title under such conditions, and hides himself, leaving Barrington to commit the obligatory crimes. He is, however, compelled to take his place, and there is a scene between him and the gallery of his ancestors, which is one of the most original effects on the stage. The predominant colour of the music is the old English ; for instance, the first opening chorus of the bridesmaids in gavotte time (E flat) and the sailor's song *à la* Dibdin.   Then comes a hornpipe and a madrigal, a sweetly pretty thing most tastefully invented, with a chaste and graceful accompaniment.   Mr. Grossmith's second song and the end of the two finales belong to the same description.   The score contains, moreover, a graceful song in waltz time for soprano (Leonora Braham), a dramatic legend for contralto, most extraordinary and highly amusing patter-trio, a very clever double chorus (you know Sullivan's favourite device of uniting two distinct subjects), a very tender little duet, a real gem for contralto and baritone, various airs and duets ; together no fewer than twenty-four numbers.

" One of the principal numbers, *the* principal, in my humble opinion, is the ghost scene above alluded to—serious, solid, the treatment of the orchestra and chorus producing a most weird and solemn effect. I wish to mention a song in three verses, orchestrated in three different ways to give emphasis to the words in a most vivid manner.   What will ' fetch ' the public is a duet in the second act between Miss Jessie Bond and Mr. Barrington, which you must hear to appreciate it, because to describe its quaintness is not easy. But if there is much serious music and more counterpoint than you would look for in a comic opera, there is much of a rollicking character, apparently written in the exuberance of high spirits.   Now you want to know which is the air Tommy protests against.   This he has confided to me in strict privacy, and I have shaken paws on keeping the secret ; so you must excuse me."

L. E.

Remarkable were the less authenticated reports

that found their way into print always "on the best
authority." One had it that the new opera was to be
Egyptian, another that the scene was laid in India.
Every outlandish place on the globe, including Tim-
buctoo, had been chosen by the author as the locale of
the play. Somebody had discovered that Miss Jessie
Bond was cast for an Ophelia part, and that George
Grossmith was to appear as a ghost; the conclusion
was that the piece was to be a Gilbertian travesty of
" Hamlet," and so, altogether, no previous production
had been so loudly heralded and gratuitously boomed
as was " Ruddygore, or the Witch's Curse." Consequently, the demand for seats on the opening night
was unprecedented, and much heartburn was felt
by hundreds of Savoy-lovers on discovering they
were not " on the list" of fortunate ticket-holders.
Enthusiasts who boasted they had never missed a
first night of any Gilbert and Sullivan opera, and
who vowed they never would be excluded, took up
positions outside the theatre in the early hours of
the eventful day. Men and women of social rank,
who on ordinary occasions were accustomed to dawdle
leisurely into their stalls, now took their places in
the queue with the professional first-nighters of pit
and gallery, caring not which door they entered, so
long as they could get inside the theatre and be
able to say they had been there. Hours before the
doors were opened every access to the Savoy, north-
wards from the Strand and southwards from the
Thames Embankment, was packed with a mass of
fevered humanity. Never before since the opening of

14

the Savoy Theatre had such a scene been witnessed. According to accounts cabled from New York some three weeks later, notwithstanding the report that "Ruddygore" was a failure in London, a similar scene was enacted outside the Fifth Avenue Theatre on the opening night of the opera. The demand for seats in America had been so great that tickets for the *première* were sold by auction and fetched fabulous prices. Such was the pitch of fame to which Gilbert and Sullivan had attained.

CHAPTER V

" RUDDYGORE "

"THE MIKADO" having been withdrawn from the Savoy on January 19th, 1887, after an uninterrupted run of 672 performances, three nights later, that is to say, Saturday, January 22nd, 1887, witnessed the production of the eighth conjoint opera of Gilbert and Sullivan. Its title was the gruesome one of—

" RUDDYGORE, OR THE WITCH'S CURSE "

AN ENTIRELY ORIGINAL SUPERNATURAL OPERA IN TWO ACTS

Dramatis Personae

MORTALS

Robin Oakapple . . MR. GEORGE GROSSMITH
    (*A Young Farmer*)
Richard Dauntless . . MR. DURWARD LELY
    (*His Foster Brother—a Man-o'-war's-man*)

Sir Despard Murgatroyd (Of
"Ruddygore)   .   MR. RUTLAND BARRINGTON
  (*A Wicked Baronet*)
Old Adam Goodheart   .   MR. RUDOLPH LEWIS
  (*Robin's Faithful Servant*)
Rose Maybud .   .   .   MISS LEONORA BRAHAM
  (*A Village Maiden*)
Mad Margaret   .   .   .   MISS JESSIE BOND
Dame Hannah .   .   .   MISS ROSINI BRANDRAM
  (*Rose's Aunt*)
Zorah   .   .   .   .   MISS JOSEPHINE FINDLAY
Ruth   .   .   .   .   .   MISS LINDSAY
  (*Professional Bridesmaids*)

GHOSTS

Sir Rupert Murgatroyd   .   .   .   MR. PRICE
  (*The First Baronet*)
Sir Jasper Murgatroyd   .   .   .   MR. CHARLES
  (*The Third Baronet*)
Sir Lionel Murgatroyd   .   .   .   MR. TREVOR
  (*The Sixth Baronet*)
Sir Conrad Murgatroyd   .   .   .   MR. BURBANK
  (*The Twelfth Baronet*)
Sir Desmond Murgatroyd .   .   .   .   MR. TUER
  (*The Sixteenth Baronet*)
Sir Gilbert Murgatroyd   .   .   MR. WILBRAHAM
  (*The Eighteenth Baronet*)
Sir Mervyn Murgatroyd   .   .   .   .   MR. COX
  (*The Twentieth Baronet*)
                              and
Sir Roderic Murgatroyd   .   MR. RICHARD TEMPLE
  (*The Twenty-first Baronet*)

Chorus of Officers, Ancestors, and Professional Bridesmaids

ACT I.—*The Fishing Village of Rederring, in Cornwall*

ACT II.—*Picture-gallery in Ruddygore Castle*
The Scenery by Mr. Hawes Craven (by permission of
Mr. H. Irving), The Military Uniforms by Messrs. Cater

& Co., from designs supplied by the Fine Art Gallery, 61,.
Pall Mall. The Ancestors by Mdme Auguste, from de-
signs by Wilhelm. The ladies' dresses by Mdme Auguste.
The incidental dances by Mr. John D'Auban.

TIME.—Early in the Present Century

The auditorium presented all the familiar features
of a Savoy *première* : all the world of literature,
science, art, politics, the law and Society, or as many
of its representatives as could be crowded in, filled the
stalls. Conspicuous in the centre were recognized
Lord and Lady Randolph Churchill. The renowned
statesman met with a mixed reception from the
"gods" in recognition of the recent revolution in
his political convictions. Close behind him sat Mr.
Labouchere, who, during the interval, accompanied the
Ex-Chancellor of the Exchequer to the smoking-room,
where, over a cigarette, they engaged in debate on some
subject even more serious than a Gilbert and Sullivan
opera.

Lord and Lady Onslow and Lord Dunraven were
present, with other peers as plentiful if not as ornate
as those who had assembled on the other side the footlights in the days of "Iolanthe." Legal luminaries
included Sir Charles Russell, Mr. Montague Williams,
Mr. Inderwick, Mr. W. J. Maclean, and Mr. (afterwards
Sir George) Lewis. The Royal Academy was represented by Sir Frederick Leighton, Sir John Millais,
Mr. Marcus Stone, Mr. Frank Holl, Mr. Whistler, Mr.
Linley Sambourne, and a host of other artists who had
come specially to review the Great Picture-gallery of
Ruddigore Castle with Hawes Craven's wondrous

sized stages of the provincial theatres by the D'Oyly Carte Touring Company. Whether or no "Ruddigore" will ever be reproduced in London remains on the knees of the gods. It is, indeed, a thousand pities that Sullivan's score, containing some of his most charming music, should be buried away in the cellar, when it might assuredly bring new joy to the present generation of music-lovers who have never heard it.

But now we may be asked, "Was 'Ruddigore' a success?" Our reply, as far as regards the music, is, "Yes—emphatically—yes." Never before was the Press more prodigal in its praise, or the public louder in its acclamation of Sullivan's workmanship. Probably the consensus of opinion was that, on the whole, "Ruddigore" contained more brilliant gems of melody set in delightful orchestration, with broader contrasts of grace and humour, than any previous Savoy opera.

If we turn to the book it would be idle to deny that the favour bestowed upon it was more qualified than the author had become accustomed to. Candidly, it is not altogether an agreeable reminiscence, but one cannot forget certain discordant, unfamiliar sounds that were only half-drowned in the flood of applause following curtain-fall. For the first time within the walls of the Savoy was heard the brutal "Boo!" of the unmannerly malcontent. It was such a novel experience that all the battalions of Savoyards wondered. By some kind sympathizers it was suggested that the contemptuous cries were not intended for the authors or the actors or the management, but rather for Lord Randolph Churchill, who chanced to be quitting the stalls at the moment Gilbert, Sullivan, and Carte were taking their "call"; but such a notion was nothing but the "precious nonsense" of too flattering Savoy-lovers. Glad as we all might have been to accept such consoling apology, it was only too obvious that, from some cause or another, "Ruddigore" had failed to convince as spontaneously as its predecessors had done. And what was the cause of the disaffection? The first act was accompanied throughout by the wild fire of applause and delight customary at the Savoy; everybody was called and recalled. But after that it seemed as though Gilbert's muse had played truant or grown dull and apathetic, or satiated with past successes, or, in other words, that his train of thought had been switched on to the wrong line and come to grief, though certainly not to fatal disaster.

Sir William acknowledged "Ruddigore" to be a caricature of what used to be known as Transpontine melodrama—a term signifying plays produced at the Surrey, the Vic., and other theatres on the south side of the Thames.

Those blood-curdling melodramas were of themselves extravaganzas of real life, unintentional satires on the virtues and vices of men and women. The question then arises how far may the travesty of an extravaganza be carried with impunity? Humour, if stretched too far, outwits itself. It becomes flat, stale, and unprofitable. Seldom has humour been more elastic than that bred by Gilbert's genius, and hardly ever was the gifted author found extending his points beyond the limits of reason and sound sense. But Gilbert's fault, if fault it can be called, lay rather in the subtlety of his brain. His wit at times sprang up from wells too deep for the ordinary mind to fathom. Here is a very striking instance in support of this theory, and, at the same time, of the density of some people's sense of humour. Will it be credited that the jolly, breezy sailor's song in " Ruddigore," the words of which shall be quoted below when we tell the story of the play, not only offended a few dull-pated British patriots who construed it as a slight on our Navy, but, worse to relate, threatened to disturb our friendly relations with France, simply because a Frenchman, the correspondent of the Paris *Figaro*, a journalist hitherto respected for his broad-minded views of British affairs, lacked the sense of humour. This person saw in Gilbert's harmless *jeu d'esprit* an insult to the French nation ; though the matter escaped becoming an international affair, it was whispered that Gilbert had received a challenge from several French officers to meet him ; but it ended in coffee and cigars.

Thus poor Sir William, fondly dreaming that his mirthful ditty, *à la* Dibdin, would be greeted with nothing but smiles, found himself between cross-fires from either side the English Channel. One may question whether, if that same song were revived in these more reasonable days, it would shock our Navy League or disturb *l'entente cordiale*. Methinks it would, rather, be accepted by all parties as a good joke.

Another negative notion that helped to prejudice the success of the piece was its title, " Ruddygore." Some prudish parents would not think of taking their

daughters to see a play with a name like that : never
—no—never, even though it had been set to music
by dear Sir Arthur Sullivan, who composed " The
Golden Legend," " The Martyr of Antioch," " Onward,
Christian Soldiers," and that lovely song " The Absent-
minded Beggar." " How ever could Sir Arthur have
dared to countenance such a name ? " " ' Ruddygore ' !
Didn't it suggest Portsmouth Hard or the East India
Docks ? "

Those dear, good, refined, squeamish people were
terribly shocked ! As for Sir William Gilbert—offering
his other cheek to the smiters, he strove to pacify them
by changing the title so far as to substitute the letter
I for Y.

Further, Gilbert made certain slight alterations in
the second act, after which the cry went forth from
the Press, " All's well with ' Ruddigore.' "

Granted that the book of " Ruddigore " was not one
of Gilbert's masterpieces, yet, seeing the opera ran for
288 performances (excelling " The Sorcerer " by 113
and " Princess Ida" by 42), the opera could hardly be
pronounced a failure.

On this question Sir William Gilbert had something
to say in a speech made by him at the O.P. Club's
" Savoyard Celebration " Dinner organized by Mr.
Carl Hentschel, the founder of the club. The entertainment took place at the Hotel Cecil on December
30th, 1906, when 450 play-goers assembled to do honour
to the distinguished author and the members past and
present of the Savoy company.

This is what Gilbert spoke :

"We were credited or discredited with one conspicuous failure—'Ruddigore, or the Witch's Curse.' Well, it ran eight months, and, with the sale of the libretto, put £7,000 into my pocket. It was not generally known that, bending before the storm of press execration aroused by the awful title, we were within an ace of changing it from 'Ruddigore' to 'Kensington Gore, or Robin and Richard were two Pretty Men.'"

CHAPTER VI

The story of " Ruddigore, or the Witch's Curse "—Superb mounting
—The acting—Jessie Bond and Durward Lely.

AMONG readers of this volume there may be many
who, never having witnessed the performance of
" Ruddigore," would like to hear what it was all about.
For their enlightenment, therefore, let me endeavour to
tell, as briefly as I may, in outline, aided by extracts
from the author's witty dialogue and sparkling lyrics,
the remarkable legend of " The Witch's Curse."

Adjacent to the Cornish village of Rederring there
stood, at the beginning of the nineteenth century,
the Castle of Ruddigore, the ancestral home of the
wicked race of Murgatroyd.   The legend attached to
the place is, early in the play, told in song by " Old
Hannah " to a crowd of village lassies, charming
maidens who, in hope of the wedding of Rose the belle
of Rederring,

> " Every day as the years roll on
> Bridesmaid's costumes gaily don."

To them Dame Hannah speaks thus :

HAN. Many years ago I was betrothed to a god-like
youth who wooed me under an assumed name.   But,
on the very day upon which our wedding was to have

been celebrated, I discovered that he was no other than Sir Roderic Murgatroyd, one of the bad Baronets of Ruddygore, and the uncle of the man who now bears that title. As a son of that accursed race he was no husband for an honest girl, so, madly as I loved him, I left him then and there. He died but ten years since, but I never saw him again.

ZOR. But why should you not marry a bad Baronet of Ruddygore ?

RUTH. All baronets are bad; but was he worse than other baronets ?

HAN. My child, he was accursed !

ZOR. But who cursed him ? Not you, I trust !

HAN. The curse is on all his line, and has been, ever since the time of Sir Rupert, the first Baronet. Listen, and you shall hear the legend.

LEGEND

" Sir Rupert Murgatroyd
His leisure and his riches
He ruthlessly employed
In persecuting witches.
With fear he'd make them quake,
He'd duck them in the lake—
He'd break their bones
With sticks and stones,
And burn them at the stake !

" Once, on the village green,
A palsied hag he roasted,
And what took place, I ween,
Shook his composure boasted ;
For, as the torture grim
Seized on each withered limb,
The writhing dame
'Mid fire and flame
Yelled forth this curse on him :

" ' Each lord of Ruddygore,
    Despite his best endeavour,
Shall do one crime, or more,
    Once, every day, for ever !
This doom he can't defy
However he may try,
        For should he stay
        His hand, that day
In torture he shall die ! '

" The prophecy came true :
    Each heir who held the title
Had, every day, to do
    Some crime of import vital ;
Until, with guilt o'erplied,
' I'll sin no more ! ' he cried,
        And on the day
        He said that say,
In agony he died !

Chorus

" And thus, with sinning cloyed,
Has died each Murgatroyd,
    And so shall fall,
    Both one and all,
Each coming Murgatroyd ! "

In dread of becoming the subject of the witch's curse,
young Ruthven Murgatroyd, heir to the Baronetcy,
flies from his ancestral home, and, assuming the
character of a country yokel, by the name of Robin
Oakapple, takes up his abode in Rederring. There he
falls in love with Rose, Dame Hannah's niece. But
he is too shy and fearful of consequences to confess
his devotion. Timely, to the village comes Richard

Dauntless, Ruthven's foster brother. To the villagers the gallant man-o'-war'sman relates in song the voyage of *The Tom Tit*. This is the lyric which gave great offence to certain over-sensitive people, specified in the last chapter.

BALLAD.—*Richard*

" I shipped, d'ye see, in a Revenue sloop,
　And, off Cape Finistere,
　　A merchantman we see,
　　A Frenchman, going free,
So we made for the bold Mounseer,
　　　D'ye see ?
We made for the bold Mounseer.

" But she proved to be a Frigate—and she up with her ports,
　And fires with a thirty-two !
　　It come uncommon near,
　　But we answered with a cheer,
Which paralysed the Parly-voo,
　　　D'ye see ?
Which paralysed the Parly-voo !

" Then our Captain he up and he says, says he,
　' That chap we need not fear;
　　We can take her, if we like,
　　She is sartin for to strike,
For she's only a darned Mounseer,
　　　D'ye see ?
She's only a darned Mounseer !

" ' But to fight a French fal-lal—it's like hittin' of a gal,
　Its a lubberly thing for to do ;
　　For we, with all our faults,
　　Why, we're sturdy British salts,

While she's only a Parley-voo
    D'ye see ?
A miserable Parley-voo ! '

" So we up with our helm, and we scuds before the breeze
    As we give a compassionating cheer ;
        Froggee answers with a shout
        As he sees us go about,
    Which was grateful of the poor Mounseer,
        D'ye see ?
    Which was grateful of the poor Mounseer !

" And I'll wager in their joy they kissed each other's cheek
    (Which is what them furriners do),
        And they blessed their lucky stars
        We were hardy British tars
    Who had pity on a poor Parley-voo,
        D'ye see ?
    Who had pity on a poor Parley-voo ! "

Robin tells his foster-brother of his shy and hopeless love, whereupon the sailor promises to assist him to gain Rose for a wife.

" Robin," says Richard, " do you call to mind how, years ago, we swore that, come what be, we would always act upon our heart's dictates—well, now, what does my heart say in this 'ere difficult situation ? Why, it says, ' Dick,' it says (it calls me Dick acos it's known me from a baby), ' Dick,' it says, ' *you* ain't shy— *you* ain't modest—speak you up for him as is '—Robin, my lad, just you lay me 'longside, and when she's becalmed under my lee, I'll spin her a yarn that will sarve to fish you two together."

15

The song that Robin then sings contains lines which have since become proverbial all the world over :

> " If you wish in the world to advance,
>   Your merits you're bound to enhance—
>   You must stir it and stump it
>   And blow your own trumpet,
>   Or, trust me, you haven't a chance."

Richard then meets Rose Maybud, and at once proves false to Robin. Following his own heart's dictates, he falls in love at first sight with the damsel. Surely a more quaint, unconventional courting scene was never witnessed on or off the stage. Rose, it must be explained, carries about with her wherever she goes a little book of Etiquette, composed, she believes, by no less an authoress than the wife of the Lord Mayor.

"It has been," says Rose, "through life my guide and monitor. By its solemn precepts I have learnt to test the moral worth of all who approach me. The man who bites his bread or eats his peas with a knife I look upon as a lost creature, and he who has not acquired the proper way of entering and leaving a room is the object of my pitying horrors "—and so on.

Thus, when the precise little Cornish maid is interviewed by Richard she is prompted by the *Book of Etiquette*, whilst the sailor steers his moral course by the compass of his heart's dictates.

The love scene is so humorous I cannot refrain from quoting it *in extenso* :

RICH. Here she comes! Steady! Steady it is! (*Enter* ROSE)—*he is much struck by her*). By the

Port Admiral, but she's a tight little craft! Come, come, she's not for you, Dick, and yet—she's fit to marry Lord Nelson! By the flag of old England, I can't look at her unmoved.

ROSE. Sir, you are agitated——

RICH. Aye, aye, my lass, well said! I am agitated, true enough!—took flat aback, my girl, but 'tis naught —'twill pass. (*Aside.*) This here heart of mine's a dictatin' to me like anythink. Question is, have I a right to disregard its promptings?

ROSE. Can I do ought to relieve thine anguish, for it seemeth to me that thou art in sore trouble? This apple—(*Offering a damaged apple*).

RICH. (*Looking at it and returning it*). No, my lass, 'taint that; I'm—I'm took flat aback—I never see anything like you in all my born days. Parbuckle me, if you ain't the loveliest gal I've ever set eyes on. There—I can't say fairer than that, can I?

ROSE. No. (*Aside*). The question is, is it meet that an utter stranger should thus express himself? (*Refers to book*). Yes—" Always speak the truth."

RICH. I'd no thoughts of sayin' this here to you on my own account, for, truth to tell, I was chartered by another; but when I see you my heart it up and it says, says it, " This is the very lass for *you*, Dick— speak up to her, Dick," it says—(*it calls me Dick acos we was at school together*)—" tell her all, Dick," it says, " never sail under false colours—it's mean! " *That's* what my heart tells me to say, and in my rough, common-sailor fashion I've said it, and I'm a-waiting for your reply. I'm a tremblin', miss. Lookye here— (*Holding out his hand.*) That's narvousness!

ROSE. (*Aside.*) Now, how should a maiden deal with such an one? (*Consults book.*) " Keep no one in unnecessary suspense." (*Aloud.*) Behold, I will not keep you in unnecessary suspense. (*Refers to book.*)

"In accepting an offer of marriage, do so with apparent hesitation." (*Aloud.*) I take you, but with a certain show of reluctance. (*Refers to book.*) "Avoid any appearance of eagerness." (*Aloud.*) Though you will bear in mind that I am far from anxious to do so. (*Refers to book.*) "A little show of emotion will not be misplaced!" (*Aloud.*) Pardon this tear! (*Wipes her eye.*)

RICH. Rose, you've made me the happiest bluejacket in England! I wouldn't change places with the Admiral of the Fleet, no matter who he's a huggin' of at this present moment! But, axin' your pardon, miss (*wiping his lips with his hand*), might I be permitted to salute the flag I'm a-goin' to sail under?

ROSE. (*Referring to book.*) "An engaged young lady should not permit too many familiarities." (*Aloud.*) Once! (RICHARD *kisses her.*)

The lovers are disturbed by the entrance of Robin, who learns the truth from Dick, whilst, much disappointed, he treats the matter with platonic unconcern. Broken-hearted as he is, Robin considers his friend has acted quite fairly in following his heart's dictates.

Rose, Richard, and Robin then join in a very charming trio, the refrain of which is:

> "In sailing o'er life's ocean wide,
>   No doubt the heart should be our guide;
>   But it is awkward when you find
>   A heart that does not know its mind."

At the end of this Rose turns away from Richard and embraces Robin. They disperse—Richard weeping.

To the village there comes Mad Margaret—a character modelled after the pattern of Ophelia. She has been the victim of one of the crimes perpetrated by Sir Despard, obedient to the curse. The poor distraught maiden is seeking for her faithless lover. The very sweet, pathetic ballad here sung by Mad Margaret may be ranked amongst Gilbert and Sullivan's brightest gems.

" To a garden full of posies
    Cometh one to gather flowers,
    And he wanders through its bowers
Toying with the wanton roses,
    Who, uprising from their beds,
    Hold on high their shameless heads
With their pretty lips a-pouting,
Never doubting—never doubting
    That for Cytherean posies
    He would gather aught but roses !

" In a nest of weeds and nettles
    Lay a violet, half-hidden,
    Hoping that his glance unbidden
Yet might fall upon her petals.
    Though she lived alone, apart,
    Hope lay nestling at her heart ;
But, alas ! the cruel awaking
Set her little heart a-breaking,
    For he gathered for his posies
Only roses—only roses ! "

                                    (*Bursts into tears.*)

Soon upon the scene enters Sir Despard, accompanied by a party of Bucks and Blades. They are all dressed in the gorgeous uniforms of military officers of the period—correct to the last button. The girls of the village express their horror of the bold, bad baronet. As he approaches them they fly from him terror-stricken, leaving him alone to moralize thus:

SIR D. Poor children, how they loathe me—me whose hands are certainly steeped in infamy, but whose heart is as the heart of a little child! But what *is* a poor baronet to do, when a whole picture-gallery of ancestors step down from their frames and threaten him with an excruciating death if he hesitate to commit his daily crime? But ha! ha! I am even with them! (*Mysteriously.*) I get my crime over the first thing in the morning, and then, ha! ha! for the rest of the day I do good—I do good—I do good! (*Melodramatically.*) Two days since, I stole a child and built an orphan asylum. Yesterday I robbed a bank and endowed a bishopric. To-day I carry off Rose Maybud, and atone with a cathedral! This is what it is to be the sport and toy of a Picture-gallery! But I will be bitterly revenged upon them! I will give them all to the Nation, and nobody shall ever look upon their faces again!

Richard Dauntless then approaches and makes known to Sir Despard that his elder brother Ruthven lives.

SIR D. Ruthven alive, and going to marry Rose Maybud! Can this be possible?

RICH. Now the question I was going to ask your honour is—ought I to tell your honour this? This is what my heart says. It says, " Dick," it says (it calls me Dick acos it's entitled to take that liberty.) " That there young gal would recoil from him if she knowed what he really were. Ought you to stand off and on, and let this young gal take this false step and never fire a shot across her bows to bring her to? No, it says, "you did *not* ought." And I *won't* ought, accordin'.

SIR D. Then you really feel yourself at liberty to tell me that my elder brother lives—that I may charge him with his cruel deceit, and transfer to his shoulders the hideous thraldom under which I have laboured for so many years! Free—free at last! Free to live a blameless life, and to die beloved and regretted by all who knew me!

Robin Oakapple and Rose Maybud, who are about to marry, then arrive to find their promised bliss suddenly blighted by Sir Despard.

SIR D. Hold, Bride and Bridegroom, ere you wed
       each other
    I claim young Robin as my elder brother.
ROBIN. (*Aside.*) Ah! lost one!
SIR D. His rightful title I have long enjoy'd,
    I claim him as Sir Ruthven Murgatroyd.

Thus at last Sir Ruthven is saddled with the witch's curse from which he had striven to escape.

In the picture-gallery of Ruddigore Castle, the walls of which are covered with full-length portraits of the baronets of Ruddigore from the times of James I., the unhappy Robin, now Sir Ruthven Murgatroyd, discusses the terrible situation with old Adam, *alias* Gideon Crawle, the faithful but wicked family steward.

ROBIN. This is a painful state of things, Gideon Crawle !

ADAM. Painful, indeed ! Ah, my poor master, when I swore that, come what would, I would serve you in all things for ever, I little thought to what a pass it would bring me ! The confidential adviser to the greatest villain unhung ! It's a dreadful position for a good old man !

ROBIN. Very likely, but don't be gratuitously offensive, Gideon Crawle.

ADAM. Sir, I am the ready instrument of your abominable misdeeds because I have sworn to obey you in all things, but I have *not* sworn to allow deliberate and systematic villainy to pass unreproved. If you insist upon it I will swear that, too, but I have not sworn it yet. Now, sir, to business. What crime do you propose to commit to-day ?

ROB. How should I know ? As my confidential adviser, it's your duty to suggest something.

ADAM. Sir, I loathe the life you are leading, but a good old man's oath is paramount, and I obey. Richard Dauntless is here with pretty Rose Maybud, to ask your consent to their marriage. Poison their beer.

ROB. No—not that—I know I'm a bad Bart, but I'm not as bad a Bart as all that.

ADAM. Well, there you are, you see ! It's no use my making suggestions if you don't adopt them.

ROB. (*Melodramatically.*) How would it be, do you think, were I to lure him here with cunning wile—bind him with good stout rope to yonder post—and then, by making hideous faces at him, curdle the heart-blood in his arteries, and freeze the very marrow in his bones ? How say you, Gideon, is not the scheme well planned ?

ADAM. It would be simply rude—nothing more. But soft—they come !

Richard and Rose enter, and are promptly condemned
by Sir Ruthven to be immured in " an uncomfortable
dungeon." This fell design is frustrated by Richard,
who came prepared for this. Unfurling a Union Jack,
he waves it triumphantly over Rose Maybud's head,
exclaiming, " The man does not live who would dare
to lay unlicensed hand upon her."

" Foiled," cried Sir Ruthven. " Foiled—and by a
Union Jack ! but a time will come, and then——"

Rose then pleads. "Sir Ruthven, have pity. In
my book of Etiquette the case of a maiden about to
be wedded to one who unexpectedly turns out to be a
baronet with a curse on him is not considered. It is
a comprehensive work, but it is not as comprehensive
as that. Time was when you loved me madly. Prove
that this was no selfish love by according your consent
to my marriage with one who, if he be not you yourself,
is the next best thing—your dearest friend——"

Robin, or rather Sir Ruthven, relents.

Left alone he soliloquizes thus :

ROB. For a week I have fulfilled my accursed doom !
I have duly committed a crime a day ! Not a great
crime, I trust ; but still, in the eyes of one as strictly
regulated as I used to be, a crime. But will my ghostly
ancestors be satisfied with what I have done, or will
they regard it as an unworthy subterfuge ? (*Addressing
pictures.*) Oh, my forefathers, wallowers in blood,
there came at last a day when, sick of crime, you, each
and every, vowed to sin no more, and so, in agony,
called welcome Death to free you from your cloying
guiltiness. Let the sweet psalm of that repentant

hour soften your long-dead hearts, and tune your souls
to mercy on your poor posterity! (*Kneeling.*)

> (*The stage darkens for a moment. It becomes
> light again, and the pictures are seen to
> have become animated.*)

The spectre of Sir Roderic (Sir Ruthven's uncle,
who, during life had been betrothed to Old Hannah,
Rose Maybud's aunt), rises in the midst of the other
baronets.   In sepulchral tone Sir Roderic sings:

" When the night-wind howls in the chimney-cowls and the bat in
  the moonlight flies,
 And inky clouds, like funeral shrouds, sail over the midnight
  skies;
 When the footpads quail at the night-bird's wail, and black dogs
  bay the moon,
 Then is the spectre's holiday—then is the ghost's high noon!

Chorus

 " Ha! ha!
 The dead of the night's high noon!

" As the sob of the breeze sweeps over the trees and the mists lie
  low on the fen,
 From grey tomb-stones are gathered the bones that once were
  women and men,
 And away they go, with a mop and a mow, to the revel that ends
  too soon,
 For cockcrow limits our holiday—the dead of the night's high
  noon!

Chorus

 " Ha! ha!
 The dead of the night's high noon!

" And then each ghost with his ladye-toast to their churchyard
    beds takes flight,
  With a kiss, perhaps, on her lantern chaps, and a grisly, grim
    ' Good-night ' ;
  Till the welcome knell of the midnight bell rings forth its jolliest
    tune,
  And ushers our next high holiday—the dead of the night's high
    noon !

Chorus

  " Ha! ha !
  The dead of the night's high noon ! "

Sir Ruthven, addressing his ancestors, says : " And
may I ask you why you left your frames ? "

SIR ROD. It is our duty to see that our successors
commit their daily crimes in a conscientious and
workmanlike fashion. It is our duty to remind you
that you are evading the conditions under which you
are permitted to exist.

ROB. Really, I don't know what you'd have. I've
only been a bad baronet a week, and I've committed
a crime punctually every day.

SIR ROD. Let us inquire into this. Monday ?

ROB. Monday was a Bank Holiday.

SIR ROD. True. Tuesday ?

ROB. On Tuesday I made a false income-tax return.

ALL. Ha ! ha !

1ST GHOST. That's nothing.

2ND GHOST. Nothing at all.

3RD GHOST. Everybody does that.

4TH GHOST. It's expected of you.

SIR ROD. Wednesday ?

ROB. (*Melodramatically.*) On Wednesday I forged
a will.

SIR ROD. Whose will ?

ROB. My own.

SIR ROD. My good sir, you can't forge your own will !

ROB. Can't I, though ! I like that ! I *did !* Besides, if a man can't forge his own will, whose will can he forge ?

1ST GHOST. There's something in that.

2ND GHOST. Yes, it seems reasonable.

3RD GHOST. At first sight it does.

4TH GHOST. Fallacy somewhere, I fancy !

ROB. A man can do what he likes with his own.

SIR ROD. I suppose he can.

ROB. Well, then, he can forge his own will, stoopid ! On Thursday I shot a fox.

1ST GHOST. Hear, hear !

SIR ROD. That's better *(Addressing ghosts.)* Pass the fox, I think ? *(They assent.)* Yes, pass the fox. Friday ?

ROB. On Friday I forged a cheque.

SIR ROD. Whose cheque ?

ROB. Gideon Crawle's.

SIR ROD. But Gideon Crawle hasn't a banker.

ROB. I didn't say I forged his banker—I said I forged his cheque.

1ST GHOST. That's true.

2ND GHOST. Yes, it seems reasonable.

3RD GHOST. At first glance it does.

4TH GHOST. Fallacy somewhere !

ROB. On Saturday I disinherited my only son.

SIR ROD. But you haven't got a son.

ROB. No, not yet—I disinherited him in advance, to save time—you see, by this arrangement—he'll be born disinherited.

SIR ROD. I see.   But I don't think you can do that.

ROB. My good sir, if I can't disinherit my own un-born son, whose unborn son can I disinherit ?

But Sir Roderic and his companion spectres are not convinced that their descendant has done his duty by the curse satisfactorily, and command him to atone for his shortcomings by carrying off a lady. If he declines he will perish in inconceivable agonies. Sir Ruthven replies that he could not do such a wicked thing as that—whereupon the ghosts torture him until he consents and apologizes.

Sir Ruthven then orders old Adam to go to the village, carry away and bring to the castle a lady.

Whilst the wicked steward is absent, Sir Despard and Mad Margaret arrive. The erstwhile crime-compelled baronet is now a sort of Methodist preacher, and Margaret, restored to sanity, is a teacher in a National school. After an amusing duet and dance they depart. Old Adam returns bringing with him, captive, Dame Hannah. The ghost of Sir Roderic again comes to earth and recognizes in the Dame his old love of long ago.

An eccentric love-scene between Sir Roderic and Dame Hannah, ending in the following charming ballad:

> " There grew a little flower
>   'Neath a great oak-tree :
>   When the tempest 'gan to lower
>   Little heeded she :
>   No need had she to cower,
>   For she dreaded not its power—
>   She was happy in the bower
>   Of her great oak-tree !
>   Sing hey,
>   Lackaday !
>   Let the tears fall free
>   For the pretty little flower and the great oak-tree !

Both

" Sing hey,
Lackaday, *etc.*

" When she found that he was fickle,
Was that great oak-tree,
She was in a pretty pickle,
As she well might be—
But his gallantries were mickle,
For Death followed with his sickle,
And her tears began to trickle
For her great oak-tree !
Sing hey,
Lackaday ! *etc.*

" Said she, ' He loved me never,
Did that great oak-tree,
But I'm neither rich nor clever,
And so why should he ?
But though fate our fortunes sever,
To be constant I'll endeavour,
Aye, for ever and for ever,
To my great oak-tree ! '
Sing hey,
Lackaday ! *etc.*"

(Falls weeping on RODERIC'S *bosom.)*
(Enter ROBIN *excitedly, followed by* BRIDESMAIDS.)

ROB. Stop a bit—both of you.

ROD. This intrusion is unmannerly.

HAN. I'm surprised at you.

ROB. I can't stop to apologize—an idea has just occurred to me. A baronet of Ruddigore can only die through refusing to commit his daily crime.

ROD. No doubt.

ROB. Therefore, to refuse to commit a daily crime is tantamount to suicide.

ROD. It would seem so.

ROB. But suicide is, in itself, a crime—and so, by your own showing, you ought none of you to have ever died at all!

ROD. I see—I understand! We are all practically alive!

ROB. Every man Jack of you!

ROD. My brother ancestors! Down from your frames! (ANCESTORS *descend*.) You believe yourselves to be dead. You may take it from me that you're not, and an application to the Supreme Court is all that is necessary to prove that you never ought to have died at all!

> (*The* ANCESTORS *embrace the* BRIDESMAIDS. *Everybody else follows their example, and so the remarkable " supernatural opera " ends.*)

Such an extravagant story, told in cold print and a necessarily brief and disjointed style, may appear less convincing and more open to unfavourable comment than when admirably performed by the Savoy company amidst the glamour of superb stage-mounting, and, above all, the magic charm of Sullivan's music. Yet, perhaps, this rough epitome may not have proved tedious, but, rather, interesting to those who learn for the first time the legend of " The Witch's Curse." Anyway, it may raise the question, among present-day lovers of the Gilbert and Sullivan operas, whether they would have felt inclined to join in the applause of the majority or in those subdued signs of disapprobation that greeted " Ruddigore " on the first night of its production.

There were two particularly noteworthy features in the performance of " Ruddigore." First to be mentioned was the acting of Miss Jessie Bond in the part of "Mad Margaret." Among the host of her admirers few had given the popular Savoy soubrette credit for such great ability as a genuine comedy-actress, for never before had the opportunity been afforded her to display her latent talent—Jessie Bond's triumph came as a surprise to all, but especially to those who were aware of the fact that her first appearance on any stage was in the insignificant part of Hebe in " H.M.S. Pinafore." So true to real life was the portrayal of Mad Margaret that Mr. Forbes Winslow, the famous authority on mental disorders, wrote a congratulatory letter to Miss Bond and inquired where she had found the model from which she had studied, and so faithfully copied the phases of insanity. No greater compliment could have been paid the actress.

Another surprise was effected by Durward Lely in the part of Richard Dauntless, the jovial man-o'-war's-man. It was truly astonishing to discover a leading tenor playing, and playing as though to the manner born, a broad comedian's part and dancing a hornpipe in such perfection as would crown him king of the fo'c'sle of the smartest ship afloat. Mr. D'Oyly Carte confessed that Lely had quite disconcerted the opinion that he had always before held, that a tenor's voice is gained solely at the expense of his brains.

CHAPTER VII

Recreations—River trips—Celebration dinners and suppers

THE Savoyards were a happy family. Away from their duties at the theatre they frequently assembled to enjoy some sort of recreation. They had their sports, notably cricket. A strong team was formed under the captaincy of Rutland Barrington, and, if I remember rightly, they generally held their own in the field.

Sullivan, Gilbert, and D'Oyly Carte, whilst ever ready to support the game with their patronage, were more strictly concerned with the runs achieved by their operas than those scored by the Savoy eleven.

Very enjoyable was the annual river picnic to which I was on more than one occasion honoured with an invitation. It took place on a summer's Sunday. The full company, under the supreme command of Mr. Carte, embarked in two commodious steam launches, one bearing the flag of the author, the other that of the composer, both flags suggesting pinafores of different design. During the voyage up-stream the boats exchanged repeated broadsides of chaff, and I am not sure that Gilbert and his merry crew always got the better of the playful duel.

On board the musician's ship, on one occasion, we were killing time by trying to concoct rhymes. Failing in one of our poetic efforts, Arthur Sullivan shouted out to his colleague, "I say, Gilbert, we are composing Limericks, and want your help; we have got as far as this:

> " That sailor who stands at the tiller
> Is in love with a girl call'd Priscilla—
> But she never was taught
> To know starboard from port "—

and now we are stuck for a last line.   Can you give us one ? "

Prompt came the reply:

> " I think your best plan is to kill her."

" Not bad," said Arthur Sullivan, " but it wouldn't look well in print."

One of the guests claiming to be a pretty good hand at Limericks, was requested to give us a sample of his own manufacture.   And this was the stuff:

> " An author named William Schwenk,
> Could never say ' Thank ' you, but ' Thenk.'
> His queer BABY rhymes
> Were so naughty sometimes
> That people inquired if he drenk."

Dead silence followed this recitation.

The Savoyards were nothing if they were not loyal to their esteemed chiefs. They were ever ready to resent any slur that might be cast on their characters. Gifted with a certain amount of intellect, they could not fail to guess who was the object of their friend's very irreverent ridicule. Accordingly the ladies of the party with one accord turned their backs upon the impertinent rhymester, presumably to express their virtuous contempt, but more possibly to hide their smiles. The male Savoyards, some of whom had, earlier in life, practised the profession of pirates somewhere down in Cornwall, and still retained bloodthirsty instincts, surrounded the culprit, threatening to keel-haul the landlubber; then with lusty lungs poured this chorus into his astonished ears :

" Don't say you're orphan, for we know that game."

The unabashed Limerick merchant calmly replied, " But, my good friends, unfortunately I am an orphan ; surely you would not hold me responsible for my parents' decease."

As soon as the murmur of disgust had died away, the irrepressible jester continued : "I am truly sorry to find that my Savoy friends are so utterly lacking in a sense of humour as to be oblivious to the innocence of my joke. At the same time I am conscious that my little poem may have appeared to some as ill-timed and not, perhaps, in the best of taste. I therefore ' beg to offer an unqualified apology.' "

Pooh Bah, who was standing by, to his manifold offices now added that of peacemaker. Stepping forward, he muttered, in his own distinct way, " I desire to associate myself with that expression of regret."

" I apologize, ladies and gentlemen," continued the poetasting guest, " on two conditions——"

" Name them," shouted the pirates in unison.

" Firstly, that you will not megaphone my Limerick to Mr. Gilbert's launch. Secondly, that you swear never to divulge the name of the author."

"We swear," cried the pirates.

Thus peace was restored. But one young lady of weak nerves had been so upset by the *émeute* that she fell into Pooh Bah's broad arms, saying, "Oh, Mr. Barrington, I do feel so unwell."

At that some wag in the bows of the boat (it sounded like George Grossmith's voice), propounded this riddle:

"What is the difference between Miss X—— and my cheroot?" Nobody gave it up; the answer was too patent to all. With one voice came the reply—"One is a woman ill, the other is a *man iller*."

Now I come to think of it, it could not have been Grossmith, seeing that G. G. never smoked Manillas.

Fortunately, the undisciplined interlude, which I have endeavoured to describe as faithfully as possible, had not been witnessed by Mr. D'Oyly Carte. Our worthy commander-in-chief had been on the bridge assisting the captain to lay the ship's course.

Anon from our author's launch came floating across the water music not always so harmonious as it might be. At the sound of it Sullivan yelled out, "Key, Gilbert, key!" The response came: "Which quay d'you mean? Where do you want us to land?"

Meanwhile Commodore Carte would sit sedately in his deck-chair puffing away at his Corona-Corona, probably reflecting what a pity it was that such sparkling wit should be wasted on the desert air of Thames Valley when it might be turned to more profitable account at the Savoy.

Our place of rendezvous for luncheon was at Penton Hook. Mooring our ships off the shore, we landed on a riverside meadow, and there proceeded to lay the cloth.

Speeches were strictly prohibited, but, needless to say, with the discussion of chicken and ham there was much debate, accompanied by a considerable amount of playful heckling.

After lunch those who were capable engaged in a game of rounders, or kiss-in-the-ring. And then, whilst Gilbert, Sullivan, and D'Oyly Carte went birds'-nesting, or searching around in hope of finding ideas for a new opera, the general company squatted on the bankside, and, following the principle of the busman's holiday, opened a concert performance of selections from the vocal scores of the Savoy operas.

Frank Cellier having purposely, and with wisdom aforethought, left his bâton at the theatre, deputed Grossmith or Barrington in turn to take his place as musical director, a duty which they carried out, as Cellier admitted, very creditably to themselves, if not always to the clear understanding of the singers.

At the first sound of the Savoyards' chorus every skiff and punt on the river within hail hastened full speed to the spot. No S.O.S. message of the present day was ever more promptly responded to. In a few minutes we found ourselves blockaded by a vast fleet of pleasure craft. The enthusiasm of the scene, the cheers and applause, reminded us somewhat of a first night at the Savoy, only that the charm of Sullivan's music was now enhanced by the environment of natural scenery and effects.

If we had yielded to every encore we should not have
reached our homes till long past the witching hour of
midnight. At this present distance of time I find it
beyond my ability to review those historic scenes of
revelry with the accuracy and graphic power of a
special correspondent.

Such samples of Savoyard holiday humour as I have
endeavoured to offer may not appear quite convincing,
nor were they calculated to set the Thames afire; yet,
be it hoped, the reader may be enabled by this snap-
shot to enter into the spirit of the scene, and to picture
the excursions and alarums of the Savoyards in the
glad days of their brotherhood.

Another custom adopted by the Savoy company as
a means of maintaining social *esprit de corps* was the
periodical holding of " family " dinner or supper parties.
These reunions were generally arranged for the specific
purpose of celebrating the successful run of an opera
or any other notable event connected with Savoy
history. The feasts were distinctly unofficial and informal to a degree. In fact, the proud, precise Savoyards
unbent for the nonce, and transformed themselves into
Bohemians of the most frivolous and irresponsible type.

" Gagging " was not only legalized but encouraged
on these occasions; but the general conversational
dialogue smacked of the Gilbertian. Such was its
infection.

The dinner or supper was confined to members of the
Company, and a few favoured attachés and camp-
followers of the Savoy who were invited as guests.

Principals and chorus, ladies and gents, foregathered

on equal footing, and contributed songs and recitations to the post-prandial entertainment. Opportunity was thus afforded the humblest and most modest chorister to display his or her shining talent which, on the stage, had been kept under a bushel, latent and undreamed of.

But, naturally, the life and soul of these festive gatherings were the chief Savoy jesters, Grossmith and Barrington. These vied with each other in enlivening our sing-song. They invariably imported samples of ware from elsewhere than the shop in which they served. Often such goods were of their own manufacture. Sometimes it was a topical song ; sometimes a humorous recitation fitted to the occasion. By way of sample of the home-made articles introduced I venture to quote some lines, a printed copy of which I recently unearthed when overhauling my collection of Savoy Souvenirs. These lines, penned in " acrostic " form, were spoken by Rutland Barrington on the occasion of a supper held at the Covent Garden Hotel on March 13th, 1887 (Queen Victoria's golden jubilee year), when the opera " Ruddigore " was running its successful course at the Savoy.

The acrostic was as follows :

> " **G** ood friends, since, by remorseless witch's curse,
> **I** must this evening perpetrate some crime,
> **L** ike base Sir Despard, only far, far worse,
> **B** ehold me—hear me, revelling in rhyme :
> **E** 'en I, the semblance of that bold, bad Bart,
> **R** evolt at pointing my poetic dart
> **T** 'wards Gilbert, Sullivan, and D'Oyly Carte.

" **C** ould Gilbert write and Sullivan compose
A song of Jubilee for the Savoy,
R ight merrily we'd sing it—tho' Heav'n knows
T here's far more Jubilee, just now, than joy—
E 'en fifty golden years have some alloy.

" **S** uch song remains unwrit, so let's, instead,
U nited sing, ' Long Life to Ruddigore ! '
L ong life to those whose wits are wisely wed ;
L ong life, Sir Arthur, Gilbert, Carte, Lenoir !
I 'm glad to see our ladies here to-night ;
V ain without them, with them is true delight.
A nd now my crime is done—forgive my verse,
N o fault of mine, but of the witch's curse."

C. B.

CHAPTER VIII

ON November 5th (an appropriate date, by the way, remembering that it was the anniversary of an event which terminated the career of another " wicked ancestor," whose name was not Murgatroyd, but Guy Fawkes) " Ruddigore" came to an end. For nearly a year following the Savoy stage was occupied by a series of revivals.

On November 12th, 1887, " H.M.S. Pinafore " was recommissioned with the following crew:

Sir Joseph Porter, K.C.B. .	MR. GEORGE GROSSMITH [1]
Captain Corcoran .	MR. RUTLAND BARRINGTON [1]
Ralph Rackstraw . .	MR. J. G. ROBERTSON
Dick Deadeye . . .	MR. RICHARD TEMPLE [1]
Bill Bobstay	MR. R. CUMMINGS
Bob Beckett . . .	. MR. RUDOLPH LEWIS
Josephine	MISS GERALDINE ULMAR
Hebe	MISS JESSIE BOND [1]
Little Buttercup . .	MISS ROSINA BRANDRAM

[1] Original characters.

This was the occasion of the first appearance at the Savoy of Miss Geraldine Ulmar, a singer and actress destined to become one of the favourite *prima donnas* of the Gilbert and Sullivan operas.

Another recruit to the Savoyard ranks was Mr. J. G. Robertson, who succeeded George Power as principal tenor, and scored success as "Ralph Rackstraw." Mr. Robertson was, if I remember rightly, a brother of Mrs. Kendal. Touching Rosina Brandram's Little Buttercup, if ever such a winsome and sweet-voiced bumboat-woman boarded Her Majesty's ships at Spithead in Victorian days, she must have taken captive the whole crew and driven a roaring trade—

> " In tea and in coffee,
> In treacle and toffee
> And excellent peppermint-drops."

It required no Gilbertian stretch of imagination to make a post-captain fall desperately in love with such " a plump and pleasing person."

It may not sound complimentary to the memory of the famous Savoy contralto if I confess that Miss Brandram's delightful Little Buttercup often reminded me of another fascinating bumboat-woman I had previously met in real life. It was at Bermuda in the early sixties, when I was a midshipman in the Royal Navy. The lady (a coloured one, by the way), who purveyed "tuck" on board H.M.S. *Orlando*, was of such a sweet, amiable disposition, and, withal, such an amusing raconteuse, that every gun-room officer in the British fleet fell a victim to her wiles.

But the middy upon whom Mrs. Dinah Browne bestowed particular favour was young Sydney Smith Dickens, youngest son of the only Charles Dickens. "Little expectations," as we nick-named him (à propos his father's story "Great Expectations," which had just about that time been published), gained the good woman's affections chiefly by his prodigious purchases of the luxuries she purveyed, such as guava jelly, rahat-lakoum, bananas, boot-laces, etc. In return for his patronage and custom, Dinah invited "Massa Dicksie" to take tea with her on shore, and I, being the lad's particular chum, was included in the invitation.

Accordingly, one afternoon to Madame Browne's private residence we repaired.

Dinah's boudoir was a clean and cosy corner in a somewhat primitive cabin home. It was neatly furnished with articles which had been salved from wrecks on the neighbouring coast—a conspicuous object being that which had once been a cottage pianoforte. The walls were adorned with a large number of photos (we called them *cartes de visite* in those days) of young naval officers, all below the rank of lieutenant. After tea our hostess entertained us with humorous anecdotes—real genuine midshipman's tales—and yielding to our persuasion sang to us some charming coon-songs in a rich, deep, but rudely cultured contralto voice.

Thence it may be understood how "Little Buttercup" of the Savoy often recalled to my mind the amiable and "gifted" Bumboat-woman of Bermuda.

"H.M.S. Pinafore" enjoyed another prosperous run

before a favouring breeze—one hundred and twenty performances, just about the number of her guns, assuming she was a three-decker of the *Victory* type. On March 17th, 1888, " The Pirates of Penzance " made their reappearance, impersonated as follows :

Major-General Stanley .	MR. GEORGE GROSSMITH [1]
Pirate King . . .	MR. RICHARD TEMPLE [1]
Samuel	. MR. R. CUMMINGS
Frederic . . .	. MR. J. G. ROBERTSON
Sergeant of Police .	MR. RUTLAND BARRINGTON [1]
Mabel	. MISS GERALDINE ULMAR
Edith	. MISS JESSIE BOND
Kate	. MISS KAVANAGH
Isabel	. MISS LAWRENCE
Ruth	MISS ROSINA BRANDRAM

" The Pirates " ran eighty nights, and on June 7th, 1888, " The Mikado " was revived for the first time—with the following *dramatis personae*.

The Mikado . . .	. MR. RICHARD TEMPLE
Nanki Poo . . .	. MR. J. G. ROBERTSON
Koko	. MR. GEORGE GROSSMITH [1]
Pooh Bah . .	MR. RUTLAND BARRINGTON [1]
Pishi Tush . . .	. MR. R. CUMMINGS
Yum Yum . . .	MISS GERALDINE ULMAR
Pitti Sing . . .	. MISS JESSIE BOND
Peep Bo . . .	. MISS SYBIL GREY
Katisha . . .	. MISS ROSINA BRANDRAM

After a run of 116 performances, " The Mikado " was again withdrawn on September 29th, 1888.

At the close of " The Mikado's " second campaign

[1] Original Characters.

Rutland Barrington terminated his engagement at the Savoy.

For just ten years the popular comedian had faithfully served under the D'Oyly Carte management. Many were the parts he had created; rich were the honours he had scored. But the time had now arrived when the actor sought new opportunities for satisfying his professional aspirations.

Barrington had been persuaded to try his hand at the attractive but risky reins of theatrical management. Backed by a friendly financier, and encouraged by the hearty good wishes of his Savoy colleagues and a host of admirers, he took the St. James's Theatre and inaugurated his management with the production of a new comedy called " The Dean's Daughter." This, proving a failure, was followed by a play written expressly for him by Mr. W. S. Gilbert. Through the author's recommendation, Miss Julia Neilson was engaged for the principal part in " Brantinghame Hall," as the piece was called. This was the début in London of Miss Neilson, who to-day, needless to relate, is numbered amongst the most gifted and distinguished of English actresses. Of the evil fortune which befel Rutland Barrington's venture, and the causes which led to his failure, particulars may be gathered from the pages of the actor's autobiography published a few years ago.

Barrington's loss was the Savoy's gain, for it was not very long before Pooh Bah, the popular, returned to the scenes of his former triumphs. Among the multitude of his friends and sympathizing acquaintances, no one felt more sorry for Barrington's bad luck

at the St. James's Theatre, no one was more pleased
to welcome him back to the Savoy, than the writer of
these present reminiscences, who for some years had
been his constant associate.

    •   •   •   •   •

The policy of revivals was more than fully justified
by the results. " H.M.S. Pinafore," " The Pirates of
Penzance," and " The Mikado " had each, in turn,
proved that it was not dead, but had simply been indulged with well-earned rest. Moreover, the interval
occupied by the reproduction of these pieces allowed
Gilbert and Sullivan leisure to turn their attention to
the preparation of a new opera. It was an opportunity
of which the author and composer did not fail to avail
themselves to the full. And the issue was " The
Yeomen of the Guard."

CHAPTER IX

"The Yeomen of the Guard"—Gilbert curbs his Pegasus—Gilbert and Sullivan's masterpiece—Sullivan's favourite opera—The lyrics—Scene between Phoebe, Meryll, and Wilfred Shadbolt—The two Savoy Jessies—Sullivan's puzzle in setting "I have a song to sing, O"—Triumph of musical construction—Peppermint Bulls'-Eyes at stage rehearsal—Tales of two Jessies.

On Wednesday, October 3rd, 1888, London was presented with Number Nine of the series of Gilbert and Sullivan's operas. The title was:

"THE YEOMEN OF THE GUARD, OR THE MERRYMAN AND HIS MAID"

Dramatis Personae

Sir Richard Cholmondeley . Mr. Wallace Brownlow
    (*Lieutenant of the Tower*)
Colonel Fairfax   . .   Mr. Courtice Pounds
    (*Under sentence of death*)
Sergeant Meryll.   . .   Mr. Richard Temple
    (*Of the Yeomen of the Guard*)
Leonard Meryll   .   .   . Mr. W. R. Shirley
    (*His Son*)
Jack Point   .   . . Mr. George Grossmith
    (*A Strolling Jester*)
Wilfred Shadbolt   .   .   . Mr. W. H. Denny
    (*Head Jailer and Assistant Tormentor*)
The Headsman .   .   .   .   . Mr. Richards
First Yeoman .   .   .   .   . Mr. Wilbraham

Y

Second Yeoman . . . . MR. MEDCALF
Third Yeoman . . . . . MR. MERTON
Fourth Yeoman . . . MR. RUDOLF LEWIS
First Citizen . . . . . MR. REDMOND
Second Citizen . . . . . MR. BOYD
Elsie Maynard . . . MISS GERALDINE ULMAR
    (A Strolling Singer)
Phoebe Meryll . . . . MISS JESSIE BOND
    (Sergeant Meryll's Daughter)
Dame Carruthers . . MISS ROSINA BRANDRAM
    (Housekeeper to the Tower)
Kate . . . . . MISS ROSE HERVEY
    (Her Niece)
Chorus of Yeomen of the Guard, Gentlemen, Citizens, etc.

The opera produced under the personal direction of
the Author and Composer.

ACT I.—*Tower Green.*
ACT II.—*The Tower from the Wharf.*

DATE.—16*th Century*

Musical Director . . MR. FRANÇOIS CELLIER
Stage Manager . . . . MR. W. H. SEYMOUR

The Scenery painted by Mr. Hawes Craven (by permission of Sir Henry Irving). The Dresses designed by Mr. Percy Anderson and executed by Miss Fisher, Madame Léon, and Mr. B. J. Simmons. Wigs by Clarkson. The Dances arranged by Mr. John D'Auban. Stage Machinist, Mr. P. White. Electrician, Mr. Lyons.

Play-goers and music-lovers were once again on the tenter-hooks of pleasurable anticipation. The three recent revivals had put a keen edge on their appetites. Expectation was quickened by the rumour that the new piece was to be of a different pattern from any of

Photo by Ellis & Walery.

MISS GERALDINE ULMAR.

Photo by Ellis & Walery.

MISS ELSIE SPAIN.

the preceding Savoy productions. And such it proved to be. The collaborators had broken entirely fresh ground. "The Yeomen" marked a very distinct departure. It seemed to indicate that Gilbert had, at last, determined upon breaking in his fiery, untamed steed. The poet had bridled and brought Pegasus down from the Helicon of unrealities to the plains of earth. Henceforth—at any rate for a while—he would canter gently on *terra firma* without appalling the senses of ordinary mortals. But the spoilt pet of Gilbert's muse chafed beneath the curb. Every now and then he seemed disposed to show the cloven hoof. Pegasus was unwilling to remain in this dull, unpoetic sphere of ours.

But Gilbert had come to realize that his best friends wanted to see and hear more of him and from a different aspect. They had been fondly hoping that some day the gifted Savoyard would hold the mirror up to nature ; not one of those terrible concave or convex quick-silver'd libellers that distort the forms of the noblest of men and the features of the fairest of women, but a perfect plate-glass, bevelled-edged mirror that should reflect people and things as they really are. Our author had learnt what was looked for, and expected of him ; and now the Savoyard chieftains had set their united wits at work to give us an opera of more rational, less fantastic quality than any they had yet produced. It was an experiment ; happily, a most successful experiment.

If a Referendum were taken, or if judgment may be safely based on the aggregate number of consecutive

17

performances, then " The Mikado " would very likely
be returned as first favourite of all the Savoy operas.
In the popular " Ring " the Japanese play undoubtedly
remains favourite to the present day. Still, it can
hardly be questioned that, as a work of pure dramatic
and musical art, " The Yeomen of the Guard " is
Gilbert and Sullivan's *chef d'œuvre*. By a select
number of the *cognoscenti* it has been pronounced the
best English light opera ever given to the stage. In
the early days of its production it was universally pre-
dicted that " The Yeomen " would be living long after
the more frivolous pieces of the Savoy répertoire were
forgotten. But there were few even among the most
devoted partisans of the Savoy who, five-and-twenty
years ago, would have dreamed that in the year 1914,
the Gilbert and Sullivan operas, with only one or two
exceptions, would be living and delighting the people
as greatly as they did in their pristine days.

" Ivanhoe," the romantic opera with which D'Oyly
Carte opened his palatial English Opera-house (now
the Palace Theatre), was of a loftier and more ambitious
type of lyric work. If it may not strictly be classified
as Grand Opera, it was generally spoken of and criti-
cized as such. But "The Yeomen of the Guard "
remained Sullivan's favourite of all his offsprings given
to the stage. Its composition yielded him more
genuine pleasure than he had found in any opera of
the topsy-turvy type. In the story of " The Merryman and his Maid " the author strikes deeper into the
mine of human sympathy ; his plot is invested with
pure pathos ; his characters are not only witty, but

wise ; they are humorous without being obtrusively
paradoxical. Many of them might have walked out of
Macaulay's "History of England," or one of those stir-
ring romances by Ainsworth or G. P. R. James which
thrilled us in our school-days. In Gilbert's story of
the "Tower of London" we seem to identify some
individuals we have met before. At any rate, we are
ready to believe they have all existed in the past.

So deftly has the librettist done his work that the
lyrics, apart from the accompanying dialogue, might
suffice to tell the story of the brave soldier condemned
to die by the headsman's axe. They describe the
prisoner's rescue from the block through the aid of a
warm-hearted woman, a simple maiden who contrives
to outwit the zealous warders of the Tower, and to
checkmate even the head jailer and assistant tormentor,
whose playthings are racks, pincers, and thumbscrews.
In plaintive verse Gilbert relates the sadder incident of
the luckless jester, poor Jack Point, whose antiquated
quips—may we call them *ambrosial* chestnuts ?—
and merry patter-songs are mingled with "sighs for
the love of a ladye." The unhappy fool's heart is
breaking for a maiden who, by the unwitting act of
saving the life, and becoming the bride, of a noble
soldier, drives to despair and death the faithful companion of her past adversity. It is only necessary to
glance through the book of the words to find the story
of "The Yeomen of the Guard" clearly and concisely
outlined in the songs and concerted numbers. This
is what a musical play should be, but seldom is. None
but a master playwright could have prepared such a

book, and assuredly " The Yeomen of the Guard " is Sir William Gilbert's masterpiece of libretti.

What delightful lyrics! Not a rhyme without reason! Not a love-song without a touch of poetry in it! Not a chorus without strong dramatic significance! What cause, then, to marvel at Sullivan's gratification when he sat down to clothe with melody such charming stanzas? Seldom has a composer been favoured with words so music-compelling. Take, for instance, the two Tenor Ballads, " Is life a boon? " in the first act, and in the second act, " Free from his fetters grim." I cannot resist the temptation to quote both these admirable lyrics. Not only may they serve to illuminate these pages, but I feel sure every reader who has ever heard them sung will welcome them here as the means of reawakening memories of their exquisite musical refrains.

It will be remembered how Colonel Fairfax, having been condemned to death, is being conducted under guard to his dungeon in the Tower. On the way he is permitted to halt and greet his old friend and comrade Sergeant Meryll, who is striving to comfort his weeping daughter—Phoebe. Let me recall the speech that precedes the song. Thus :

PHOEBE. (*Aside to* MERYLL.) Oh, father, father, I cannot bear it!

MER. My poor lass!

FAIR. Nay, pretty one, why weepest thou? Come, be comforted. Such a life as mine is not worth weeping for. (*Sees* MERYLL.) Sergeant Meryll, is it not? (*To* LIEUT.). May I greet my old friend? (*Shakes* MERYLL'S

hand). Why, man, what's all this ? Thou and I have
faced the grim old king a dozen times, and never has
his majesty come to me in such goodly fashion. Keep
a stout heart, good fellow—we are soldiers and we know
how to die, thou and I. Take my word for it, it is
easier to die well than to live well—for, in sooth, I have
tried both.

BALLAD.—*Fairfax*

" Is life a boon ?
   If so, it must befal
   That Death, whene'er he call,
Must call too soon.
   Though fourscore years he give,
   Yet one would pray to live
Another moon !
   What kind of plaint have I,
   Who perish in July ?
   I might have had to die,
Perchance, in June !

" Is life a thorn ?
   Then count it not a whit !
   Man is well done with it ;
Soon as he's born,
   He should all means essay
   To put the plague away ;
And I, war-worn,
   Poor captured fugitive,
   My life most gladly give—
   I might have had to live
Another morn ! "

The second song occurs when Colonel Fairfax finds
himself free from his dungeon, but bound by conjugal
ties to which, for the purpose of the plot, he has been
compelled to submit.

COL. FAIRFAX. So I am free ! Free, but for the cursed
haste with which I hurried headlong into the bonds
of matrimony with——Heaven knows whom ! As far
as I remember, she should have been young ; but
even had not her face been concealed by her kerchief,
I doubt whether in my then plight I should have taken
much note of her. Free ? Bah ! The Tower bonds were
but a thread of silk compared with these conjugal
fetters which I, fool that I was, placed upon mine own
hands ! From the one I broke readily enough—how
to break the other !

SONG.—*Fairfax*

" Free from his fetters grim—
    Free to depart ;
Free both in life and limb—
    In all but heart !
Bound to an unknown bride
    For good and ill ;
Ah, is not one so tied
    A prisoner still ?

" Free, yet in fetters held
    Till his last hour,
Gyves that no smith can weld,
    No rust devour !
Although a monarch's hand
    Had set him free,
Of all the captive band
    The saddest he ! "

From a casket full of such rich gems it is not easy to
select one more lustrous than another. But as a
sample of exquisite coquetry, as an illustration of the
wiles of a saucy maiden humouring, to his destruction,
the attentions of a repulsive wooer, let me commend

that delightful comedy scene between Phoebe Meryll and Wilfred Shadbolt, the baboonish jailer. Phoebe, in order to secure the keys of the cell in which Colonel Fairfax is imprisoned, proceeds to captivate her loathsome lover with the make-believe of reciprocated affection.

(PHOEBE *has slyly taken bunch of keys from* WILFRED's *waistband and hands them to* SERGEANT MERYLL, *who enters the Tower, unnoticed by* WILFRED).

WILFRED. Ha! ha! I am a mad wag.
PHOEBE. (*With a grimace.*) Thou art a most light-hearted and delightful companion, Master Wilfred. Thine anecdotes of the torture-chamber are the prettiest hearing.
WILFRED. I'm a pleasant fellow an' I choose. I believe I am the merriest dog that barks. Ah, we might be passing happy together.
PHOEBE. Perhaps. I do not know.
WILFRED. For thou wouldst make a most tender and loving wife.
PHOEBE. Aye, to one whom I really loved. For there is a wealth of love within this little heart—saving up for—I wonder whom? Now, of all the world of men, I wonder whom? To think that he whom I am to wed is now alive and somewhere! Perhaps far away, perhaps close at hand! And I know him not! It seemeth that I am wasting time in not knowing him.
WILFRED. Now say that it is I—nay! suppose it for the nonce. Say that we are wed—suppose it only—say that thou art my very bride, and I thy cheery, joyous, bright, frolicsome husband—and that, the day's work being done, and the prisoners stored away

for the night, thou and I are alone together—with a long, long evening before us !

PHOEBE. (*With a grimace.*) It is a pretty picture—but I scarcely know. It cometh so unexpectedly—and yet—and yet—*were* I thy bride——

WILFRED. Aye ! wert thou my bride—— ?

PHOEBE. Oh, how I would love thee !

BALLAD.—*Phoebe*

" Were I thy bride,
Then the whole world beside
    Were not too wide
        To hold my wealth of love—
    Were I thy bride !

" Upon thy breast
My loving head would rest,
    As on her nest
        The tender turtle-dove—
    Were I thy bride !

" This heart of mine
Would be one heart with thine,
    And in that shrine
        Our happiness would dwell—
    Were I thy bride !

" And all day long
Our lives should be a song :
    No grief, no wrong
        Should make my heart rebel—
    Were I thy bride !

" The silvery flute,
The melancholy lute,
    Were night-owl's hoot
        To my love-whispered coo—
    Were I thy bride !

MR. C. H. KENNINGHAM.

MR. W. H. DENNY.

" The skylark's trill
Were but discordance shrill
    To the soft thrill
        Of wooing as I'd woo—
    Were I thy bride ! "

(MERYLL *re-enters; gives keys to* PHOEBE, *who
    replaces them at* WILFRED'S *girdle, un-
    noticed by him.*)

" The rose's sigh
Were as a carrion's cry
    To lullaby
        Such as I'd sing to thee,
    Were I thy bride !

" A feather's press
Were leaden heaviness
To my caress ;
    But then, of course, you see,
    I'm not thy bride ! "

(Exit PHOEBE.)

WILFRED. No, thou'rt not—not yet ! But, Lord,
how she woo'd ! I should be no mean judge of wooing,
seeing that I have been more hotly woo'd than most
men. I have been woo'd by maid, widow, and wife.
I have been woo'd boldly, timidly, tearfully, shyly—
by direct assault, by suggestion, by implication, by
inference, and by innuendo. But this wooing is not
of the common order ; it is the wooing of one who
must needs woo me, if she die for it !

(Exit WILFRED.)

Who that witnessed this scene as originally played
by Mr. W. H. Denny and Miss Jessie Bond can ever
forget the effect it had upon the audience ? Once again

the fascinating little Savoy soubrette displayed admirable skill as a comedy actress.   Nothing could be more coquettish, more artistically artful than the manner in which the cunning Phoebe wheedled and deceived the unsuspecting Cerberus.   This is altogether one of the most amusing scenes in the opera, and never fails to meet with rapturous applause.

During the last revival of " The Yeomen of the Guard" at the Savoy the part of Phoebe was sustained by Miss Jessie Rose so charmingly that not only old Savoyards but Sir William Gilbert himself declared the second Jessie to be in every respect a worthy successor to Jessie the First as Queen of Savoy Soubrettes.

Sir Arthur Sullivan used to confess that the most puzzling musical problem that he was ever called upon to solve was the setting of the duet between Jack Point and Elsie Maynard.   The lyric which holds the keynote of the sad story of " The Merryman and his Maid" Gilbert had constructed on the model of the nursery rhyme, " The House that Jack Built."   The stanza, " I have a song to sing, O " comprises four verses ; to each succeeding verse two lines are added. Thus, while the first verse is of *seven* lines only, the last verse is extended to *thirteen* lines.   It will be admitted that, as a rule, the composer of an ordinary drawing-room ballad finds an insuperable difficulty in setting it if the verses are not minutely alike in metre and number of lines ; he requires that each verse shall contain the same precise quantity of dactyls and spondees in the same strict sequence, otherwise his muse will not awake to the occasion.   This being so, will any one be surprised to learn that it took Sullivan a full fortnight to set to music Gilbert's very out-of-the-common lyric ? It kept poor Sir Arthur awake at night, and, when a friend called and found him in a semi-demented state, he would moan out in melancholy tone, "My dear fellow, I have a song to set O, and I don't know how the dickens I'm going to do it ? " However, as we all know, Sullivan accomplished it at last, if not to his own entire satisfaction, to the wonder and delight of everybody else. Musicians alone can appreciate the intricacy of his task, and the masterly way in which he fulfilled it, especially as regards the elaborate and diversified orchestration with its pathetic drone pervading it throughout.

" I have a song to sing, O," may not be considered by every one the gem of the opera, but that it is a trjumph of musical construction all will admit. Moreover, it is the song that is first quoted whenever " The Yeomen of the Guard" is mentioned.

Over the contemplation of this delightful opera one would gladly linger beyond the allotted time and space. But already it may be thought that I have wandered beyond the domain of happy reminiscences into the more prosaic field of dry, critical review. And so, lest we depart yet further from the purpose of the present volume, let me bring this chapter to a close with an anecdote which " The Yeomen of the Guard " recalls to mind.

It was timorously whispered into my ears by Miss Jessie Rose. The young lady hesitated before beginning the story ; she feared that her gossip might

be calculated to "give Sir Arthur Sullivan away," but
I assured her that, if the tale was a good one against
himself, Sullivan was certain to have repeated it.
In like assurance I hazard its publication here.

One day, during the rehearsal of "The Yeomen of
the Guard" for its first revival at the Savoy, François
Cellier, who was coaching the chorus, noticed that some
of the ladies were not singing out with their usual
power and clear accent. On his reproving them for
what he conceived to be slackness and inattention, his
lecture was received with subdued laughter. Feeling
annoyed, the musical director approached Miss Jessie
Rose, whom he imagined to be the ring-leader, and
asked for an explanation of this revolt, saying he
could not put up with such breach of discipline. Miss
Rose, trying to assume a serious countenance, spluttered
forth, "Well, Mr. Cellier—you *must* forgive us; it is
quite impossible to sing with our mouths full." Sullivan, then coming to Cellier's side, said, "Don't scold
the ladies, François—it's all *my* fault! Miss Rose is
quite right; nobody can sing with a mouth full."
Then, taking from his overcoat pocket a box of Maynard's famous peppermint bulls'-eyes, he extended
it to Cellier, saying, "You try! accept one of these
Elsie Maynards." François, smiling, placed the sweet-
meat in his mouth and muttered, "I think the best
thing we can do is to take a few bars' rest for refreshment."

During the pause Jessie Rose, who, added to her
other accomplishments, possessed poetic fancy, scribbled
on the fly-leaf of her score the following lines :

MISS JESSIE ROSE.

MISS RUTH VINCENT.

" How doth the bull's-eyed peppermint
Delight the singer's throat !
It gives a charming mezzo-tint
To sweet soprano note."

This *poem* falling into Sir Arthur's hands, he re-marked that, if it were not for fear of making Sir William jealous, he might set the words to music.

" Oh please—please, Sir Arthur—*don't* do that," pleaded the poetess, all the time thinking to herself— " If only he would ! "

It must be added that such frivolous interludes were very exceptional at the Savoy rehearsals, where, as we have before mentioned, strict attention to business was the general rule. This fact may be emphasized by repeating something told me by that other popular Savoy soubrette—" Jessie the First," as we have called her. Miss Jessie Bond has assured me that the only time she can remember ever seeing Sir Arthur Sullivan cross was when she sang a *crotchet* instead of a *quaver*.

Both the above items of tittle-tattle relating to the loved and respected *maestro* help to illustrate alike the generous nature and the amiability of Sir Arthur Sullivan.

CHAPTER X

A SKILFUL *chef* will arrange his ménu from day to day
with studious care to gratify his patrons' taste for
variety. In like manner did our Three Savoyards, in
the preparation of each succeeding programme, show
their regard for the value of contrast. For example :
had " The Yeomen of the Guard " followed immediately
on the heels of " Ruddigore," so serious a play might
not have proved as acceptable as it did after a *réchauffé*
of lighter pieces had whetted the public appetite for
more substantial fare.

But on no occasion that I can recall was contrast
more evident or more agreeable than when we were
given " The Gondoliers."

In " The Yeomen " the author had touched the deepest chords of human sympathy. The story of " The Merryman and his Maid " was rich in genuine pathos relieved by wit and humour of that pure kind which is without the sting of satire, void of that caustic ridicule from which it had been imagined no Gilbertian libretto could ever be free. In his latest opera Gilbert had shown how he could paint true portraits of people as cleverly as he could sketch caricatures. The Savoy author had proved how, from behind the grinning mask of his own eccentric comedy, he could behold and study men and women as they actually live and move and have their being. He could see and read and depict their characteristics as faithfully as any ordinary dramatist or poet. But Gilbert's pet hobby was shooting with his own patent catapult at folly as it flies. Just for a while he seemed to have wearied of losing himself in the clouds. He had ceased to gaze down from giddy heights, and no longer indulged in the practical joke of showering grains of mustard and pepper upon the pigmy people who swarmed like ants beneath him.

He had become content for a day to seek among ordinary mortals for characters whom the least imaginative play-goer could identify as true types of humanity. Around them he would weave a plot and story perfectly consistent with the realities of life. And so, as we have seen, he gave us his masterpiece of opera-libretti—" The Yeomen of the Guard."

But now, after a year spent beneath the grey, grim walls of the Tower of London, Gilbert, with his ever willing colleagues Sullivan and Carte, determined to transport us away from scenes of gloom and grief to realms of sunshine and mirth. Ah! thought all Savoyards, "What a delightful, exhilarating change it will be!"

Sullivan, well used to the varying moods and vagaries of his gifted friend, waits ready with his lyre to accompany him once more into the regions of Topsy-turvy-dom. The composer has simply to change his key from the minor, which had been in keeping with the sad story of unhappy Jack Point, to the major key, which shall better befit the songs of the Sunny South whither the co-labourers are bound.

Away they hie together, Gilbert with his wallet bulging with brilliant ideas, Sullivan with his brain-cells bubbling over with streams of melody. Away they journey southwards until " To Venetia's shores they come."

They have left far behind them in the chill North those stern-visaged, medieval-looking Yeomen of the Guard, the solemn warders of the Tower ; and now they find themselves surrounded by cheery Venetians ; gay and gallant gondolieri with smiling, sweet-voiced contadine. Above them a clear cerulean sky ; beneath them sparkling waters. Everywhere around them brilliant colour, music, song, dance, laughter. What a change ! with such environment how can the Savoy humorists be other than light-hearted, not to say exuberantly frolicsome ? How can they fail with such material ready at hand to produce a play that shall charm their friends at home with a glimpse of Italian glories ; an opera that shall set dull London once more singing and dancing to their merry tunes for many a month to come ?

And now, in silvery Venice, Gilbert listens to a tale concerning a kingdom called Barataria, whose throne is vacant. He then chances across various quaint characters that will just suit his " book." First, he discovers the eccentric, impecunious Duke of Plaza-Toro, a grandee of Spain who is in process of forming himself into a Limited Liability Company. ("What a part for Grossmith!" thinks our author. "But— Grossmith has deserted us.")

His grace has just arrived in Venice with the Grand Duchess and their charming daughter Casilda—and suite. The suite in attendance on the courtly party consists of one individual, a handsome youth named Luiz, who, naturally enough, has fallen desperately in love with the pretty Casilda. Now (in his mind's eye), Gilbert sees approaching Don Alhambra del Bolero, the Grand Inquisitor.

" The very man I was looking for ! Why, bless my lucky star, if this worthy person is not the very image of Denny ! Capital! we'll soon get our plot and characters together."

To Sir Arthur Sullivan Mr. Gilbert then presents all these distinguished personages—and their suite. The author has already secured an option on all the shares in " The Duke of Plaza-Toro Co., Ltd."

Our ever-ready composer forthwith proceeds to measure them all for music—just as a court tailor in Bond Street fits a Duke or an Earl with robes of rank.

One thing is quite certain, the Duke and Duchess of

18

Plaza-Toro will be perfectly suited with appropriate serio-comic numbers, and Sullivan has made up his mind that the lovely Casilda shall have a delicious love-duet with the handsome Luiz as soon as the " musical suite" is permitted to cast aside that "delicately modulated instrument" (the drum) of which he is said to be a "past-master." Gilbert has whispered to Sullivan: "You see, I intend that Luiz shall eventually turn out to be the rightful heir to the throne of Barataria."

" Ah, splendid idea that ! so original ! " remarks Sullivan *sotto voce*. I suppose you will want a coronation march. " Eh ? Well—perhaps—but—no—I think we will crown him off. But I'll tell you what we must have, and that is a grand dance."

" Yes—quite so ! say a cachucha! and for how many ? Oh, the full strength of the company, I should say."

Sir Arthur makes a note : " Cachucha omnes."

" And now," continues Gilbert, "we must select half a dozen clever, good-looking gondoliers. One of them must be a fine, rotund, sturdy fellow, a character that would suit Rutland Barrington, don't you know ? "

" Ah yes—that's important—Barrington will be rejoining us ; we must certainly find a good model for Rutland. He must be a gondolier with a fine voice, and know how to use it—but not too much music, please ! You won't forget—Barrington——"

" Yes—yes, I know what you were going to say. I've got my eyes on two handsome brothers, Giuseppe and Mareo Palmieri, the pick and flower of all the gondoliers—just the very part for Courtice Pounds and Rutland Barrington. Then, next item, half a dozen specially selected contadine—must be pretty, graceful, able to sing and dance the cachucha, fandango, bolero, etc. Having secured all these as patterns for our players, we will place them all together in our united brain-pans, and, *hey presto!*—there we are— our *dramatis personae* are chosen, our plot is laid. It may not be a very strong plot."

" Not as strong as ' The Yeomen's,' I imagine ? " queried Sullivan.

" Well no—perhaps not; but still, let's hope strong and coherent enough for our Savoy friends. Then, think of the colour! with all these picturesque costumes and scenic accessories, what pegs on which you will hang some of your daintiest musical *morceaux*, old friend." (Sir William was always a sure prophet !)

" Yes," replied Sullivan, " I quite appreciate the situation. You know how I revel in this glorious atmosphere. The man who fails to find inspiration in Venice or the Riviera is no artist. He may enjoy being punted about in a gondola by moonlight; he may be devoted to these charming contadine; but, I repeat, he is no artist if he does not become inspired as you and I must be."

This brief description of the manner in which the plot and story of " The Gondoliers " was conceived and worked out may, very likely, not be accepted by everybody as—

> " A tale quite free from every doubt,
>   All probable, possible shadow of doubt,
>   All possible doubt whatever."

Well, supposing it is not absolutely authentic, is it not, at least, easy to imagine how Gilbert and Sullivan may have proceeded on something like the lines we have ventured to suggest ? At any rate, "The Gondoliers," with the King of Barataria, the Duke and Duchess of Plaza-Toro, their daughter, and suite, came to reign conjointly at the Savoy, where London play-goers hastened to become their faithful and devoted subjects.

Nobody will want to be told further details of Gilbert's strange romance of "The Gondoliers." Probably to every reader of this book the bright little opera has long been familiar. If not, they and their children and their children's children will have many an opportunity of making the acquaintance of the cheery Venetians, if not at the Savoy, at some other theatre of the British Empire, for, if I am not too optimistic, "The Gondoliers" and every other of the Gilbert and Sullivan répertoire will be running through generations yet to come.

Here is the original cast of—

THE GONDOLIERS, OR THE KING OF BARATARIA

As presented at the Savoy Theatre, London, on Saturday, December 7th, 1889.

DRAMATIS PERSONAE

The Duke of Plaza-Toro . MR. FRANK WYATT
(*A Grandee of Spain*)
Luiz   .   .   .   . MR. WALLACE BROWNLOW
(*His Attendant*)
Don Alhambra Del Bolero . . MR. W. H. DENNY
(*The Grand Inquisitor*)

MISS ESTHER PALLISER.

MISS FLORENCE PERRY.

2761

Marco Palmieri	.	.	MR. COURTICE POUNDS
Giuseppe Palmieri	.	.	MR. RUTLAND BARRINGTON
Antonio .	.	.	.	.	MR. METCALF
Francesco.	.	.	.	.	.	MR. ROSE
Georgio .	.	.	.	.	.	MR. DE PLEDGE
Annibale .	.	.	.	.	.	MR. WILBRAHAM

(Venetian Gondolieri)

| The Duchess of Plaza-Toro | | MISS ROSINA BRANDRAM |
| Casilda . | . | . | . | . | MISS DECIMA MOORE |

(Her Daughter)

Gianetta .	.	.	.	MISS GERALDINE ULMAR [1]
Tessa	.	.	.	.	MISS JESSIE BOND
Fiametta .	.	.	.	.	MISS LAWRENCE
Vittoria .	.	.	.	.	MISS COLE
Giulia .	.	.	.	.	MISS PHYLLIS

(Contadine)

| Inez | . | . | . | . | . | MISS BERNARD |

(The King's Foster-mother)

Chorus of Gondoliers and Contadine, Men-at-Arms, Heralds, and Pages

ACT I.—*The Piazzetta, Venice*
ACT II.—*Pavilion in the Palace of Barataria*

The Dresses designed by Mr. Percy Anderson and executed by Monsieur Alias, Madame Léon, and Messrs. B. J. Simmons & Co. The Dances arranged by Mr. W. Warde.

| Conductor | . | . | . | MR. FRANÇOIS CELLIER |

Special interest was attached to the production of "The Gondoliers" altogether apart from its own qualities as an opera.

---

[1] The part of Gianetta was later in the run taken by that charming artiste, Miss Esther Palliser.

For the first time since the series of Gilbert and
Sullivan operas began at the Opera Comique in
November 1877, the name of George Grossmith was
absent from the programme.   After a period of
twelve years' uninterrupted service and repeated
triumphs, the popular comedian had grown weary
of the monotony of long runs.   Moreover, he was
persuaded that, from a financial point of view, he
could do better for himself as a public entertainer.
For some time past he had contemplated seceding
from the D'Oyly Carte management, but had been
induced to remain at the Savoy for the run of " The
Yeomen of the Guard."   Grossmith can hardly have
regretted having done so, seeing that in the part of
" Jack Point " he found wider scope for the display
of his powers as a real jester of jesters and legitimate
actor than had ever previously been afforded him.
When one comes to reflect on the final scene in which
Grossmith played the chief part on the Savoy stage, the
refrain of his swan-song, " I have a song to sing, O,"
mingles with the echo of that livelier ditty, " He
never would be missed," with which he amused us in
" The Mikado."   If ever Koko had secretly placed
his own name on that historical list of undesirables,
the public was not found to endorse such condemnation.   " Gee-Gee " was in truth greatly missed from
his post of honour in the ranks of the Savoyards.
Happily, his place was taken by that versatile actor,
singer, and dancer, Frank Wyatt, who, as the Duke of
Plaza-Toro, scored an instantaneous success.   But
perhaps the best solatium given for the loss of George

Grossmith was the return to the Savoy of Rutland Barrington. The hearty welcome back accorded to the favourite Savoyard must have been soothing balm to the wounds occasioned by his luckless campaign at St. James's Theatre.

Another new-comer and great acquisition to the Savoy company was Miss Decima Moore, who, in the part of Casilda, made her first important appearance on the London stage, and at once captivated all hearts by her sweet singing and winsome personality.

It is doubtful if the walls of the Savoy had ever resounded with such ringing peals of laughter as those which greeted the introduction of " The Gondoliers " on the first night. A wild thunderstorm of applause raged throughout the theatre from rise to fall of curtain. At first it was a deep roar of delight, then for a few seconds a subdued rumble of restrained mirth ever crescendo until it burst again into a louder roar. Gilbert had this time provided the Savoyards, both before and behind the footlights, with just the very feast they were hungry for. The actors, the actresses, and the musicians seemed to revel in the humour of the play. The audience forgot they were on the banks of murky, muddy Thames. Gilbert, the magician, had transported them in a body to sunny Venice.

Plot ! Who worried about a plot ? It was quite joy enough to bask beneath Italian skies and watch the frolics of those delightfully irresponsible people singing, dancing, and indulging in the wittiest conversation that even the Savoyards had ever listened to.

As for Sullivan's music, it could only be likened to a

moorland stream rippling and leaping in its course over the pebbly reaches, pausing anon at the still and restful pools of deeper melody, only again to ripple with sparkling laughter downwards to the sea.

"The Gondoliers," from the gladsome opening chorus of Contadine to the Finale, is throughout replete with charming variety and striking contrasts. Take, for instance, the quaint patter-song of Giuseppe, one of the supposititious twin Kings of Barataria, wherein he describes the responsibilities of his exalted rank:

> " Rising early in the morning,
> We proceed to light our fire ;
> Then, our Majesty adorning
> In its work-a-day attire,
> We embark without delay
> On the duties of the day."

And so on for some sixty lines, each line accompanied by some facetious comments from the orchestral instruments, and a titter from the audience, who drank in every syllable rendered by Rutland Barrington in his own clear, inimitable diction. Close upon this follows that Sullivanesque gem of gems, "Take a pair of sparkling eyes," sung by Courtice Pounds with all the delicacy and finished art of which he is a past-master.

Take, again, the famous Chorus and Cachucha Dance, which so fascinates and enraptures an audience that they demand and re-demand it again and again until the dancers have no breath left to continue singing. Then, after Don Alhambra, in a humorous song, has

pointed a moral to the conjoint Kings to the effect
that—

> " In short, whoever you may be,
> To this conclusion you'll agree—
> When every one is somebodee
> Then no one's anybody "—

comes that remarkable illustration of masterly con-
trapuntal composition which only Sullivan could have
written :

> " In contemplative fashion
> And a tranquil frame of mind,
> Free from every kind of passion,
> Some solution let us find."

But when every song and concerted number in " The
Gondoliers " is a joy, the reviewer is too apt to lose his
way in a maze of delightful memories, and fails to find
his path out in time to resume the task that still remains before him in other directions.

Sullivan, to all seeming, revelled in the composition
of this, the tenth opera of the famous series. Yet,
strange to relate, Sir Arthur often declared that " The
Gondoliers " gave him more trouble to compose than
any of his previous stage works, not even excepting
" H.M.S. Pinafore," which he wrote whilst suffering
all the time with agonies of physical pain. It may
surprise those who imagine that these light comic
operas were, to the musician, little more than " pot-
boilers" to learn that they caused Sullivan far more
anxious labour and anxiety than his " Martyr of
Antioch " or " The Golden Legend," for, as Sir Arthur

explained, the score of an opera requires so much alteration when brought to stage rehearsal. Not only has the composer to satisfy the author, but the music must fit the singers' capabilities, and be set to suit every situation ; whereas, in the composition of an oratorio, one may "gang his ain gait" guided only by his sympathetic muse.

Such facts are seldom realized by an audience, who, if they ever pause to consider the construction of an opera, do so only to marvel how the author and composer have contrived together to make the piece go with such smooth, clockwork precision.

Glancing through a vast collection of press notices of "The Gondoliers," I find amid the loud chorus of praise one, and one only, discordant note. Again it came from the dramatic critic (!) of a sporting journal. Could it have been that same perverse individual who, as previously related, so utterly condemned "Iolanthe" as publicly to confess that he would sooner witness a Punch and Judy show at a street corner ? It is difficult to believe that any other sane person, professing to be a judge of music and the drama, could have conscientiously published such a scathing "review" as that from which I cannot refrain quoting. The critique, be it noted, appeared in print some six or seven weeks after the production of "The. Gondoliers." It is, in my humble opinion, most amusing, if not edifying, reading.

"Whilst others rush wildly for a first glimpse of the latest Gilbert and Sullivan piece, I," quoth this very

captious critic, " always put off going as long as I can ;
I want as much grace as possible between whiles in
order to forget the previous production and the production before that. . . . I am tired, as an all-round
play-goer, of the perpetual sameness of the Savoy
methods ; they weary me to the point of absolute
dulness.   They were well enough when they were
new, and may be well enough now to those who do not
go to the theatres very often. . . . I have seen no other
piece of late which made me feel so little lively, except
' The Dead Heart ' at The Lyceum.   I was more
amused by the public than by the opera.   The house
was crowded, but it seemed to me less like an audience
than a congregation.   They had heard of Gilbert and
Sullivan, and had come to worship at their shrine as
they would go on Sunday to sit under Stopford Brooke,
or Dr. Parker, or Mr. Spurgeon.   They offered one
another half their books of the words, as good people
do when you are put into a strange pew at church.
What is more, they looked at their books rather than
at the stage, and followed the songs with awe and the
singularly wordy dialogues with reverence.   Sometimes they smiled audibly, but not when the author
was at his best, and occasionally they even laughed
outright—when the gallery set the example.   It was,
as it were, the adoration by a sect of some prophet
adopted for the sake of a good character, but known
very little of personally."

And so on, in the same strain for three or four columns.

Thus, you will observe, the critic launched his
caustic darts not only at the play, but also at his companion play-goers, who numbered many hundreds.

Of course, every play-goer is entitled to his own
opinion of a play, whether he has paid for his seat or

been admitted by an order; but I think I shall not be singular in my judgment that, when a professed critic goes out of his way to condemn works that have in the past been so universally approved, and which still live to delight the multitude, that critic is unworthy of his responsible vocation. Happily, such presumptuous false reports have but slight influence on public opinion : a few incontrovertible facts may be mentioned in proof of this, so far as concerns "The Gondoliers."

On the anniversary performance of " The Gondoliers," the theatre was crowded with an audience as brilliant, as representative, and as enthusiastic as that which had assembled on the first night. On this occasion, by the way, the opera was conducted by the composer, and every lady in the auditorium was presented by the management with a floral bouquet.

" The Gondoliers " remains to this day one of the most popular of the operas played by the D'Oyly Carte Opera Company on tour.

" The Gondoliers " met with the warmest recognition of Royalty. The Prince and Princess of Wales, with all the Royal Family, paid repeated visits to the Savoy during the run of the piece, His Royal Highness expressing his opinion that this was the best of the Gilbert and Sullivan operas.

On Friday, March 6th, 1891, a Command Performance of " The Gondoliers " was given at Windsor Castle before Her Majesty Queen Victoria, this being the first theatrical entertainment to take place at Court since the death of the Prince Consort.

WATERLOO CHAMBER, WINDSOR CASTLE.

Stage set for performance of "The Gondoliers" before Her Majesty Queen Victoria, March 6th, 1891.

284]

When the score of " The Gondoliers " was published by Chappell & Co., twelve men were kept packing from morn till night, and on the first day 20,000 copies (eleven wagon loads) of the vocal score alone were despatched. But the printing-machines were still kept going at high pressure, and the first order executed by the publishers, including the pianoforte score, the vocal score, the dance, and other arrangements reached over 70,000 copies.

For five hundred and fifty-four consecutive performances " The Gondoliers " ran at the Savoy, and brought to the managerial exchequer a sum exceeding that earned by any preceding opera.

These few incidental notes I would specially commend to the writer with whom I have, in the spirit of enthusiasm, dared to cross pens. But now, in order to remove the smart of any wounds that our duel may have inflicted, let me end this chapter with an anecdote concerning the composer of " The Gondoliers."

One evening, Sir Arthur Sullivan, whilst watching the performance for a few minutes from the back of the dress-circle, thoughtlessly, or " in contemplative fashion," commenced humming the melody of the song then being given, whereat a sensitive old gentleman— a musical enthusiast—turned angrily to the composer and said, " Look here, sir, I paid my money to hear Sullivan's music—not yours." Sullivan used often to repeat this tale against himself, candidly confessing that he well deserved the rebuke.

CHAPTER XI

NAPOLEON I. used to say " the best diplomacy is
to speak the truth." Another great leader of men,
George Washington, (to wit,) made it a rule, as we were
all informed in our youth, never to tell a lie. Both are
excellent precepts, no doubt; but perhaps an equally
wise diplomacy is, whenever it is possible, to keep
silence concerning any subject about which it may appear ungracious to utter a word. Unfortunately, of the
three suggested courses, the conscientious historian is
compelled by virtue of his office to observe the Napo-
leonic code. If his chronicles are to be credited with
truth, his every chapter may not be *couleur de rose*.
He must sometimes allude to unpleasing incidents,
which have long been the subject of public gossip.

Every one would have rejoiced, none more than the
present writer, if the countless happy reminiscences of
the Savoy might have continued unsullied by the
shadow of a regret.

For full fourteen years the brilliant Savoy Triumvirate had worked together as harmoniously as success-

fully. They had given the public ten delightful operas, in return for which the public had given each of the Trio a fortune far exceeding any that had previously been reaped by a theatrical manager, author, or composer. It seemed as though death alone could ever dissolve so strong and prosperous a partnership. But, alas, it was otherwise decreed.

Whilst " The Gondoliers " was at the flood-tide of success it was whispered abroad that the good ship of the Savoy had sprung a leak. For a while nobody would credit the report. But, if it was true, still it was hoped that, sailing as it was in such calm and prosperous seas, there was little danger of the vessel's foundering.

Unfortunately, however, two of the chief officers had squabbled; the third could do nothing but stand by and endeavour to cast oil upon the troubled waters. But all in vain. The rift, instead of being patched up and securely caulked, as it might easily have been, was allowed to widen into a dangerous rent. Could it be believed ? Gilbert and D'Oyly Carte had actually quarrelled, whilst Sullivan, although he took no active part in the dispute, was compelled to adhere to one side or the other. Believing Gilbert to be the aggressor, Sullivan decided to abide by Carte.

" And what," it will be asked, " what was it all about ? "

The answer is, Next to nothing ! A storm had burst in a tea-cup. A little more of the sugar of mutual regard, a few added drops of the milk of human kindness, and all bitterness would have been removed from the cup. But, unhappily, Mr. Gilbert was possessed of a will that could never brook opposition and a temper that he could not always control. And so the breeze that had sprung up increased to a gale, and the gallant pleasure-ship was eventually stranded.

All the world wondered ! Varied and vague were the stories set afloat ; but, perhaps, none more absurd or incredible than the true story which, seeing it was such a momentous incident in the history of the Savoy, may not here be passed over in silence. The *casus belli* was—a carpet !

It appears that Mr. D'Oyly Carte, as duly authorized business manager of the firm, conceived it to be, not only politic, but right and proper, to minister to the comfort of clients through whose patronage and support their business had thrived so remarkably. Accordingly Mr. Carte purchased, among sundry other items of furniture for the renewal and repair of the theatre, a carpet. The carpet, *et cetera*, were in the usual course charged to the joint account. Sir Arthur Sullivan, on his part, raised no objection to the outlay, and, for the sake of peace, did his utmost to persuade Mr. Gilbert to take a similar view of the matter. But Mr. Gilbert remained obdurate in his opposition to such lavish expenditure. He was of opinion that a new carpet, costing £140, would not draw an extra sixpence into the exchequer, that the theatre was so crowded nightly that no one could possibly tell or care a jot how the floor was covered. Mr. Gilbert thought it was sheer waste of money. He was then politely reminded that, by the terms of their partnership agreement, he had no voice in the matter. Whereupon our author waxed exceeding wroth, went to law against his old friends and comrades, and, parting company with the Savoyards, formed a troupe of clever "Mountebanks," and became their chief conjointly with one of the most delightful of Bohemians, most amiable of men and most charming of composers—whose name was Alfred Cellier.

Thus the great Savoy partnership was dissolved in the hey-day of its success. Great was the consternation, bitter the regret that spread throughout the dramatic and musical world.

But now, with all gladness, let us hasten to leap over the dull period of a few years to find The Three reunited at the Savoy, where, in October 1893, their twelfth opera " Utopia Limited," was produced, to the delight of all Savoyards.

Before proceeding to deal with events and incidents that occupied what may be described as the Gilbert and Sullivan interregnum at the Savoy, it may be pleasing to all if this chapter of unhappy memories is brought to a close with a quotation from a speech made by Sir William Gilbert at a dinner given on December 30th, 1906, by the O. P. Club, under the presidency of Mr. Carl Hentschel, founder of the club. The feast was organized specially to celebrate the revival of the operas at the Savoy.

Speaking in response to the toast in his honour, Sir William said :

"The magnificent compliment paid him that evening
19

CHAPTER XII

WITH the dissolution of the Savoy partnership, Mr. D'Oyly Carte found himself in a position as unenviable as that of the Commander-in-Chief of an army corps who has lost one of his most valued and reliable generals of division—Gilbert had resigned his post, and Sullivan, although he still remained faithful to the Savoy, was without a libretto, and at a loss to discover a librettist. After a while, however, Sydney Grundy, one of the ablest and most scholarly of contemporary English dramatists, supplied the composer with an acceptable "book." Thereupon Sir Arthur commenced setting "Haddon Hall."

But, seeing that it must be a long time before the Grundy-Sullivan opera would be ripe for production, D'Oyly Carte, before the termination of "The Gondoliers" run, made a gallant attempt to find a piece that might carry on the traditions of his theatre; ultimately he accepted a new opera called "The

Nautch Girl," written by George Dance, with lyrics
by Frank Desprez (author of several clever "curtain-
raisers" at the Savoy), and the music by Edward
Solomon, a composer of great popularity in his brief
day, a musician possessed of the gift of tunefulness
with more than an average measure of fanciful and ingenious power of orchestration. Obviously it was a
very thankless, invidious task for any author or composer to be called upon to follow Gilbert and Sullivan
at the Savoy. But here Mr. Carte's clever generalship
was displayed. He recognized in Dance and Solomon
apt disciples of Gilbert and Sullivan, and deemed it
wise to entrust his interests to such men rather than
to those who might take a wide departure from the
Savoy line of humour.

The general opinion expressed regarding " The
Nautch Girl" on its production on June 30th, 1891,
was to the effect that the Dance-Solomon work, although inferior to, was none the less a very acceptable
substitute for, an opera by the more celebrated collaborators upon whose style it was fashioned. The
strong family likeness noticeable between " The Nautch
Girl" and some of its predecessors at the Savoy was
intensified by the presence in the cast of some of the
famous Savoyards of the old brigade : notably Rutland Barrington (admirably fitted with a part as the
Rajah of Chutneypore), Jessie Bond, Courtice Pounds,
Frank Thornton, and W. H. Denny. A notable new-
comer to the Savoy was Miss Leonora Snyder, a sweet-
voiced American soprano whom D'Oyly Carte had
chanced upon in New York.

"The Nautch Girl" enjoyed a prosperous run of 199 performances, and on January 29th, 1892, Mr. Carte revived Solomon's opera, "The Vicar of Bray,"[1] which not long previously had achieved success at another theatre. In this piece we were introduced to another clerical incumbent of the Savoy stage. If not altogether as popular as Dr. Daly, D.D., of "The Sorcerer," yet the character afforded Rutland Barrington further opportunity of poking fun at a dignitary of the rival profession in his own inimitable and pardonably irreverent way. It might, with truth, be remarked that the clever Savoy comedian became, by the versatility of his art, the prototype of that historical Vicar of Bray who gained preferment through being all things to all, men, no matter what king, Gilbert or a lesser monarch, might reign at the Savoy.

Following the exit of "The Vicar," on June 10th, 1892, the doors of the Savoy remained closed for a period of three months, such a lengthy interval never having occurred since the opening of the theatre in 1881.

To turn now, for a moment, to consider what Gilbert had been doing since he quitted the Savoy ; as mentioned in the last preceding chapter, Sir Arthur Sullivan's former colleague had turned to Alfred Cellier to compose the music of his new piece, "The Mountebanks," which opera was produced at the Lyric Theatre under the management of Mr. Horace Sedger, on Monday, January 4th, 1892. That event, it may perhaps be remarked, comes hardly within the strict bounds of Savoy reminiscences. Nevertheless, if we re-

[1] Written by Sydney Grundy.

member how "The Mountebanks" was the creation of one of the three famous Savoyards in collaboration with the clever composer who, in the earliest days of the Gilbert and Sullivan operas, aided their cause by his valued service as musical director—it would be less reasonable here to omit than to include reference to the Lyric Theatre's production. The mention of Alfred Cellier's final composition will awaken in the minds of many of his surviving friends memories sad and painful. All will recollect how, when his heavy task approached completion, Cellier was overtaken by a mortal sickness against which he fought with heroic courage. Compelled by physical suffering and weakness to lay aside his pen at intervals, he persevered with indomitable pluck until his undertaking was accomplished. Little did the audience who listened with delight to the sparkling melodies of "The Mountebanks" imagine that they were the composition of a dying man. But so it proved—Alfred Cellier had given to the world his "swan-song."

I recall the hour when poor Alfred Cellier—one of my dearest friends—worn out with the toil and excitement of a lengthy rehearsal, sought my companionship at a little club where we used to foregather. There, falling upon a couch at my side, he gave way to a painful fit of hysteria—sure sign of exhausted strength. Alfred Cellier, alas! was not spared to witness the success of his final work. Almost on the eve of the production of "The Mountebanks" one of the noblest-hearted and most unostentatious of men was carried to his last earthly resting-place in

Norwood Cemetery.   Among letters cherished and bequeathed by Alfred Cellier's brother François, is one which I have been privileged to read.   It came from Sir Arthur Sullivan, who, on hearing of Alfred's death, wrote from Paris on December 29th, 1892, thus:

> " DEAR FRANK,
>   " I can hardly see the paper for the tears which are in my eyes at the dreadful news just received by telegram.   Poor dear old Alfred! my old school-fellow and friend! the most lovable creature in the world. . . ."

Every one who knew Alfred Cellier will endorse those sentiments, that came from the depths of Arthur Sullivan's heart.   Marvellous was the similarity in natural disposition of our two greatly beloved English composers.

.   .   .   .   .

Let us now bring back our " reminiscences " to the Savoy.

On Saturday, September 24th, 1892, Mr. D'Oyly Carte presented—if one may use the Frohmannic phrase, unknown in Victorian days—" the light English opera in three acts, entitled, ' Haddon Hall,' written by Sydney Grundy, composed by Arthur Sullivan." The company included several old-established and popular Savoyards ; the cast and programme of the opera read as follows:

CHARACTERS

John Manners . . .	MR. COURTICE POUNDS
Sir George Vernon , , ,	MR. RICHARD GREEN

Oswald	MR. CHARLES KENNINGHAM
(*Royalists*)	
Rupert Vernon . . .	MR. RUTLAND BARRINGTON
(*Roundhead*)	
The McCrankie	MR. W. H. DENNY
Sing-song Simeon . .	MR. RUDOLPH LEWIS
Kill-joy Candleman . . .	MR. W. H. LÉON
Nicodemus Knock-knee . .	MR. A. FOWLES
Barnabas Bellows-to-mend . . .	MR. G. DE PLEDGE
(*Puritans*)	
Major-domo	MR. H. GORDON
Dorothy Vernon . . .	MISS LUCILLE HILL
Lady Vernon . . .	MISS ROSINA BRANDRAM
Dorcas	MISS DOROTHY VANE
Nance	MISS NITA COLE
Gertrude	MISS CLARIBEL HYDE
Deborah	MISS FLORENCE EASTON

Chorus of Simples and Gentles

ACT I.—THE LOVERS

SCENE.—*The Terrace* (W. Telbin)

" The green old turrets, all ivy thatch,
    Above the cedars that girdle them rise,
The pleasant glow of the sunshine catch,
    And outline sharp on the bluest of skies."

ACT II.—THE ELOPEMENT

SCENE I.—*Dorothy Vernon's Door* (Hawes Craven)

" It is a night with never a star,
    And the hall with revelry throbs and gleams ;
There grates a hinge—the door is ajar—
    And a shaft of light in the darkness streams."

SCENE II.—*The Long Gallery* (J. Harker)

ACT III.—The Return

Scene.—*The Ante-chamber* (W. Perkins)

Note.—*The clock of Time has been put forward a century, and other liberties have been taken with history.*

The Opera produced under the Stage-direction of Mr. Charles Harris and the Musical Direction of Mr. François Cellier. The Dances arranged by Mr. John D'Auban. The Costumes designed by Mr. Percy Anderson and executed by Madame Auguste, Madame Léon, Mr. B. J. Simmons, Messrs. Angel & Son, and M. Alias. Wigs by Clarkson. Properties by Mr. Skelly. Stage Machinist, Mr. Peter White.

It is more easy to imagine than describe the scene of enthusiastic welcome that greeted the return of Sir Arthur Sullivan to the Savoy. Mingled with the usual loyal sentiments of admiration and regret was a large measure of sympathy with the *maestro* in the trouble and anxiety he had endured through the loss of his valued coadjutor. Exceptional also was the interest attached to the advent of the new librettist, and hardly less was the confidence shown that, in Sydney Grundy, Arthur Sullivan had chosen a worthy collaborator. Another Gilbert was not looked for ; neither was any imitation of the Gilbertian style expected from an author who had already won high reputation by the distinct originality and clever construction of his stage-plays. Every play-goer felt confident that whatever Grundy had to say would, so far as touched dialogue, be worth listening to. As regards the lyrics, the composer was, surely, the best judge of their merit ; it was enough that Sullivan had found them acceptable.

Accordingly, it was with pleasant anticipation that the Savoyards crowded into the theatre to obtain a first view of "Haddon Hall." If at curtain-fall their brightest hopes had not been fully realized, neither the critics nor the general public found cause for dissatisfaction with the new bill of fare set before them. Per haps the style of the orthodox dramatist appeared somewhat too old-fashioned for the unconventional Savoy. Grundy's story bore the flavour of Harrison Ainsworth, and although, according to a note printed in the programme, "The clock of time has been put forward a century, and other liberties taken with history," the Royalists and Roundheads and Puritans of the prescribed period were not sufficiently advanced in their views and dispositions to win the ardent affections of players, especially Savoyards, towards the end of the nineteenth century.

Another feature of Grundy's play not reconcilable with every one's taste was the obtrusive Scot, "The McCrankie from the Isle of Rum." Admirably as the character was impersonated by W. H. Denny, McCrankie became a wee bit o'a nuisance. To many in an audience the Scotch dialect in a light English opera is as unacceptable as the screak of bagpipes in a London drawing-room. It is, of course, simply a matter of taste. Still, the wisest policy of a playwright is to cater for the majority.

But, after all, if the truth were known, the chief fault found in "Haddon Hall" was that it was another

G. and S. opera, but that the G. stood not, this time, for Gilbert, but Grundy. Few play-goers have been so blinded by prejudice as the Savoyards.

Gilbert and Sullivan were their idols; they could worship none other. Touching this point, and the attitude of the critics, Sydney Grundy, stout, honest, British dramatic yeoman that he ever was, let fly a " telling " shot in a very caustic letter to the papers. Thus wrote the author of " Haddon Hall " :

" SIR,
" As a humble but sympathetic student of dramatic and musical criticism may I venture to suggest that a short bill be introduced into Parliament making it a penal offence to supply the Savoy theatre with a libretto? Having regard to the magnitude of the crime, the punishment, which, of course, should be capital, might be made at the same time ignominious and painful. Should the libretto be so impertinent as to be successful, I would respectfully · suggest ' something lingering with boiling oil in it,' if so humble a person as I may be permitted a quotation.
Yours, etc.,
" SYDNEY GRUNDY."

But, despite all " irreconcilable antagonism," Grundy's " Haddon Hall " proved sufficiently attractive to fill the Savoy Theatre for no fewer than 204 performances. At any other theatre it might have achieved still greater success. " Haddon Hall " remains a popular favourite with amateur societies, and its revival on the London stage might be interesting and remunerative. As regards the music ; Sullivan proved

Winter Lodge. Addison Road. W
16 March, 1914.

My dear Bridgeman,

My "impressions" of Sullivan — certainly; but in "a dozen lines" — impossible! And (1) "as a composer." My impressions, who know not one note of music from another! This fact he would never believe. "How is it you can always recognise mine?" "Whenever I hear a wave of melody that suggests an ocean of harmony, I know that's Sullivan".

However little the critics thought of my libretto, I have the satisfaction of knowing that it pleased my collaborator. He never tired of telling me what a pleasure it was to him to set my words. Yet we did not always agree. Of all important numbers, I invariably submitted at least two versions; & he invariably chose the one I should have rejected. "What's the matter with the others?" I once snapped. "Nothing," he said; "but I've been setting them for fifteen years."

(2) "As a man." To work with him, was a precious privilege; & to think of him, is an abiding joy.

Sincerely yours,
Sydney Grundy.

FACSIMILE LETTER FROM SYDNEY GRUNDY TO CUNNINGHAM BRIDGEMAN.

that, although no longer coupled in harness with a lyric steed of the same high mettle and spirit as the one with whom he had been running for fifteen years, his muse, instead of turning sulky, was as bright as ever, and continued to carry the composer along in the same ceaseless, unbroken canter, leaving behind him as he went the echo of sweet melodies.

CHAPTER XIII

NEXT on the list of Savoy productions came a piece called " Jane Annie, or the Good Conduct Prize." Such a title might lead one to suppose that it was a farcical comedy. It was nothing of the sort, it was labelled, " A new and original English Comic Opera," bearing the names of J. M. Barrie and A. Conan Doyle as the authors and Ernest Ford as composer. Reminiscences of " Jane Annie " are not, altogether, of the most agreeable kind. To the present generation who, probably, have never heard of " Jane Annie " of the Savoy, it will sound like heresy to speak in derogatory terms of any work by such distinguished knights of the pen as the present Sir James Matthew Barrie and Sir Arthur Conan Doyle. But those among us of riper years who have followed with interest the respective careers of those two richly gifted writers, and who, during the past quarter of a century or more, have enjoyed the many delightful fruits of their genius, can only pause to wonder if it

can be true that the J. M. Barrie who gave the stage
" The Little Minister " in 1897 and " Peter Pan " in
1904, to be brought back to cheer us at every succeeding Christmas-tide, was the very same J. M.
Barrie who wrote " Jane Annie " in 1893 ; and can it
be possible that his collaborator in that weird, amateurish effusion was, in very truth, the same A. Conan
Doyle who amazed our seven senses with " The Adventures of Sherlock Holmes " in 1891, who contributed to the stage " A Story of Waterloo," that
charming, dramatic sketch that helped the fame of
Henry Irving in 1900 ?

Can, we ask ourselves again, can the part-author
of " Jane Annie " have been that delightful story-
teller who has enriched our libraries with scores of
volumes of romance, novels, poems, and songs that
will live ? If one trusted to memory alone, doubt on
the subject might yet prevail, but there, on the Savoy
playbills, in cold print we read, " Jane Annie, or the
Good Conduct Prize," written by J. M. Barrie and
A. Conan Doyle. I doubt not that both authors
would be thankful if every record of that abortive
Savoy opera might be committed to the flames. Perhaps they would have thought it kinder and more
considerate on the part of the present writer to leave
their ill-fated heroine alone and undisturbed in her
unhallowed grave. Fain would he have done so, but
the obligation, sometimes an ungracious one, of the
historian is to chronicle, without fear or favour, all
incidents relating to the subject in hand. Hence poor,
hapless " Jane Annie " is dragged perforce into the

varied chronicles of the Savoy. The best atonement that can be offered for seeming disrespect shown to the greatly respected authors will be to say nothing further about a work which they themselves would be ready to confess was unworthy of their pens.

Unfortunately, again, the praise to be bestowed upon the music of " Jane Annie " must be qualified. Mr. Ernest Ford won considerable reputation as a clever musician, and since he was, if I remember rightly, a pupil of Sir Arthur Sullivan's, it is easy to understand how he became so inoculated with his master's manner and themes that he could not tear himself away from them far enough to allow him to give rein to his own imaginative powers as a composer. True, Sullivan was a perfect model for a student to copy, but a too close copy of the master was less than acceptable, especially to Savoyards. Taken altogether, " Jane Annie " was the most perplexing phenomenon ever presented by D'Oyly Carte's management. For once the usually wide-awake *impresario* must have been caught napping when he accepted and produced such a poor, vapid, uninteresting work.

For the sake of reference we append a list of the *dramatis personae* of—

JANE ANNIE, OR THE GOOD CONDUCT PRIZE

A Proctor	.	.	.	MR. RUTLAND BARRINGTON
Sim	.	.	.	.	MR. LAWRENCE GRINDLEY
Greg	.	.	.	.	MR. WALTER PASSMORE
(*Bulldogs*)				
Tom	.	.	.	MR. CHARLES KENNINGHAM
(*A Press Student*)				

Jack . . . . Mr. Scott Fishe
    (*A Warrior*)
Caddie . . . . Master Harry Rignold
    (*A Page*)
First Student . . . Mr. Bowden Haswell
Second Student . . . Mr. Herbert Crimp
Third Student . . . Mr. Sidwell Jones
Miss Sims . . . Miss Rosina Brandram
    (*A Schoolmistress*)
Jane Annie . . . Miss Dorothy Vane
    (*A Good Girl*)
Bab . . . . . Miss Decima Moore
    (*A Bad Girl*)
Milly . . . . . Miss Florence Perry
Rose . . . . . Miss Emmie Owen
Meg . . . . . Miss Jose Shalders
Maud . . . . . . Miss May Bell
    (*Average Girls*)

Schoolgirls, Press Students, and Lancers

Produced under the Stage Direction of Mr. Charles Harris, and the Musical Direction of Mr. François Cellier.

The Scene is obviously laid round the corner from a certain English University Town.

ACT I.—*First Floor of a Seminary for the Little Things that grow into Women.* (Mr. W. Perkins.)

There will be an interval of about twenty minutes between the Acts.

ACT II.—*A Ladies' Golf Green near the Seminary.* (Mr. W. Telbin.)

TIME.—*The Present*

One night elapses between the Acts.

" Jane Annie " languished on for fifty days before departing this life on July 1st, 1893, lamented by a

20

select clan of true and faithful Caledonian golf enthusiasts, who had found "prodeegious" diversion in cheering the several humorous allusions to " caddies " and " niblicks," " drivers " and " putters," with which the opera was enlivened.   To those of the audiences uninitiated in the noble game of golf the word "bunker" sounded so much like " bunkum " as to tickle their risible faculties.   But, of course, that last remark is intended as a " stage aside."

.   .   .   .   .

After the demise of poor " Jane Annie " the Savoy Theatre was again closed for three months.   During the interval desponding Savoyards were cheered by the glad tidings that all estrangement between Gilbert and Sullivan had disappeared.   It became known that Sir Arthur, having recovered from an alarming illness, was now, in the seclusion of his home at Weybridge, busy at work on the composition of a new Gilbertian comic opera, and that his old friend and colleague, who had been at Homburg to get rid of the gout, had returned to Grim's Dyke, his lovely home at Harrow Weald.   Both giants were reported to be thoroughly refreshed and in full vigour, armed and ready to enter upon another campaign on the field of their many past victories.   Thus the hopes of their faithful followers were to be realized.   The ending of much despair had come.

Although two years had passed since the unhappy break-up of the Triumvirate, not a few of the most devoted admirers of the renowned three had clung stedfastly to the belief that Gilbert, Sullivan, and

D'Oyly Carte must eventually come together again. It had been proved beyond doubt that the author and composer were essential to each other; that, united, they prospered, divided they fell! D'Oyly Carte too, despite his heroic efforts, had found that only Gilbert and Sullivan could fill the Savoy.

It was no reflection on the skill and ability of those other clever authors and composers whose works had in turn been exploited by the enterprising manager during the interregnum. Each, whilst acting in the thankless post of *locum tenens*, had yielded of his best, and, generally, the best had been very good, but not precisely to the fastidious taste of the Savoyards.

Since the withdrawal of "The Gondoliers" in June 1891, there had been more frost than sunshine surrounding Mr. Carte's pretty theatre; ghosts of departed joys had intruded to mar the merriment of Savoy audiences. But now the spring was returning, the singing of birds would soon be heard by Thames Embankment. As, day by day, there appeared preliminary paragraphs in the papers confirming the first report and adding particulars, reliable and otherwise, of the *rapprochement* which had been brought about, players declared it was "quite like old times." Soon it became known that rehearsals had actually begun; that a remarkably gifted American soprano had been engaged as *prima donna*, and that the names of several old Savoy favourites were included in the cast of the new opera. Truly, it was the most gladsome news that had come to arouse the lethargic theatrical world for many a long day. Intense was the excite-

ment, unprecedented the rush of applicants for first-
night seats.   That unholy carpet, with all the trouble
it had occasioned, was trodden upon and obliterated
from memory.   Gilbert, Sullivan, and D'Oyly Carte
smiled again, and England rejoiced.   No happier
event in the eventful annals of the Savoy could ever
be chronicled than the re-enthronement of the popular
monarchs in October 1893.

CHAPTER XIV

A RED-LETTER day in the calendar of the Savoy was Saturday, October 7th, 1893. " There was a sound of revelry by night " which shook the walls of the re-lighted playhouse. It was the great re-gathering of the clans, the glad reunion of Savoyards.

To inaugurate the event, the popular *lever-de-rideau* concerts were revived by the pit and gallery chorus. Society in the stalls and boxes was entertained, as in the old days, with reminiscences of " H.M.S. Pinafore," " The Pirates," " Patience," and " Iolanthe." Even the critics threw off their masks of apathetic unconcern and abandoned that air of boredom common to the cult. The most profound and solemn academic was seen to smile and exchange an affable nod with the distinguished somebodies that crowded the theatre. Everybody said to every other body, " Isn't it a treat ? " And all before the opera had begun ! Although the leading press representatives had been present at the dress rehearsal the day before, they one and all seemed glad to have been invited to sit the piece out a second time, if only to discover whether the public would endorse or controvert the reviews they had already prepared for publication.

All the familiar scenes of a Savoy *première* were re-enacted, but enthusiasm on this occasion seemed to be accentuated. The audience resembled a ship's company who, just come off a long voyage, half starved on salt junk and weevilled biscuits, look forward with greed to a good, square meal ashore.

But now the well-known form of Sir Arthur Sullivan is seen creeping bashfully, it may be nervously, through the dim, cellar-like opening from beneath the stage to the front of the orchestra. The beloved *maestro* looks pale and worn by recent illness and the fag of long rehearsals, but once again, with characteristic modesty, patience, and indomitable pluck, he faces the host of his faithful worshippers. In response to their cheers of welcome Sir Arthur bows, and bows, and bows again until at length, in very pity for him, the cry of " Hush ! " subdues the frantic shouts of delight. The overture begins ; after a few opening bars, my neighbour on the right nudges me and whispers, " The same good old Sullivan." " Yes," I whisper back, " it is the master's voice," whereat my neighbour on the left, whispers " H'sh ! " One is afraid to breathe, a cough would bring down frowns from every part of the house. The stillness of enchantment reigns throughout the playing of the overture. There is no mistaking the maker's name on the fabric of the music. It bears the hall-mark of excellence. The shuttle is flying through warp and woof, weaving the texture of pure, silver melody ; the overture ends. Another volley of cheers from the front ! we open the book of the words of " Utopia Limited, or The Flowers of Progress." The amber satin curtains part, revealing a beautiful palm-grove in the gardens of King Paramount's Palace. There we are introduced to a group of lovely maidens, who bear a strong resemblance to those we remember meeting in " Iolanthe " and " Patience." They are lying lazily about the stage and enjoying themselves in lotus-eating fashion the while they sing a dreamy opening chorus, a lyric essentially Gilbertian and Sullivanesque.

" In lazy languor, motionless,
  We lie and dream of nothingness :
    For visions come
    From Poppydom
      Direct at our command :
Or, delicate alternative,
In open idleness we live,
    With lyre and lute
    And silver flute,
      The life of lazyland !

SOLO.—*Phylla*

" The song of birds
    In ivied towers ;
      The rippling play
      Of waterway ;
The lowing herds ;
    The breath of flowers ;
      The languid loves
      Of turtle-doves—
These simple joys are all at hand
Upon thy shores, O Lazyland."

(*Loud applause and cries of " Encore."*)

A few words of dialogue spoken by a minor character indicate at once that our author has remained faithful to his own familiar vein of facetious humour. We are assured that Gilbert's quiver has been refilled with keen, pointed shafts of good-humoured satire, and we know he is going to launch them against his own country, or, rather, against the super-pride, the mock-heroic sentiments of his English compatriots—we recognize his aim at once :

CALYNX. Good news ! Great news ! His Majesty's eldest daughter, Princess Zara, who left our shores five years since to go to England—the greatest, the most powerful, the wisest country in the world—has taken a high degree at Girton, and is on her way home again, having achieved a complete mastery over all the elements that have tended to raise that glorious country to her present pre-eminent position among civilized nations !

SALATA. Then in a few months Utopia may hope to be completely Anglicized ?

CALYNX. Absolutely and without a doubt.

MELENE. (Lazily.) We are very well as we are. Life without a care—every want supplied by a kind and fatherly monarch, who, despot though he be, has no other thought than to make his people happy—what have we to gain by the great change that is in store for us ?

SALATA. What have we to gain ? English institutions, English tastes, and—oh, English fashions !

CALYNX. England has made herself what she is because, in that favoured land, every one has to think for himself. Here we have no need to think, because our monarch anticipates all our wants, and our political opinions are formed for us by the journals to which we subscribe. Oh, think how much more brilliant this dialogue would have been if we had been accustomed to exercise our reflective powers! They say that in England the conversation of the very meanest is a coruscation of impromptu epigram!

It is enough. We perceive that Gilbert is looking upon England and English institutions through the green spectacles of a jealous foreigner. His intention is to pour ridicule upon the Jingoism of the average Briton, and we know that Gilbert will succeed where any other author, daring the attempt, would come to utter grief.

Some of us may feel inclined to cry, "Shame on such unpatriotism!" whilst all the time we laugh and applaud and say to ourselves, "After all, it sounds very much like the truth, and Gilbert has such a clever knack of swamping nasty grey powders in nice black-currant jam."

Gilbert, Sullivan, and D'Oyly Carte had, of course, read in the papers, from time to time, such uncomplimentary, discouraging remarks as, for instance, "Surely we have had enough of these topsy-turvy operas—when is the nauseating stuff to be put a stop to?" But the three Savoyards knew their public better, and were satisfied that if, indeed, anybody was nauseated, it was not by the fare provided at the Savoy, but by the weakness of the digestive organs of a few lack-a-daisical individuals, who failed to appreciate the dainty dishes set before them. In other words, they had no sense of humour. Mr. Carte was assured that a vast majority of his patrons preferred what they now began to call the " old-fashioned Savoy operas" to any of that other sort which he had lately been exploiting, and so he was only too glad when Gilbert and Sullivan provided him with yet another topsy-turvy piece, perhaps the topsy-turvyest piece they had ever produced.

The remarkable reception accorded to "Utopia" confirmed the wisdom of the managerial policy. This, the twelfth Gilbert and Sullivan opera, was generally acknowledged to be one of the best of the series. The subject gave Gilbert fine scope for skittish treatment. Our author could hardly have conceived a funnier idea than that of the King of some sea-girt isle, unmarked in any chart or map, a fantastic monarch who, having determined to adopt the manners and customs, the fads and fashions, of " the greatest, the most powerful, the wisest country in the world," sends his daughter to Girton to study the elements that have tended to raise England to her proud position.

In grotesque characterization, in mirthful situations, in wit and humour of dialogue and graceful rhythmic song-words, Gilbert proved that he had not yet exhausted the resources of his peculiar genius. The interval of rest away from the theatre had, it seemed, refreshed his muse, and although, at the early rehearsals of the play, the author, still suffering from gout, had to be wheeled about the stage in a bathchair, the perfect production of the new opera testified that Gilbert remained without a rival in the skill of stage-management.

Those of my readers to whom " Utopia " is an unknown quantity would very likely be glad to be told something further about the eccentric King Paramount, who sought to remodel his Court on the ceremonial lines of the Court of St. James's ; but the story would appear insipid and uninteresting unless told in Gilbert's own inimitable way.

The best that can be done here is to quote a few samples of the dialogue and lyrics, from which some idea may be gathered of the plot and incidents of the piece, of the quality of the stanzas which inspired Sullivan to draw from his inexhaustible well of melody some of the sweetest conceptions.

Let us take, first, a duet between Nekaya and Kalyba, the twin daughters of King Paramount, girls about fifteen years old, who have been " finished " by " a grave, and good, and gracious English lady, and are now to be exhibited in public " that all may learn what, from the English standpoint, is looked upon as maidenly perfection.

In very modest and demure manner they stand with their hands folded and their eyes cast down as they introduce themselves thus :

> BOTH. Although of native maids the cream,
> We're brought up on the English scheme—
>   The best of all,
>   For great and small,
>   Who modesty adore.
>
> NEK. For English girls are good as gold,
> Extremely modest (so we're told),
> Demurely coy—divinely cold—
>   KAL. And we are that—and more.
> To please papa, who argues thus—

All girls should mould themselves on us,
    Because we are,
    By furlongs far,
        The best of all the bunch.
We show ourselves to loud applause
From ten to four without a pause—
    NEK. Which is an awkward time because
        It cuts into our lunch.

        BOTH. Oh, maids of high and low degree,
    Whose social code is rather free,
    Please look at us and you will see
    What good young ladies ought to be !
    NEK. And as we stand, like clockwork toys,
A lecturer whom papa employs
    Proceeds to praise
    Our modest ways
        And guileless character—
    KAL. Our well-known blush—our downcast eyes—
Our famous look of mild surprise
    NEK. (Which competition still defies)
        KAL. Our celebrated ' Sir ! ! ! '
Then all the crowd take down our looks
In pocket memorandum-books.
    To diagnose
    Our modest pose
        The Kodaks do their best :
    NEK. If evidence you would possess
Of what is maiden bashfulness,
You only need a button press—
    KAL. And *we* do all the rest.

Gilbert's faith in the histrionic capabilities of tenors,
as a body, was not great ; yet, strange to tell, he sometimes entrusted to the leading tenor some of the most
comical "business" of the piece, with song-words of
such subtle wit as to require a singer possessed of a

full sense of humour to give adequate point to them. This paradoxical feature of Gilbertian methods was notably illustrated in " Ruddigore," where, as we have seen, a broad comedian rôle was admirably played by Durward Lely.

And now, again, in " Utopia " the usually conventional sentimental love-scene between the principal tenor and the *prima donna* was so humorous as to call forth laughter as spontaneous as any heard throughout the opera. The author's words may, indeed, have been the chief factor of the fun, but they needed a comedian to turn them to good account, and Mr. Charles Kenningham, the Savoy tenor of that period, proved himself an excellent comedian. But then, it must be remembered how Gilbert possessed the faculty of transforming any sort of vocalist—aye, even a " tenor-stick "—into a competent actor. But in order that what I am trying to convey may be the better understood, the song and the scene in question are here presented. It occurs at the opening of the second act :

RECIT.—*Fitzbattleaxe*

" Oh Zara, my beloved one, bear with me !
Ah, do not laugh at my attempted C !
Repent not, mocking maid, thy girlhood's choice—
The fervour of my love affects my voice !

SONG

" A tenor, all singers above
(This doesn't admit of a question),
Should keep himself quiet,
Attend to his diet,
And carefully nurse his digestion ;

But when he is madly in love
 It's certain to tell on his singing—
  You can't do chromatics
  With proper emphatics,
 When anguish your bosom is wringing !
When distracted with worries in plenty,
And his pulse is a hundred and twenty,
And his fluttering bosom the slave of mistrust is,
A tenor can't do himself justice.
 Now observe—(*sings a high note*),
You see, I can't do myself justice !

" I could sing, if my fervour were mock—
 It's easy enough if you're acting—
  But, when one's emotion
  Is born of devotion,
 You mustn't be over-exacting.
One ought to be firm as a rock
 To venture a shake in *vibrato*,
  When fervour's expected,
  Keep cool and collected,
 Or never attempt *agitato*.
But, of course, when his tongue is of leather,
And his lips appear pasted together,
And his sensitive palate as dry as a crust is,
A tenor can't do himself justice.
 Now observe—(*sings a cadence*),
It's no use—I can't do myself justice ! "

ZARA. Why, Arthur, what *does* it matter ? When the higher qualities of the heart are all that can be desired, the higher notes of the voice are matters of comparative insignificance. Who thinks slightingly of the cocoa-nut because it is husky ? Besides (*demurely*) you are not singing for an engagement (*putting her hand in his*), you have that already !

FITZ. How good and wise you are ! How unerringly

your practised brain winnows the wheat from the chaff, the material from the merely incidental!

ZARA. My Girton training, Arthur. At Girton all is wheat, and idle chaff is never heard within its walls.

A splendid specimen of a Gilbertian love-scene; a perfect parody of the silly ways of young lovers in general, and tenor lovers in particular. Need it be added how thoroughly Sullivan entered into the spirit of the fun, intensifying the humour of every line by the mirth-provoking devices of his musical instruments?

Following upon this amusing lyric, in agreeable contrast came the following graceful—

DUET

ZARA. " Words of love too loudly spoken
    Ring their own untimely knell;
Noisy vows are rudely broken,
    Soft the song of Philomel.
Whisper sweetly, whisper slowly,
    Hour by hour and day by day;
Sweet and low as accents holy
    Are the notes of lover's lay.

FITZ. " Let the conqueror, flushed with glory,
    Bid his noisy clarions bray;
Lovers tell their artless story
    In a whispered virelay.
False is he whose vows alluring
    Make the listening echoes ring;
Sweet and low when all-enduring
    Are the songs that lovers sing."

CHAPTER XV

"UTOPIA" CONTINUED

Cast of the opera—A new Savoy *prima donna*—Début of Miss Nancy McIntosh—More samples of Gilbert's lyrics and dialogue—"Utopia" a popular success—Utopian Court Drawing-room—Displeasure in high places.

BEFORE proceeding further to review the latest Gilbert and Sullivan opera, let us record the cast of—

"UTOPIA LIMITED, OR THE FLOWERS OF PROGRESS"

King Paramount the First   MR. RUTLAND BARRINGTON
   (*King of Utopia*)
Scaphio   .   .   .   .   MR. W. H. DENNY
Phantis .   .   .   .   .   . MR. JOHN LE HAY
   (*Judges of the Utopian Supreme Court*)
Tarara   .   .   .   . MR. WALTER PASSMORE
   (*The Public Exploder*)
Calynx .   .   .   .   . MR. BOWDEN HASWELL
   (*The Utopian Vice-Chamberlain*)

IMPORTED FLOWERS OF PROGRESS

Lord Dramaleigh .   .   .   MR. SCOTT RUSSELL
   (*A British Lord Chamberlain*)
Captain Fitzbattleaxe . MR. CHARLES KENNINGHAM
   (*First Life Guards*)
Captain Sir Edward Corcoran, K.C.B.
   (*Of the Royal Navy*)   MR. LAWRENCE GRINDLEY

Mr. Goldbury . . . . MR. SCOTT FISCHE
   (*A Company Promoter, afterwards*
     Comptroller of the Utopian Household)
Sir Bailey Barre, Q.C., M.P. . MR. ERNEST BLACKMORE
Mr. Blushington . . . MR. HERBERT RALLAND
   (*Of the County Council*)

The Princess Zara . . . MISS NANCY McINTOSH
   (*Eldest daughter of King Paramount*)
The Princess Nekaya . . MISS EMMIE OWEN
The Princess Kalyba . . MISS FLORENCE PERRY
   (*Her younger Sisters*)
The Lady Sophy . . MISS ROSINA BRANDRAM
   (*Their English Gouvernante*)
Salata . . . . . MISS EDITH JOHNSTON
Melene . . . . . MISS MAY BELL
Phylla . . . . . MISS FLORENCE EASTON
   (*Utopian Maidens*)

   ACT I.—*A Utopian Palm-grove*
   ACT II.—*Throne-room in King Paramount's Palace*

(Mr Hawes Craven by permission of Mr. Henry Irving)
Stage Director . . . MR. CHARLES HARRIS
Musical Director . . . MR. FRANÇOIS CELLIER

   Stage Manager, Mr. W. H. Seymour. The Dances arranged by Mr. John D'Auban. The Utopian Dresses designed by Mr. Percy Anderson, and executed by Miss Fisher, Madame Auguste, and Madame Léon. Uniforms by Messrs. Firmin & Sons, also by Mr. B. J. Simmons and Messrs. Angel & Sons. The Presentations by Madame Isabel Bizet-Michau. The Court Dresses by Messrs. Russell & Allen. The Judges' Robes by Messrs. Ede & Son.The Ladies' Jewels by The Parisian Diamond Company. The Wigs by Mr. Clarkson. The properties by Mr. Skelly. Stage Machinist, Mr. P. White.
   The Opera produced under the sole direction of the Author and Composer.
21

It was with a loud flourish of trumpets that Miss Nancy McIntosh, the pretty American soprano, made her début on the operatic stage in the part of " The Princess Zara."

A native of Cleveland, Ohio, Miss McIntosh had come to London to study singing under Mr. George Henschel, and it was at concerts directed by that famed professor that his pupil became favourably known to the musical public.

Gilbert, having been charmed by the singing and personality of the young artiste, introduced her to Sullivan and D'Oyly Carte, the result being her engagement as principal soprano in the new Savoy opera. Highly laudatory press notices, in advance, led the public to anticipate a triumphant first appearance at the Savoy. That their brightest expectations were fully realized can hardly be admitted. As a singer gifted with a beautiful voice, Miss McIntosh was readily acknowledged to be a great acquisition to the Savoy; but as an actress she was found to be unripe. She had much to learn before she could attain to that mark which distinguishes the professional from the amateur. It is, invariably, a mistake to exalt a novice at one step to the front rank. Such faith, without sure foundation, seldom results in anything but disappointment to all concerned. Far wiser is it to allow an artist to graduate and earn degree than to thrust honours upon the shoulders of one unprepared to carry them. So it might have been with Mr. Gilbert's clever *protégée*. The leading lady's part in " Utopia " was an exacting one, even for an experienced actress,

Photo by Ellis & Walery.

MISS NANCY MACINTOSH.

Photo by Ellis & Walery.

MISS FORTESCUE.

322]

so that it would have been little less than marvellous if a budding débutante, beset with nervousness and the excitement of the occasion, had achieved unqualified success.

Such critical observations must not be taken as ungracious reflections on the artistic merits of the young *prima donna*; they are simply intended to convey some impression of the reason why Miss Nancy McIntosh failed, in a measure, to achieve at the outset the triumph all her friends had hoped to witness.

And now to quote another delightful number from the book of "Utopia." Would that with Gilbert's poetical words we might give Sullivan's lovely setting of the unaccompanied chorus:

> " Eagle high in cloud-land soaring,
>   Sparrow twittering on a reed,
> Tiger in the jungle roaring,
>   Frightened fawn in grassy mead;
> Let the eagle, not the sparrow,
> Be the object of your arrow,
>   Fix the tiger with your eye,
>   Pass the fawn in pity by.
> Glory then will crown the day;
> Glory, glory, anyway! "

Was it not against the eagles and tigers of society who prey upon poor humanity, those base beings and the evils they beget, that Gilbert aimed the arrows of his satire? To the fawns, the gentler things of creation, he was ever gentle. It was thus that glory crowned his day.

Another particularly happy song was one in praise of English girls :

" A wonderful joy our eyes to bless,
In her magnificent comeliness,
Is an English girl of eleven-stone-two,
And five-foot-ten in her dancing-shoe !
　　She follows the hounds, and on she pounds—
　　　　The ' field ' tails off and the muffs diminish—
　　Over the hedges and brooks she bounds
　　　　Straight as a crow, from find to finish.
　　At cricket, her kin will lose or win—
　　　　She and her maids, on grass and clover,
　　Eleven maids out—eleven maids in—
　　　　And perhaps an occasional ' maiden over ' !
Go search the world and search the sea,
Then come you home and sing with me.
There's no such gold and no such pearl
As a bright and beautiful English girl !

" With a ten-mile spin she stretches her limbs,
She golfs, she punts, she rows, she swims—
She plays, she sings, she dances, too,
From ten or eleven till all is blue !
　　At ball or drum, till small hours come
　　　　(Chaperon's fan conceals her yawning),
　　She'll waltz away like a teetotum,
　　　　And never go home till daylight's dawning.
　　Lawn-tennis may share her favours fair—
　　　　Her eyes a-dance and her cheeks a-glowing—
　　Down comes her hair, but what does she care ?
　　　　It's all her own and it's worth the showing !
Go search the world, etc.

" Her soul is sweet as the ocean air,
For prudery knows no haven there ;

To find mock-modesty, please apply
To the conscious blush and the downcast eye.
Rich in the things contentment brings,
  In every pure enjoyment wealthy,
Blithe as a beautiful bird she sings,
  For body and mind are hale and healthy.
Her eyes they thrill with right good-will—
  Her heart is light as a floating feather—
As pure and bright as the mountain rill
  That leaps and laughs in the Highland heather !
Go search the world, etc."

Then let us take the stanza that forms the Finale to the opera. In this it seemed as though the author wished to offer some atonement for the ridicule he had been pouring upon his own country, and to show that he could from his heart say with Byron, " England, with all thy faults, I love thee still."

FINALE

ZARA. " There's a little group of isles beyond the wave—
  So tiny, you might almost wonder where it is—
That nation is the bravest of the brave,
  And cowards are the rarest of all rarities.
The proudest nations kneel at her command ;
  She terrifies all foreign-born rapscallions ;
And holds the peace of Europe in her hand
  With half a score invincible battalions !
    Such, at least, is the tale
    Which is borne on the gale,
     From the island which dwells in the sea.
    Let us hope, for her sake,
    That she makes no mistake—
     That she's all she professes to be !

KING. "Oh may we copy all her maxims wise,
  And imitate her virtues and her charities ;
And may we, by degrees, acclimatise
  Her parliamentary peculiarities !
By doing so we shall, in course of time,
  Regenerate completely our entire land—
Great Britain is that monarchy sublime,
  To which some add (but others do not) Ireland.
    Such, at least, is the tale, etc."

From the point of view both of the Press and of the public, "Utopia" was a great success, and it proved itself to be so by filling the Savoy Theatre for 245 days. Why then, it may be asked, has the piece never been revived, like nearly all the other G. and S. operas? Possibly the only true answer lies in the fact that King Paramount's playful parody of the English Court caused grave displeasure in high places, so that to repeat the offence would be beyond the bounds of loyalty, wise policy, or good taste, even though in later days the subject might not be received in the same serious, grey light that dimmed the glories of "Utopia" twenty years ago. The evil was found in a too faithful but highly coloured representation of Princes and Princesses, noblemen and statesmen, household officials and others, modelled, as it were, from real life at St. James's. In the belief that such scenes excited ridicule, Gilbert's fantasy was taken as an affront, and so deeply resented that no member of the English Court was known to pay a second visit to "Utopia."

It may be interesting to the present generation—I

trust it may not be considered indiscreet—if we extract from the libretto the entire scene which, although it did not bring upon Gilbert a charge of *lèse-majesté*, was held to be, at least, wanting in respect to Royalty and High State.

KING. (*Addressing members of his Cabinet.*)   Gentlemen, our daughter holds her first Drawing-room in half an hour, and we shall have time to make our half-yearly report in the interval.   I am necessarily unfamiliar with the forms of an English Cabinet Council; perhaps the Lord Chamberlain will kindly put us in the way of doing the thing properly, and with due regard to the solemnity of the occasion.

LORD DRAMALEIGH.   Certainly—nothing simpler. Kindly bring your chairs forward—His Majesty will, of course, preside.

> *They range their chairs across stage like Christy*
> *Minstrels.*   KING *sits* C., LORD DRAMA-
> LEIGH *on his* L., MR. GOLDBURY *on his*
> R., CAPT. CORCORAN L. *of* LORD DRAMA-
> LEIGH, CAPT. FITZBATTLEAXE R. *of* MR.
> GOLDBURY, MR. BLUSHINGTON *extreme*
> R., SIR BAILEY BARRE *extreme* L.

KING. Like this ?

LD. DRAM. Like this.

KING. We take your word for it that all is right. You are not making fun of us ?   This is in accordance with the practice at the Court of St. James's ?

LD. DRAM. Well, it is in accordance with the practice at the Court of St. James's Hall.*

KING. Oh ! it seems odd, but never mind.

* The Hall in London, where the Moore and Burgess Christy Minstrels performances were given.

Song.—*King*

Society has quite forsaken all her wicked courses,
Which empties our police-courts, and abolishes divorces.
Chorus. Divorce is nearly absolute in England.
King. No tolerance we show to undeserving rank and splendour;
For the higher his position is, the greater the offender.
Chorus. That's a maxim that is prevalent in England.
King. No peeress at our Drawing-room before the Presence passes,
Who wouldn't be accepted by the lower middle classes.
Each shady dame, whatever be her rank, is bowed out neatly.
Chorus. In short, this happy country has been Anglicized completely!
It really is surprising
What a thorough Anglicizing
We have brought about—Utopia's quite another land ;
In her enterprising movements
She is England—with improvements,
Which we dutifully offer to our mother-land!
King. Our city we have beautified—we've done it willy-nilly—
And all that isn't Belgrave Square is Strand and Piccadilly.
Chorus. We haven't any slummeries in England!
King. We have solved the labour question with discrimination polished,
So poverty is obsolete and hunger is abolished.
Chorus. We are going to abolish it in England.
King. The Chamberlain our native stage has purged, beyond a question,
Of " risky " situation and indelicate suggestion ;
No piece is tolerated if it's costumed indiscreetly.
Chorus. In short, this happy country has been Anglicized completely!
It really is surprising, etc.
King. Our Peerage we've remodelled on an intellectual basis,
Which certainly is rough on our hereditary races.
Chorus. We are going to remodel it in England.
King. The Brewers and the Cotton Lords no longer seek admission,
And Literary Merit meets with proper recognition.

CHORUS. As Literary Merit does in England !

KING. Who knows but we may count among our intellectual chickens

Like you an Earl of Thackeray and p'raps a Duke of Dickens—

Lord Fildes and Viscount Millais (when they come) we'll welcome sweetly.

CHORUS. In short, this happy country has been Anglicized completely !

It really is surprising, etc.

(At the end all rise and replace their chairs.)

KING. Now, then, for our First Drawing-room. Where are the Princesses ? What an extraordinary thing it is that, since European looking-glasses have been supplied to the royal bed-rooms, my daughters are invariably late !

LD. DRAM. Sir, their Royal Highnesses await your pleasure in the ante-room.

KING. Oh. Then request them to do us the favour to enter at once.

MARCH. *Enter all the Royal Household, including (besides the Lord Chamberlain) the Vice-Chamberlain, the Master of the Horse, the Master of the Buckhounds, the Lord High Treasurer, the Lord Steward, the Comptroller of the Household, the Lord-in-Waiting, the Groom-in-Waiting, the Field Officer in Brigade Waiting, the Gold and Silver Stick, and the Gentlemen Ushers. Then enter the three Princesses (their trains carried by Pages of Honour), Lady Sophy, and the Ladies-in-Waiting.*

Thereupon followed an exact, a too faithful representation of a Court Drawing-room; and this it was that caused all the trouble. It was a great pity, seeing that " Utopia, or The Flowers of Progress," was one of the brightest and wittiest of Gilbert's books, whilst the score was rich in songs that all who heard them would like to hear again. Some of them may be numbered amongst Sullivan's purest gems of melody.

In connection with the rehearsals of "Utopia" an anecdote is told of Charles Harris, the Stage Director. Like his *confrère*, Richard Barker, Charlie Harris, whilst brusque and rough in manner, was very kind-hearted. Drilling the company in the Court Drawing-room scene, he had great difficulty in prevailing on one of the ladies to adopt the attitude of grace becoming the occasion. At length he called her to his side and said : " Look here, my dear, you mustn't walk as if you were going to fetch your father's supper-beer. Bear in mind, you are passing before the King and Queen." The timid girl, abashed, was nigh weeping, but Harris, in gentler tone, continued : " All you want is a little confidence, my dear. I suppose you haven't much money about you ? " The girl replied : " Not—very— much, Mr. Harris." Then " Charlie " handed her a sovereign, saying, " Well, put that in your purse and let's try again. Now walk as if you were a marchioness with heaps of gold in your pocket." The inducement having the desired effect, the poor girl blushingly thanked Harris and offered back the sovereign. " No, my dear, you keep that," said Charlie ; " go and dine like a Duchess, and to-morrow, when you rehearse, you will be fit to present at Court ! "

Here is another characteristic story of Charles Harris,

who, as is generally known, was brother to Sir Augustus
Harris.   He had been witnessing a dress rehearsal
at Drury Lane.   On his return to the Savoy D'Oyly
Carte asked him how things had gone.   Harris replied,
" Awful ! everything is in a perfect state of *Kudos*."

" Utopia," after a run of 245 performances, was withdrawn on June 9th, 1894.

The most pleasant incident of the memorable first
night of " Utopia " was the enthusiastic reception of
Gilbert and Sullivan when they took their " Call," and,
appearing before the curtain, shook hands in token of
the renewal of their friendship.   It was a touch of
sentiment that went straight home to the hearts of
all Savoyards, and evoked shouts of joy sincere and
unrestrained.

CHAPTER XVI

FOLLOWING the withdrawal of " Utopia " on June 9th,
1894, the tide of fortune began to ebb. Failure followed upon failure. All Mr. Carte's plucky efforts to
find a piece to the liking of his patrons were in vain.
First he tried an English adaptation of André Messager's
" Mirette," an opera comique which had met with
great success in Paris, but here it proved unacceptable,
and was withdrawn after forty days, and the theatre
remained closed for two months. Yet so great was
D'Oyly Carte's faith in the attractiveness of Messager's
music that he ventured to produce a second version of
" Mirette," but with no better success than had attended the first edition. French opera was not what
was wanted at the Savoy.

Then followed the Burnand-Sullivan comic opera,
" The Chieftain," a glorified version of the same
author's " Contrabandista," a one-act musical piece,
produced by German Reed at St. George's Hall in

1867. " The Chieftain " was allowed but short life, and not a very merry run of ninety-six nights. Nothing would satisfy the Savoyards but Gilbert and Sullivan. All other authors and composers were as heretics. And it must be the conjoint work of their favourites, otherwise the piece would not be a genuine Savoy Opera. Accordingly the ever-obliging Manager recalled a second time " The Mikado," and that popular potentate again proved the greatness of his sway. People swarmed to renew the acquaintance of " Pooh-Bah," " Koko" & Co., those grotesque Japanese serio-comics whose welcome would never wear out. For 127 nights mirth and laughter reigned once more at the Savoy. Meanwhile, a new opera by Gilbert and Sullivan had been in rehearsal. Strange to relate, the preliminary announcement of the piece did not create the usual wave of excitement. The Savoyards seemed to be growing apathetic in their attitude even towards their great high-priests. Could it be that recent failures had caused them to lose faith in the Savoy management, and that now they were following the instincts of rats that scuttle from a sinking ship ? The suggestion was absurd. If only the new opera should prove as good, or even half as good, as " The Mikado," or " The Gondoliers," apathy would promptly change to the old enthusiasm. And so, yet hoping for the best, they patiently awaited the production of " The Grand-Duke, or the Statutory Duel."

The first performance took place on Saturday, March 7th, 1896. Too soon it was found that hopes were doomed to disappointment. The bright wedding-chorus which opened the opera was full of promise and put everybody into a happy mood. Sullivan had returned to cheer the town, as he alone could do, with his exhilarating music. But whilst the audience turned over the leaves of "The Book" they grew more and more listless. Where was the sparkling, effervescent Gilbertian wit that had tickled their fancy without failing for the past twenty years? Surely this was not the same Gilbert who had given them just a dozen masterpieces, with which none but the most captious critics had found reasonable fault. Did the evil lie in the fact that "The Grand-Duke" bore the fatal number thirteen, or, what did it all mean? The weakness was not with the *dramatis personae*, for the cast included many old-established favourites—Rosina Brandram, Emmie Owen, Rutland Barrington, Walter Passmore, Scott Russell, and Charles Kenningham. No stronger company could Savoyards have wished for. To the list was added the name of Madame Ilka von Palmay, a charming Hungarian soprano, whose pretty suspicion of a foreign accent gave agreeable colour to a remarkably clear English enunciation. The new *prima donna*'s talents could not be rightly gauged by the part she had to play in such a vapid, uninteresting opera. Then further, although no one could foretell it, the minor parts were filled by artistes whose names, in later days, were to be entered on the roll of popular Savoy favourites. Among these were Ruth Vincent, Jessie Rose, Florence Perry, and C. H. Workman. Individually and collectively the company, coached and drilled to the usual Savoy pitch of perfection, worked right loyally and well; but they could not import life into the dry bones of "The Grand-Duke," nor could Sullivan's most sparkling ripple of melody lift the piece out of the stagnant slough of Gilbert's un-Gilbertian humour. It was evident that our author's muse was sick or sulky when he wrote "The Grand-Duke." No one could believe that Gilbert's mine of fun fantastic was worked out. Yet it was possible !

It would be a thankless task and quite unnecessary to dwell longer on an event that cannot be included amongst happy reminiscences of the Savoy. Still less pleasant is it to reflect that "The Grand-Duke" was the last work of the famous collaborators. Far happier would our retrospect have been if, before those amber, satin curtains of the Savoy, Gilbert and Sullivan might together, hand in hand, have made their final bow amidst the loudest shouts of triumph that had ever rewarded their labours. But it was not to be.

Thus "The Grand-Duke" won the unenviable distinction of scoring the shortest run of all the Gilbert and Sullivan operas. The total number of performances was one hundred and twenty-three.

After the extinction of His Highness, back came the marvellous "Mikado" to save the situation and restore the fame of its author. This, the third revival of the Japanese opera, continued to hold the stage for 226 consecutive performances. Since its original production in 1885, "The Mikado" had now been played at the Savoy alone no fewer than 1,141 times. The one-thousandth performance was celebrated, in gala fashion, by an audience resembling that of a first night. The theatre was beautifully decorated with scarlet and gold chrysanthemums, and "All was right as right could be," under the fourth dispensation of the "Most humane Mikado that ever did in Japan exist." A noteworthy incident attached to this revival was the retirement from the stage of Miss Jessie Bond. During a period of nearly twenty years, this clever little lady, by her talents as an actress and singer and still more so by the charm of her personality, had captivated the hearts of all Savoyards, and now, on her entering into "the felicity of unbounded domesticity," Miss Bond's departure was accompanied by the hearty good wishes of her colleagues and a multitude of friends in front of the curtain.

And now, "The Mikado" having retired to rest for a while, we were to witness the accession of yet another monarch on the Savoy stage.

The production of "His Majesty, or the Court of Vingolia," written by Mr. F. C. Burnand and composed by Sir Alexander Mackenzie, was anticipated with keen interest. For the first time the distinguished Mus. Doc. entered the domain of comic opera. Every music-lover knew that Sir Alexander might be trusted to do nothing that was not in the highest degree musicianly. With such an expert librettist as the Editor of *Punch*, the famous Principal of the Royal Academy of Music would, it was confidently thought, have the assistance of a most worthy colleague. Much, then, was expected from such collaboration. But, alas! all

MY CARD O' GOOD WISHES

The little maiden, all unknowing,
Hail from a hidden summer,
Changed to a sort of Japanese fairy.

The proud of Savoy,
This little maid call'd Britt-Sing.
Him to you now on Jenny's wing
And this is the message she made bring—

XMAS
85

From

MISS JESSIE BOND'S CHRISTMAS CARD, 1885.

336]

such hopes and expectations proved futile. For some reasons, which it would be impertinent to try to explain, Burnand's style of humour failed to appeal to a Savoy audience. In the right order of things it should have been otherwise, since, by strange coincidence, Mr. Francis Cowley (now Sir Francis C.) Burnand, is descended from an old Savoyard family. "His Majesty" was far from the brightest inspiration of the witty author of "Happy Thoughts," who in this, his latest work, was assisted by Mr. R. C. Lehmann, his clever colleague on the staff of *Punch*. Burnand's "Court of Vingolia" lacked the brilliancy and vitality of Gilbert's "Utopian Court," or that of the "Kingdom of Barataria," in which the "Merry Gondoliers" frolicked and flourished for five hundred gladsome days. In brief, "His Majesty" was not up to the mark as a libretto. It was wanting in a quality most likely to evoke humour from any serious composer, so that it may justly be said that Sir Alexander Mackenzie was too heavily handicapped by his librettist. His music throughout "His Majesty" was full of life and spirit, rich in grace, charm, and variety; but it was not quite bright and sparkling enough for the purpose of Savoy Opera.

The composer's superb instrumentation and beautiful choral effects were better suited to Grand Opera. Nothing finer than the Finale to the first act was ever heard at the Savoy. Sir Alexander truly gave us of his best, but, to quote the words of a musical critic, "The musician's best is not always the best in the ears of an ordinary British theatrical audience. Such

22

fine orchestration was above the understanding of the Savoyards."

Many music-lovers, after hearing the music of " His Majesty," expressed regret that Mackenzie's opera " Colomba" had not been produced by Mr. D'Oyly Carte at the English Opera-house. It might well have been included in the required répertoire, which, if it had been established, might have changed the destinies of the palatial theatre built by Carte for such specific purpose.

The character of His Majesty, Ferdinand the Fifth, was represented by George Grossmith, who made his reappearance at the Savoy after an absence of nearly eight years. But the popular comedian, finding the part unsuitable to him, resigned it after a few performances, and his place was taken by Mr. H. A. Lytton, who scored his initial success at the Savoy, where, in later revivals of the Gilbert and Sullivan operas, he established his fame by his admirable acting and singing in various parts.

After a reign of sixty-one days, " His Majesty " was dethroned, and on May 5th, 1897, " The Yeomen of the Guard " was revived for the first time. This charming opera was as welcome as the spring flowers that were just then blooming in the Thames Embankment Gardens.

" The Yeomen " again drew crowded audiences to the Savoy up to November 20th, 1897. After a short recess, Mr. Carte put on " The Grand-Duchess " ; but, notwithstanding the fascinations of Florence St. John in the title-rôle, Halévy and Offenbach's " Grand-Duchess " proved as unattractive as Gilbert and

Sullivan's "Grand-Duke." The most interesting consequence of this revival was the opportunity it afforded of drawing comparison between the English and the French masters of light opera. However much opinions in the wider world may have differed regarding the comparative merits of the two composers, it was quite certain that, at the Savoy, Offenbach in all his brilliancy did not succeed in dimming the glory of Sullivan. If, at the time, any play-goer questioned that fact, the enthusiasm which greeted the return of "The Gondoliers" must have convinced them that Sir Arthur Sullivan still reigned King Paramount in the hearts of British music-lovers.

We have sometimes heard Sullivan described as "The English Offenbach." According to a statement contained in a letter from Sir Arthur to his friend Mr. B. W. Findon, the very absurd, ill-considered epithet was invented by Mr. G. A. Macfarren. That the learned Professor did not intend it as a compliment to his gifted British contemporary is obvious. By most of us it is accepted in the reverse sense ; by many such facetious comparisons are resented as an affront, a slur on Sullivan's fame. There is an unmistakable savour of jealous spleen and ill-natured irony in the phrase "The English Offenbach." And it is much to be regretted that Macfarren should have handed the term down to posterity in the pages of the "Encyclopaedia Britannica." Musical savants in France have never, so far as we know, returned the compliment by calling Offenbach "The French Sullivan." They are wiser and more polite across the Channel. Our French friends doubtless recognized the absurdity and questionable taste of linking together the names of two composers so distinct in their musical style and method. But then, it may be remarked, music-lovers in France have been far less prodigal in their praise of Sullivan than we English have been in our admiration of Offenbach. The comparison is entirely uncalled for!

"The Grand-Duchess," when previously performed in England, had given musical play-goers great pleasure, but, although Offenbach's effervescent, bubbling music was appreciated for a brief season at the Savoy, it soon became stale, flat, and unprofitable. Accordingly, after ninety-nine performances, the French piece was withdrawn and on March 22nd, 1898, "The Gondoliers" came back to hold the Savoy stage for a few weeks pending the production of "The Beauty Stone."

The casts of the operas mentioned in this chapter will be found in the Appendix at the end of the book.

Photo by Ellis & Walery.

MISS EMMIE OWEN.

Photo by Ellis & Walery.

MISS LULU EVANS.

340]

CHAPTER XVII

" THE BEAUTY STONE "

Collaboration of Pinero, Comyns Carr, and Sullivan—Romantic Musical Drama—Good music *v.* bad music—Old and new music—Sir Alexander Mackenzie's esteem for Sir Arthur Sullivan—Letter from Sir Alexander—His Sullivan lectures—The present author airs his personal views—" The Golden Legend "—A letter from Sullivan—Pinero's libretto—Comyns Carr's lyrics—" Beauty Stone " unsuited to Savoy—Ruth Vincent—Pauline Joran—Walter Passmore plays " The Devil "—Emmie Owen, " The Dare-devil."

AFTER a brief run of the revived " Gondoliers " a great revolution took place at the Savoy. King Ridicule was driven from his throne ; laughter holding both his sides was silenced for a time, whilst " The Devil " usurped authority and strove to bring back to the stage the spirit of superstitious romance which so enthralled and, it is assumed, delighted play-goers in the Middle Ages.

For some time it had been rumoured that Mr. Pinero had undertaken to supply Sir Arthur Sullivan with a libretto ; great, then, was the interest awakened. What, it was asked, might we not expect from the conjoint work of England's most brilliant living dramatist and her favourite living composer? A work of art it was bound to be. Accordingly, when it became

known that Pinero and Comyns Carr, with Sullivan,
had completed a Romantic Musical Drama, curiosity
knew no bounds. The scenes of enthusiasm that
always attended a Savoy *première* have more than
once been described in this volume, but the writer can
recall no occasion when greater excitement prevailed
than on this first night of " The Beauty Stone." Never
in the proud annals of the Savoy had a more brilliant
nor a more eager and impatient audience assembled,
and when, on opening their programmes, people saw
that Walter Passmore was going to play " The Devil,"
everybody expected lots of good fun. So frantic and
continuous were the cheers that greeted Sir Arthur
Sullivan's reappearance in the Conductor's Chair that
many moments elapsed before the popular *maestro* was
allowed to raise his bâton. When at length he did
so, there came a mighty hush to proclaim the intense
interest with which the house settled down to listen
for the first time to the overture to " The Beauty
Stone." A few bars, and it needed not the presence
of the chief in the orchestra nor his name on the programme to identify the composer with its ever-haunt-
ing melodies, which so many have tried to emulate, but
have only succeeded in caricaturing. And Sullivan's
muse appeared to have been refreshed and invigorated
by his sojourn in the Riviera, from whence our composer had recently returned for the rehearsal of his
new opera.

I have been sometimes asked to define the difference
between good music and bad music. Being neither a
theoretical nor a practical musician, and, indeed, a

most consummate ignoramus concerning the canons
of the musical art, all that I have been able to reply
has been that to me all music that delights one's
natural senses, quickens the pulse and appeals to the
inner consciousness—may we not call it the soul ?—is
good ; whilst that which sounds incongruous and un-
expressive of words or thoughts is bad. Such old-
fashioned notions will doubtless bring down upon me
the scorn and derision of musical prophets !

But my most indulgent readers may remind me
that this is hardly the place to air my views on a
subject regarding which I confess myself a dunce. My
excuse for such temerity must be that I am a devout
lover of music—music that charms my senses, as
Sullivan's has ever done. Thus, regardless of ridicule,
I grasp the opportunity here afforded me of expressing
my humble but honest opinion that the music has
been the main artery of the life of the Savoy operas.
Moreover, I am just now smarting from the tongue-
pricks of a distinguished American *littérateur*, a man,
perhaps, as ignorant as myself of the rudiments of
music. He confessed that he liked some of Sullivan's
music—in fact, he thought many of his songs were
quite " O.K." ; but that, to compare Sullivan favourably, as a composer, with Offenbach was absurd,
nothing but insular prejudice. Over a Martini cock-
tail we agreed to differ. On the other hand, it is some
consolation to find my untutored judgment supported
by the academical observations of some of our highest
and best respected musical critics. Take, for instance,
the opinion of that serious and learned musical savant,

Mr. W. S. Rockstro, who writes thus: "The predominant quality in Sullivan's light opera music is reverence for art, conscientious observance of its laws in little things." Further, in support of the cause I am pleading, let me call as a witness one who at the present period is an acknowledged Field-Marshal in the army corps of British musicians—Sir Alexander Mackenzie, Principal of the Royal Academy of Music.

In ready response to my request, Sir Alexander, with characteristic kindness and good nature, has favoured me with a few lines bearing testimony to the admiration and esteem in which he held his departed friend and colleague, Sir Arthur Sullivan. I cannot do better than give a facsimile reproduction of the distinguished Professor's letter.

It was my great privilege and pleasure to attend those "Sullivan Lectures" which Sir Alexander Mackenzie delivered at the Royal Institution in May 1901, just six months after the death of Sir Arthur. Although thirteen years have intervened, I still retain the deep impression made upon my mind by the scholarly and graceful words uttered by a living master of music in praise and honour of the master departed. It is to be regretted that such clever and delightful essays on the life-work of Sullivan should remain on the shelf, and I have therefore ventured to suggest to Sir Alexander Mackenzie that he should publish them for the benefit and pleasure of posterity.

Such reliable expert judgment as that I have been quoting above strengthens my own amateurish faith, and I think I shall be supported by every British lover

Dear Cunningham Bridgeman.

You ask me to add a line
or two on the subject of your book, and I
cannot do better than quote the concluding
words of my lectures on the life and work of
our late friend.

"A personal imprint, perhaps more
delicate and elegant than strong, is
visible on the many pages he has left us.
And by virtue of their individual stamp,
he held the power of gaining and retaining
the ear and heart of the people.
By that, he has been also fully acknowledged
by an overwhelming majority of
contemporary writers and musicians.....
Whether he himself was completely
satisfied with the sum of his life's
labour, we shall never know. But,
humanly speaking, he ought to have
been as happily content with it, as is
the nation in the possession of the
works of Arthur Sullivan."

And with all good wishes
Believe me
Yours very faithfully
A. C. Mackenzie

London. March 4th. 1914.

FACSIMILE LETTER FROM SIR ALEXANDER MACKENZIE TO CUNNINGHAM
BRIDGEMAN.

344]

of music when I say that it is not easy to discover in Sullivan's operas any music that is not good. To me, Sullivan's was always real music, pure and most convincing music, music that must touch a sympathetic chord in a sensitive soul, unless, peradventure, it be of that unhappy mortal described by Shakespeare :

> " The man that hath no music in himself,
>   Nor is not moved with concord of sweet sounds,
>   Is fit for treasons, stratagems, and spoils."

Sullivan's melodies, " the concord of sweet sounds " that flow incessantly through his instrumentation, have always had the same effect upon my emotions, whether the music I have listened to has been the " In Memoriam " overture, " The Golden Legend," " The Mikado," or any of his lighter works, with their feast of delightful, solemn, pathetic, or humorous harmonies.

After attending the first performance in London of " The Golden Legend " at the Albert Hall—November 15th, 1886—I was so deeply impressed with the beauty of the work that, before retiring to rest that night, I could not resist an impatient desire to express my admiration and offer my congratulations to Sir Arthur. By the following day's post I received from the composer a note so characteristic of Sullivan's genial, responsive nature that I would further adorn this chapter with a facsimile reproduction.

But now to return to " The Beauty Stone." Here, once more, Sullivan displayed the remarkable versatility of his genius, Pinero's quaint, old-world story, culled by the author's fervid imagination from an incident of the year 1408 related by Froissart, brought inspiration to the composer, while Dr. Comyns Carr's lyrics, if they did not reach the highest flight of poetry, more nearly approached it than is often found to be the case with operatic libretti. Carr's verse was never unpoetical ; it was always smooth and rhythmical. But Sullivan, after having so long yoked his muse to Gilbert's very crisp, pithy, and ever-varying lyrics, was sometimes puzzled by his new librettist's lengthy stanzas and extremely elongated lines. Yet Sullivan succeeded in clothing them in some of his boldest and most masterly music.

Taken altogether, " The Beauty Stone " was a work of genuine art, one that any author or composer might be proud to put his name to. Yet it failed to attract, and was withdrawn after fifty performances. This ill-success was, doubtless, partly due to the indisposition of the disciples of Gilbert and Sullivan to accept any entertainment that disturbed the traditions of their popular temple. The Savoy was not the right place for this Romantic, musical drama. " The Beauty Stone " required a wider setting, a more elaborate mounting, and a numerically stronger company than was possible on the Savoy stage. Had the piece been written and composed seven years earlier it might, after a certain amount of reconstruction, have been found suitable to place on the répertoire of the English Opera-house—that répertoire which D'Oyly Carte had projected, but, unfortunately, failed to create. But in 1891 " The Beauty Stone,"

1. QUEEN'S MANSIONS.
VICTORIA STREET. S W

17. Nov. 1896

My dear Bridgman.

Pray believe that your enthusiastic and eloquent praise of my work gave me the quickest pleasure. I am not yet hardened enough to be indifferent to the kindness of a friend.

yours sincerely
Arthur Sullivan.

FACSIMILE LETTER FROM SIR ARTHUR SULLIVAN TO CUNNINGHAM BRIDGEMAN.

like the renowned Spanish fleet, "could not be seen because it was not yet in sight."

And so it came to pass that the Pinero-Carr-Sullivan opera was numbered with many another admirable work that has failed through misadventure. It is truly lamentable to reflect how once again so much arduous labour proved in vain. More especially is it to be regretted that one of Sir Arthur Sullivan's most charming scores should lie buried, its music unheard by the multitude, but never to be forgotten by the comparative few whose privilege it was to listen to its beautiful numbers. There are probably some old Savoyards who will find particular pleasure in recalling that exquisite song of the blind heroine, poor Laine (admirably impersonated by Miss Ruth Vincent), who, left alone in her misery, invokes the pity of the Blessed Virgin thus :

> " Mother of Jesu, at thy feet I cry ;
> I do not crave for love
> That so my heart may live,
>   Else what am I ?
> Nay, and if God above
> Hath naught of love to give,
>   I fain would die."

The scene may be remembered. As though in answer to the maiden's prayer, the Devil, disguised as a holy friar, enters and presents the cripple with the magic gem, on which, he sings,

> " Once trod the Virgin's feet, and, since that hour,
> This silent particle of precious stone—
> A relic rescued from the wreck of time—

Hath so much virtue, that on man or maid,
Whoe'er it be who owns it, there doth fall
The gift of perfect Beauty."

This brief quotation will suffice to indicate the quality of the work, and to show how widely this opera differed from all that had preceded it at the Savoy. The following is the cast of—

THE BEAUTY STONE

As produced by Mr. R. D'Oyly Carte at the Savoy Theatre on Saturday, May 25th, 1898.

Philip, Lord of Mirlemont	Mr. George Devoll
Guntran of Beaugrant	Mr. Edwin Isham
Simon Limal	Mr. Henry A. Lytton
Nicholas Dircks	Mr. Jones Hewson
Peppin	Mr. D'Arcy Kelway
A Seneschal	Mr. Leonard Russell
A Lad of Town	Mr. Charles Childerstone
Baldwyn or Ath	Mr. J. W. Foster
Lords of Serault, Velaines, and St. Sauveur	Mr. Cory James / Mr. H. Gordon / Mr. J. Ruff
The Devil	Mr. Walter Passmore
Laine	Miss Ruth Vincent
Joan	Miss Rosina Brandram
Jacqueline	Miss Emmie Owen
Loyse, from St. Denis	Miss Madge Moyse
Isabeau, from Florennes	Miss Minnie Pryce
Barbe, from Bovigny	Miss Ethel Jackson
A Shrewish Girl	Miss Mildred Baker
A Matron	Miss Ethel Wilson
Saida	Miss Pauline Joran

Unhappily for the well-doing of his venture, Mr.

Photo by Robinson, Dublin.

MISS PAULINE JORAN.

Photo by Ellis & Walery.

MADAME ILKA VON PALMAY.

348]

Carte, yielding to the persuasion of an influential friend
and professed authority, had engaged two American
singing actors who had come to London armed with
highly flattering testimonials. These gentlemen proved
to be, both as actors and singers, incapable of doing
justice to the very important parts with which they
were entrusted. They certainly made their mark on
public opinion, but it was not the mark desired ; in
fact, it was such a smudge as seriously to jeopardize
the success of the piece. Apart from these, no stronger
company of artists could have been desired. Notable
amongst them were Miss Pauline Joran, unquestionably the finest *prima donna* ever seen on the Savoy
stage, and Miss Ruth Vincent, who for the first time
was given the opportunity of displaying those exceptional talents which have since brought her, especially
as a vocalist, to the front rank of her profession. A
word must be said concerning Pinero's "Devil" as
portrayed by Walter Passmore. Of course, every man
who ever troubles to think of him must form his own
conception of the spirit of evil; but, to me, the impish
being who caused such mischief with "The Beauty
Stone" had, with all his mediaeval grotesqueness
which the author intended he should possess, too
much of the low-comedy mortal in his composition.
His tricks were more supernatural than his personality. The Pineroic Prince of the Power of Darkness bore a distinct family likeness to Goethe's
Mephistopheles, but lacked his courtly suavity and
that will-power which made Faust his slave. The
Devil who appeared at the Savoy for a brief season

was neither so princely, nor so gentlemanly, nor so sorrowful as Miss Marie Corelli's Satan, whilst, seeing that his omnipotence over vain mortals was dependent upon a pebble, one could not easily exalt him above the rank of a demon-king in pantomime. I dare say I was very dense in my perception, but I could not make up my mind whether Pinero had misconceived the character or the clever comedian, Walter Passmore, was too conscientious a Christian to take the Devil's part even in a stage-play. Be this as it may, it must be admitted that Passmore, aided by the fascinating, clever soubrette, Emmie Owen, whose spirited acting proved her to be the perfect personification of a dare-devil, succeeded in imparting agreeable relief to a too sombre, although exceedingly interesting, romantic musical drama.

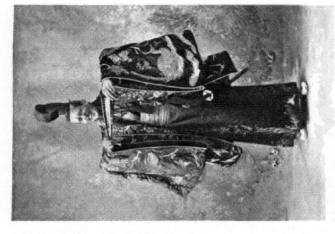

MR. SCOTT FISCHE.

MR. WALTER PASSMORE.

350]

CHAPTER XVIII

"THE BEAUTY STONE" was withdrawn on July 16th, 1898, and until the end of that year the Savoy stage was occupied by revivals of "The Gondoliers" and "The Sorcerer," with "Trial by Jury." Then came "The Lucky Star," a comic opera in three acts. The author-in-chief's name was not divulged, but the lyrics were written by Adrian Ross and Aubrey Hopwood, the music by Ivan Caryll. The piece was supported by a strong company including Walter Passmore, Henry A. Lytton, Robert Evett, Isabel Jay, Emmie Owen, and Jessie Rose; but "The Lucky Star" scarcely succeeded in justifying its title as far as it concerned the management. The opera met with only moderate success, and was taken off after a run of one hundred and forty-three performances. "H.M.S. Pinafore" was then revived a second time and enjoyed another prosperous run of one hundred and seventy-four days, extending to November 25th, 1899.

It was at this period that Sir Arthur Sullivan found a new collaborator in the person of Captain Basil

Hood, whose name as a dramatic author and librettist had already become favourably known to the public by several successful productions, notably " Gentleman Joe," " The French Maid," and " Dandy Dan," to all of which pieces the music had been composed by Walter Slaughter.   The present writer may claim to have been partly instrumental in bringing Basil Hood to the footlights of London.

In the year 1886, when Captain (then Lieutenant) Hood was serving with his regiment (the Princess of Wales's Own Yorkshire) in Ireland, a fellow officer of his showed me a sample of his early attempts at playwriting.   It was a " Blue Beard" pantomime, written for and played by officers and men of his regiment.   I can well remember that the book of the words was elaborately printed in blue, with an emblematic design of a huge golden key on the cover.

Professing in those days to be a dramatic critic, I, not without trepidation, undertook to read the novice's play.   Often previously my sensitive nerves had been sorely tried through accepting the thankless office of friendly judge and adviser.   But to my pleasure I soon discovered that the latest author of " Blue Beard" was capable of more ambitious work than writing amateur pantomime.   Basil Hood's rhymed dialogue was polished, bright, and witty, his song-words were full of refined humour, his verse somewhat reminiscent of his namesake, Tom Hood.

Having made Hood's acquaintance, I introduced him, first, to my friend Wilfred Bendall, a clever composer with whom I had collaborated in several one-act operettas. Hood and Bendall then prepared a little musical piece called "The Gypsies," which was accepted and produced by Sir Augustus Harris. Eventually Wilfred Bendall suggested to Sir Arthur Sullivan (whose secretary he was) that in Hood he might find a capable and worthy coadjutor. Sullivan and Hood then met, and the outcome was—

THE ROSE OF PERSIA, OR THE STORY-TELLER AND THE SLAVE

Characters

The Sultan Mahmoud of Persia	MR. HENRY A. LYTTON
Hassan . . .	MR. WALTER PASSMORE
(*A Philanthropist*)	
Yussuf	MR. ROBERT EVETT
(*A Professional Story-teller*)	
Abdallah . . .	MR. GEORGE RIDGWELL
(*A Priest*)	
The Grand Vizier . . .	MR. W. H. LEON
The Physician-in-Chief .	MR. C. CHILDERSTONE
The Royal Executioner .	MR. REGINALD CROMPTON
Soldier of the Guard . .	MR. POWIS PINDER
The Sultana Zubeydeh . .	MISS ISABEL JAY
(*Named "Rose-in-Bloom"*)	
"Scent-of-Lilies" . . .	MISS JESSIE ROSE
"Heart's Desire" . . .	MISS LOUIE POUNDS
"Honey-of-Life" . . .	MISS EMMIE OWEN
(*Her Favourite Slaves*)	
"Dancing Sunbeam" .	MISS ROSINA BRANDRAM
(*Hassan's First Wife*)	
"Blush-of-Morning" . .	MISS AGNES FRASER
(*His Twenty-fifth Wife*)	
"Oasis-in-the-Desert" . .	MISS MADGE MOYSE
"Moon-upon-the-Waters" .	MISS JESSIE POUNDS
"Song-of-Nightingales" . .	MISS ROSE ROSSLYN

23

" Whisper-of-the-West-Wind "   MISS GERTRUDE JERRARD
(*Wives of Hassan*)

Chorus, ACT I.—*Hassan's Wives, Mendicants, and Sultan's Guards.*
ACT II.—*Royal Slave-girls, Palace Officials, and Guards.*

Produced under the personal direction of the Author and Composer, and under the stage direction of MR. R. BARKER.

Musical Director   .   .   MR. FRANÇOIS CELLIER

ACT I.—*Court of Hassan's House*
ACT II.—*Audience Hall of the Sultan's Palace*
(W. Harford)

The costumes designed by MR. PERCY ANDERSON
Stage Manager   .   .   .   MR. W. H. SEYMOUR

The Dances arranged by Mr. W. Warde (by kind permission of Mr. George Edwardes). Dresses by Miss Fisher, Madame Auguste, Madame Léon, and Mr. B. J. Simmons. Stage Machinist, Mr. P. White. Electrician, Mr. Lyons.

The opera was produced on November 29th, 1899, and on the first night was found to fulfil the bright hopes entertained that the new collaboration would be effective. " The Rose of Persia " was an unqualified success. No opera since " The Gondoliers " had been so agreeable to the taste of Savoyards, and great were the expectations awakened.

As a matter of course, the critics pronounced Basil Hood to be a close imitator of Gilbert. Every author who dared to write smart, pithy dialogue, or whose lyrics were above average merit, was charged with the misdemeanour of Gilbertianism. Sometimes. no doubt,

Photo by Ellis & Walery.

MISS AGNES FRASER.

Photo by Ellis & Walery.

MISS LOUIE POUNDS.

354]

the accusation was merited, but as regards Basil Hood
it was not justified. His quaint Eastern story was
obviously inspired by Omar Khayyám. The title, the
characterization, the names of the *dramatis personae*—
all smacked of the ancient Persian story-teller, and
very skilfully had the author preserved the atmosphere
of the East. The lyrics were gracefully conceived,
rich in poetic fancy, and in thorough harmony with
the scene. There was not a stanza unworthy of Sullivan's setting ; indeed, the beauty of the music told
how the composer had found inspiration in the words.

Among the many gems of " The Rose of Persia "
let us recall some of the most memorable.

First came that fine song for Abdallah :

> " When Islam first arose,
> A tower upon a rock."

Then followed the song of " Dancing Sunbeam,"
superbly sung by Rosina Brandram :

> " Oh, Life has put into my hand
>   His bunch of keys,
>   And said, ' With these
>   Do aught you please !
> But one door only, understand,
>   Is not for thee—
>   Societee !
> The Key of Gold will open wide that door-way ;
> But recollect, that one way is not *your* way ! '
>   So, like a Peri at the gate
>   Of Fashion-land,
>   I have to stand—
>   The sport of tantalizing Fate ! "

One of the most popular numbers of the opera was that sung by Robert Evett :

> " I care not if the cup I hold
>   Be one of fair design,
>   Of crystal, silver, or of gold,
>   If it containeth wine."

Another charming ballad was that with which " Heart's Desire " (Louie Pounds) opened the second act :

> " Oh, what is Love ?
>   A song from heart to heart ;
> When each doth complement
>   Its counterpart."

But the crowning song came last in the opera. It is sung by Hassan, whose life depends upon his succeeding in telling the Sultan an interesting story which must have a happy ending.

This was the song :

> " There was once a small Street Arab,
>   And his little name was Tom :
> And he lived in Gutter-Persia
>   Where such arabs all come from :
> And, like little Gutter-Persians
>   (Ev'ry one and one and all),
> His spirits were elastic
>   As an india-rubber ball !
>
> " And all day long he sang a song,
> A merry little ditty as he danced a cellar-flap :
>   ' The life I lead is all I need,
> And I know no better ! '—the lucky little chap !

" Now among the bricks and mortar
     Did his little life-time pass ;
He had never seen a flower
     Nor a single blade of grass :
But one day he found a daisy,
     And he thought that simple thing
Was a wondrous flow'r from heaven,
     And he took it to the King !

" He meant no wrong, but through the throng
He struggled to the Sultan, and laid it on his lap
     (That simple weed—he did, indeed),
For he knew no better—the foolish little chap !

" But the Sultan gravely thanked him,
     Saying, ' Would that I had eyes
To see a simple daisy
     As a gift of Paradise !
I will not now reward thee,
     Or exchange thy humble lot—
For riches would but rob thee
     Of a wealth that I have not ! '

" So all day long he sang his song,
That merry little ditty as he danced a cellar-flap :
     ' The life I lead is all I need ! '
For he knew no better—the lucky little chap ! "

SUL. Is the story finished ?

HAS. That is only the beginning, O King. That little boy was myself—and the Sultan was your father —and the story I have been telling to the slave, which she has been telling to the Sultana, is the story of my own life—and, O King, this is the point : you have yourself commanded that the story—which is my life —is to have a happy ending.

Sul. By the beard of my grandfather, you have played an odd trick upon me!

Has. It is the odd trick, O King, that wins the game!

This plaintive story, sympathetically told by Walter Passmore to the accompaniment of Sullivan's ear-haunting melody, touched not only the Sultan's heart but the heart of the Savoy audience. No happier ending to his play could the author have conceived.

"The Rose of Persia" held the Savoy stage until June 28th, 1900, and numbered two hundred and twelve performances.

An incident associated with the production of this opera recurs to my mind. One day I happened to meet Sullivan coming from rehearsal. He was looking worn and worried. I anxiously inquired the cause of his dejection. "My dear fellow," he replied, "how would you feel if, whilst you were in the throes of rehearsing an opera, you were called upon to set ' The Absent-minded Beggar' for charity? That's my trouble! All day long my thoughts, and at night my dreams, are haunted by the vision of a host of demon-creditors pursuing me with the cry, ' Pay—Pay—Pay'! It puzzled me to compose Gilbert's ' I have a song to sing O,' but that was child's-play compared to the setting of Kipling's lines. If it wasn't for Charity's sake I could never have undertaken the task."

It was not very long after that meeting that I sat beside Sir Arthur's bed, where he lay seriously ill. Notwithstanding acute suffering, with characteristic kindness he granted me an interview with special reference to an entertainment at the Crystal Palace which, through his influence, I had been commissioned to prepare. It was with a heavy heart I parted from my old friend. I could not get rid of a sad foreboding that we had met for the last time. And so, alas, it proved to be!

CHAPTER XIX

IN order to allow Hood and Sullivan time to prepare another opera, Mr. D'Oyly Carte now revived, a second time, " The Pirates of Penzance," which popular piece again drew crowded audiences for a period of five months. Then came the first revival of " Patience." Nineteen years had passed since this opera was transferred in its pristine state from the Opera Comique to inaugurate the opening of the Savoy Theatre. It was generally believed that " Patience " was dead and buried for ever ; that the play had perished with the mock aestheticism on which it was a playful skit. Bunthorne and Grosvenor, if not quite forgotten, had become the mere shadows of ancient types, grotesque characters who had greatly amused us in 1881 and 1882. It was, therefore, questioned whether the point of Gilbert's satire would or would not be understood and appreciated by a later generation who knew not Maudle, Postlethwaite, or the Cimabue Browns, and, perhaps had never heard of the worshippers of the sunflower and the lily.

It was in consequence of such doubt that "Patience" had not, like all the other notable Gilbert and Sullivan successes, been revived until now. But on November 17th, 1900, "Patience" came back from the grave as sweet and winsome and as guileless as ever, to flirt in turn with her childhood's playfellow, Archibald "The All-right," and Bunthorne, the "Aesthetic sham." Both false disciples of the Oscar Wilde cult, the "idyllic" and the fleshly "all-but" poets returned to pose and flop and utter "platitudes in stained-glass attitudes," whilst close on their heels followed the adoring "twenty love-sick maidens, love-sick still against their will," and all as limp and clinging as they were twenty years ago; in fact, precisely as they had prophesied they would be, and probably will be twenty years hence.

Then, just as the audience was beginning to weary of the silly maidens with their amorous sighs and yearnings, back marched the gallant 35th Dragoon Guards; on to the stage they tramped to the enlivening quick-step "The Soldiers of our Queen"; they came in time to save the situation, to cause dismay amongst the idiotic members of the "Inner Brotherhood" and to rouse their friends in front to tumultuous applause. And what a welcome we of the old Brigade gave them one and all! Some of us had been wondering whether we should identify any of the *dramatis personae* as our cheery companions of days gone by. We feared that the "greenery-yallery, Grosvenor gallery" poets would appear to us too rusty, musty, and out of date, as flat and stale as the incidents and institutions referred to in their topical patter. We half expected that the love-sick maidens would have lost their power to charm as they used to do, and that even the village milkmaid, Patience, might now, instead of fascinating, annoy us by her superlative innocence. Then, again, the entire cast of characters was new; we should sorely miss old faces. Where could another Patience be found worthy to compare with Leonora Braham ? Where another Lady Angela as delightful as Jessie Bond ? What would Bunthorne and Grosvenor be without Grossmith and Barrington ? But all such anxious doubts were quickly dispelled. The opera was as fresh and full of vitality as ever. Rest had given new lease of life to all the characters ; they seemed to have borne the burthen of twenty years better than ourselves, and their perennial youth rejuvenated the oldest amongst us. Isabel Jay, with her admirable singing and graceful personality, though she could not chase away happy memories of the original Patience, we welcomed, admired, and felt grateful for. Rosina Brandram, less massive than her predecessor, succeeded in getting as much fun as ever out of the part of Lady Jane, and her glorious, rich contralto voice added, as it ever did, to the charm of Sullivan's music. Walter Passmore and Henry Lytton lessened our regret at the loss of former favourites. In short, as regards the company and the general production, we could find nothing at all to grumble at.

But perhaps the greatest astonishment felt by old Savoyards was the enthusiastic reception accorded the aesthetic opera by the younger generation. Here and there in the book a word or two had been altered, quite unnecessarily, to bring the piece up to date; such, for instance, as the substitution of "Tuppeny Tube" for "Threepenny Bus," and "Lord Roberts" for "Sir Garnet," who, by the way, was still living in honoured retirement as Lord Wolseley. These trifles, however, in no way hindered the success of the revival. Every Gilbertian quip, familiar to some of us, went straight to the ears of those who heard it for the first time. The tangled affections of the conscientious milkmaid and her poet-suitors, the alternate adoration of Bunthorne and Grosvenor by the rapturous damo- sels, the amorous propensities of Lady Jane, and the quaint efforts of the Dragoon Officers to become aestheticized—all these things won laughter and ap- plause no less hearty than in former days.

But, as we once before suggested, there could be little doubt that it was chiefly through Sullivan's tuneful music that "Patience" captivated the hearts of all, both old and young alike. "Prithee, pretty maiden," "The Magnet and the Churn," "Love is a Plaintive Song," with its exquisite Valse refrain, Lady Jane's burlesque ballad, "Silvered is the raven hair"—in fact, all the old favourite songs were re- demanded again and again, despite Frank Cellier's efforts to subdue unreasonable encores. But the gem of all, the unaccompanied sestette, "I hear the soft note of an echoing voice," came back to our senses with the fragrant sweetness of a long-cherished but half-forgotten melody. To the ears of the younger people this perfect specimen of a part-song was a new and abiding joy.

Taken altogether, the resurrection of "Patience" was one of the most remarkable events in the whole history of the Savoy. Its success was as unqualified as it had been unexpected. But, unhappily, mingling with our pleasure was keen regret.

In the first place, Sir Arthur Sullivan was too unwell to appear, and to conduct as was his custom on first nights; and when at curtain-fall Gilbert and D'Oyly Carte took their "Call," they both limped on the stage supported by stout walking-sticks, reminding us of Chelsea pensioners. The author was again the victim of his old enemy, the gout; but the esteemed manager's case was of a more serious nature. Mr. Carte was in the throes of intense suffering; he had been for some time prey to an illness that was too soon afterwards to have a fatal ending.

Wednesday, November 7th, 1900, will remain for ever memorable in the annals of the Savoy, since on the evening of that day two of the members of the famous Triumvirate made their last bows to their patrons, associates, and friends, whilst the third of the veteran chiefs lay sick and—though we little dreamed it then—dying.

So, whilst mirth and laughter reigned within the walls of the Savoy, black clouds were gathering overhead. And only too soon they were to break!

On Thursday, November 22nd, 1900, the sad tidings went forth that Sir Arthur Sullivan was dead. "The sweetest singer of his generation" had passed away in the early hours of that morning. Deep and sincere was the grief felt throughout Great Britain, and every English-speaking nation of the world.

By the kind sanction of my friend and fellow-scribe, Mr. B. W. Findon, I am permitted to quote from his admirable work, "Sullivan and His Operas." Mr. Findon, who claimed not only close friendship but blood relationship with the composer, gives the following interesting account of Sullivan's last days of life, the incidents attending his illness, and the causes which, humanly speaking, accelerated the end :

"The early part of the year (1900) Sullivan had spent at Monte Carlo, where his life was one of quiet routine and mild enjoyment. He would work throughout the afternoon, and, after a late dinner, would go to the Casino and indulge in a little play for an hour or so, and then retire to his hotel. He avoided all gaiety, and was content with the society of one or two friends.

"The summer months he spent at Walton-on-Thames, and there he devoted himself to composition with the energy and concentration for which he was ever remarkable. It would have been well had he remained at Walton until the approach of winter made it desirable for him to return to his London home. But he had a fancy to go to Switzerland, and there the mischief began which had so fatal a termination.

"Grand scenery and Nature's loveliness possessed an irresistible fascination for Sullivan, and it was his delight to sit in the open in the evenings after dinner and pensively contemplate the wonders around him. It had been his habit in past years, and, so far as he saw, there was no obstacle in the way of his gratifying a favourite custom. He forgot, however, that age makes dangerous what youth can do with impunity. The night-air was sweet and refreshing, but its breath proved fatal to him. A troublesome cold was followed by bronchitis, and, as soon as he could travel with safety, Sullivan returned home. All then might have been well, but on October 29th he exposed himself to a piercing wind in order to see the return (from South Africa) of the City Imperial Volunteers. The bronchitis reappeared more acutely than before, and told its worst tale on a heart which, already weak, gave way under the strain imposed upon it. Between six and seven a.m. on Thursday, November 22nd, he partook of a light breakfast, and there was nothing in his condition to alarm those attending him. At about half-past eight he partially raised himself in bed, and complained of a pain in his heart. His nephew placed his arms around him, and assistance was promptly forthcoming, but the Pale Messenger had arrived, and Sullivan, in obedience to his inexorable summons, passed peacefully away on the Feast Day of St. Cecilia."

It had been Sullivan's desire that he should be buried close to his mother in Brompton Cemetery, but so earnest was the wish expressed by his distinguished compatriots and the public in general, that England's well-beloved musician should be laid in our National mausoleum, that widespread was the satisfaction when it became known that the Dean and Chapter of St. Paul's had readily acceded to the request made to them.

At eleven o'clock on Tuesday, November 27th, the

funeral procession set forth from Victoria Street, Westminster, on its mournful way, first to the Chapel Royal, St. James's, where, by command of the Queen, part of the Burial Service was to take place, and thence to St. Paul's. Throughout the line of route flags drooped at half-mast, whilst beneath them people crowded in their thousands, bare-headed and in silence, waiting to pay their last tribute of respect and gratitude to the lamented master whose genius had done so much to brighten their lives for the past five-and-twenty years.

Into the Royal Chapel, where Arthur Sullivan had begun his career as a chorister, was borne the casket containing his remains. On either side stood men and women famous in society and the wider world of Art in all its branches. The Queen was represented by Sir Walter Parratt, Master of Music, who was the bearer of a wreath with the inscription: "A mark of sincere admiration for his musical talents from Queen Victoria." Sir Hubert Parry represented the Prince of Wales; the German Emperor was represented by Prince Lynar, Attaché of the German Embassy; Prince and Princess Christian by Colonel the Hon. Charles Eliot, and the Duke of Cambridge by General Bateson.

Among the congregation at the Chapel Royal were seen the United States Ambassador; the Earl and Countess of Strafford; Theresa, Countess of Shrewsbury; the Countess of Essex; Lord Glenesk; Lord Rowton; Lord Crofton; Lady Catherine Coke; the Dean of Westminster; Lady Bancroft; Lady

Barnby ; Mr. Arthur Chappell ; Mr. and Mrs. F. C.
Burnand ; Mr. Arthur W. Pinero ; Mr. Haddon
Chambers ; Lieutenant Dan Godfrey ; Signor Tosti;
Mr. George Grossmith ; Mr. Rutland Barrington ; Miss
Macintyre ; Mrs. Ronalds ; Canon Duckworth ; Lady
Lewis ; Miss Ella Russell ; Mr. Augustus Manns;
Mr. Charles Wyndham ; Captain Basil Hood ; the
Chairman and Secretary of Leeds Musical Festival;
and Representatives of various British Musical Asso-
ciations.

The Pall-bearers were Sir Squire Bancroft, Mr.
François Cellier, Colonel A. Collins (one of the Royal
Equerries), Sir Frederick Bridge, Sir George Lewis,
Sir Alexander Mackenzie, Sir George Martin, and
Sir John Stainer.

The chief mourners were Mr. Herbert Sullivan
(nephew), Mr. John Sullivan (uncle), Mrs. Holmes,
and Miss Jane Sullivan (nieces), Mr. Wilfred Bendall
(Sullivan's secretary), Mr. B. W. Findon, Mr. Edward
Dicey, Mr. C. W. Mathews, Mrs. D'Oyly Carte, Dr.
Buxton Browne, Mr. Arthur Wagg, Mr. Fred Walker,
Mr. Dreseden and Sir Arthur's servants.

Much to their regret, neither Mr. Gilbert nor Mr.
Carte was able to attend the funeral. The first was
on the Continent for the benefit of his health, the
second was laid up by serious illness. The present
writer also, having been absent from London at the
time, has not the advantage of an eye-witness to give
a graphic description of the funeral obsequies of his
old friend ; and so, rather than attempt to paint the
picture from imagination, he gladly avails himself

again of the courtesy of his brother-author who is so generous as to lend the aid of his experience.

In these sympathetic words, Mr. Findon describes the scenes and incidents in which, as a chief mourner, he took part at the Chapel Royal and St. Paul's Cathedral :

" . . . As the casket was borne into the Chapel, it was impossible to avoid thinking of those days when Sullivan himself had worn the gold and scarlet coat of a Chapel Royal Chorister, and his sweet young voice had rung through the sacred edifice. Then the world and its honours lay before him, but we doubt if even in the most sanguine moments of impulsive boyhood he imagined the greatness that one day would be his, or that his bier would pass within those honoured walls amid the silent demonstration of a mourning people. The anthem, ' Yea, though I walk through the valley of the shadow of death,' from his oratorio ' The Light of the World,' was beautifully sung, and the pathos of the music bathed many a face in tears, and touched a tender spot in more than one loving heart. Another of the dead master's exquisite thoughts, ' Wreaths for our graves the Lord has given,' brought the Service at the Chapel Royal to an end, and the procession passed on its way to St. Paul's Cathedral, which was crowded with sympathetic spectators.

" Clerical etiquette and cathedral dignity compelled the beginning of the Burial Service anew, and when the coffin had been lowered into the crypt there came the most poignant moment of the long ceremonial.

" Close to the open vault sat the members of the Savoy Opera Company, including his life-long friend, Mr. François Cellier, who had been associated as *chef d'orchestre* with all his comic operas, and, after

24

the Benediction had been given, they sang in voices charged with emotion the touching chorus, 'Brother, thou art gone before us,' from 'The Martyr of Antioch.' The effect was quite remarkable, inasmuch as it was one of those incidents which come but rarely in a life-time."

It was not in London alone that people mourned for Arthur Sullivan on that November day. Throughout Great Britain and Ireland, on the Continent of Europe, in America and farther across the seas, thousands of fond and grateful hearts ached with grief at the thought that England's dear master of melody had passed away into the silent land. From high-born personages and from people of low estate came floral emblems, wreaths, crosses, and lyres innumerable. Conspicuous among them was a beautiful harp of purple blossoms with strings—one broken—of white violets. To this offering was attached a card bearing the inscription:

In Memoriam

ARTHUR SEYMOUR SULLIVAN

Born 13 May, 1842. Died 22 Nov., 1900

FROM MR. D'OYLY CARTE'S " ROSE OF PERSIA " TOURING
COMPANY IN TOKEN OF THEIR AFFECTIONATE REGARD

Dear Master, since thy magic harp is broken,
   Where shall we find new melodies to sing ?
The grief we feel may not in words be spoken ;
   Our voices with thy songs now heav'nward wing.
Whilst on thy tomb we lay this humble token
   Of love which to thy memory shall cling.

BELFAST,
   24th November, 1900.

These simple lines but half expressed the love and esteem in which Sir Arthur Sullivan was held by all whose privilege it was to have been associated with him, and to have served, however humbly, his proud and brilliant life-cause.

A line borrowed from Moore's poem on the death of Sheridan might well be applied to Sullivan—

". . . Who ran
Through each mode of the lyre and was master of them all."

CHAPTER XX

IT may not be out of place in these personal reminiscences to narrate how the sad tidings of Sullivan's death reached my ears. I had arrived in Dublin as Mr. D'Oyly Carte's press representative in connection with the tour of "The Rose of Persia," and on the morning of November 22nd, in pursuance of my official duties, I called at the office of *The Irish Times* and interviewed one of the sub-editors. Speaking of Sullivan's precarious health, I had just stated that, according to latest reports from headquarters, the composer had recovered strength sufficiently to enable him to resume work on his new opera, to be called "The Emerald Isle," when our conversation was interrupted by a telephone call. Then, like a bolt from the blue, came the message, "Sir Arthur Sullivan died at nine o'clock this morning!"

This was one of the strangest coincidences, as it was, truly, the saddest one in my experience.

In the Irish capital the sad news created great lamentation, for the music-loving people of Ireland always claimed Sullivan as one of their kindred, and, further, the knowledge that the subject of the new opera upon which he was engaged was Irish intensified sympathetic interest in the sorrowful event.

As in London, so in Dublin, the anxious question arose, "What will now become of 'The Emerald Isle' ? "

It soon became known that a large portion of the music was left unfinished by Sullivan. Three songs in the first act and five in the second act had not been set, and, with the exception of numbers 1 and 2 scored by Sir Arthur, the whole of the opera remained to be harmonized and orchestrated. General satisfaction followed the announcement that, by request of the author, Basil Hood, and Mr. Carte, the task of completing the score had been undertaken by Edward German.

In due course "The Emerald Isle" was finished, and, appropriately, on St. Patrick's Day the opera was placed in rehearsal at the Savoy, under the personal direction of the author, assisted by Richard Barker.

Although Mr. Carte was in too weak a state of health to take any active part in the work of preparation, everybody rejoiced to learn that the patient showed signs of wonderful improvement ; accordingly it was fondly hoped that the esteemed manager's strength would be sufficiently restored to allow him to witness the production of the piece. But it was not to be; a few days later Mr. Carte had a serious relapse, and his distinguished medical attendant, Sir

Thomas Barlow, pronounced him to be in a critical state.

On April 3rd, four months and a half after the death of Sir Arthur Sullivan, Richard D'Oyly Carte, the second of the famous Triumvirate, passed away in his London residence, No. 4, Adelphi Terrace, in the fifty-seventh year of his age.

To musical London and a large sphere beyond the news of the death of the popular impresario came with a great shock. All Savoyards and associates of the Savoy felt they had lost a friend, one to whom they were indebted for a multitude of past joys.

In the year 1844 D'Oyly Carte was born in Soho. His grandfather fought at Waterloo with "The Blues"; his father was a member of Rudall and Carte, a well-known firm of musical-instrument makers. His mother, descended from a Suffolk branch of the D'Oyly family, was the daughter of a clergyman on the staff of the Chapels Royal. After passing through University College School, Richard D'Oyly Carte matriculated at London University, but in deference to the wish of his parents he abandoned the "higher education" and entered his father's business.

It was at the beginning of the year 1873 that I made the acquaintance of Mr. Carte. Our first meeting came about in this way: whilst confined to bed for nearly a year in the Royal Naval Hospital, Plymouth, through an accident contracted in the service, I was guilty of writing a three-act comedy, entitled "Shipmates." Greatly to my astonishment, the play was accepted by a theatrical manager for production in the provinces; whereupon, with the unblushing assurance of a budding dramatist, I went straightway to Arthur Sullivan and asked him if he would do me the favour to compose the music of a song incidental to my comedy.

Sullivan, being busily engaged on his oratorio " The Light of the World," was unable to oblige me, but he gave me a letter of introduction to Mr. Frederic Clay, one of the most kind-hearted and genial men it was ever my pleasure to meet. Clay very promptly set my song, and a day or two later, when I called to see him at his office in the Treasury, he conducted me from thence up Whitehall to Craig's Court, and there introduced me to Mr. Carte, whose firm at once published the song called, by the way, " Lover Mine." This happy incident was the beginning of a lasting friendship, and formed another link in the chain of circumstances that eventually drew me into the family circle of the Savoy.

For the public at large it is hardly possible to realize to what extent the remarkable success of the Savoy pieces was due to D'Oyly Carte. His post of duty resembled that of Chief Engineer on a great ocean liner. He was seldom seen " on deck." It was only on first nights that he gave his patrons the opportunity of gazing upon him. But, all the while, it was owing to his skill and ceaseless care in the control of the motive power that the good pleasure-ship, *The Savoy*, with its rich argosy of mirth and melody, voyaged safely past the breakers and shallows that sometimes beset its usually calm and prosperous voyage. Without D'Oyly Carte's business instinct, his knowledge, sagacity, tact, and good taste, Gilbert and Sullivan might never have succeeded in emancipating the English stage from the vulgar inanities of those badly adapted, coarse *réchauffés* of French *opéra bouffe* which were served up *ad nauseam* to play-goers of the unenlightened 'sixties.

If only for his achievement in cleansing the Augean Stables of our theatres, the name of D'Oyly Carte must always remain honoured in the history of the English stage. Carte's energy and enterprise knew no bounds, but seldom did his ambition o'erleap itself. Perhaps, indeed, the only occasion where his judgment proved at fault was, not so much in the building of his palatial English Opera-house, as in believing that British operatic composers would be forthcoming when a suitable theatre was ready for them.

It was a mistake to launch " Ivanhoe," to embark his fortunes on what was, admittedly, a bold experiment, without first providing a means of rescue in the shape of other operas to follow. But for this error in judgment, Carte's splendid aim to establish English opera might have been achieved—who can tell ? Nevertheless, despite the failure of his scheme, the promoter was deserving of the greatest credit for his plucky venture, whilst Mr. Carte's financial ability in extricating himself from the undertaking was very remarkable.

To a casual observer D'Oyly Carte's true character

and disposition was a problem not easy to solve. His customary attitude was that of a shy or nervous man. Whilst conversing with him, a stranger might not unreasonably imagine that he was indifferent to the subject under discussion; he gave one the impression that his thoughts were wandering far away. His response often sounded vague and pointless, as though to signify that the matter did not interest but rather bored him to talk about. But all the while he was carefully weighing every word, twisting and turning its value over in his mind. His methods of transacting business were quite out of the common order, and not always easy to comprehend for any but his trusty adjutants and servants, all of whom could testify to the wisdom and soundness of his instinct.

Carte possessed a keen sense of humour, yet, whether listening to or telling a funny story, his countenance never betrayed appreciation of the joke. Not a muscle of his face relaxed; he seemed as emotionless as the Sphinx. But behind the veil of apathy he laughed to his own heart's content.

These reflections recall to mind an anecdote Carte used to tell against himself. It may be a " chestnut," but it is, I think, a digestible one.

One day he had arranged to lunch with his old friend and colleague, Mr. Michael Gunn, at Romano's in the Strand. Gunn, after waiting for him some minutes, sent a young messenger across to the Savoy to remind Carte of the appointment. The youth found his way down to the stage, where an audition was taking place. He tried to approach the busy manager, but was abruptly told he must wait his turn. Whilst standing amongst the crowd, listening to the voice-trials, the messenger suddenly became stage-struck, and, believing he could sing as well as most of them, he thought he might venture to enter the competition. Accordingly, as soon as his turn came, he advanced boldly to the pianoforte, and was asked by the chorus-mistress what he would sing. Without hesitation he replied, " I am an Englishman." This well-known song from " H.M.S. Pinafore " he rendered to the best of his ability, but, as Carte afterwards related, the accent of Romano's employé was much too Italian to belong to an Englishman, and he advised the young *buffo profundo* to apply at Covent Garden Opera-house. But the climax of the story came when the young man got back to Romano's.

Mr. Gunn inquired what had kept him so long away, and if he had brought an answer from Mr. Carte.

" No, sir," he replied, " I could not get near the gentleman, but—*I've had my voice tried.*"

D'Oyly Carte was a man of the most refined artistic taste, a virtue richly inherited by his sole surviving son, Mr. Rupert Carte. His home in Adelphi Terrace was furnished in a manner admirably in keeping with the decorative designs of Adam, with Angelica Kauffman medallions which enriched the walls and ceilings. In this connection a story is told of a certain art connoisseur who, calling upon Mr. Carte, was so lost in admiration of the surroundings of one of the rooms as to be led to betray weakness in critical judgment. After studying, with the air of an expert, the chimney-piece, he remarked: " Ah! we shall never see such workmanship as that again!" Carte very considerately refrained from informing his guest that the chimney-piece he so greatly admired had been recently designed and fitted to match the modern appointments of the room.

His library and billiard-room were decorated by Whistler, an old friend of D'Oyly Carte and his wife. Whistler personally mixed the paints for these rooms. Literary, artistic, and theatrical friends of Mr. Carte remember with pleasure the delightful " yellow " room at Adelphi Terrace, with its French windows overlooking the Thames.

Of all the beautiful articles of furniture in his London house, that which Mr. Carte valued beyond all others was a luxurious sofa, the gift of Sir Arthur Sullivan. It was upon this he was lying when he breathed his last.

Mr. D'Oyly Carte was twice married and left two sons—the eldest, Lucas, a barrister, who died in 1907, the other, Rupert, present chairman of the Savoy Hotel and owner of the performing rights of the Gilbert and Sullivan operas and the D'Oyly Carte Opera Company.

To his second wife, formerly Miss Cowper Black, better known as Helen Lenoir, Mr. Carte was in a large measure indebted for his remarkable success, but to this subject further reference will, it is hoped, be made before the close of this book.

Richard D'Oyly Carte was buried, in accordance with his request, at Fairlight, Hastings, the funeral being conducted privately. A handsome Memorial Window in the Savoy Chapel Royal testifies to the esteem in which he was held by all who knew him.

CHAPTER XXI

THE D'OYLY CARTE TOURING COMPANY

Discipline and *esprit de corps*—Unabated enthusiasm in the provinces
—A Classic Acting-Manager—No " fish " stories admitted—Fred
Billington's views and experiences—Gilbert and Sullivan operas in
America, Africa, and the Continent—English theatre orchestras
compared with German—State subsidy—George Grossmith and
George Thorne—Johannesburg—An absconding dresser—Billington
and Workman robbed—François Cellier's visits to Africa—Henry
A. Lytton—Gilbertian actor of many parts—Touring—Its bright
and its dark side—Company snowed up—Leicester Tunks's birth-
day supper-party—The Gilbert and Sullivan operas in Oxford and
Cambridge.

FIVE years have passed since the last performance of
a Gilbert and Sullivan opera took place at the Savoy,
but during that period Londoners have had frequent
opportunities of renewing the acquaintance of their
old favourites through the medium of the D'Oyly
Carte Touring Company at suburban theatres.   At
the present moment a widespread appeal is being
made for the revival of the operas at their old home
or in some other West End theatre where, it is suggested, an annual season of Gilbert and Sullivan
would prove sufficiently attractive to ensure a profitable return.   There are, doubtless, many difficulties
in the way of carrying out the scheme which do not
enter into the consideration of the public.   Whether

Mr. Rupert D'Oyly Carte is disposed to entertain the proposition, or to rest content with the periodical visits of his country company to outer London, remains a Cabinet secret.

It might not unreasonably be imagined that the members of the touring company, principals and chorus alike, would grow stale and slack by constant repetition of the operas, week in, week out, during eleven months of every year ; but seldom is there to be noticed any falling away in the quality of the performances. Under close managerial watchfulness and unrelaxing discipline, the high traditions of the Savoy are upheld. But above and beyond that, there exists a strong *esprit de corps*. Like the units of a crack regiment, the D'Oyly Carte actors and actresses are proud of their flag and jealous to defend its honour and their own reputation. If it were otherwise they would long ago have worn out their welcome in the provinces, seeing that in Manchester, Liverpool, Leeds, Sheffield, Newcastle, Glasgow and Edinburgh—in fact, in all the big towns visited by the company—play-goers are no whit less critical and exacting, perhaps more so, than those of the metropolis. But there is no sign of enthusiasm abating. Everywhere the Red and Black preliminary posters of the " D'Oyly Carte Repertory Company " awaken glad anticipation, and the theatres are crowded throughout the period of their stay. My own personal experience of " the Road " being comparatively limited, I invited Mr. Henry E. Bellamy, who, for twenty years or more, has held the position of Acting-

Photo by Dover Street Studios.

MR. C. H. WORKMAN.

Photo by S. Laighieri.

MR. H. E. BELLAMY.

Manager, D'Oyly Carte Touring Co.

Manager, to contribute any interesting data relating to his tours. I hoped, for instance, that he might be able to give an estimate of the number of miles he has traversed whilst journeying through Great Britain, Ireland, and also South Africa, where he has thrice captained the company. I went so far as to tempt him to divulge a state secret by informing the public as to the approximate amount of £ s. d. he had taken since he entered the service. But all in vain ; my friend, who is not generally of a bashful or reserved disposition, yet ever discreet, replied that the mathematical problems I had set him were beyond his ability to solve. I should have remembered that classics are his forte, and that, if I desired to brighten my book with a few choice Latin quotations, Henry Bellamy was the man to supply them. He very kindly offered to contribute any amount of prime fishing stories if they would be of any use, but, thanking him, I remarked that I should be sorry to discount the pleasure of the multitude who delight in listening to, even if they do not always credit, the tales of his piscatorial adventures. Further, I assured him that my object was to include in these pages nothing but the truth, the whole truth, and—no fish stories.

Mr. Fred Billington I found much more ready to oblige, and, in response to my request for a few notes, the genial comedian denied himself the pleasure of a round on the golf-links in order to prepare an outline sketch of his views and experiences in connection with the D'Oyly Carte Company.

Fred Billington is one of the most popular " strolling

players " of his day.   His name is one to conjure with
in every part of the country, and any incidents relating
to his career as a Gilbert and Sullivan actor will be
interesting to a large number of play-goers.

Mr. Billington joined the D'Oyly Carte Company
in 1879, making his first appearance at the Standard
Theatre, Shoreditch, as Bill Bobstay, boatswain's
mate of " H.M.S. Pinafore," and has ever since
then remained staunch to the Savoy Operas.
He has played Pooh Bah well over three thousand
three hundred times, this number including performances in England, America, and the continents of
Europe and Africa.   He has twice gone with the
Company to South Africa, and, the veteran adds: "I
have paid one official visit to Balmoral, where I had
the honour of presenting Pooh Bah to Her Majesty
Queen Victoria."

No one who has witnessed Billington's clever
character-study of the Gaoler in " The Yeomen of
the Guard " will be surprised to learn that Shadbolt
is his favourite part.   It is certainly his best part,
one that might have been designed expressly for him,
so perfectly does it suit his dry and unctuous style
of humour.

Touching his personal impressions of provincial
audiences, Billington pronounces them to be, as a
rule, good everywhere, but he awards the palm to
the Northern towns.

" In Edinburgh, Aberdeen, Glasgow, and Newcastle," he says, " the strongest evidence of ap-

MR. H. A. LYTTON.

MR. FRED. BILLINGTON.

preciation is shown. In the Midlands also, the operas meet with loyal support. Yorkshire, my native county, I cannot speak so well of, except, perhaps, Sheffield. Sheffield, by the way, was the very first town to understand Gilbert's humour ! But I must not forget our good Irish friends and patrons, who always give us such warm welcome that we look forward to our periodical visits to Dublin and Belfast with infinite pleasure. Provincial audiences are variable in every way. This makes touring interesting. We never know what to expect. Fresh audiences, fresh orchestras, towns, theatres, dressing-rooms, lodgings and hotels, all offer such constant variety that there is no likelihood of getting stale, as one is prone to become after a long run in London, where to be given a good part in a successful play is often a misfortune to the actor. He finds himself transformed into a star, and immediately fancies he has reached heaven, where there is no necessity to work hard for a living ; and so he often gets careless and acquires a contempt for the provinces where he has probably learnt his business.

" Appreciation of Gilbert and Sullivan is also variable. The audiences in some towns are apathetic ; Gilbert's wittiest sayings are received as solemnly as if they were sermons from the Reverend Doctor Dryasdust, but in those towns of the North which I have specified and also in Ireland, the people are very loyal to ' Ours,' and, if I am not mistaken, they will continue to be so long after you and I are forgotten.

" Africa I liked immensely. Life there is so entirely different from what one is accustomed to at home or in France, Germany, or America—I mean not only theatrical but social and general life. But the towns lie so far apart that railway journeys are not only trying to one's nerves and patience, but lay a heavy

25

tax on the managerial exchequer. Johannesburg is the best town in South Africa for business, but sorry is the lot of the management that does not draw crowded houses there. Failing to do so means a very heavy loss on a big company like our own. Fortunately, we hit the bull's-eye of popular taste, and Manager Bellamy left the town a wealthier man than when he entered it.

"In Cape Town, Durban, Maritzburg, Pretoria and Bloemfontein, the theatres, if packed at ordinary prices, only just enable a big company to pay expenses.

"Touching American audiences," Billington continues, "they are, as every British actor knows, splendid people to play to. If you give them a good show they shower honours upon you, but if you fail to please them they tell you so in plain words, and their language is sometimes worthy of Limehouse. I'm thankful to say I got on very well with them. Pooh Bah was quite to their liking.

"Whilst in the States we also tried 'Ruddigore.' This was a frost; the Americans were not for taking any witch's curses. As for 'The Gondoliers,' as everybody knows, across the herring-pond the opera was known as 'The Gone-dollars.'

"Business on the Continent was variable. We played 'Mikado,' 'Pinafore,' 'Patience,' and 'Trial by Jury' in Germany, Holland, Austria, and Bavaria. To Berlin we returned four times to appear either at the Walner or the Krolls Theatre. One notable feature of our German audiences was their enthusiastic reception of Sullivan's music, especially his concerted pieces; on the other hand, Gilbert's humour was nowhere understood. Such a specimen of a man-o'-war sailor as Dick Deadeye of 'H.M.S. Pinafore,' the Press remarked, would never be admitted into the German Imperial Navy, and if 'Trial by Jury' was

Doyly Carte Company in Africa

386]

a sample of English law proceedings, they preferred their own methods.

" On the Continent the orchestras, everywhere, were magnificent, numbering never less than forty, sometimes as many as eighty, and all excellent players.

" The inadequacy of our English provincial orchestras is terrible. Only the most hardened artist can witness, unmoved, the murder of Sullivan's scores, when twenty instruments have to do the work of sixty or seventy. Our native instrumentalists may be, doubtless they are, individually as proficient as the foreigners, but to compare the numerical strength of an ordinary English provincial orchestra with those found even in second or third-class German theatres is as unfair as it is absurd, seeing that, in Germany, theatre bands are subsidized by Government. Sullivan did what he could to try and persuade the powers that be to adopt the foreign policy, but English Home Rule, as regards music or any other branch of art, was not to be discussed or interfered with.

" During my thirty-six years' association with the Gilbert and Sullivan operas I have acted with thirty-six Josephines in ' Pinafore ' ; sung under thirteen conductors, including Sullivan himself and Alfred Cellier ; I have been cast with a dozen Jack Points, one of whom was George Thorne, who actually created some of what are known as ' The Grossmith ' parts. In witness whereof ' The Referee ' some years ago, in answer to a correspondent, said : ' Yes, George Grossmith was the original Jack Point, but George Thorne created the part.' A paradox only to be disentangled by those who knew George Thorne."

Such are Mr. Billington's interesting and instructive notes. But our old friend omits to mention a serio-comic incident which occurred to him in South Africa.

The story, as related to me by Mr. C. H. Workman, concerns an affair which occurred in Johannesburg, where, we have been informed, a pile of money was taken by the management.

Billington and Workman shared a dressing-room at the theatre, and were waited upon by the best and smartest dresser that had ever fallen to their lot. He was an Englishman, so they naturally trusted him. But their over-confidence proved costly to them. One " Treasury " night before leaving Johannesburg, when, at the end of the performance of " The Mikado," Koko and Pooh Bah returned to their room to disrobe, no dresser was to be found, nor were their purses, watches, and other valuables. Their estimable attendant had left without saying " Good-bye."

Billington, I am told, gave vent to his wrath in some of his choicest Yorkshire vernacular ; Workman was equally vehement in a minor key. However, as soon as they had resumed their ordinary twentieth-century attire, Billington observed, " Thank the Lord, Workie, we won't have to tip him this week."

François Cellier, who twice accompanied the D'Oyly Carte Company to South Africa, used to say that those trips were among the most pleasant events of his life.

Next in seniority to Fred Billington in the existing D'Oyly Carte Touring Company comes Henry Lytton, who made his first appearance in Gilbert and Sullivan's opera as a member of the Savoy Chorus in 1884. It was not until three years later that he was promoted from the ranks. His opportunity came when he was called upon, at a few hours' notice, to play Robin Oakapple in " Ruddigore "—the part vacated by George Grossmith a few nights after production. His success determined Mr. Carte to entrust him with the leading comedian's rôles on tour. Ten years later he was suddenly recalled to the Savoy, again to relieve Grossmith, who had resigned his part in Sir Alexander Mackenzie's opera, " His Majesty." From that time onward, with intervals, during which he fulfilled other engagements away from the Carte management, Lytton has appeared in all the Savoy revivals, and, when these came to an end, returned with the company to the provinces, where he has long been an established favourite. As a versatile actor his record is remarkable.

To mention only a few of Mr. Lytton's achievements. In " The Sorcerer " he has succeeded Barrington as the Vicar; in " H.M.S. Pinafore " he has played Captain Corcoran and Dick Deadeye; in " The Pirates of Penzance," the Major-General and the Pirate King; Grosvenor in " Patience "; Strephon in " Iolanthe "; in " The Mikado " he has appeared both in the title-rôle and as Ko-Ko; in " The Gondoliers," Giuseppe Palmieri, and also the Duke of Plaza Toro; and in " The Yeomen of the Guard " he has played, in turn, Wilfred Shadbolt and Jack Point.

This list, incomplete as it is, will suffice to show

Lytton's extraordinary aptitude to assume and successfully to portray characters of varying and very distinct type. It has been the bad fortune of this clever and hard-working comedian never to create a part in a Savoy opera. All the more is it to his credit that his name should have become eminent on the list of famous Savoyards.

Theatrical touring is not all pleasure, play, and picnic. Sometimes, indeed, it is as arduous and irksome as army campaigning. During the summer months when the company is visiting seaside places and holiday resorts, the members' lot is far from an unenviable one, but the reverse side of the picture is seen when the dark, chill days of winter return. Sunday after Sunday, no matter what the weather or the conditions of health or inclination, the actors and actresses are called upon to bustle off, bag and baggage, to continue their route to the next town. Often the journey across country is very long and tedious, such, for example, as that from Plymouth to Sheffield, or from Portsmouth to Edinburgh. But the arrangements made conjointly by the Acting-Manager and the railway companies for special train-service are so admirably regulated and timed that there is seldom any cause for complaint. There are, necessarily, occasions when the patience and endurance of the hardest campaigner is severely tried.

Let me recall one very exceptional adventure.

About five years ago, the D'Oyly Carte Company were snowed up for more than twelve hours whilst journeying from Dundee to Aberdeen. A fierce

MR. LEICESTER TUNKS.

Photo by Morrison, Edinburgh.

MISS BEATRICE BOARER.

blizzard was raging, and the poor girls of the company, who, on the evening before, had been basking as Contadine on " Venetia's sunny shore," had now to endure the rigours of an Arctic climate. The journey, under normal conditions, being comparatively a short one, few members of the company had provided themselves with so much as a bun or a biscuit for refreshment. Heaven only knows what would have become of them had not Providence, in the person of Mr. Leicester Tunks, one of the joint Kings of Barataria, come to the rescue. Fortunately, it so happened that it was Tunks' birthday, and to celebrate the anniversary he had invited several of his colleagues to sup with him on arrival at Aberdeen. Knowing that theatrical landladies are not always to be relied upon in emergency, he had taken the precaution to bring with him from Dundee a Gargantuan steak-and-kidney pie,·together with sundry confections for which the constituency of our Admiralty's First Lord is noted, and a bottle or two of the best Highland Blend, Bottled Bass, *et cetera*. Accordingly, the popular baritone's birthday party, which took place in the train at midnight, if not quite in keeping with the traditions of supper at the Savoy, was not to be despised by the most fastidious. Nobody was heard to grumble at the absence of knives and forks ; one and all forgot they were buried in a snowdrift, and everybody declared that Leicester Tunks deserved the Carnegie reward for noble service done in saving his fellow-travellers from starvation.

In no town visited by the D'Oyly Carte Opera

Company do they meet with a heartier welcome than in Oxford and Cambridge. The 'Varsity men, dark blues and light blues alike, rush in crowds to the theatre with excitement only less intense than that they show at their boat-race or cricket-match at Lords. In fact, if truth be told, their enthusiasm at those annual meetings is more veiled and circumspect than when they assemble to greet " The Mikado." They are splendid audiences to play to : dons, proctors or undergraduates, one and all alike listen intently throughout, and, appreciating every point of the opera, the elders mop their eye-glasses, dimmed with the breath of their delight, whilst the students roar their applause as only British youths can do. In Oxford and Cambridge the Gilbert and Sullivan operas not only are accepted as the highest type of theatrical entertainment, but have long been acknowledged as classics and honoured as such.

MISS LOUIE RENÉ.

Photo by Peterson's, Glasgow.

MISS CLARA DOW.

CHAPTER XXII

CONCERNING AMATEURS

Influence of the Gilbert and Sullivan operas upon amateur acting—
Establishment and growth of operatic and dramatic societies—
Business control and discipline puts an end to the old style of
" go-as-you-please "—A few tales about unprofessional players.

AMONG the many extraneous influences of the Gilbert
and Sullivan operas on all branches of society at
large, none is more remarkable than the impetus they
have given to amateur performances.

In days previous to the "Pinafore" period, the
amateur actor and actress were looked upon as quacks
and interlopers, and as such treated with sublime
contempt and ridicule by the profession. But all
is changed. Amateur societies have become a powerful adjunct and support to the culture of music and
the drama. They are now accepted as useful training-
schools for the legitimate stage, and from the volun-
teer ranks have sprung many present-day favourites.
Well-organized institutions exist in every part of the
country. Progressing from strength to strength, they
have grown so strong and independent that they
admit to their circle none but qualified aspirants to
stage honours. Advancing still further, some of the

leading operatic and dramatic clubs engage the services of London theatrical agencies to co-operate with them in forming the strongest available cast of principals for the drama or opera they select for performance. That this state of things is attributable in a very large measure to the popularity of, and the infectious craze for performing, the Gilbert and Sullivan operas can hardly be questioned. To establish this theory it is only necessary to study Douglas's Directory, a useful publication issued by the National Amateur and Dramatic Association, founded in February 1899. This admirably compiled booklet contains, among sundry other items of information, a complete list of performances given in all towns where *bonâ fide* Amateur Societies exist in affiliation with the National Association. From this it will be gathered how vastly the Savoy operas transcend all others in the number of performances given.

To Mr. Howard J. Hadley, the Honorary General Secretary of the Association, I am indebted for some convincing statistics. I cannot do better than quote from Mr. Hadley's letter :

" With the aid of Douglas's Directory (1914) I find there are about thirty-six Operatic Societies in London and district, of which about twenty would be playing Gilbert and Sullivan operas in any one year, giving an average of five performances for each society. This would amount to one hundred performances in the year.

" As to the provinces, there are about three hundred and twelve Operatic Societies, and of these about one hundred and seventy-three produce Gilbert and Sullivan operas, and, given an average of five performances, the total would be eight hundred and sixty-five performances : altogether, nine hundred and sixty-five in one year for the United Kingdom.

"With regard to our Association, of which I can speak with more certain knowledge, out of a total of one hundred and seventy-seven Operatic Societies, about seventy-six of these produce Gilbert and Sullivan operas and average five annual performances each, the total amounting to three hundred and eighty representations.

"The Birmingham Amateur Opera Society is, I think, one of the oldest in the kingdom, and has, between the years 1886 and 1914, given about one hundred and twenty performances of Gilbert and Sullivan operas, and the Worcester Amateur Operatic Society comes a good second. Formed in 1892, it has up to the present time (1914) given nearly eighty performances of the operas under the stage direction of one man, viz. Mr. Shelford Walsh (a Worcester man). This, I think, is a record.

"The chief beauty and the greatest attraction which these operas possess is that they are absolutely 'clean'; the quiet humour is abundant and inimitable, whilst the music has a lingering, lilting leaven about it which is absolutely delightful, and always makes one long for more. I think one's whole being feels the better after an evening with Gilbert and Sullivan opera. It is ever a most satisfying, exhilarating feast.

"A fact not unworthy to mention is that Societies affiliated to our Association have contributed to charities no less a sum than £54,000, and maintain many beds in local infirmaries. This alone may be said to justify their existence."

This rough statement, coming from unimpeachable authority, will astonish all who before were ignorant of the wonderful march made by the army of amateurs. That their advance continues whilst their ranks increase in strength, I have received further assurance from Mr. W. Sims-Bull, stage-manager of the Savoy during Mr. Workman's régime, who, by virtue of his experience and practical knowledge of the requirements of the Gilbert and Sullivan operas, is much sought after by Amateur Societies as Stage-coach and producer.

Mr. Bull relates how in the year 1882 his father applied to Mr. D'Oyly Carte for permission to perform " Iolanthe " in Cheltenham. Mr. Carte's reply was in the negative. The Savoy manager did not, at that time, feel justified in encouraging amateurs; he believed that their expenses could not possibly be covered by receipts, whilst, on his part, he was not in a position to forego or reduce the author's fee. Five years later, when the application was renewed and permission granted, " Iolanthe " was performed in the Winter Gardens, Cheltenham, and from the profits a substantial sum was handed over to a local charity.

Mr. Sims-Bull remarks how, everywhere, even in the small towns, amateurs have come to realize that strict discipline and business methods are indispensable at rehearsal, and that every part must be suitably cast. This marks a wide departure from the conditions existing not so very long ago.

Some of Sims-Bull's experiences with amateurs are very amusing. For instance, at a rehearsal of " Pinafore," the gentleman cast for Captain Corcoran conceived the brilliant idea of chasing Dick Dead-eye round the quarter-deck with a bladder at the end of a stick, after the fashion of a clown in pantomime ; the actor was quite sure it would get the laugh of the evening, but the manager assured him that the use of bladders on board " H.M.S. Pinafore " was contrary to the Gilbertian articles of war.   On another occasion a feeble-voiced tenor, whose opinion of himself was far superior to his artistic ability, objected to a stage-cloth because it destroyed the ring of his notes.

A young lady without the slightest pretensions to shine either as singer or actress was given the part of Elsie Maynard in " The Yeomen of the Guard," by virtue of her father being Mayor of the Borough ; whilst the part of Phoebe in the same opera was allotted to an elderly spinster who could afford to pay for the position, and insisted upon her skirt being made long enough to cover her ankles.

In " The Gondoliers," the lady impersonating Casilda had, a few months previously, entered the bonds of matrimony ; it was accordingly rather disconcerting when in singing the lines—

> " But, bless my heart, consider my position,
> I am the wife of one, that's very clear "—

the word " condition " was substituted for " position."

But slips of the tongue are not confined to amateurs. Miss Jessie Bond, for example, confesses to one strange *lapsus linguae.* It occurred in "Patience," where she had to speak the line—

"Retribution like a poisèd hawk came swooping down upon the Wrong-doer."

Instead of "poisèd hawk" Miss Bond said "hoisèd pawk." To some it may have suggested that Lady Angela's thoughts were in the clouds, intent on solving the problem "might pigs fly"!

Anecdotes relating to the eccentricities and conceits of the old school of amateurs might fill a bulky volume, but, finding how few pages remain before this present book must close, we may not further enlarge on the subject.

But, by the way, I must not omit to mention the fact that the best amateur performance of a Gilbert and Sullivan piece I ever witnessed was that of "The Mikado," given by the Dunedin (New Zealand) Operatic Society. The staging may not have been in strict conformity with the Savoy Prompt-book, still, there was nothing so irreverent as would have vexed the mind of the author had he been present. The refined acting of the principals, their clear enunciation, and the grouping of the Chorus showed that the Company had been carefully drilled by one who had become acquainted with Gilbertian traditions. But it was chiefly as singers that the New Zealand Amateurs shone. A better Chorus I have never heard. Listening to them for the first time, I was astounded by the volume of rich tone and the admirable phrasing; still more remarkable was it to note how nearly

Sullivan's *tempo* was observed throughout the performance. It may seem incredible that Gilbert and Sullivan should be so thoroughly understood and reverenced in that far-away Dominion; but New Zealand has been made well acquainted with the Savoy operas by the periodical visits of the travelling companies controlled by the late J. C. Williamson, who leased the Australasian rights in the pieces.

CHAPTER XXIII

BUT now to return to the Savoy. With the death of Sir Arthur Sullivan, closely followed by that of Mr. D'Oyly Carte, this volume might, not untimely, end. But there yet remain events and incidents connected with the story of the Savoy under the D'Oyly Carte management which may, without creating an anti-climax, form the subject of our concluding chapters. The last of the famous Triumvirate, Sir William Gilbert, yet lived and, although he had, since the production of " The Grand-duke," ceased to take an active interest in Savoy affairs, he was still at hand ready to assist in the supervision of the revivals of his pieces from time to time.

But the sole management of the Savoy now devolved upon Mrs. D'Oyly Carte, under whose responsibility " The Emerald Isle, or the Caves of Carrig-Cleena," was produced on Saturday, April 27th, 1901, with the following cast :

MR. RICHARD BARKER.

MR. W. SIMS BULL.

Photo by Ellis & Walery.

Savoy Stage Managers.

Characters

The Earl of Newtown, K.P. . . MR. JONES HEWSON
(*Lord Lieutenant of Ireland*)
Dr. Fiddle, D.D. . . . . . MR. R. ROUS
(*His Private Chaplain*)
Terence O'Brian . . . MR. ROBERT EVETT
(*A Young Rebel*)
Professor Bunn . . . MR. WALTER PASSMORE
(*Shakespearian Reciter, Character
Impersonator, etc.*)
Pat Murphy . . . . MR. HENRY A. LYTTON
(*A Fiddler*)
Black Dan . . . . . MR. W. H. LEON
Mickie O'Hara . . . . MR. C. EARLDON
(*Irish Peasants*)
Sergeant Pincher . . . . MR. R. CROMPTON
Private Perry . . . . MR. P. PINDER
(*H.M. 11th Regiment of Foot*)
The Countess of Newtown . MISS ROSINA BRANDRAM
Lady Rosie Pippin . . . MISS ISABEL JAY
(*Her Daughter*)
Molly O'Grady . . . MISS LOUIE POUNDS
(*A Peasant Girl*)
Susan . . . MISS BLANCHE GASTON-MURRAY
(*Lady Rosie's Maid*)
Nora . . . . . MISS LULU EVANS
Kathleen . . . . MISS AGNES FRASER
(*Peasant Girls*)

Irish Peasants and Soldiers of 11th Regiment of Foot
ACT I.—*Outside the Lord-Lieutenant's Country Residence*
ACT II.—*The Caves of Carrig-Cleena*
(W. HARFORD)
PERIOD.—*About a Hundred Years Ago*
*Produced under the Personal Direction of the Author, and under
the Stage-direction of* MR. R. BARKER.
Musical Director . . . MR. FRANÇOIS CELLIER
26

The libretto of "The Emerald Isle" was pronounced to be altogether worthy of the author of "The Rose of Persia." Captain Basil Hood had conceived an interesting story of Irish rural life, with its picturesque scenes of peasant bhoys and pretty colleens clad in the costumes of a century ago. In admirable contrast to these merry-hearted rustics of "the disthressful counthree" were introduced an aristocratic Lord-Lieutenant and his high-born wife, neither of whom ever discoursed in anything but Shakespearean blank verse. These magniloquent Vice-Royalties were escorted, wherever they went, by a gallant Devon Regiment in their curious uniforms of the Georgian period. A capital character-sketch of a sturdy Devonian was that of Sergeant Pincher, played to the life by Mr. Reginald Crompton, himself a native of the land of loveliness and clotted cream. The Sergeant's song and chorus, composed by Edward German and rendered in broad Devonshire dialect, was one of the hits of the piece. Basil Hood's lines may not appeal to all readers, but, coming, as I do, from the wild west-country parts, I feel impelled to quote stanzas so thoroughly characteristic of the land.

Now this be the song of the Devonshire men
  (With a bimble and a bumble and the best of 'em !)
And the maids they have left on the moor and the fen—
  There was Mary Hooper and Mary Cooper and Jane Tucker
  and Emily Snugg and Susan Wickens and Hepzibah Lugg
  and pretty Polly Potter and the rest of 'em !

The Sergeant he came a-recruiting one day
  (With a bimble and a bumble for the best of 'em !)

And the maids cried " Alack ! " when the men went away—
   There was Thomas Perry and Thomas Merry and Jan Hadley
   and Timothy Mudd and Harry Budgen and Oliver Rudd and
   Ebenezer Pincher and the rest of 'em !

So the men marched away in their bright scarlet coats,
Though they shouted " Hooray ! " they had lumps in their throats,
And the maids fell a-crying, as maids often do,
Saying, " Oh, will our lovers be faithful and true ? "

But some day they will march into Devon, and then
   (With a bimble and a bumble and the best of 'em !)
All the maids will be taking the names of the men—
   There'll be Mary Perry and Mary Merry and Jane Hadley and
   Emily Mudd and Susan Budgen and Hepzibah Rudd and
   pretty Polly Pincher and the rest of 'em !

The Sergeant he may come recruiting once more
   (With a bimble and a bumble for the best of 'em !)
There will always be Devonshire men for the war—
   There'll be young Tom Perry and young Tom Merry and young
   Hadley and little Tim Mudd and young Hal Budgen and a
   juvenile Rudd and a little Ebenezer and the rest of 'em !

From these brief notes it will easily be seen how far
the author showed his appreciation of the value of
contrasts in colour and characterization.

Whilst the sympathy of all Savoyards was, naturally,
with Basil Hood in the loss he had sustained through
the death of his gifted colleague so shortly after they
had begun successful collaboration, cause to con-
gratulate the author was forthcoming when it was
found with what masterly skill and taste Edward
German had completed the score left unfinished by
Sullivan. Distinct in their individual style as were

the two composers, Sullivan and German alike possessed
the strain of what we must call, for lack of a more
technically correct description, " motherland melody."
Thus, Hood's well-turned lyrics, both the graceful
and the humorous, were set to music by German in a
tone that blended as perfectly as could be expected
with the numbers composed before his death by Sir
Arthur Sullivan. Every lover of Sullivan will remember that "The Emerald Isle" contains the master's
swan-song :

> " ' Come away ' sighs the Fairy voice,
> · ' Come follow me to Carrig-Cleena !
> ' For there I make all aching hearts rejoice,
>   Come—come away.' "

Although thirteen years have passed since it was
heard at the Savoy, the refrain of that beautiful melody
must often haunt the ears and awaken a pathetic
memory in the mind of every one who listened to it.

I am here reminded of an incident which occurred
during the rehearsal of " The Emerald Isle." One
morning, whilst Mrs. D'Oyly Carte was surveying the
stage proceedings from the heights of the upper circle,
one of the ladies of the company, observing the figure
through the dim light of the auditorium, directed the
attention of the stage-manager, Richard Barker, to
what she supposed to be an intruder. Barker, who was
a bit of a wag in his way, glanced upward, and, mistaking his worthy manageress for one of the theatre
charwomen engaged on her duties, replied : " Never
mind her, my dear, she won't hurt—it's only the *Fairy*

Cleaner!" A moment later Mrs. Carte, from the front row of the circle, called down: "Mr. Barker, might I suggest that——" "Good heavens!" gasped the stage-manager, "it's the Missus!"

Shortly after the production of "The Emerald Isle," Mrs. D'Oyly Carte let the theatre to Mr. William Greet, who continued the run of the Hood-Sullivan-German opera with great success before sending the piece on tour with the full Savoy Company.

I happened to be again in Dublin during the visit of "The Emerald Isle" company. There was some doubt as to the kind of reception the opera would meet with at the hands of Irish play-goers. On the opening night, led by curiosity, I took up a position at the back of the pit of the Gaiety Theatre, and anxiously awaited events. Strange to relate, all the points which it was feared might touch the sensibilities of the Dublin people met with nothing but hearty applause. All went smoothly until the general dance, which occurs in the second act. Then, because it was supposed the jig-step was not quite correct, or that the girls lifted their heels too high, a torrent of boo-ing burst upon the house. A sympathetic Patrick standing immediately in front of me shouted out in a lusty voice: "Arrah nhow! Can't ye be aisy if on'y out of rishpect for the dead composer?" To which another voice responded: "Eh Sorr, an' an Oirishman too he was, so he was!" This appeal had a magic effect on the rowdies, and the performance continued without further disturbance.

Let the truth be told: there are no more devout

lovers of the Gilbert and Sullivan operas than the warm-hearted people of The Emerald Isle.   And sound critics they are, too !

Mr. William Greet, during his tenancy of the Savoy, produced, in succession to " The Emerald Isle," first, Hood and German's charming opera, " Merrie England," and, after that, another musical play of a lighter type, "The Princess of Kensington," by the same author and composer.

On resuming management in December 1906, Mrs. D'Oyly Carte began a series of Gilbert and Sullivan revivals under the personal stage-supervision of the author.   These revivals, which continued, with occasional intervals, up to March 1909, beyond proving the wonderful vitality of the operas, were uneventful; yet it may be interesting to record one or two memorable incidents that marked the period which was, alas! to bring to a close the active managerial régime of Mrs. D'Oyly Carte.   For instance, on Saturday, August 24th, 1907, which date ended a successful eight months' season, the management celebrated the occasion by providing a mixed *réchauffé* of tit-bits from the Savoy Repertory.   The entertainment, which took the form of a Wagnerian " Ring " performance, opened at 4 o'clock in the afternoon with Act I. of " The Yeomen of the Guard," followed by the second act of " The Gondoliers."   After an interval of an hour and a quarter, the amber curtains were withdrawn, to reveal the second act of " Patience " ; and then Mrs. Carte sprung an agreeable surprise upon the audience.

The evening's programme announced two items only—selections from "Patience" and "Iolanthe"; great, then, was the shout of applause when the familiar Overture to "The Mikado" was heard; greater still the rapture when a scene from the popular piece was interpolated. The promised revival of the Japanese opera had a short time previously been cancelled in deference to considerations of State Diplomacy, but now, the conditions being changed, the public were privileged to enjoy a dainty *bonne-bouche* from their favourite dish. It was a very happy thought of Mrs. D'Oyly Carte's, and was greatly appreciated by the audience.

A complete chronological list of the last Savoy Revivals, with the cast of each opera, will be found in an Appendix at the end of this book. It may be useful for reference. The success which attended those presumably final performances encourages the belief that an annual season of a Gilbert and Sullivan Répertoire in Central London would prove as re- munerative to the management as it would be accept- able, assuredly, to the thousands of metropolitan play-goers who at the present time are crying out in their hunger for another feast of their favourite fare.

In March 1909, Mr. C. H. Workman, having acquired from Mrs. D'Oyly Carte a short lease of the Savoy, entered upon the management of that theatre. The clever comedian had made a host of friends and admirers by his triumphs in the "Grossmith" parts. Of his Jack Point it is worthy to note that Sir William

Gibert, in a public speech, expressed his opinion in the following complimentary terms :

" In Mr. Workman we have a Jack Point of the finest and most delicate finish, and I feel sure that no one will more readily acknowledge the triumph he has achieved in their old parts than his distinguished protagonist, Mr. George Grossmith, and his immediate predecessor, Mr. Passmore."

Under such auspices, and with such credentials, there seemed every reason to hope that success might reward Workman's plucky venture. At the same time, remembering Mr. D'Oyly Carte's experience at the Savoy away from Gilbert and Sullivan, one needed great faith to venture the prediction that Mr. Workman, or even a more experienced manager, would overcome the prejudice that existed against the production at the Savoy of any operas other than those of the famous Savoyards. Unhappily, such doubts and fears proved to have been only too well founded. The most notable event connected with Workman's period of management was the production of Sir William Gilbert's last opera, called ".Fallen Fairies." Pitiful it is to record the fact that, although Gilbert's libretto was rich in his own quaint humour and poetic fancy, and Edward German's music as charming as it always was and ever must be, the " Fallen Fairies " failed to enchant play-goers, and thus brought Workman's reign to an untimely end.

After reflecting on misfortune, it is always good to try to scare away the ghost of vain regrets with the

recital of a humorous story; and "Workie," as his
familiars call him, possesses a goodly stock of funny
tales quite apart from those of "Fallen Fairies." Here
is one I am permitted to repeat. It was during a
rehearsal of "The Yeomen," the situation occurring
when poor Jack Point, in a gay and frivolous mood
for the moment, is found with his arms around the
necks of Elsie and Phoebe and striving to kiss each
girl in turn. Gilbert suggested that the comedian
was rather overdoing the caressing business; whereupon Workman respectfully remarked: "Ah! yes, I
see, Sir William. You would not kiss them more than
once?" "Oh! indeed I would," was Gilbert's
prompt retort, "but perhaps, from the public point
of view, one kiss might be enough for *you* to give."

On May 29th, 1911, all London was shocked by
the appearance of news-placards announcing the
"Sudden death of Sir William Gilbert." Within an
hour the tragic tidings had spread to the most dis-
tant British Colonies. Sir William, it was said, on
reaching his home in Harrow Weald, fagged out by
an arduous day in town, sought in his wonted way to
refresh his limbs with an open-air bath in the lake
within the grounds of Grim's Dyke. Whilst swimming
he was stricken with heart-failure. Promptly rescued
from the water, he was carried to his room, but life
was extinct. The last of the renowned Triumvirate
had passed away, following his old colleague to the
Land beyond Life's border.

CHAPTER XXIV

SIR WILLIAM GILBERT

It may not be very generally known how Sir William Gilbert became a hero at the early age of four. For the story of the tiny boy's exciting adventure the present writer is indebted to Miss Edith A. Browne's clever character-study of Gilbert.

During a visit to Naples with his parents the child, whilst out for a morning's ramble with his nurse, was captured by brigands, who restored him in exchange for a "pony." One may readily surmise that, had our Savoy author fallen into the hands of banditti some forty or fifty years later, the price of his ransom would have been increased to a very large number of "monkeys."

I have never heard it suggested that it was upon the Naples romance that Gilbert based his story of "The Pirates of Penzance," but it is not unlikely that, whilst engaged in framing the character of Ruth, the piratical maid of all work, the author's thoughts reverted to his old nurse, who was so weak and simple-minded as to believe the plausible tale of the two nice Neapolitan gentlemen who told her that they had been requested by the boy's father to fetch him.

Almost as soon as Gilbert had learnt to write he began scribbling rhymes, but from his parents he re-

Photo by Dover Street Studios.

SIR WILLIAM GILBERT COMING FROM REHEARSAL.
" Perhaps his brain is addled, and it's very melancholy."—*Iolanthe.*

ceived no encouragement. His father, at one time a "middie" in the Indian Navy, was himself the author of one or two works that failed to attract the public. Probably on that account he had no faith in his son's literary ability. At the same time it was his intention to send the youth to Oxford, but the outbreak of the Crimean War upset such plans, and led to Mr. W. S. Gilbert being appointed to a clerkship in the Privy Council Office. Gilbert did not take kindly to his clerical work, and afterwards declared that his appointment was the worst bargain the Civil Service Commissioners ever made. On the strength of a legacy he was enabled to enter the Bar, but his restless spirit would not be curbed sufficiently to allow him to shine in the dull grey firmament of the law. And so, finding himself all but a briefless barrister—such an one as he describes in "Trial by Jury"—he soon threw off his wig and gown, and, instead of marrying " a rich attorney's elderly ugly daughter," he took to journalism, and wrote the "Bab Ballads," which later inspired him to write opera libretti. Such is the brief epitome of Sir William Gilbert's life, before the day when he met Arthur Sullivan.

My first personal introduction to Gilbert dates back to the year 1874. It took place whilst travelling homewards one night on the Underground Railway from Charing Cross to Kensington. I had been spending the evening at the old Prince of Wales's Theatre, enjoying once again the exquisite performance of Marie Wilton and Mr. S. B. Bancroft (as they were then named on the playbills) in Gilbert's charming dramatic sketch

"Sweethearts." Naturally we talked "shop," and more particularly about "Sweethearts."

Although I cannot boast the close intimacy with Gilbert that it was my privilege to enjoy with Sir Arthur Sullivan, at this moment, after spending so many pleasant days, as they seem to have been, in his companionship whilst engaged on this little history, I cannot bring my personal reminiscences to a close without alluding to the genial manner in which he always greeted me, and the kind words of encouragement he tendered after witnessing some of my small dramatic essays. "Praise from Sir Hubert Stanley is praise indeed," and a complimentary word from Sir William Gilbert was to be proudly welcomed and fondly cherished by the humblest of neophytes.

A notable instance of Gilbert's kindness is related by the well-known actor-manager, Mr. Edward Compton, who confesses his indebtedness to Sir William for his first London appearance in particularly auspicious circumstances. The occasion was the benefit performance given at Drury Lane Theatre in March 1877 in aid of a Testimonial Fund to the veteran comedian, Mr. Compton. The part of Evelyn in "Money" was to have been played by Henry Irving, but that distinguished actor being unable to appear, at Gilbert's suggestion the committee entrusted the important rôle to the beneficiaire's son, young Edward Compton, who had but recently joined the profession. In the cast were such notabilities as Marie Wilton, Madge Robertson, Ellen Terry, Hare, Kendal, Bancroft, Benjamin Webster, William Farren and David James.

Grim's Dyke.
Harrow Weald.

19 Nov. 1903

Dear Cellier

Many thanks for
your good wishes. Personally
I'm rather sick of birthdays —
I've had so many of
them.

A Gilbert is of no use
without a Sullivan — + I
can't find one!

Kindly yours

W S Gilbert.

FACSIMILE LETTER FROM SIR WILLIAM GILBERT TO FRANÇOIS CELLIER.

412]

Such a send-off seldom falls to the lot of a budding actor. It was accordingly a feather in his cap when Edward Compton scored a great success, and he has not forgotten to be grateful to Sir William Gilbert for the opportunity thus afforded him of displaying the talents inherited from his father.

It would require a book as bulky as this present volume to contain the numberless humorous anecdotes told of the Savoy author. Many of his *bons mots*, apart from those which have appeared in print, have become " as familiar as household words," but what the world at large knows least about concerning Sir William Gilbert is that beneath his autocratic, self-willed, Caesarean attitude which sometimes gave offence, there beat a kindly, sympathetic heart, ever responsive to the cry of distress or an appeal from those in need. If all his generous acts might be recorded yet another volume would be needed to hold them ; but this Sir William would have set his face against, for he " liked to do kind deeds by stealth," and felt very angry if they were ever found out.

All Savoyards were much gratified to learn the tidings of Gilbert's knighthood, which honour was conferred upon him by King Edward VII on July 15, 1907.

Sir William Gilbert's funeral was unaccompanied by pomp and circumstance. By his own request his body was cremated, and the casket containing his ashes was borne to the grave in the picturesque churchyard at Stanmore by his friends Mr. Rowland Brown and Mr. Herbert Sullivan, nephew to Sir Arthur, amidst a vast assembly of notabilities in the world of art.

...e Savoy
...ntion to seek
...chly earned. To
...possibility. To stop
...top living. The greatest
...e at her desk trying to solve
...s which came before her from
...o, notwithstanding failing health,
... spirit of indomitable energy that
...her, Mrs. Carte continued to give un-
...ion to the minutest details of business
...ith her Touring Company and other mat-
...ich she was personally concerned. Nothing
...aunt her courage. To the advice and appeals of
...nearest and dearest to her, who watched with
...iety the gradual decline of her physical strength,
...he would not listen : her hand found work to do, and
...she must do it with all the might she yet retained.
Mrs. Carte's mind was too large, too strong for the
frail body that possessed it. Thus, month after month,
year succeeding year, the brave woman struggled
patiently against the evil that was draining the life-
blood from her veins. Rallying from illness again and

falls to the lot of a budding

a feather in his cap when

reat success, and he has

Sir William Gilbert for

of displaying the

this present

anecdotes

mots,

have

hat

Photo by Ellis & Walery.

MRS. R. D'OYLY CARTE.

CHAPTER XXV

TRIBUTE TO MRS. D'OYLY CARTE

ON retiring from the active management of the Savoy in 1909, it was far from Mrs. Carte's intention to seek the rest and ease which she had so richly earned. To her nature idleness was an impossibility. To stop working would have been to stop living. The greatest pleasure of her life was to be at her desk trying to solve the innumerable problems which came before her from hour to hour. And so, notwithstanding failing health, maintained by the spirit of indomitable energy that had never failed her, Mrs. Carte continued to give unrelaxed attention to the minutest details of business connected with her Touring Company and other matters in which she was personally concerned. Nothing could daunt her courage. To the advice and appeals of those nearest and dearest to her, who watched with anxiety the gradual decline of her physical strength, she would not listen : her hand found work to do, and she must do it with all the might she yet retained. Mrs. Carte's mind was too large, too strong for the frail body that possessed it. Thus, month after month, year succeeding year, the brave woman struggled patiently against the evil that was draining the life-blood from her veins. Rallying from illness again and

Photo by Ellis & Walery.

MRS. R. D'OYLY CARTE.

CHAPTER XXV

TRIBUTE TO MRS. D'OYLY CARTE

On retiring from the active management of the Savoy in 1909, it was far from Mrs. Carte's intention to seek the rest and ease which she had so richly earned. To her nature idleness was an impossibility. To stop working would have been to stop living. The greatest pleasure of her life was to be at her desk trying to solve the innumerable problems which came before her from hour to hour. And so, notwithstanding failing health, maintained by the spirit of indomitable energy that had never failed her, Mrs. Carte continued to give unrelaxed attention to the minutest details of business connected with her Touring Company and other matters in which she was personally concerned. Nothing could daunt her courage. To the advice and appeals of those nearest and dearest to her, who watched with anxiety the gradual decline of her physical strength, she would not listen : her hand found work to do, and she must do it with all the might she yet retained. Mrs. Carte's mind was too large, too strong for the frail body that possessed it. Thus, month after month, year succeeding year, the brave woman struggled patiently against the evil that was draining the life-blood from her veins. Rallying from illness again and

Photo by Ellis & Walery.

MRS. R. D'OYLY CARTE.

CHAPTER XXV

ON retiring from the active management of the Savoy in 1909, it was far from Mrs. Carte's intention to seek the rest and ease which she had so richly earned. To her nature idleness was an impossibility. To stop working would have been to stop living. The greatest pleasure of her life was to be at her desk trying to solve the innumerable problems which came before her from hour to hour. And so, notwithstanding failing health, maintained by the spirit of indomitable energy that had never failed her, Mrs. Carte continued to give unrelaxed attention to the minutest details of business connected with her Touring Company and other matters in which she was personally concerned. Nothing could daunt her courage. To the advice and appeals of those nearest and dearest to her, who watched with anxiety the gradual decline of her physical strength, she would not listen : her hand found work to do, and she must do it with all the might she yet retained. Mrs. Carte's mind was too large, too strong for the frail body that possessed it. Thus, month after month, year succeeding year, the brave woman struggled patiently against the evil that was draining the life-blood from her veins. Rallying from illness again and

414

Photo by Ellis & Walery.

MRS. R. D'OYLY CARTE.

CHAPTER XXV

On retiring from the active management of the Savoy in 1909, it was far from Mrs. Carte's intention to seek the rest and ease which she had so richly earned. To her nature idleness was an impossibility. To stop working would have been to stop living. The greatest pleasure of her life was to be at her desk trying to solve the innumerable problems which came before her from hour to hour. And so, notwithstanding failing health, maintained by the spirit of indomitable energy that had never failed her, Mrs. Carte continued to give unrelaxed attention to the minutest details of business connected with her Touring Company and other matters in which she was personally concerned. Nothing could daunt her courage. To the advice and appeals of those nearest and dearest to her, who watched with anxiety the gradual decline of her physical strength, she would not listen : her hand found work to do, and she must do it with all the might she yet retained. Mrs. Carte's mind was too large, too strong for the frail body that possessed it. Thus, month after month, year succeeding year, the brave woman struggled patiently against the evil that was draining the life-blood from her veins. Rallying from illness again and

Photo by Ellis & Walery.

MRS. R. D'OYLY CARTE.

again, she would creep back to her desk to deal with some business minutes which having, necessarily, been neglected during an interval of pain, had been worrying her sensitive mind. Of death she had no fear; her one desire seemed to be to leave nothing undone which she might yet do. If it might be she would die in harness. But the unequal fight was soon to end. After lingering for a long while on the borderland between life and death, Mrs. Carte, or more correctly at this point to call her by the name which became hers by a second marriage in 1902, Mrs. Stanley Carr Boulter, passed away on Monday, May 5th, 1913.

In the introductory chapter of this book Mrs. D'Oyly Carte was rightly described as the *Dea ex machina* of the Savoy, and more than once in the course of our Reminiscences passing allusion has been made to the silent part played in the Gilbert and Sullivan operas by one of the most gifted of women. But only those who enjoyed the personal acquaintance of Mrs. Carte can estimate her true worth. To her marvellous talent of organization was mainly due the success that attended not only the Savoy Theatre but several other ventures, notably the Savoy Hotel, in the building and establishment of which she was largely concerned. In the direction of all matters Mrs. Carte's initiatory judgment always held precedence, her advice and suggestions were invariably adopted. Seldom, if indeed ever, was a woman found to possess such a thorough knowledge of the principles of sound finance, with absolute mastery of details either with respect to the intricate figures of a financial statement or the most subtle and involved clauses of a legal document.

But Mrs. Carte was not only a woman of business: she possessed artistic taste of the highest order, and was a good judge of the capabilities of those who sought professional engagements at the Savoy. Her benevolence was widely known, but its extent can never be told. Her liberality was, at all times, governed by good judgment, but from " the low prayer and plaint of want " she never turned away her ear.

King Edward VII bestowed upon Mrs. D'Oyly Carte the Order of Mercy ; but, greatly prizing as she did the royal honour, to her kind heart it must have been a greater pride to feel how she had won the esteem and love of a multitude of men and women who, professionally engaged at the Savoy, had experienced at her hands true acts of friendship, sympathy, and encouragement to brighten their days of toil and anxiety.

As a tribute to the memory of Mrs. D'Oyly Carte, let me be permitted to quote the words of her old friend and colleague, Mr. George Edwardes, thus : " A more wonderful woman it was never my lot to know.   It was my privilege to work with Miss Helen Lenoir under Mr. Carte for a considerable time, and I never ceased to marvel at her great energy and inexhaustible activity. *The whole fabric of the Savoy truly rested upon her.*"

Mrs. Carte was greatly distressed as one after another of many faithful servants and coadjutors of long years' standing was taken from her side by death.   Of those who survived her at the Savoy, the chief were François

MR. G. A. RICHARDSON.

Photo by Eckhardt, Clapham.

MR. W. BECKWITH.

Cellier and George A. Richardson. The first has since passed away, the other still continues in his secretarial post at the Savoy, where also a few humbler servants of many years remain to speak in grateful words their praise of the good mistress whose loss they so deeply lament.

I have recently chanced to read an article which appeared in the *Sketch* shortly after the death of Mrs. D'Oyly Carte ; thinking that it may be of special interest to American lovers of the Gilbert and Sullivan operas, and that they may be pleased to be reminded of the woman to whom they were in no small measure indebted for the organization of the performances in the United States, I venture to borrow the following paragraph from its pages :

" Miss Helen Lenoir (now Mrs. D'Oyly Carte) was the indefatigable head of the Carte Bureau in Broadway, hard by the Standard Theatre, where most of the Gilbert-Sullivan operas were produced, Charlie Harris being the clever stage-manager. When it is stated that Mr. Carte not only sent out the entire company from England, as well as all the dresses, the scenery alone being painted from models in New York, it may readily be imagined what immense labour was placed upon Miss Lenoir. Of course she was in constant cable communication with London, for singers are ' kittle cattle,' and often by sheer tact she saved the situation when things looked hopeless. It cannot be said that the Carte invasion was looked upon with favour by the native managers, but they were quite cute enough to

27

perceive that the public appreciated the carefully produced works from England better than their own slipshod affairs. And then they began to amend their ways, and have now turned the tables on us. They owe a deep debt of gratitude to Mr. and Mrs. D'Oyly Carte for showing them the right path in which to tread. And they have trod it with great and increasing profit."

   •   •   •   •   •

But now, in conclusion, let me confess that this, the final chapter of our book of reminiscences, has been the most difficult one of all to write. I have wanted to say so much, and, for lack of space, have been compelled to say so little, and that all so unworthily of my greatly esteemed friend Mrs. Carte. At the same time, as I have recently been reminded by Mr. Stanley Boulter when I ventured to suggest how greatly his gifted wife's biography would be prized by the public, Mrs. Carte—as we must still, for custom's sake, call her—was of such an extremely modest and unostentatious disposition that she was always averse to being publicly spoken of or written about. Yet, it may be asked, what volume touching the Savoy could be considered complete that did not contain some personal reference to one who was the " be all " and " end all " of the institution ?

I would add that the same sense of self-dissatisfaction as that expressed regarding this chapter vexes my mind with regard to the present volume from beginning to end. I am conscious of having left unsaid many things that might, with advantage, have been said on a subject so inexhaustible as the Savoy and the

Savoyards. Better, perhaps, to have erred thus, than to have written anything that might, with better judgment and wisdom, have remained unwritten. I have no vain excuse to offer for my shortcomings, but in mitigation of sentence may I not plead for the indulgent sympathy of my readers in the loss I was called upon to sustain by the untimely death of my old friend and collaborator, François Cellier?

CONCLUSION

A few weeks ago, in the " Princess Ida " room of the Savoy Hotel, it became my happy fortune to join a reunion of a few survivors of the Old Brigade of the D'Oyly Carte Army Corps.   With three of the number I made acquaintance at the Opera Comique in 1878 when " H.M.S. Pinafore " was launched.   These were Miss Jessie Bond, the original Hebe, Miss Julia Gwynne, one of the brightest of the bevy of sisters, cousins, and aunts, and Mr. (now Sir George) Power who created the part of Ralph Rackstraw.   The fourth of the party of Victorian Savoyards was Miss Leonora Braham, who joined the company in 1881, to win fame in the title-rôle of " Patience."

Over luncheon we cheerily chatted of those days of long ago when we were all young people, and now I, a veteran camp-follower, could not but observe that the four merry-hearted survivors had, one and all, borne the burthen of years as wondrously as had those Gilbert and Sullivan operas at whose christening they had stood sponsors just a third of a century ago.   During our repast it was suggested that, as a final illustration of this present book, nothing might be more appropriate than a picture of the survivors at the base of

Photo by The Record Press.

the statue to Sir Arthur Sullivan, upon which we gazed down from the windows of the hotel. Accordingly, a photographer having been requisitioned, the party adjourned to the Victoria Embankment and were straightway snapshotted. Here, by the way, to avoid any possible misconception, it may be advisable to point out that the central figure of the group—that immediately beneath the bust of Sullivan—does *not* represent one of the survivors; it is, in fact, the symbolic form of "Grief" modelled in bronze; and so, fair lady-readers, pray spare your blushes.

A courteous, full-bodied sergeant of police who kept the space clear for the artist, was greatly interested in the operations. "Lor, bless you, sir," said he, ". don't I remember all those plays—partic'lar that one where some of my profession had to tackle those Pirates of Penzance, I think they called themselves? —and they were real life-like constables, they were, sir. Opera Comic?—No, sir, I hadn't joined the force in those days; 'twas later on, at the Savoy Theatre over there, sir, that I saw them, when Mr. Passmore took *my* part—meaning the Sergeant's, sir—and I couldn't a'done it better myself, and, believe me, sir, the truest words I ever heard spoke on the stage was, ' A p'liceman's lot is not a 'appy one.' I sometimes sing that song to my missus when she ain't feeling very well. Thank you, sir, I hope the picture'll come out all right. Good afternoon, ladies! Good day, sir!"

It was much to be regretted that neither Barrington nor Passmore was present to acknowledge the sergeant's compliments.

THE SORCERER

	Opera Comique. Nov. 17, 1877.	Savoy, Oct. 11, 1884.	Savoy, Sept. 22, 1898.
Sir Marmaduke Pointdextre	Mr. Richard Temple	Mr. R. Temple	Mr. Jones Hewson
Alexis	" Bentham	" Durward Lely	" R. Evett
Dr. Daly	" Rutland Barrington	" R. Barrington	" H. A. Lytton
Notary	" Fred. Clifton	" Lugg	" Leonard Russell
John Wellington Wells	" Geo. Grossmith	" Geo. Grossmith	" W. Passmore
Lady Sangazure	Mrs. Howard Paul	Miss Rosina Brandram	Miss Rosina Brandram
Aline	Miss Alice May	" Leonora Braham	" Ruth Vincent
Mrs. Partlet	" Everard	" Ada Doree	" Ethel McAlpine
Constance	" Giulia Warwick	" Jessie Bond	" Emmie Owen

H.M.S. PINAFORE

	Opera Comique. May 25, 1878.	Savoy, Nov. 12, 1887.	Savoy, June 6, 1889.	Savoy, July 14, 1908.
The Rt. Hon. Sir Joseph Porter, K.C.B.	Mr. Geo Grossmith	Mr. Geo. Grossmith	Mr. W. Passmore	Mr. C. H. Workman
Captain Corcoran	" R. Barrington	" R. Barrington	" H. A. Lytton	" R. Barrington
Ralph Rackstraw	" Geo. Power	" J. G. Robertson	" Robert Evett	" H. Herbert
Dick Deadeye	" R. Temple	" R. Temple	" R. Temple	" H. Lytton
Bill Bobstay	" F. Clifton	" R. Cummings	" W. H. Leon	" Leicester Tunks
Bob Beckett	" Dymott	" R. Lewis	" Powis Pinder	
Josephine	Miss Emma Howson	Miss Geraldine Ulmar	Miss Ruth Vincent	Miss Elsie Spain
Hebe	" Jessie Bond	" Jessie Bond	" Emmie Owen	" Jessie Rose
Little Buttercup	" Everard	" Rosina Brandram	" Rosina Brandram	" Louie René

PIRATES OF PENZANCE

	Opera Comique. April 3, 1880.	Savoy. Mar. 17, 1888.	Savoy. June 30, 1900.	Savoy. Dec. 1, 1909.
Major-General Stanley	Mr. Geo. Grossmith	Mr. Geo. Grossmith	Mr. H. A. Lytton	Mr. C. H. Workman
Pirate King	" R. Temple	" R. Temple	" Jones Hewson	" H. A. Lytton
Samuel	" G. Temple	" R. Cummings	" H. W. Leon	" Leo Sheffield
Frederic	" Geo. Power	" J. G. Robertson	" Robert Evett	" H. Herbert
Sergeant of Police	" R. Barrington	" R. Barrington	" Walter Passmore	" R. Barrington
Mabel	Miss Marion Hood	Miss Geraldine Ulmar	Miss Isabel Jay	Miss Dorothy Court
Edith	" Julia Gwynne	" Jessie Bond	" Lulu Evans	" Jessie Rose
Kate	" Lillian La Rue	" Kavanagh	" Alice Coleman	" Beatrice Boarer
Isabel	" Neva Bond	" Lawrence	" Agnes Fraser	" Ethel Lewis
Ruth	" Emily Cross	" Rosina Brandram	" Rosina Brandram	" Louie Rene

PATIENCE

	Opera Comique. April 23, 1881.	Savoy. Nov. 7, 1900.	Savoy. 1907.
Colonel Calverley	Mr. R. Temple	Mr. Jones Hewson	Mr. Frank Wilson
Major Murgatroyd	" Frank Thornton	" W. H. Leon	" Richard Andean
Duke of Dunstable	" Durward Lely	" R. Evett	" Harold Wylde
Reginald Bunthorne	" Geo. Grossmith	" W. Passmore	" C. H. Workman
Archibald Grosvenor	" R. Barrington	" H. A. Lytton	" John Clulow
Bunthorne's Solicitor	" G. Bowley	" H. C. Pritchard	
Lady Angela	Miss Jessie Bond	Miss Blanche Gaston Murray	Miss Jessie Rose
Lady Saphir	" Julia Gwynne	" Lulu Evans	" Marie Wilson
Lady Ella	" M. Fortescue	" Agnes Fraser	" Ruby Gray
Lady Jane	" Alice Barnett	" Rosina Brandram	" Louie Rene
Patience	" Leonora Braham	" Isabel Jay	" Clara Dow

IOLANTHE

	Nov. 25, 1882.	Dec. 7, 1901.	June 14, 1907.	Oct. 14, 1908.
Lord Chancellor	Mr. Geo. Grossmith	Mr. W. Passmore	Mr. C. H. Workman	Mr. C. H. Workman
Earl of Mountararat	" R. Barrington	" Powis Pinder	" Leicester Tunks	" Frank Wilson
Earl of Tolloller	" Durward Lely	" R. Evett	" H. Herbert	" Harold Wylde
Private Willis	" Charles Manners	" R. Crompton	" Leo Sheffield	" Overton Moyse
Strephon	" R. Temple	" H. A. Lytton	" H. A. Lytton	" H. A. Lytton
Queen of Fairies	Miss Alice Barnett	Miss Rosina Brandram	Miss Louie Rene	Miss Louie Rene
Iolanthe	" Jessie Bond	" Louie Pounds	" Jessie Rose	" Jessie Rose
Celia	" M. Fortescue	" Agnes Fraser	" Dorothy Court	" Violet Lander
Leila	" Julia Gwynne	" Isabel Agnew	" Beatrice Boarer	" Beatrice Meredith
Fleta	" Sybil Grey	" Hart Dyke	" Ethel Lewis	" Violet Frampton
Phyllis	" Leonora Braham	" Isabel Jay	" Clara Dow	" Clara Dow

427

PRINCESS IDA

	Jan. 5, 1884.
King Hildebrand	Mr. Rutland Barrington
Hilarion	" Henry Bracey
Cyril	" Durward Lely
Florian	" Charles Ryley
King Gama	" Geo. Grossmith
Arac	" R. Temple
Guron	" Warwick Gray
Scynthius	" Lugg
Princess Ida	Miss Leonora Braham
Lady Blanche	" Rosina Brandram
Lady Psyche	" Kate Chard
Melissa	" Jessie Bond
Saccharissa	" Sybil Grey
Chloe	" Heathcote
Ada	" Lilian Carr

THE MIKADO

	Mar. 14, 1885.	June 7, 1885.	July 11, 1896.	April 28, 1908.
The Mikado	Mr. Richard Temple	Mr. R. Temple	Mr. Scott Fischer	Mr. H. A. Lytton
Nanki Poo	,, Durward Lely	,, J. G. Robertson	,, Chas. Kenningham	,, Stafford Moss
Koko	,, Geo. Grossmith	,, Geo. Grossmith	,, Walter Passmore	,, C. H. Workman
Pooh-Bah	,, Rutland Barrington	,, R. Barrington	,, R. Barrington	,, R. Barrington
Go To	,, R. Cummings	,, R. Lewis	—	,, F. Drawater
Pish Tush	,, F. Bovill	,, R. Cummings	,, Jones Hewson	,, Leicester Tunks
Yum Yum	Miss Leonora Braham	Miss Geraldine Ulmar	Miss Florence Perry	Miss Clara Dow
Pitti Sing	,, Jessie Bond	,, Jessie Bond	,, Jessie Bond	,, Jessie Rose
Peep Bo	,, Sybil Grey	,, Sybil Grey	,, Emmie Owen	,, B. Boarer
Katisha	,, Rosina Brandram	,, Rosina Brandram	,, Rosina Brandram	,, Louie Rene

RUDDIGORE

	Jan. 22, 1887.			Jan. 22, 1887.
Robin Oakapple	Mr. George Grossmith	Rose Maybud		Miss Leonora Braham
Richard Dauntless	,, Durward Lely	Mad Margaret		,, Jessie Bond
Sir Roderic Murgatroyd	,, Richard Temple	Dame Hannah		,, Rosina Brandram
Sir Despard Murgatroyd	,, Rutland Barrington	Zorah		,, Josephine Findlay
Old Adam Goodheart	,, Rudolph Lewis	Ruth		,, Lindsay

THE YEOMEN OF THE GUARD

Character	Oct. 3, 1888.	May 5, 1897.	Dec. 8, 1906.	Mar. 1, 1909.
Sir Richard Cholmondeley	Mr. Wallace Brownlow	Mr. Jones Hewson	Mr. A. Johnstone	Mr. Leo Sheffield
Colonel Fairfax	" Courtice Pounds	" C. Kenningham	" Pacie Ripple	" H. Herbert
Sergeant Meryll	" Richard Temple	" R. Temple	" Overton Moyle	" R. Temple
Leonard Meryll	" W. R. Shirley	" Scott Russell	" Henry Burnard	" Lawrence Legge
Jack Point	" Geo. Grossmith	" W. Passmore	" C. H. Workman	" C. H. Workman
Wilfred Shadbolt	" W. H. Denny	" H. A. Lytton	" J. Clulow	" R. Barrington
Elsie Maynard	Miss Geraldine Ulmar	Miss Ilka von Palmay	Miss Lilian Coomber	Miss Elsie Spain
Phoebe Meryll	" Jessie Bond	" Florence Perry	" Jessie Rose	" Jessie Rose
Dame Carruthers	" Rosina Brandram	" Rosina Brandram	" Louie Rene	" Louie Rene
Kate	" Rose Hervey	" Ruth Vincent	" Marie Wilson	" B. Boarr

THE GONDOLIERS

Character	Dec. 7, 1889.	Mar. 22, 1898.	July 18, 1898.	Jan. 24, 1907.	Jan. 18, 1909.
Duke of Plaza Toro	Mr. Frank Wyatt	Mr. W. Elton	Mr. W. Elton	Mr. C. H. Workman	Mr. C. H. Workman
Luis	" Wallace Brownlow	" Jones Hewson	" Jones Hewson	" A. Johnstone	" Leo Sheffield
Don Alhambra Del Bolero	" W. H. Denny	" Walter Passmore	" W. Passmore	" J. Clulow	
Marco Palmieri	" Courtice Pounds	" C. Kenningham	" R. Evett	" Pacie Ripple	" R. Barrington
Giuseppe Palmieri	" Rutland Barrington	" H. A. Lytton	" H. A. Lytton	" Richard Green	" H. Herbert
Duchess of Plaza Toro	Miss Rosina Brandram	Miss Rosina Brandram	Miss R. Brandram	Miss Louie Rene	Miss Louie Rene
Casilda	" Decima Moore	" Ruth Vincent	" Ruth Vincent	" Marie Wilson	" Blair Spain
Gianetta	" Geraldine Ulmar	" Emmie Owen	" Emmie Owen	" Lilian Coomber	" Jessie Rose
Tessa	" Jessie Bond	" Louie Henri	" B. Gaston Murray	" Jessie Rose	" Ethel Lewis
Fiametta	" Lawrence	" Ethel Jackson	" Ethel Jackson	" ——	" B. Boarr
Vittoria	" Cole	" Jessie Rose	" Mildred Baker	" ——	" Adrienne Andrean
Giulia	" Phyllis	" Margaret Moyse	" Margaret Moyse	" ——	" Amy Royton
Ines	" Bernard	" Jessie Pounds	" Jessie Pounds		

THE NAUTCH GIRL

June 30, 1891.

Punka	Mr. Rutland Barrington
Indra	„ Courtice Pounds
Pygama	„ Frank Thornton
Bahoo Curree	„ F. Wyatt
Bumbo	„ W. H. Denny
Chinna Louis	Miss Jessie Bond
Sullie	„ Saumarez
Cheetah	„ Laurence
Hollie Beebee	„ L. Snyder
Bonyan	„ Louise Rowe
Kaka	„ Annie Cole
Tippera	„ Cora Tinnie

THE VICAR OF BRAY

Jan. 28, 1892.

Rev. William Barlow	Mr. Rutland Barrington
Rev. Henry Sandford	„ Courtice Pounds
Thomas Merton, Esq.	„ Richard Green
Mr. Bedford Rowe	„ W. H. Denny
John Dory	„ W. S. Laidlaw
Peter Piper	„ Bowden Haswell
Samuel Spicer	„ F. Barrett
First Huntsman	„ J. Wilbraham
Second Huntsman	„ Rudolph Lewis
Mrs. Merton	Miss Rosina Brandram
Nelly Bly	„ Mary Duggan
Cynthia	„ Louise Rowe
Agatha	„ Annie Cole
Blanche	„ Cora Tinnie
Rose	„ Janet Watts
Gertrude	„ Nellie Kavanagh
Winifred	„ Lenore Snyder

HADDON HALL

Sept. 24, 1892.

John Manners	Mr. Courtice Pounds
Sir George Vernon	„ Richard Green
Oswald	„ Chas. Kenningham
Rupert Vernon	„ Rutland Barrington

The McCrankie	Mr. W. H. Denny
Sing Song Simeon	„ Rudolph Lewis
Dorothy Vernon	Miss Lucille Hill
Lady Vernon	„ Rosina Brandram
Dorcas	„ Dorothy Vane
Nance	„ Nita Cole
Gertrude	„ Claribel Hyde
Deborah	„ Florence Easton

JANE ANNIE

May 13, 1893.

A Proctor	Mr. Rutland Barrington
Sims	„ Lawrence Grindley
Greg	„ Walter Passmore
Tom	„ Charles Kenningham
Jack	„ Scott Fischе
Miss Sims	Miss Rosina Brandram
Jane Annie	„ Dorothy Vane
Bab	„ Decima Moore
Milly	„ Florence Perry
Rose	„ Emmie Owen
Meg	„ Jose Shalders
Maud	„ May Bell

UTOPIA

Oct. 7, 1893.

King Paramount	Mr. Rutland Barrington
Scaphio	„ W. H. Denny
Phantis	„ John Le Hay
Tarara	„ Walter Passmore
Calynx	„ Bowden Haswell
Lord Dramaleigh	„ Scott Russell
Capt. Fitzbattleaxe	„ Charles Kenningham
Capt. Sir Edward Corcoran . . .	„ Lawrence Grindley
Mr. Goldbury	„ Scott Fischе
Mr. Blushington	„ Herbert Ralland
Princess Zara	Miss Nancy McIntosh
Princess Nekaya	„ Emmie Owen
Princess Kalyba	„ Florence Perry
The Lady Sophy	„ Rosina Brandram
Salata	„ Edith Johnston
Melene	„ May Bell
Phylla	„ Florence Easton

MIRETTE

July 3, 1894.

The Baron van den Berg	MR. RICHARD TEMPLE
Gerard de Montigny	,, SCOTT FISCHE
Picorin	,, COURTICE POUNDS
Bobinet	,, WALTER PASSMORE
Francal	,, JOHN COATES
Bertuccio	,, SCOTT RUSSELL
Mirette	MISS FLORENCE ST. JOHN
Bianca	,, FLORENCE PERRY
Zerbinette	,, EMMIE OWEN
The Marquise de Montigny	,, ROSINA BRANDRAM

THE CHIEFTAIN

Dec. 12, 1894.

Count Vasquez de Gonzago	MR. COURTICE POUNDS
Peter Adolphus Grigg	,, WALTER PASSMORE
Ferdinand de Roxas	,, SCOTT FISCHE
Sancho	,, RICHARD TEMPLE
José	,, M. R. MORAND
Pedro Gomes	,, SCOTT RUSSELL
Blazzo	,, BOWDEN HASWELL
Escatero	,, POWIS PINDER
Pedrillo	MASTER SNELSON
Inez de Roxas	MISS ROSINA BRANDRAM
Dolly	,, FLORENCE PERRY
Juanita	,, EMMIE OWEN
Maraquita	,, EDITH JOHNSTON
Anna	,, ADA NEWALL
Zitella	,, BEATRICE PERRY
Nina	,, ETHEL WILSON
Rita	,, FLORENCE ST. JOHN

THE GRAND-DUKE

Mar. 7, 1896.

Rudolph	MR. WALTER PASSMORE
Ernest Dummkopf	,, C. KENNINGHAM
Ludwig	,, RUTLAND BARRINGTON
Dr. Tannhauser	,, SCOTT RUSSELL
The Prince of Monte Carlo	,, SCOTT FISCHE
Viscount Mentone	,, CARLTON

Ben Hashbaz	.	.	.	.	.	.	MR. WORKMAN
Herald	.	.	.	.	.	.	„ JONES HEWSON
The Princess of Monte Carlo	.	.	.	MISS EMMIE OWEN
The Baroness von Krakenfeldt	.	.	.	„ ROSINA BRANDRAM
Julia Jellicoe	.	.	.	.	.	MADME. ILKA VON PALMAY
Lisa	.	.	.	.	.	.	MISS FLORENCE PERRY
Olga	.	.	.	.	.	.	„ MILDRED BAKER
Gretchen	.	.	.	.	.	.	„ RUTH VINCENT
Bertha	.	.	.	.	.	.	„ JESSIE ROSE
Elsa	.	.	.	.	.	.	„ ETHEL WILSON
Martha	.	.	.	.	.	.	„ BEATRICE PERRY

HIS MAJESTY

Feb. 20, 1897.

Ferdinand the Fifth	.	.	.	.	MR. GEO. GROSSMITH
Count Cosmo	.	.	.	.	„ SCOTT RUSSELL
Baron Vincentius	.	.	.	.	„ JONES HEWSON
Baron Michael	.	.	.	.	„ EARLDON
Prince Max	.	.	.	.	„ C. KENNINGHAM
Mopolio	.	.	.	.	„ FRED BILLINGTON
Boodel	.	.	.	.	„ W. PASSMORE
Herr Schinppenhammer	.	.	.	„ BRYAN
Chevalier Klarkstein	.	.	.	„ H. CHARLES
Adam	.	.	.	.	„ C. H. WORKMAN
Princess Chloris	.	.	.	MISS ILKA VON PALMAY
Duchess Gonzara	.	.	.	„ McCAULEY
Dame Gertrude	.	.	.	„ BESSIE BOUSILL
Helena	.	.	.	.	„ JESSIE ROSE
Dorothea	.	.	.	.	„ RUTH VINCENT
Claudina	.	.	.	.	„ MILDRED BAKER

THE GRAND-DUCHESS

Dec. 5, 1897.

Grand-Duchess	.	.	.	.	MISS FLORENCE ST. JOHN
Wanda	.	.	.	.	„ FLORENCE PERRY
Isa	.	.	.	.	„ RUTH VINCENT
Olga	.	.	.	.	„ JESSIE ROSE
Charlotta	.	.	.	.	„ BEATRICE PERRY
Fritz	.	.	.	.	MR. C. KENNINGHAM
Prince Paul	.	.	.	.	„ H. A. LYTTON
Baron Puck	.	.	.	.	„ W. ELTON
Nepornus	.	.	.	.	„ GEO. HUMPHREY
General Boom	.	.	.	.	„ WALTER PASSMORE

28

Baron Grog . . . . . . Mr. C. H. Brookfield
Carl . . . . „ C. H. Workman
Colonel Marcobrun . . . . . „ Scott Fische
Captain Hocheim . . . . . „ Cory James

THE BEAUTY STONE

May 28, 1898.

Philip, Lord of Mirlemont . . . . Mr. George Devoll
Guntran of Beaugrant . . . . „ Edwin Isham
Simon Limal . . . . . . „ Henry A. Lytton
Nicholas Dircks. . . . . . „ Jones Hewson
Peppin . . . . „ D'Arcy Kelway
A Seneschal . . . . . . „ Leonard Russell
A Lad of Town . . . . . . „ Charles Childerstone
Baldwyn or Ath . . . . . „ J. W. Foster
Lords of Serault, Velaines, and St. Sauveur . „ Cory James, Mr. H. Gordon, and Mr. J. Ruff
The Devil . . . . . . „ Walter Passmore
Laine . . . . Miss Ruth Vincent
Joan . . . . „ Rosina Brandram
Jacqueline . . . . . . „ Emmie Owen
Loyse, from St. Denis . . . . „ Madge Moyse
Isabeau, from Florennes . . . . „ Minnie Pryce
Barbe, from Bovigny . . . . „ Ethel Jackson
A Shrewish Girl . . . . . „ Mildred Baker
A Matron . . . . . . „ Ethel Wilson
Saida . . . . „ Pauline Joran

THE LUCKY STAR

Jan. 7, 1899.

King Ouf the First . . . . . Mr. Walter Passmore
The Baron Tabasco . . . . . „ Henry A. Lytton
Siroco . . . . „ Fred Wright, Jun.
Kedas . . . . „ Frank Manning
Tapioca . . . . „ Robert Evett
Cancan . . . . „ Leonard Russell
Princess Laoula . . . . . Miss Ruth Vincent
Aloës . . . . „ Isabel Jay
Oasis . . . . „ Jessie Rose
Asphodel . . . . „ Madge Moyse
Zinnia . . . . „ Mildred Baker
Adza . . . . „ Katie Vesey
Lazuli . . . . „ Emmie Owen

THE ROSE OF PERSIA

Nov. 29, 1899

The Sultan Mahmoud of Persia	Mr. Henry A. Lytton
Hassan	„ Walter Passmore
Yussuf	„ Robert Evett
Abdallah	„ George Ridgewell
The Grand Vizier	„ W. H. Leon
The Physician-in-Chief	„ C. Childerstone
The Royal Executioner	„ Reginald Crompton
Soldier of the Guard	„ Powis Pinder
The Sultana Zubeydeh	Miss Isabel Jay
" Scent-of-Lilies "	„ Jessie Rose
" Heart's Desire "	„ Louie Pounds
" Honey-of-Life "	„ Emmie Owen
" Dancing Sunbeam "	„ Rosina Brandram
" Blush-of-Morning "	„ Agnes Fraser
" Oasis-in-the-Desert "	„ Madge Moyse
" Moon-upon-the-Waters "	„ Jessie Pounds
" Song-of-Nightingales "	„ Rose Rosslyn
" Whisper-of-the-West-Wind "	„ Gertrude Jerrard

THE EMERALD ISLE

April 27, 1901.

The Earl of Newtown	Mr. Jones Hewson
Dr. Fiddle, D.D.	„ R. Rous
Terence O'Brien	„ Robert Evett
Professor Bunn	„ Walter Passmore
Pat Murphy	„ H. A. Lytton
Black Dan	„ W. H. Leon
Mickie O'Hara	„ C. Earldon
Sergeant Pincher	„ R. Crompton
Private Perry	„ Powis Pinder
Countess of Newtown	Miss Rosina Brandram
Lady Rosie Pippin	„ Isabel Jay
Molly O'Grady	„ Louie Pounds
Susan	„ Blanche Gaston Murray
Nora	„ Lulu Evans
Kathleen	„ Agnes Fraser

INDEX

Printed by Hazell, Watson & Viney, Ld., London and Aylesbury, England.

Lightning Source UK Ltd.
Milton Keynes UK
UKHW020304100223
416720UK00002B/425

WIRED

WIRED

CONTEMPORARY ZULU TELEPHONE-WIRE BASKETS

by David Arment and Marisa Fick-Jordaan
photographs by Andrew Cerino

published by S/C EDITIONS • SANTA FE
distributed by MUSEUM OF NEW MEXICO PRESS • SANTA FE
distributed in Africa by DAVID KRUT PUBLISHING • JOHANNESBURG

ACKNOWLEDGMENTS

To Jim, for taking me on my first trip to Africa, which changed our lives,
and for helping me find a way to turn a good idea into reality;
and to Trisha, for her passion for Africa and for her support—it can be done!
—David Arment

To Jan and Jan-Paul, and for Margaret Daniel, who has helped all the way.
—Marisa Fick-Jordaan

This book was made possible by the generous
support of the Wilson Education Foundation.

The Wilson Education Foundation (WEF) was set up to endow financially
disadvantaged high school graduates in the United States with
four-year college scholarships, as well as to provide scholarships and
other educational or medical assistance to organizations worldwide.
The WEF is currently funding specific initiatives to improve schools in rural South Africa.
The WEF has also become involved in the fight against AIDS, and the administration
of care and support to children whose lives are affected by AIDS.
More information about the WEF can be found at www.wilsoneducationfoundation.org.

Proceeds from the sale of this book benefit the Wilson Education Foundation.

previous pages, left:
BLACK-AND-WHITE PLATE WITH INITIALS E. M.
Elliot Mkhize
324 x 290 mm
Collection of David Arment

opposite page:
BHEKI SIBIYA DEMONSTRATING THE HARD-WIRE WEAVING TECHNIQUE
Photographed at the BAT Centre
January 2004

CONTENTS

**THIS BOOK WOULD NOT HAVE BEEN POSSIBLE
WITHOUT THE GENEROUS SPONSORSHIP OF:**

Doug & Lisa Allen

Bartel Arts Trust

Bergamo Fabrics

Barbara Buzzell

Lynn Caldwell

Susan & Vance Campbell

Melissa M. Carry, M.D., P.A.

Casa Nova

Todd Davis & Chris Richter

Natalie Fitz-Gerald

Susan & Charles Fradin

Carolyn Franklin & Roger Polan

Thelma Glassman

Marcella M. McDaneld

Emily & Herman Mauney

George & Christie Mazuera

*Curtis B. Medford & Trikes
    Wallcovering Source*

In memory of Pete & Micky Pedersen

Jim Rimelspach

Beth, Bob, Lindsey, & Lauren Sawyer

Kelly & Carol Trimmer

Susan Tonjes

Joan Warren & Steve Grady

Trisha Wilson

Wilson and Associates

previous pages, left:
HARD-WIRE BOWL
Alice Gcaba
120 × 380 mm

opposite page, clockwise from top left:
SOFT-WIRE BOWL
Joseph Msomi
190 mm diameter, Private Collection
SOFT-WIRE BOWL
Artist unknown
165 mm diameter, Private Collection
SOFT-WIRE BOWL
Joseph Msomi
190 mm diameter, Private Collection
SOFT-WIRE BOWL
Artist unknown
180 mm diameter, Private Collection

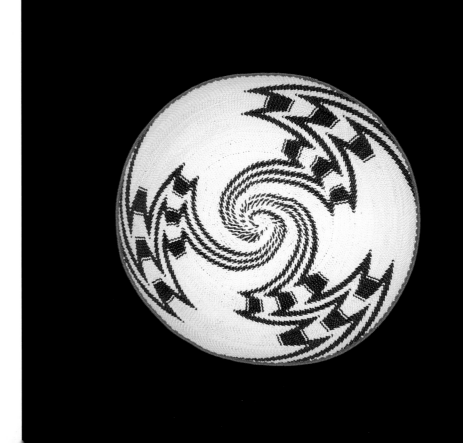

WHY THE WIRE PLATES?

At its heart, this book tells a story, which is long overdue, about the traditions and resourcefulness of a group of Zulu weavers and the individuals who helped turn a craft into fine art. The objects of this art form—the baskets, sticks, bottles, and other wire pieces—are a collector's dream. Traveling through South Africa on the safari circuit, one has time for a stopover in the cities, Johannesburg, Cape Town, and Durban, to do some shopping. The attraction of these beautiful objects is clear, and they are to be found in many an overweight bag checked in for flights back to the United States or Europe.

A photograph in a brochure for tourists was my first exposure to telephone-wire baskets. Colorful and distinctive, they stood out from the typical tourist curios of carved giraffes and beaded jewelry. This was during the early 1990s, and the few baskets that were available had designs of simple zigzags and swirls. The colors were basic, and the wire was in many cases truly recycled from scrap dealers and the local telephone lines. The quest began.

I started collecting baskets—when I could find them—on annual trips to South Africa. I began to seek out sources and to follow the development of the art. Soon I noticed that

opposite page:

WHY THE WIRE PLATES?
Bheki Dlamini
345 mm diameter
Collection of Paul Mikula

simple figures started showing up in the baskets. Letters and words were integrated into the work and the color and design became more complex and artistic. My passion became intense, and I found myself tracking down baskets from New York to Paris, and broadening my collection to include other quirky and historic Zulu wire objects. Little did I know at the time that my personal interest was so closely aligned with the development of the baskets into an art form and the beginning of an international marketing effort by the BAT Shop (an arts and crafts development center) in Durban. While I was busy collecting, Marisa Fick-Jordaan was, unbeknownst to me, working with the weavers of Siyanda (a residential area outside Durban), helping to turn an rural craft into an art form and supplying baskets to Art Africa and other shops. Sharing a passion for telephone-wire baskets, we needed only to connect.

A close mutual friend, Marianne Fassler, the icon of South African fashion, brought us together. We visited Siyanda together; a hot awakening for a Texan used to high rises and air-conditioned everything. Then, on a steamy evening in Durban after an exceptional day, we plotted this book over whisky prawns.

There was very little formal documentation on the baskets and we knew that a book on telephone wire had to be written. We had our storytellers, Marisa herself and Paul Mikula, who were there in the beginning, encouraging and promoting. Karel Nel, associate professor of fine art at the University of the Witwatersrand, while battling malaria, agreed to write the foreword in order to provide some context for the baskets and to explain their connection to the development of wire-working in southern Africa. The baskets and objects spoke for themselves and we gained access to collections in South Africa as well as in the United States.

But the process is only a minor part of the story. This book is about the development of the craft, about the weavers, the Siyanda community, the collectors, and the beautiful works of art. This book is about how a group of people came together, elevating a rural craft to a new and exciting urban art form that has acquired well-deserved international recognition and acclaim.

—David Arment

RE-WIRED

Transformations of the wire-working traditions in the southern African region

by Karel Nel

Within the southern African context, wire has for eons been associated with the manufacture and embellishment of high-status objects. During our own time wire has, to a large degree, lost its value or specialness and is taken much for granted. But this was not always so. The skills required for drawing wire in Africa were both highly complex and extraordinarily labor-intensive, which meant that a piece of wire was, traditionally, a rare and expensive commodity. Early examples of wire as a valuable trade item are to be found in the currencies produced in the Cross River region of Nigeria from the sixteenth through the eighteenth centuries: these short lengths of drawn wire were bundled and traditionally bound and bent into a U shape. They were often found at archeological sites, and are associated specifically with burials.

In southern Africa, too, wire, often in the form of tightly wound anklets and bracelets, is found in archeological sites, once again mainly in association with burials. An opulent use of drawn copper and brass is to be found in the woven wire-work that embellished important personal objects during the nineteenth and early twentieth centuries, particularly among Zulu speakers and other, related, Nguni groups. For example, small gourd snuff containers

were frequently decorated with brass and copper wire in refined, geometric patterns, an indication of the social significance of these small objects and of their association with the *amadlozi* (ancestral spirits).

Copper and brass were highly valued commodities throughout Africa—and southern Africa was no exception. Here, particularly in the Zulu court, Shaka, Dingaan, and a succession of leaders centralized and controlled access to the metal. This meant that the metals were used for high-status objects associated with centralized power, among them the *ingxotha,* the brass cuff-like ornaments awarded for bravery, and the heavy brass beads known as *ndondo,* worn only by those held in high esteem in the kingdom. Finely woven wire was used to decorate significant objects, such as staffs of office and ceremonial batons, particularly during the period of the great military might of Shaka and the Zulu empire. Many fine examples of objects adorned in this manner were collected during the Anglo-Zulu Wars and taken back to Britain. In recent years considerable numbers of these artifacts have been brought back to and are now included in important public collections such as those of the Johannesburg Art Gallery, the Standard Bank Collection of African Art at the University of the Witwatersrand, the Durban Art Gallery, the National Gallery in Cape Town, and the Campbell Collections in Durban.

A major aesthetic revolution occurred in Nguni culture when small, brightly colored glass beads were introduced by early European traders and missionaries. These beads, manufactured in Bohemia, were imported in large quantities for trade and barter. They, like the metals, were largely controlled by the ruling power, at least until the mid-1850s, when the royal monopolies started to wane. The introduction of the beads led to the development of a complex visual language within the beadwork, signaling group identity, social and marital status, and other nuanced information—all through the evolution of intricate geometric patterns and specific color sequences.

These beads inevitably found their way onto the traditional *izimbenge* (baskets used as pot lids). The pots in which traditional beer was brewed were closely associated with the ancestral realm and so, by association, were the *izimbenge,* which kept dust from the beer and protected this sacred substance. It is therefore not surprising that these baskets were embellished with the precious beads, an indication of their importance and of their ritual connection with the *amadlozi.*

In time, this complex visual language would form the basis of the patterns that emerged in the new wire-basket tradition, which developed in the 1980s as the *imbenge* (a single basket) and its associated beadwork played a pivotal role in the evolution of the craft. The use of telephone wire for *izimbenge* locked together three traditions in a new syntax (see images page 18). Firstly, the copper wire, the high-status commodity used to embellish traditionally important objects, had become a valuable substitute for grass in the great basket-making tradition, shifting the very nature of the object itself. Secondly, the traditional form of the *imbenge* was adopted initially for the new baskets, which only later became considerably larger and shallower (hence their description as "plates")—or, at times, deeper. Thirdly, the colored, plastic sheathing of the wire introduced a wide variety of colors into the equation, displacing the traditional bead embellishment and resulting in rich, regularly textured surfaces with numerous chromatic shifts. The complex, geometric patterns that evolved in the new wire baskets have their ancestry in traditional patterns, but require of the weavers an understanding of the mathematics inherent in those patterns.

There was traditionally a strong, gendered relationship in Zulu culture to both the manufacture and use of specific objects: wood carving and metal forging or casting were very much part of the male domain; working with clay, in the making of pots, and intricate beadwork were traditionally part of the female domain. Basket weaving is an interesting anomaly; it seems to have been practiced by both men and women and the custom is still followed in the weaving of wire baskets. Weaving with copper wire might be expected to fall, if loosely, into the male domain of metal working; the complex colored syntax of woven patterns might be expected to be associated with the female domain of beadwork.

Most traditional items were produced for a specific use within a prescribed cultural context and often bore strong ritual overtones that were deeply embedded in the matrix of the culture. The Nguni cultures of southern Africa were by and large nomadic, with cattle central to both the culture and its economy. The cattle were at the very heart of perceptions of self-worth, the means of social reciprocity, the sacred link to the ancestral world, the *amadlozi,* and were above all, a barometer of social order and stability. The nomadic life style associated with cattle keeping meant that personal possessions were necessarily few. Such objects as were made and kept would, also necessarily, be small and useful—a headrest, a milk pail, a meat platter, pots, *izimbenge* and other baskets, small snuff containers, beadwork, and ceremonial sticks. These few items, though, were of great significance. They were made with great attention to both form and detail and sometimes were embellished with particular care. In a nomadic culture there is no place for the grand pieces of furniture, large paintings, bronzes, or other artifacts of this order that are generally considered by Westerners as art.

THREE GOURDS COVERED IN WIRE
Artist unknown
20th century
h: 62, 85, and 77 mm
Collection of the Phansi Museum, Durban

The objects, by nature small, domestic, and personal, rather than large, public, and institutional, were therefore almost invisible to most Westerners as legitimate expressions of artistic impulse and, consequently, were relegated to the status of mere craft or cultural artifact; the region was understood to have produced no art. This colonial attitude persisted and has changed only slowly despite serious studies of the complex value systems underpinning seemingly everyday objects. Nonetheless, consolidated private and public collections have helped to create a body of material that now allows people to compare and contrast works and to begin to recognize a gestalt for the southern African work.

These opportunities have produced a change in the assessment of the objects, with the collections migrating from ethnographic museums to art museums and a concomitant shift in the perceptions of scholars and the public. This reevaluation, and the understanding that there is, indeed, a southern African aesthetic, has lead to a renewed interest in the objects, with the work being regarded less as craft and more as art. Traditional nineteenth-century southern African pieces now change hands for astronomical sums in the major auction houses in New York and Paris.

TWO ALUMINUM WIRE BRACELETS
Artist unknown
20th Century
60 x 60 and 145 x 80 mm
Collection of the Phansi Museum, Durban

That this new appreciation has clearly had an effect on contemporary production is to be seen in this sumptuous publication. As new markets opened up for early traditional pieces, so too a market has opened for the contemporary. In the past, pieces produced specifically for the Western market were curios, that is objects that no longer had any purpose within the context of traditional ritual, but were strategically adapted to the demands of another market and a different aesthetic. The fact that the objects were being produced for a new market altered their form, function, and aesthetic. The same kinds of changes are apparent in the evolution of the modern wire basket.

We see in this publication that, where distinctive objects of high quality are produced within a broad framing context, the function and symbolic significance of the *izimbenge* have largely evaporated; new demands and changing functions have altered the form and aesthetic of the baskets. This change is mirrored in the *imbenge* itself. No longer the traditional small bowl, of which the convex, upper surface was the more important and most finely decorated, the contemporary *izimbenge* have wide, flared bowls and flattened platter-like forms, with decorated interior, concave surfaces. They have become more like roundels or flat works that may easily be hung on walls. Losing their traditional functionality entirely, they have become more like paintings as they have been adapted for the Western fine-art market.

These shifts have come about only after many years of mentoring and encouragement by an array of dedicated individuals who have been passionate about ensuring that this rich tradition and extraordinary skill continue to thrive, and who have made it possible for the weavers to develop their skills to create these remarkable objects and to make a living. The evolution of these changes is chronicled, both visually and verbally, in this publication. The nurturing guidance of some of the people who are part of this evolution is legendary and I cherish the memories of those whom I have had contact with or met over the years, particularly Jo Thorpe of the African Art Centre in Durban, Tessa Katzenellembogen and Creina Alcock, whose early encouragement laid the foundation of much of what was to come, Marisa Fick-Jordaan of the BAT Centre, whose innovation and steadfastness have carried a tide of talent into the new century. The establishment of the FNB Vita Craft Now awards—by which outstanding practitioners of the art have been encouraged and singled out, among them Elliot Mkhize, Ntombifuthi Magwasa, Zama Khanyile, and Vincent Sithole—has affirmed the importance of their work locally, nationally, and internationally.

This book celebrates the efflorescence of skill and creativity associated with wire work. It focuses on the innate ability of traditional artists and craftspeople to reinvent their skills and aesthetics in response to the introduction of new materials, adapting and developing them to their own ends and creating an astoundingly innovative beauty, addressing tradition and change, and literally reinventing the past.

opposite page, clockwise from top left:

COPPER BOWL WITH PEARL BEADS
Artist unknown
178 mm diameter
Collection of David Arment

COPPER WIRE OVER ALUMINUM-WIRE BOWL
Thulani Ngubane
241 mm diameter
Private Collection

COPPER-WIRE BOWL
Elias Mshengu
336 mm diameter
Private Collection

"WOVEN" COPPER-WIRE PLATE
Lindelani Ngwenya
336 mm diameter
Collection of David Arment

SONG OF PRAISE

by Paul Mikula

In traditional Nguni society, all newcomers are introduced
or introduce themselves by describing their origins,
their families, their achievements, and their circumstances.

Important people have their own praise singers to do this for them.

Let us sing the praises of these baskets, which nowadays they call plates,
so that everyone will be familiar with their background and history.

*These are wire baskets—telephone-wire baskets—made by the Nguni people
to sell to the* abalungu *(white people) and* abafunduki *(foreigners).
Recently our own people have started to buy them as presents for visitors.*

*They call these baskets art, although we do not have a word in our vocabulary for "art."
We do have many words for "beauty" and for how well things are made. We use those
words for these baskets: they are absolutely beautiful and extremely well made. One
needs only to hold one to appreciate it. They are made from the fine telephone wires*

opposite page:
CLAY ZULU BEER POTS WITH TELEPHONE-WIRE *IZIMBENGE*
Artists unknown
20th century
Beer Pots: Collection of the Phansi Museum, Durban
Izimbenge: Collections of David Arment, Marisa Fick-Jordaan,
and the Phansi Museum, Durban

that are found inside larger plastic- or rubber-sheathed cables,
which we used to get from scrap-metal merchants or
from our friends who worked on telephone installations.

We call the wire scoobie wire.

In making the baskets, one is limited to the ten colors normally found
in the large cables: white, brown, green, yellow, gray, pink, blue, red,
black, and purple. In addition there are wires of those same colors
and either a horizontal stripe or a ring coding, so that there is an even bigger choice for
the installation engineer and for the basket maker.
In the old days a basket maker, usually a Zulu-speaking night watchman
with time on his hands, would hunt down a piece of cable
and then produce his objects in ever duller colors,
until he had used up even the most unexciting colors,
the striped and banded and brown wires generally coming last.

The telephone wire itself is made up of a thin plastic skin over single copper core. This
makes it extremely strong and so may be pulled tight when woven into the basket. These
scoobie wires, originally covered in rubber and subsequently in
PVC (polyvinyl chloride), have been available in South Africa since the 1930s,
although we really only started using them for baskets in the 1950s.
One still sees many old telephone-wire objects about, such as walking sticks banded with
wire or bottles covered from head to toe
in beautifully woven scoobie-wire dresses.

Because organic pigments were used in the older wires, the colors
were sensitive to ultraviolet light. They quickly became bleached out and the
coating became brittle. Later, inorganic, mineral-based pigments were used;
the colors lasted longer and the coating remained flexible.
It is easy to see which piece is new and which is old,
unless an old item has been hidden in the dark corner of a
kist (wooden chest), just to fool some innocent research student.
Some artists today no longer use telephone wire at all, preferring to
use panel wire because it is even thinner and has a diameter of only 0.22 mm.
Some makers even have wire especially made for them.
No more looking for scraps and making baskets from whatever could be found, no sir!
Many of today's artists specify the colors and the thicknesses of their materials.

opposite page:
THREE TELEPHONE-WIRE PLATES
Artists unknown
310 mm diameter, Collection of the Phansi Museum, Durban
330 mm diameter, Campbell Collections, Durban
260 mm diameter, Collection of the Phansi Museum, Durban

Isn't that wonderful!

The telephone wire is only a part of the basket.
The structure of a basket is based on a spiral of thick wire around which
the thinner telephone wire is wound and held together with tight loops
also of telephone wire. This is what we call the hard-wire technique.
This particular technique is as old as grass basket making itself; wire has been
substituted for the various grasses of the core and the palm leaves used for binding.

There is another, more complex way of making a bowl: the soft-wire technique,
which is based on the traditional method of covering walking sticks and snuff
containers with various metal wires, a method that is still used
for covering walking and traditional dancing sticks and bottles.
A cover of telephone wire is plaited (braided) over a bowl- or plate-shaped object,
and then the mold is removed. Objects made according to this method
do not have the inherent strength of those made with a heavy-wire core,
but the technique produces marvelous diagonal designs,
although the variety is limited, and a much lighter product.
In these days of air freight and international tourists,
that has become an important consideration.

Because the technique based on a structural core permits a great variety of designs,
it is unlikely to be supplanted. The core wire used today is generally made of
galvanized mild steel and ranges from approximately 0.6 through 1.2 mm in diameter.
Available in rolls at hardware stores, it is easy to bend and holds its shape well.
Before the 1960s, the core wire used was generally 19 S.W.G. (standard wire gauge) ordi-
nary mild steel wires, which turn black with age and eventually rust away.

Wire weaving as a craft was first used for walking sticks and bottles,
but the true ancestor of wire weaving as an art is the imbenge, *the beer pot lid.*
Traditionally this lid, woven of grass and palm leaf,
is one of the most important household objects in the Zulu homestead
because it covers the ukhamba (clay beer pot).
It allows the beer to breathe and prevents dive-bombing kamikaze insects
from intoxicating and possibly obliterating themselves in the beverage.

Among the Nguni people the drinking of beer is a quasi-sacred event because
it is done to honor the amadlozi (ancestral spirits), *who are themselves not*
averse to partaking in the celebrations and for whom a special little pot is set

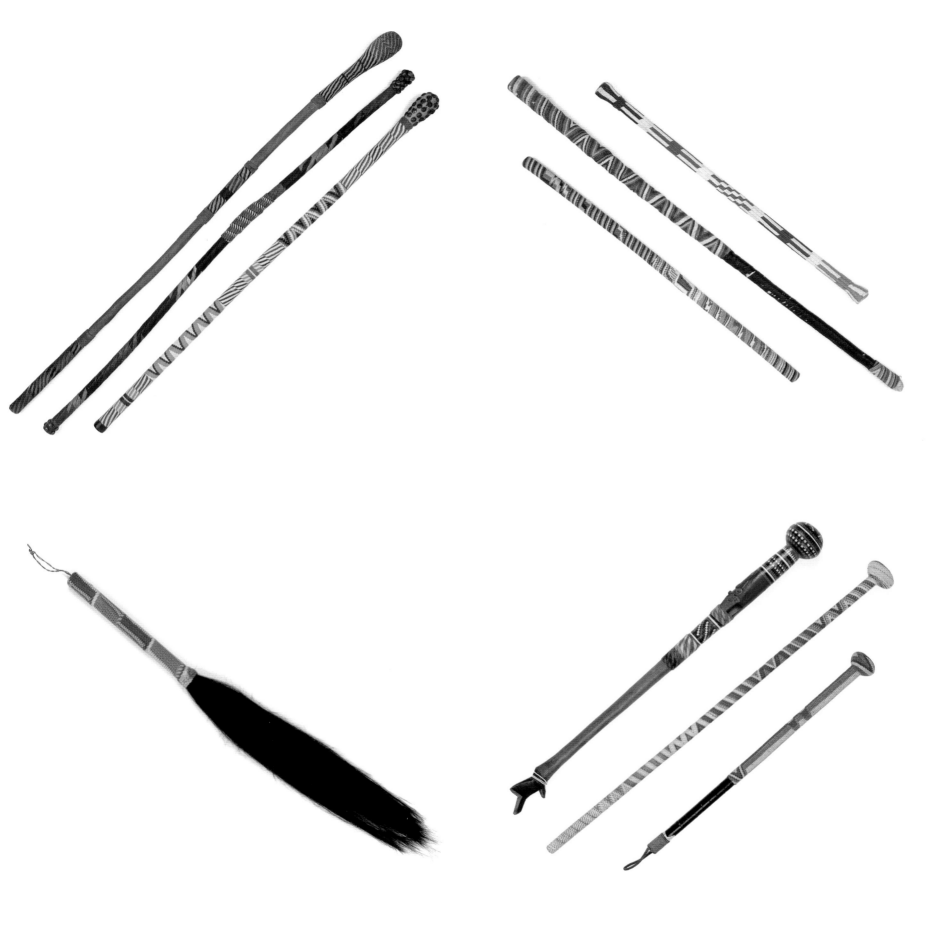

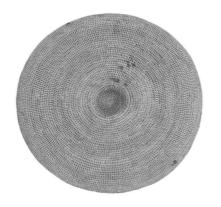
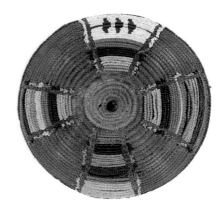

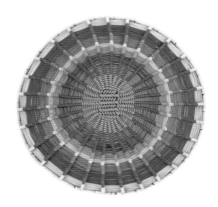
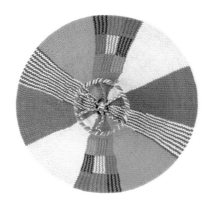

aside on the umsamo (domestic altar) of the home.
Very strict rules and etiquette are followed in the brewing, drinking,
and presentation of the beer. It deserves only the most beautiful containers and lids.
To my mind there is nothing more beautiful than a sumptuous
fat clay ukhamba burnished to a magnificent shine,
in the deepest black of the amadlozi,
elegantly decorated with just a few amasumpa
(a traditional decorative element of raised "warts" or bumps) here and there,
and crowned with a beautifully made grass imbenge, which has been lovingly
decorated by the woman of the house in the colors of the clan.

During the rural depression of the 1970s attempts were made to revitalize
the vanishing basket-making craft in Zululand in order to create jobs.
But plastic containers had long since replaced the various
baskets that were traditionally used around the home.
The only basket still being made was the imbenge.
It was probably the amadlozi then, who had refused to let that tradition die. Entrepreneurs
who went to the countryside and the hostels to sell plastic
beer pots soon declared bankruptcy; and the small enamel bowls they offered
just could not replace the izimbenge as covers for the pots.
These imbenge-making skills survived and it was soon possible to resurrect the craft, and
expand market for these baskets, which today has become the main source of livelihood
for the thousands of brave mothers and grandmothers
who are the backbone of our rural communities.

Not that time stood still for these objects or communities.
Nguni culture is totally inclusive, constantly on the lookout for new skills and
materials, new ways of doing things; of making them even more exciting and beautiful.
This quest applies to dress, to dance, to music, and to crafts.
One can imagine the return of the prodigal son from iGoli—Johannesburg,
Gauteng, the city of gold—where he had toiled underground in the mines for a year.
He would be laden with technological wonders: a radio,
a wind-up gramophone, widely flared, multicolored bell-bottom trousers,
many glass beads, and a roll of telephone wire. This was grass of another sort.
As thin as the finest grass, stronger than the ilala palm leaves, and more
colorful than the best dyes obtained from local roots and leaves
or even those from the chemist (pharmacist) in the nearest town.

Until the introduction of the core of mild steel wire, small bundles of grass continued to be used as the coil, as they had in the past. The telephone wire, which replaced the ilala palm, was used to decorate and bind the basket together.

Traditionally baskets of all sorts were made by men, and only very occasionally by women, and were sold at local markets.
These baskets would then be taken home and decorated with beadwork by the women.
The decorations were individual and the decorator more or less exuberant, but the women would generally use only certain color codes and local symbols of the region and or the clan.
The codes themselves might change over time, with the exclusion or addition of colors, symbols, or writing.
These changes make for a fascinating study and help to identify and locate baskets and beadwork in particular clan areas and in time.

Why the codes change is often difficult to establish.
For instance, we still do not understand why the seven colors of the isishunka pattern used in the Msinga region of KwaZulu-Natal suddenly made way for the isithembu colors, with the addition of bright yellow, and then later for the simpler but more colorful umzansi patterns, or the phalafini pattern, for that matter.
Each is distinct and different and associated with small local clan villages or the shop or event at which they may have originated.
Other trails are easier to follow.
When, for some reason—war, lack of transport, deteriorating roads, poverty—the people of the highlands stop trading with those in the lowlands, the age-old exchange of grasses and palm leaves stops.
Replacement materials have to be found.
One is wool, which is strong, colorful, and available.
The use of a new material soon results in new designs and new, local color codes. Beads are no longer essential as the decoration may be stitched right into the object.

None of those changes and inevitable developments altered the traditional function of the imbenge. The real revolution occurred in Johannesburg, that much hated, much loved city, the origin of everything, all the evil in the world and all the knowledge, and the rural communities' link to the universe.
iGoli is where all real men spent their youth and acquired their wisdom, be it political, technological, or artistic. It is where decisions were made about hairstyles and about how much knee a young married woman should show under her cowhide

above, top:
CLAY BEER POT WITH GRASS *IMBENGE* COVERED WITH BEADS
175 x 225 mm (pot), 60 x 180 mm (*imbenge*), Collection of Jim Rimelspach

above, bottom:
COILED TELEPHONE WIRE OVER GRASS BOWL
Artist unknown
345 x 175 mm, Collection of the Phansi Museum, Durban

marriage skirt. From here great global ideas, gathered from movies, abafundisi (teachers), friends, and magazines, were transformed and transferred to the remotest corners of the rural areas.

Working with metal had always been the domain and the responsibility of men as has been the caring for the cattle, erecting the structure of the home, working with grass and leather, and providing the security of the family at home. It was traditionally women who worked with earth, made the pots, plastered the huts, planted the crops, did the beadwork, brewed the beer, cooked, and had the children. The new metal imbenge fitted well into this division of labor.
Most of South Africa's gold mines are clustered around the Witwatersrand, with Johannesburg as the fulcrum. Each mine was operated as a fiefdom, with a mine manager in charge of a small town totally dedicated to it. Management and skilled staff lived in colonial luxury.
The hard underground work was mostly reserved for migrant laborers from the rural areas, who worked on short-term contracts and lived in single-sex hostels.
This system, first begun on the diamond mines in Kimberly during the 1870s, continues to this day, although in a more humane and dignified way.
While it produced many social ills, it did produce a society in which the allocation of jobs by gender could not exist.
There were no women to make pots, do the beadwork, cook, or sew.
Soon the most wonderfully decorated patchwork clothes and decorated baskets were being produced.

The domain of the male was perpetuated when the baskets were decorated with the colorful wire and sewing machines were used to make the clothes.
Cooking became the grilling of meat and steaming of maize meal—South Africa's favorite meal to this day—eaten standing up. Honor could thus be maintained.
Only pottery remained in the female domain and soon a thriving trade developed, with the clay izinkhamba (beer pots) being delivered to the miners, and the decorated wire izimbenge being made in iGoli and exported back to the villages.
In this way the humble imbenge now found its way back home totally transformed, much more beautiful and durable; and it was no longer necessary to have the women decorate it to make it special.
Many other materials were tried along the way, among them plastic bags cut into strips, sisal string, and garden nursery twine, but these did not find a market. Only the scoobie wire and the grass izimbenge survive today.

above, top:
HORN, WOOD, COPPER WIRE & TELEPHONE WIRE SNUFF BOTTLES
Artist unknown, h: 150 mm and 130 mm, Private Collection

above, bottom:
TELEPHONE-WIRE HARD HAT
Shadercke Ntuli
280 x 220 x 130 mm, Private Collection

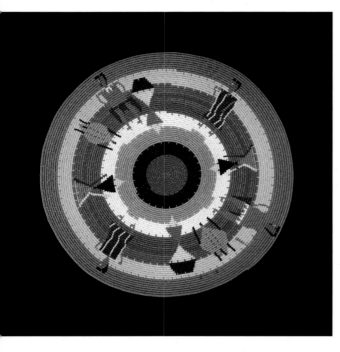

TELEPHONE-WIRE PLATE
Bheki Dlamini
310 mm diameter
Collection of David Arment

*Originally the mines were organized and organized themselves by tribe and clan,
and the old traditions were adhered to, each home area retaining
its own color and design combinations and preferences.
In izimbenge from the Umvoti area, for instance, white and blue wire was used.
Closer to Durban, very strong geometric designs were preferred.
The items were sold at special markets, of which the Mai Mai market
in central Johannesburg was probably the most famous.
It was at this market that the prodigal son would stock up before returning home.
A large kist, beautifully decorated, with mirrors and glued-on prints of the
Kaiser Chiefs soccer team or of Jesus and Mary, or both, would be loaded with
beads, blankets, izimbenge, and other wonders of technology made from the finest materials available—plastic and Perspex—insulation tape in different colors, bicycle reflectors,
maybe even a bicycle, aluminum wire, and many other treasures.
It was expected of a young man, especially if he were returning to get married,
to be generous to his own and his future wife's family.*

*Wire imbenge making is hard work, man's work.
It takes skill, strength, and time.
It was ideal for those who protect and guard us during the long and
lonely nights, the night watchmen. Fearless, feared Zulu night watchmen!
These were the great, great, great grandchildren of the majestic Cetshwayo,
who whipped the British army at iSandlwana in 1879.
Wire weaving became their industry.
While some specialized in the covering of bottles and knobkerries
(sticks used as weapons), most went for the imbenge market.
They shared their skills willingly and one would often see small groups of
heavily clad night watchmen in their cast-off army greatcoats clustered
around a fire made in a cut-off, perforated oil drum, keeping warm and working
at their beautiful baskets, discussing designs and techniques and, one hoped, keeping an
ear out and eyes open for the odd scebenga (bad guy), who would be trying to get into the
back door, possibly to steal telephone wire to sell to night watchmen.*

*One can picture similar groups of men, centuries ago, even before
Shaka founded the nation, in deepest Zululand, also sitting around the fire,
keeping warm and decorating their dancing and
walking sticks with copper, bronze, and iron wire.
Melting, casting, and hammering the metal, they were producing*

22

brass beads, gauntlets, arm rings, wire, and spears.
They were always on the lookout for new metals and other material for decorations.
Iron was mined locally, but most other treasures trickled in from north and east
Africa or from the missionaries and later from the colonial merchants in barter trade. Many
an elephant was sacrificed on the altar of vanity.

When I and many others discovered the izimbenge, we were taken
by their beauty and entirely dismissed their function.
We preferred the inside of the imbenge—turned over, it is like a bowl—and
tended to look at the designs from that side.
We wanted them to hang on the wall—they were just too beautiful to be hidden away—and
we wanted them bigger and flatter; the baskets were becoming plates.
At night we waited outside Fast Sails, a small factory, to find out if
Elliot Mkhize or Bheki Dlamini had produced another masterpiece.
Or we would go to the African Art Centre in Durban to find out if
another genius basket maker had been discovered.
For more than two decades, the proprietors of the Art Centre had nurtured the
grass-roots artists and encouraged them to show and sell their work to a wider public.
Most of the artists were very poor, often out of work, and struggled to buy the wire. When
times were particularly bad, in the 1980s, I even "inherited" a number
of homeless basket makers, who settled in at my architecture offices.
Then in 1992 we launched the Bartel Arts Trust (BAT), funding an art center
and development projects, workshops, and residential facilities.
Soon a whole group of wire-basket makers moved there
and we could reclaim our office.

Some brought their wives and children and
soon the gender barrier was entirely dissolved.
Women were making wire baskets and two young men,
Thami Jali and Clive Sithole, were making wonderful pots!
Marisa Fick-Jordaan established the BAT Shop and took over.
She wanted the baskets bigger still, and flatter, and wilder.
She pushed the artists and found the buyers.
She gave them all courage and helped them unearth their talents—
and soon they took flight and magic happened and a new art form was born.

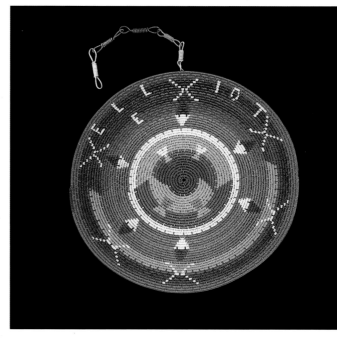

"ELLIOT" BASKET
Elliot Mkhize
210 mm diameter
Collection of the Phansi Museum, Durban

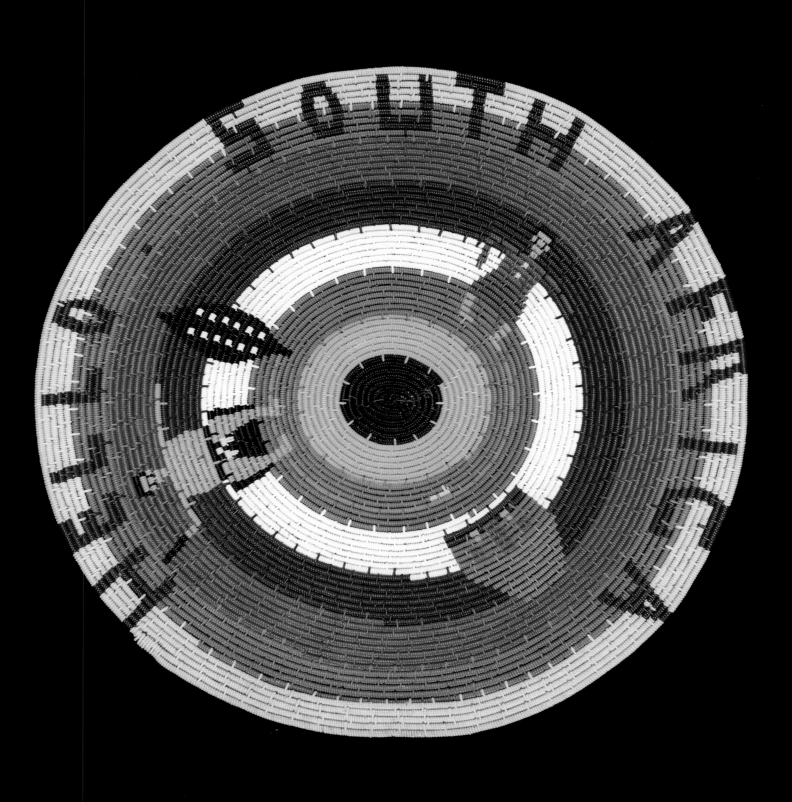

TRANSITIONS
by Marisa Fick-Jordaan

1

When Bartel Arts Trust (BAT) and Nedbank Arts and Culture Trust were launched simultaneously in 1994, this was the major arts event of the year in South Africa. And when Paul Mikula, the founding trustee of the Bartel Arts Trust, appeared in full Batman regalia on the stage, the arts community was delighted. This momentous happening was certainly eclipsed by the inauguration of Nelson Mandela as the first democratically elected president of post-apartheid South Africa, and this election brought a newfound sense of optimism to the country after decades of despair and isolation.

A few months later, I went to the BAT Centre to buy my first telephone-wire basket. Ducking under scaffolding and climbing over piles of concrete bricks, I managed to locate Bheki Dlamini and his pregnant wife, Dudu Cele, in a back room adjacent to the future visual arts studio. Then, with Dudu's *Hello South Africa* basket under my arm, I bumped into Mike van Graan, the director of BAT, who jokingly asked if I were looking for a job. "Never!" I replied. Not eight months later I would be persuaded to set up the BAT Shop and telephone-wire weaving would become part of my daily existence and an all-consuming passion. Never is a long time, as they say.

opposite page:
HELLO SOUTH AFRICA
Dudu Cele
285 mm diameter
Collection of Marisa Fick-Jordaan

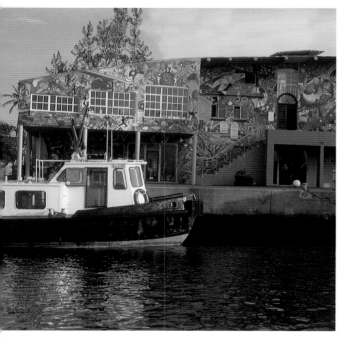

My foray into the craft world started when, as a fashion designer in the early 1990s, I had started exploring the possibility of using Zulu beadwork for clothing that was to be marketed under the African Legacy label. There were hardly any books available for reference, so for inspiration I borrowed old beadwork pieces from Jo Thorpe, the doyenne of African art, who was then at the African Art Centre. Expecting Jo to disapprove of my commercial, trendy interpretations of a cultural legacy, I was surprised when she encouraged me, saying that the Zulu crafters were ready to work in new directions.

In the first week after the shop opened, Bheki Dlamini arrived with a handful of students from the Siyanda community—Albert Dlamini, Anamaria Dlamini, Zodwa Maphumulo, Ntombifuthi Magwasa, and Elliot Ndwandwe—all urging me to buy their wire baskets. The master weaver Elliot Mkhize soon brought his wares and many early photographs show this little band proudly posing in front of the cobalt blue wall that was dedicated to showcasing what, to my mind, was the most distinctive, vibrant, exciting, contemporary art form.

All the early baskets were of the traditional *imbenge* (beer pot) size, very small, around 190 millimeters in diameter, and although here and there a figure, a car, or a hut appeared, the predominant motif was variations of what we called the Zulu *imbali* (flower), a pattern of radiating rings with points or petals. To make their work more marketable, we showed the weavers books, including carpet designs and art and design magazines to inspire them to work in new shapes and sizes. With some direction on design, the weavers began developing more complex geometric patterns that were initially inspired by Zulu beadwork, particularly the complex patterns from the Nongoma district and Zulu earplug designs from Msinga.

The annual BAT calendars celebrating traditional Zulu artifacts became a major source of inspiration and were proudly displayed in urban shacks and rural homesteads. Exhibitions at the BAT Centre showcasing the best examples of traditional Zulu material culture from private collections encouraged a renewed pride in local design. When additional colors became available, as a result of the BAT Shop ordering custom hues from suppliers, traditional combinations were used, but later weavers began to experiment with a wider color palette as these were also made available. We placed an emphasis on the development of individuality, and the weavers began producing increasingly sophisticated and intricate abstract geometric designs, working well outside the boundaries of traditional Zulu patterning.

Each name was prominently displayed when baskets were placed for sale or on exhibit at the BAT Shop. By giving credit to the weavers, we were encouraging them to develop an individual style and attribution became a useful tool when we were obliged to decline work of poor quality. Often we were offered baskets that had been woven in unattractive and dull colors, but they included innovative design elements and we began to understand that the basic materials of this craft were difficult to obtain. Scrap-metal merchants were hounded for "scoobie wire," the PVC-coated copper telephone wire that the weavers were using. In my naiveté, celebrating the innovative use of a recycled material, I had no idea at the time of the side effects of this craft: the increasing theft of copper-wire cables and the problems the theft caused in the entire community, but more immediately to Telkom, the company that provided telephone service in the country, and to the rural farmers who depended on it. International patrons appreciated and purchased the baskets; the locals, including government officials, had to be appeased for the resulting disruption in telephone service.

In May 1996 I was asked to curate *WIRED*, the first exhibition of telephone-wire baskets in the Menzi Gallery at the BAT Centre. The media publicity and critical acclaim for the exhibition helped to create a wider local audience. As sales increased rapidly, so did our group of Siyanda weavers. Twenty minutes drive from Durban, Siyanda (the optimistic name means "we are moving forward") is a sprawling informal settlement adjacent to one of the largest townships outside the city of Durban. The core residents of the community settled in Siyanda after political violence during the 1980s forced them to abandon their original homes. Supported by the BAT Shop, this community has become the center of telephone-wire weaving. Within two years, the weaving group had grown to about seventy people and several imaginative and talented artists emerged from this community.

The craft spread when neighbors and family members were taught to weave, and despite the attitude of most newly urbanized young men toward what they perceived to be "women's work," they, too, appreciated the possibility of staying at home, using their hands, and earning incomes—a far cry from waiting to pick up employment here and there in the formal sector. Unlike other craft forms that are practiced exclusively by either men or women, and in which skills are passed down through tradition, the Siyanda project was, and remains, the domain of a disparate group of men and women of all ages, most of whom had no prior crafting skills.

Acknowledging the growing market for distinctly South African products, and realizing the potential for generating an income by producing handmade craftwork, the South African government decided to make the so-called cultural industries a priority. The government began providing financial support for training and encouraging partnerships with internal and external development agencies. From the start, the modernization of the craft and the

THE INFORMAL SETTLEMENT OF SIYANDA
Outside of Durban, South Africa
Photograph by David Arment

development of the products were driven by the market. Feedback from the market was crucial: product, price, quality, and on-time delivery are what the market wants. The BAT Shop has helped to build the market by encouraging the weavers to be innovative, to expand their designs, and to produce baskets of high quality. We also believe that it is important to build sustainable relationships with all the people we deal with.

As a result of the initial success, the group had grown too big to go on as it had begun, with a mentor for each weaver. To continue improving the designs and quality of the baskets, we asked the Masibambane Trust, which was established to support economic development projects, to fund formal workshops at the BAT Centre. Elliot Mkhize was brought in to teach technique, and we made suggestions about the design of the baskets and offered lessons on the important issue of money management. In 1998 our efforts were rewarded when Ntombifuthi Magwasa won the prestigious FNB Vita Craft Now Award for her wire basket. Telephone-wire basketry had made the leap from curio to art craft.

For our first attempts at what might be called mass production, the weavers were asked to repeat designs that had proved popular in the shop. Once the weavers could reproduce those designs to a standard size, we presented a sample of their work to the interior designer Boyd Ferguson, of the interior design firm Cecile and Boyd, who was at the time designing the innovative Singita Lodge, located in the Sabi Sand Reserve, adjacent to the Kruger National Park in South Africa. What we showed him was a flat tray with a rim. His response was entirely enthusiastic and has led to one of our most successful and continuing collaborations. The tray itself, which is used as a decorative under plate for the table settings, has become a classic product that has been mentioned in many editorials on the subject of design and illustrated in articles about the interior design of the lodge. As Cecile and Boyd have worked on new lodges for the Singita Private Game Reserve, new designs have been developed for the under plates and, because they are offered for sale in the boutiques attached to the lodges, they are providing a steady income for the weavers while gracing tables around the world.

In 1997 the French contemporary artist Hervé Di Rosa traveled to South Africa at the invitation of the newly established French Institute of South Africa. After visits to Johannesburg and Cape Town, he arrived at the BAT Centre in search of master crafters with whom he could collaborate on his project *Autour du Monde*. Finding that Johannesburg and Cape Town were relatively devoid of traditional craft, he was enthusiastic about the number of people practicing Zulu crafts in the Durban area. Here he saw people working in several traditional and transitional techniques, from wood burning and

opposite:
THE ELEMENTS OF LIFE, 1998
Design by Hervé Di Rosa
Woven by Zodwa Maphumulo
800 mm diameter, Private Collection
Photograph by Pierre Schwatrz

sculpting to plastic-bag weaving. Initially he wanted to use them all, but in the end he focused on telephone-wire weaving, beadwork, and wood carving. He launched a collaboration titled Dirozulu. In selecting Durban and BAT as the eighth step of his world tour, he was also drawn by the diverse Asian, Zulu, and European influences on the cultural landscape of Durban—its harbor reminded him, he said, of Sète, the city in the south of France where he had been born.

Although the baskets in their contemporary form are artworks, the weavers had not ventured much beyond the original bowl or lid shape. Hervé needed a larger, more traditionally flat canvas for his designs and had no interest in the functional applications of the technique. He was able to expand the possibilities of the form and to increase the diameter of the new, mandala shape from about thirty to ninety centimeters (approximately twelve to thirty-five inches), but his innovation was limited by the circular weaving process, which prescribed the shape of his canvas and elements of his designs. He also discovered that telephone-wire weaving technique is quite rigid in its possibilities and that certain forms and intervals that were an intrinsic part of his designs were simply impossible to make. So he adapted the designs and, when all the bumps were ironed out, the process picked up momentum. Small mock-ups of the new designs were made and then enlarged at a printing shop. Hervé then specified the design parameters, selected a telephone-wire palette of around fifteen colors, and art happened, a cross-fertilization of universal imagery and local icons. The fruits of Di Rosa's two-year collaboration with Vincent Sithole, Simon Mavundla, Alice Gcaba, Zodwa Maphumulo, and Elliot Ndwandwe, were exhibited in May 2000 at the Menzi Gallery at the BAT Centre and in July 2000 at the Standard Bank Gallery in Johannesburg. Shortly thereafter two Dirozulu mandalas were included in *Passage d'exotisme,* the fifth Lyon Biennale. I served as project director for the collaboration, an experience that expanded my view of the possibilities for the baskets in terms of both scale and design.

On a visit to Mdukutshani in rural Msinga, I discovered not only a kindred spirit in Creina Alcock, who was leading a similar design and marketing project, but also the existence of a telephone-wire weaving project at Waayhoek, near Ladysmith in central KwaZulu-Natal, midway between Durban and Johannesburg. In 1988 Tessa Katzenellembogen had taught flood survivors from the Waayhoek resettlement community to weave telephone-wire bowls using the soft-wire technique traditionally used by Zulu night watchmen to cover sticks and to make *izimbenge* (beer-pot lids). This soft-wire technique, by which the wire is woven around a mold or template, is less labor intensive than the coiled technique used

THE BAT SHOP
Durban, South Africa

for both the under plates mentioned above and the coiled, hard-wire, master-weave baskets. Many of the traditional zigzag-design bowls produced by the Waayhoek community were marketed to galleries in Johannesburg and to international museum stores.

By the time I found out about this group, Tessa was living in London, and many of the weavers had, as a result of violence and problems with land settlement in the area, moved back to Msinga, where they had lived before being forcibly moved under apartheid. In addition to the zigzag-design bowls, Tessa had developed eggs and bowls made of copper wire and glass beads, and under Creina's watchful eye and direction, these objects have become classics in South African and international craft markets. Hoping to find a new market for this work, we arranged that the BAT Shop would sell a set of four small bowls in various styles and colors, some of solid colors, some with a simple swirl design in two or more colors. This was our first step in the design of a commercial range of baskets.

In 1998 representatives from Black Dog, a newly formed company based in Paris marketing craft products from South Africa, visited Durban. Recognizing the potential to expand the range offered by the BAT Shop, they offered to help develop a very different object: a large bowl with a flat bottom, a shape we have named our lampshade design, which would fuse traditional craft skills with minimalist contemporary design.

At the time, only two weavers were skilled in this technique of weaving the telephone wire over a mold, there was only one master mold, and the supply of materials was limited. The design concepts proved a challenge even to the masterful Jaheni Mkhize. Nonetheless, a mold manufacturer was found and funding made available for the development of skills. Contracted to run a series of workshops to teach new weavers, Jaheni managed to expand the project to include twenty members of the Mkhize family and several friends from the Greytown area, about three hours from Durban.

These lampshade baskets were initially marketed only through Black Dog, and were bought by Donna Karan for her store in New York and were sold at the Musée des arts décoratifs in Paris. After two years, with production capacity at a minimum and demand growing, the BAT Shop took control of marketing, registered the name zenzulu as a trademark, and continues to update and expand the range annually. The objects produced by this design symbiosis have received many accolades, including an Elle Decoration International Design Award in 2002. For recent designs, glass beads and natural seeds have been used together with the telephone wire, and the colors are continuously updated. The design has also been used in a range of fashion accessories and Christmas ornaments.

In late 1998 a visit by the Australian curator Christina McGuiness to establish an artist's exchange program with the Artists Foundation of Western Australia, led to an invitation to attend and exhibit at the Perth International Arts Festival in 2000. Only two artists would be attending and, in an attempt to keep the selection democratic, we arranged a competition and exhibition to coincide with our annual BAT Shop end-of-year party. The Masibambane Trust stepped forward with a generous offer for the prize money. After much deliberation by an independent jury, the work of Vincent Sithole and Ntombifuthi Magwasa was selected and they were invited to Perth. The competition proved to be a great motivation to many other emerging weavers. Zama Khanyile, for instance, won a merit award for a small basket that was to give a taste of what was to come later in her career.

The start of the new millennium saw us winging our way to Australia with enough wire baskets, as well as a few recycled-tin cars and airplanes, to fill the two gallery floors of the Moore's Building in Fremantle. After two years of planning and fundraising, the *Durbs to Freo Wire and Metal Act* became a reality. Arriving on Australia Day, the two Zulu artists had their first taste of a full-blown fireworks display. We were all feted and in the media spotlight for two weeks. With bumper attendances and a sellout show, our first international exhibition was a resounding success.

Invited by the French Institute to curate an exhibition, *Contemporary Zulu Basketry,* at the Alliance Française Gallery in Johannesburg at the end of 2000, we managed to extend the scope of the exhibition to include traditional *ilala* palm basketry from Hlabisa and copper-wire baskets from Msinga. Since its inception, the BAT Shop had forged close ties with the well-known *ilala* palm basket weavers in northern KwaZulu-Natal. The Masibambane Trust again provided the prize money to be awarded for the best baskets at the exhibition. The emerging master weaver Simon Mavundla took the honors in the telephone-wire section. Elias Mtshengu and Ngakhelaphi Mkhize, members of the original Waayhoek project, won the first and second prizes for their copper-wire baskets.

A fortuitous visit to the *Contemporary Zulu Basketry* exhibition by the director of the OXO Tower Wharf and Gallery, in London, served as inspiration for the suggestion that an exhibition of contemporary South African craft might form part of the promotional Celebrate South Africa month in London and throughout the United Kingdom. Works by Alice Gcaba and an installation of the BAT Shop's zenzulu range of contemporary wire baskets were selected for the exhibition, titled *Bowled Over,* that opened at the OXO Gallery in May 2001.

"BAT CENTA"
Tholiwe Ntsele
370 mm diameter
Collection of Marisa Fick-Jordaan

Spreading our wings even further that year, we were invited, sponsored under the Chicago Sister Cities International Program, to exhibit and be the cultural anchor at "Listen to Africa," a conference aimed at highlighting sustainable and innovative development in Africa. This became a memorable experience in more ways than one, as we arrived in Chicago the night before the planes slammed into the Twin Towers on the morning of September 11, 2001. We would like to believe that the colorful telephone-wire baskets on show helped to lift spirits in the aftermath of the tragic events that affected us all.

Continuing the tradition of excellence, Zama Khanyile and Vincent Sithole have joined Ntombifuthi Magwasa and Elliot Mkhize on the FNB Vita Craft Now Awards roll of honor. More opportunities to exhibit internationally are opening up as collectors and museums increasingly acknowledge that the boundaries between what is called *art* and what is called *craft* are being blurred, given that the latter is as valid as the former in representing authentic and vital expression.

Notwithstanding its direction and expansion of the design of objects, the BAT Shop continues to acknowledge and, more importantly, to nurture the unique and original creativity of the artists it works with. Despite harsh social conditions, many creative individuals have managed to put their talents to productive use. Crafters are earning sustainable incomes and many of them are the sole breadwinners in extended families. After decades of benign neglect, Siyanda is being transformed under an urban-renewal program. Water and electricity are being installed, the roads improved, and brick-and-mortar houses will replace the shack dwellings. This is exciting and long overdue, of course, but in some way it is sad in that much of the textured character, individual expression, and innovation in the use of building materials will necessarily disappear. Weaving skills are now being passed on to the next generation. In ten years, coiled telephone-wire basket weaving has become a traditional craft in an urban area where none existed before. My hope is that chickens will continue to scratch in the dust and that the design inspiration that has long been drawn from rural pasts will not be lost as Siyanda itself changes.

opposite:
COLORFUL SWIRL & ZIGZAG BOWLS
zenzulu
Private Collection

THE MASTER WEAVERS **2**

What began as a craft of utility has become, through the dedication of a small group of weavers in a rural community in Zululand, an art form. With the encouragement of their advocates and collectors, a few weavers have taken this craft to the next level, creating a uniquely African artistic expression.

Many people now weave baskets, but a few talented artists have risen above the rest, weaving wire into art. We call them the master weavers, the artists who have contributed something very special to this form. It is they who are appreciated as today's finest weavers of telephone wire.

It started with a few weavers who really were the night watchmen, Elliot Mkhize, Bheki Dlamini, and Alfred Ntuli. Later, masters such as Zodwa Maphumulo, Dudu Cele, Ntombifuthi Magwasa, Alice Gcaba, and Robert Majola joined the ranks and quickly received recognition in South Africa and internationally. Now those pioneers have been joined by a new group of weavers whose work has a contemporary flair: Simon Mavundla, Vincent Sithole, Zama Khanyile, Bheki Sibiya, Jaheni Mkhize, and Mboniseni Khanyile.

opposite page:
JAHENI MKHIZE DEMONSTRATING THE SOFT-WIRE WEAVING TECHNIQUE
Photographed at the BAT Centre, January 2004

Not only do these master weavers provide a legacy of beautiful baskets, but also they have been instrumental in handing down their skills to their friends, family, and the next generation. This is truly an African form of community development, the key to the craft economy that provides income and self-sufficiency for a large community of weavers. These are the masters today, but the art form continues to develop and we look forward to new weavers, who will continue to push the art form forward.

opposite page:
BHEKI SIBIYA DEMONSTRATING THE HARD-WIRE WEAVING TECHNIQUE
Photographed at the BAT Centre, January 2004

DUDU CELE

Born 1970, Port Shepstone, KwaZulu-Natal
Died 2002, Durban

Photograph by William Raats

Dudu began weaving in the early 1990s, learning to weave from her husband, Bheki Dlamini. Although her initial work was similar to his, it did not take long for her to develop her own patterns and figures, including the integration of more animals and natural themes.

Dudu's work is well described as being full of riotous colors and oozing individual expression. She had a passion for celebrating life and occasion in her work, and her baskets showcase images of soccer championships and other such events. Her soft spot for a little romance shows in the red hearts that creep into many of her designs. One basket pays tribute to Nelson Mandela and Graca Machel, and features a luxury car, a honeymoon hotel, cheerleaders, and the *QE2*, on which the distinguished couple sailed to Cape Town.

Like Bheki, she loved including script in her weaving. Celebratory greetings containing birthday, Valentine, and Christmas wishes were her favorite. Because the quality of her lettering was high and her English literacy skills were good, she was always the first weaver who came to mind when the BAT Shop received private or corporate requests that included lettering.

Dudu is represented in the Durban Art Gallery and Gertrude Posel collections, and in numerous private collections in South Africa and abroad. In 1996 she participated in the group exhibition *Jabulisa: The Art of KwaZulu-Natal,* at the Standard Bank National Arts Festival in Grahamstown. The exhibition also toured to the Durban Art Gallery and the Tatham Art Gallery in Pietermaritzburg. Dudu died of AIDS-related complications in 2002.

opposite page:
PLATE COMMEMORATING THE WEDDING
OF NELSON MANDELA & GRACA MACHEL
Dudu Cele
400 mm diameter, Collection of Marisa Fick-Jordaan

following pages, left, clockwise from top left:
JUMPING IMPALA
Dudu Celi
336 mm diameter, Private Collection

GIRAFFE AND OTHER ANIMALS
Dudu Celi
300 mm diameter, Collection of Trisha Wilson

HAPPY BIRTHDAY
Dudu Celi
390 mm diameter, Collection of Jim Rimelspach

AMATUWASA
Dudu Cele
310 mm diameter, Collection of Marisa Fick-Jordaan

following pages, right:
MAPANSULA DANCE
Dudu Cele
290 x 275 mm, Collection of Marisa Fick-Jordaan

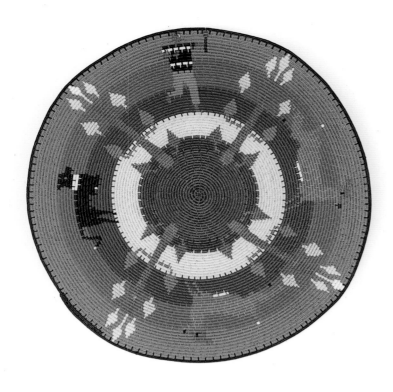
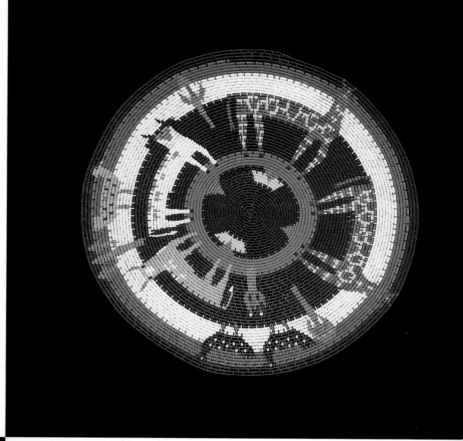
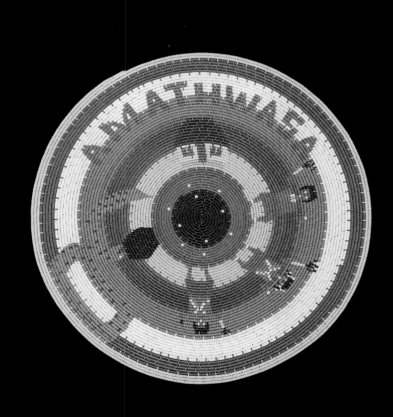

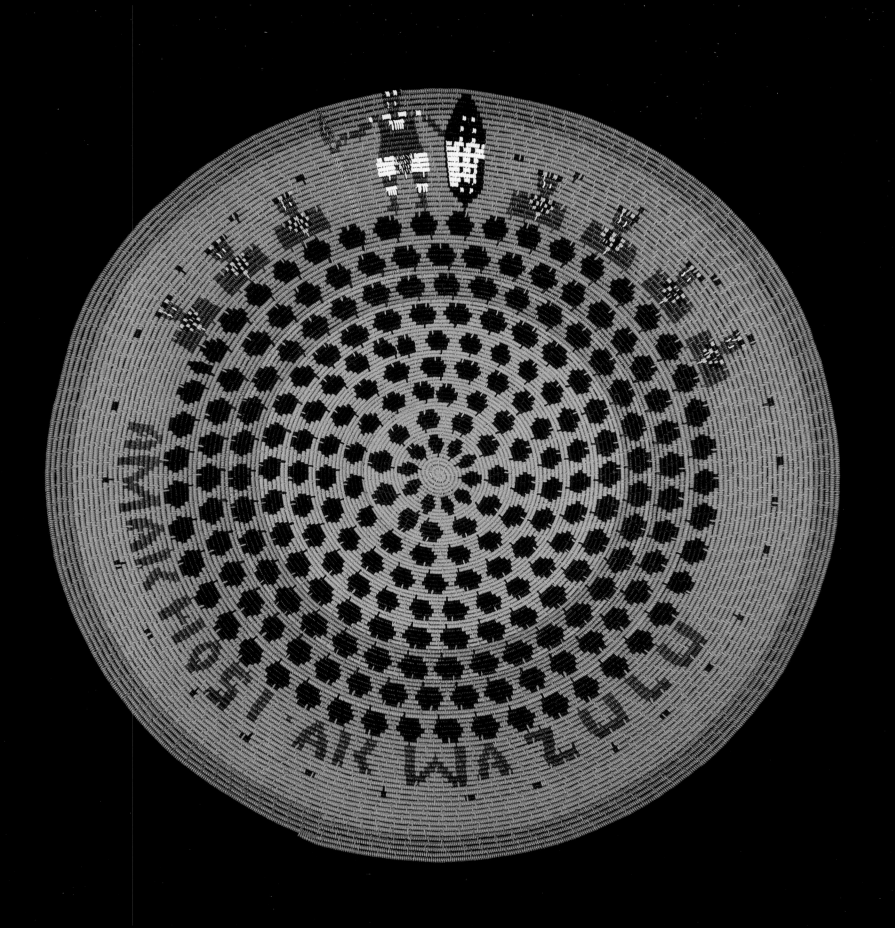

BHEKI DLAMINI

Born 1957, Esikhawini, KwaZulu-Natal
Died 2003, Durban

Photograph by William Raats

Bheki was a great storyteller who would share his stories for hours with anyone who would listen. Luckily this wonderful ability extended beyond the oral tradition and into his weaving. He began weaving in1987 and was the second master weaver to emerge. When he began weaving he used traditional Zulu patterning, but soon incorporated figurative work and circular rings. Being the first weaver to introduce figures into his designs, he made a name for himself by using the basket as a canvas. Transcending the merely decorative, he wove landscapes and stories into his work, dealing with subjects that ranged from traditional Zulu culture through national sports celebrations.

He was a proud traditionalist, committed to the new South Africa, and a fierce sports fanatic, with a particular love for soccer and big sporting events. His works *Umthakathi, Amathwasa, Bafana Bafana,* and *Rugby World Cup*, among others, spell this out quite loudly. With such zest for life, Bheki was consistently inventing imagery and he never repeated designs. Each of his works is unique.

Also distinctive in Bheki's work was his use of text. He was the first weaver to incorporate it into his works as a matter of course, using the technique to title his designs and as part of the overall storytelling process. While many other weavers found that incorporating script into the design of their baskets was a major challenge, Bheki took up the challenge and made it his trademark.

Bheki's work began to get gallery attention in 1994. That year Kim Saks showed some of his works at an exhibition in her Johannesburg gallery. In 1995 Bheki and his wife, Dudu Cele, were caretakers at the BAT Centre. At the Centre's opening exhibit, Bheki, who came to the opening in traditional Zulu costume, exhibited a bowl that he had woven incorporating a Zulu flower and three figures. He was naturally charming and his talent was so apparent that he quickly became one of the artists most frequently represented in exhibitions. In 1996 he exhibited at the KwaZulu-Natal Biennale, and that same year his work was selected for the South African contemporary art exhibition at the Mermaid Gallery in London. This was his first major recognition.

opposite page:
AMAKHOSI AKWAZULU
Bheki Dlamini
470 mm diameter
Collection of David Arment

Like many of the weavers, Bheki arrived in Durban to look for a job. Luckily for the residents of Siyanda, he settled there and came to play a pivotal role in their lives. He found work as a delivery man at Fast Sails, a sail-manufacturing business in Durban. There, during his breaks, he socialized with Elliot Mkhize, a security guard who made use of the time by weaving. Bheki watched, learning the skills. Back in Siyanda he shared these skills with others, and became pivotal to the early growth of the craft.

Bheki died of cancer in 2003. He lives on in his work, in his storytelling, and in the new traditions of the wire-weaving skills he shared with many of his fellow weavers.

opposite page, clockwise from top left:
UMSHADO WESIZULU
Bheki Dlamini
500 mm diameter
Collection of the Phansi Museum, Durban

ZULU WARRIORS
Bheki Dlamini
412 mm diameter
Private Collection

PARTY TIME
Bheki Dlamini
342 mm diameter
Collection of Trisha Wilson

UDWENDWE LUKAKOTO
Bheki Dlamini
368 mm diameter
Private Collection

following pages, left:
MADIBA (NELSON MANDELA) AND GRACA GO TO PARLIAMENT
Bheki Dlamini
470 mm diameter
Collection of Marisa Fick-Jordaan

following pages, right:
BOWL WTH ZULU FLOWER PATTERN AND FIGURES
Bheki Dlamini
130 x 130 mm
Collection of Marisa Fick-Jordaan

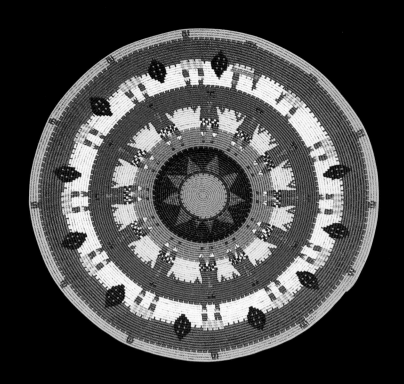

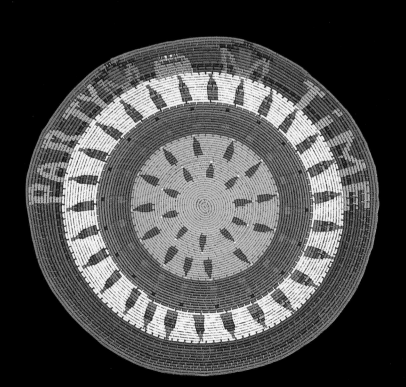

ALICE GCABA

Born 1956, Flagstaff, Eastern Cape

Alice grew up in a rural community, left school after grade four, and began helping her family with the farming. In 1975 she moved from the Eastern Cape to Durban, looking for employment. She found domestic work in Greenwood Park, where she worked for twenty years until her employers died. After their deaths she survived by working as a hawker in Durban, until she began producing telephone-wire baskets in 1996.

In Durban, Alice moved from the rural community of Inanda to KwaMashu (a suburb outside Durban), before settling in Siyanda, where she was one of the first residents. Luckily, she settled next door to Mavis Njokweni, who, like so many of the other weavers in Siyanda, generously shared her skills with Alice. A year later, Alice began selling her work to the BAT Shop.

Her style of baskets is unmistakable. Typically she uses a bright base color and adds many randomly placed figures to her plates and bowls. She weaves the icons of her South African world, both rural and urban, into her baskets, and her figures include people, huts, houses, lizards, and various other animals. When she works with patterns she often uses an interesting interplay of colors between positive and negative. Consistently working with bright and vibrant colors, Alice has created a quirky style.

In addition to her figurative design elements, Alice has become a master of form, creating not only plates, but also a deep and precise hard-wire bowl. This shape is a challenge to weave, and Alice does it with ease.

An independent woman who lives alone, Alice provides for herself and also supports her extended family back in the Eastern Cape. Like many of the other weavers, she has taught a core of Siyanda women to weave.

opposite page:
LARGE BLACK PLATE WITH FIGURES
Alice Gcaba
476 mm diameter, Collection of David Arment

following pages, left:
RED PLATE WITH FIGURES
Alice Gcaba
362 mm diameter, Private Collection

WHITE PLATE WITH FIGURES
Alice Gcaba
420 mm diameter, Collection of David Arment

PURPLE BOWL WITH FIGURES
Alice Gcaba
368 mm diameter, Collection of David Arment

BLUE PLATE WITH FIGURES
Alice Gcaba
420 mm diameter, Private Collection

following pages, right:
PURPLE BOWL WITH FIGURES
Alice Gcaba
368 mm diameter, Collection of David Arment

ZAMA KHANYILE

Born 1971, Empangeni

Zama's story is one of perseverance, and is the stuff of fairy tales—a politically correct Cinderella-meets-Pygmalion story. Zama had a low-wage job at a restaurant at Durban Station. She wished for better things and always kept an eye open for something better. And one day it came to her. She read a news story about Ntombifuthi Magwasa, a settlement dweller who had won the big FNB Vita Craft Now Award for her telephone-wire baskets.

Zama immediately began weaving baskets to try to sell to the BAT Shop. Her early baskets were, in a word, *terrible*, and the BAT Shop bought none. For six months she persisted, making poor-quality baskets and begging the buyers to take her wares, "even for little money." She would arrive on sale days, timid, her face all but obscured under a hat, lurk behind all the other weavers, and hide her mouth behind her hand when she spoke. But she never gave up.

Then came the competition to select entries for the Perth International Arts Festival. The judges spotted a basket they liked. It displayed quality and a good sense of design. In a word, it was beautiful. So it was selected, and off it went to Perth. When Marisa checked the pricing on the basket, she found that Zama, so used to disappointment, had severely underpriced it. Marisa raised the price by 400 percent and it sold. In addition, Zama won a small cash prize in the competition.

After the festival, Zama arrived to be paid for her basket. When she received her money, she burst into tears. It was the most money she had ever earned in her life, and probably one of the first times she had ever felt validated. She has been weaving incredible baskets ever since. She began experimenting with imagery and soon after made a basket decorated with cows. After that, Marisa showed her some wrapping paper illustrated with leopards. She incorporated the animals into her next work, complete with three-dimensional whiskers. Subsequently she produced a series of spotted-cat baskets, and now,

opposite page:
PLATE WITH MULTICOLOR CATS
Zama Khanyile
508 mm diameter
Collection of David Arment

working on quite a large scale, includes figures, birds, and trees. It seems there is no stopping Zama, whose name, incidentally, means "to try"!

Since her success in Perth and receiving a merit award at the FNB Vita Craft Now Awards in 2002, Zama's work has become much sought after and she has become a full-time weaver. Her confidence level has increased along with her prices. Though she still lives in KwaMashu, where she learned to weave from her neighbor Vusi Khanyile, her life is a far cry from those days in the restaurant.

opposite page, clockwise from top left:
TURQUOISE PLATE WITH ANIMALS AND FIGURES
Zama Khanyile
540 mm diameter
Collection of Melanie Cohen

BLACK-AND-WHITE COWS
Zama Khanyile
490 mm diameter
Private Collection

RED PLATE WITH FIGURES AND HOUSES
Zama Khanyile
540 mm diameter
Collection of David Arment

LEOPARDS
Zama Khanyile
400 mm diameter
Collection of David Arment

MBONISENI KHANYILE

Born 1967, Eshowe

Mboniseni is very independent, has a strong personality, and, like an archetypal artist, can be decidedly stubborn. He always arrives to sell his wares on the wrong day and he usually does so late on a Friday afternoon, when the buyers are tired and ready to go home. When questioned about his sense of timing, he remains unfazed, smiles or laughs, and simply continues the negotiation process. It's a skill he must have learned from a tough start in life.

In 1984 he left Emasunelwini High School in Eshowe, having completed only grade nine. This qualification did not get him very far, and he soon found himself working as a farm laborer, cutting sugar cane. With very little prospect of other work coming along, Mboniseni had no choice but to continue working as a laborer. He did so for eleven years until, in 1995, he decided to move to Durban in search of better pay. In Durban he found piece-work in the construction industry and as a cleaner.

In 1996 he moved to the more affordable settlement of Siyanda and began a new life in the midst of the Siyanda weavers. The move was life changing. Many of their neighbors were weaving for a living, and it was not long before his girlfriend, Bongiwe Doyisa, began learning to weave. She in turn taught him. He quickly learned how to make *izimbenge* (beer pot lids), and in 1997 he stopped doing piecework and began weaving full time. That same year he began supplying the BAT Shop.

Mboniseni says that the success of his neighbors Zodwa Maphumulo, Ntombifuthi Magwasa, and Simon Mavundla, was an inspiration to him, and that as he had excelled at craft at school, he felt he could be a success too.

Today he is known for his frog designs and for his brightly colored geometrics. He is skilled at including text in his designs, and as a result he has secured quite a number of commissions from collectors and the corporate sector. A number of his designs include AIDS slogans.

opposite page:
ORANGE FROGS
Mboniseni Khanyile
420 mm diameter
Private Collection

following pages, left:
RED FROGS AND BUTTERFLIES
Mboniseni Khanyile
410 mm diameter
Private Collection

following pages, right:
AIDS KILLS
Mboniseni Khanyile
390 mm diameter
Private Collection

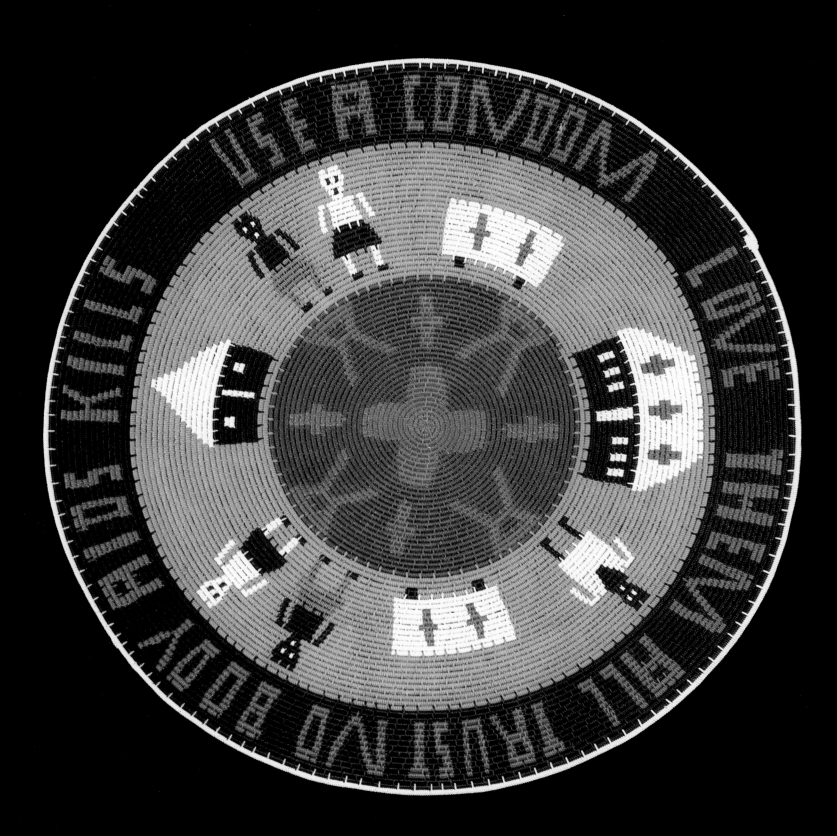

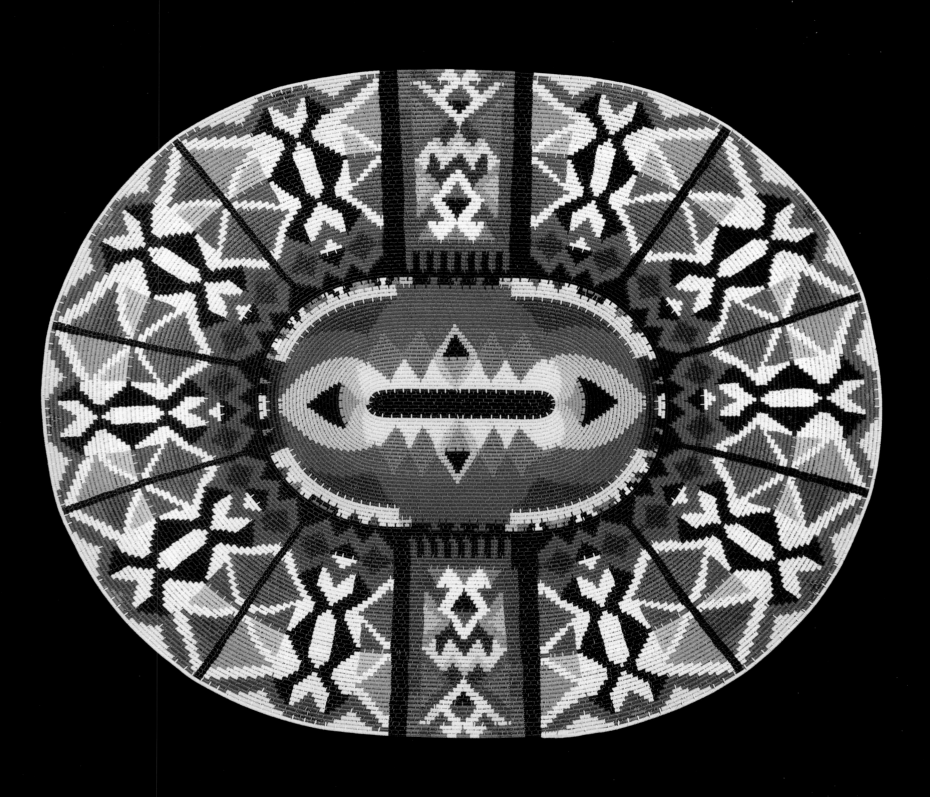

NTOMBIFUTHI MAGWASA

Born 1965, Nongoma, KwaZulu-Natal

Ntombifuthi wove her first basket in 1993, after being taught how to weave by her neighbor Anamaria Dlamini in Siyanda. She had a natural talent for the craft and soon developed an unusually complex sense of color and balance in her designs. Inspired by the colors of the wire and how the colors work together, she experiments constantly with new patterns and scale. She looks for inspiration in books, magazines, and in the colors and patterns she sees around her. Her designs range from traditional Zulu patterns to bold contemporary patterns that reflect a melding of Zulu and Ndebele traditions.

Early on in her work Ntombifuthi displayed an exceptional talent. Marisa noted this at once and encouraged her to refine the shapes and sizes of her baskets and to develop her designs. Then Marisa lent her an embroidery book that included stunning designs on kelim carpets. Ntombifuthi was immediately interested in the complex patterns and designs. She kept the book for three months and returned with a basket showing the beginnings of her now-famous design style, a complex relationship of foreground to background.

In 1998 Ntombifuthi won the top prize in the prestigious FNB Vita Craft Now awards, South Africa's principal craft competition. The prize brought significant recognition for her and, by association, for all the telephone-wire weavers of Siyanda. Today she is an internationally recognized artist whose work is represented in many public and private collections locally and internationally.

But it was not all smooth sailing for Ntombifuthi. Like many South Africans, she has had her fair share of hardships. She was born in Nongoma into a conservative rural Zulu family, where her life was governed by set social, economic, and gender constraints. When she completed grade three, her father took her out of school and she was put to doing what is referred to as women's work. In the Magwasa family, she says, it was custom that girls did not go to school.

opposite page:
LARGE OVAL ABSTRACT PLATE
Ntombifuthi Magwasa
515 x 425 mm
Collection of David Arment

Luckily Ntombifuthi realized quite early that her lack of education was going to be a stumbling block in life. Influenced by her sister's skill at craft, and by economic necessity, she began a journey to find a means of making a living. The journey took her through a dressmaking course, into a milkshake flavor factory, and on into the world of telephone-wire basket weaving.

While living in Siyanda she met Bheki Sibiya, to whom she has taught the weaving technique. They are now married and have a family. Today the woman who once had never left her province, who once had never boarded a plane, describes herself as a businesswoman and a full-time artist. You may catch Ntombifuthi between baskets, at awards ceremonies and exhibitions, on flights to Cape Town and Chicago, Johannesburg and Perth, or simply enjoying her favorite curry at home in Durban.

opposite page:
ABSTRACT PLATE
Ntombifuthi Magwasa
450 mm diameter
Collection of Marisa Fick-Jordaan

following pages, left, clockwise from top left:
ABSTRACT PLATE
Ntombifuthi Magwasa
413 mm diameter
Private Collection

ABSTRACT PLATE
Ntombifuthi Magwasa
450 mm diameter
Collection of David Arment

ABSTRACT PLATE
Ntombifuthi Magwasa
440 mm diameter
Private Collection

ABSTRACT PLATE
Ntombifuthi Magwasa
476 mm diameter
Collection of David Arment

following pages, right, clockwise from top left:
ABSTRACT PLATE
Ntombifuthi Magwasa
370 mm diameter
Private Collection

ABSTRACT PLATE
Ntombifuthi Magwasa
375 mm diameter
Collection of Trisha Wilson

ABSTRACT PLATE
Ntombifuthi Magwasa
365 mm diameter
Collection of Marisa Fick-Jordaan

ABSTRACT PLATE
Ntombifuthi Magwasa
390 mm diameter
Collection of the Phansi Museum, Durban

ROBERT MAJOLA

Born 1946, Eshowe, KwaZulu-Natal

Robert Majola traveled to Durban from the Eshowe area in 1982 looking for work. Unlike many other weavers, he did find employment and more than two decades later he is still working full time with Portnet, the National Port Authority, at the harbor in Durban. He produces baskets in his spare time.

Back in the early 1990s Robert noticed a fellow commuter from KwaMashu who spent his train journeys weaving objects from telephone wire. Fascinated by this occupation, Robert took informal lessons from the man during their daily trips. But the skill did not come easily; his tutor used an *usungulu* (a long needle) in his work, which Robert could not seem to master. Eventually, the man (whose name Robert does not know) let him use his hands, which is when, Robert says, everything started.

Since he began weaving, Robert, like many weavers, has collected his wire supplies from the scrap yards. The variety in his sources has influenced his use of colors, his palette ranging from primary to pastel colors, depending on what he can obtain. He does occasionally rely on formal suppliers for specific colors for special orders.

For molds he still uses the now-rusty, conventionally styled enamel bowls that he bought years ago from African trading stores in the rural areas. He works on these molds and has developed a unique soft-wire weave, creating small bowls with markedly geometric patterns. He creates between four and six pieces a week

He arrived at the BAT Shop soon after it opened in August 1995. Ever since then he has been a regular supplier, arriving to sell during his lunches, tea breaks, and on Saturdays. He jokes that he has to sneak away from work to deliver his bowls. That said, he is very proud of his success and has brought his boss and coworkers in to see that he really does sell his work at the BAT Shop.

opposite page, left to right:
FOUR SOFT-WIRE BOWLS
Robert Majola
140, 170, 140, and 170 mm diameter
Collection of Magda van der Vloed

ZODWA MAPHUMULO

Born 1960, Port Shepstone, KwaZulu-Natal

Zodwa Maphumulo works as a full-time artist from her home in the settlement of Siyanda outside Durban. She was the first woman to learn telephone-wire basket weaving in 1992, and has since developed her weaving skills into a fine art. She enjoys local and international recognition and was chosen to represent South Africa at the Smithsonian Folk Art Festival in Washington, D.C., in 1999. Between 1998 and 2000 she worked on the Dirozulu project with the French artist Hervé Di Rosa. Visitors to the New Orleans Jazz Festival in 2004 were given the opportunity to meet her—she was one of twenty South African art crafters invited to attend and exhibit at the festival.

Zodwa's work is respected for a number of reasons. She is an expert weaver renowned for her high-quality baskets that include both geometric and figurative elements incorporating people and animals. She has developed unique elephant and dog characters, inspired by and adapted from the carpet designs she was shown. Her images of schoolgirls and of Zulu women have become her signature. Her form, too, is important: she has perfected a sophisticated and elegant shape for her plates, which have developed into a unique bowl structure. When it comes to color, she loves working with both pastels and brights but is particularly fond of pink, yellow, and purple.

Her success has taken her a long way. Born in 1960, she is the daughter of farm laborers. Like so many other children, she left school at an early age, having completed only grade six. She moved to Durban in 1980, at the age of twenty, and settled in KwaMashu, where she worked as a domestic servant for a black nurse. In 1984 she moved to Siyanda, built herself a shack, and took work as a domestic tog worker (a casual laborer) in neighboring Newlands East. She worked there from 1984 to 1992. Although life was still tough, the move to Siyanda was to be fortuitous.

At the settlement she encountered Bheki and Albert Dlamini, two of the handful of weavers at the time. Tired of poorly paid work, she spent time learning and developing her

opposite page:

YELLOW BOWL WITH FIGURES

Zodwa Maphumulo
470 mm diameter
Collection of David Arment

skill with Bheki and Albert. Bheki helped her find a market for her baskets through Paul Mikula, and in 1992 she left her job and began weaving full time. In 1995 Bheki introduced Zodwa to the BAT Shop. She laughs as she tells the story. Apparently Bheki dragged her and the four other Siyanda weavers down to the harbor by taxi from Siyanda. He had them traipsing under freeways, through the traffic, over railroad lines, and along the water's edge to find the shop. This was the start of a long relationship with Marisa and the BAT Shop, which continues to this day.

opposite page:
COUPLES
Zodwa Maphumulo
400 mm diameter
Collection of Marisa Fick-Jordaan

following pages, left, clockwise from top left:
SCHOOL GIRLS
Zodwa Maphumulo
408 mm diameter
Collection of David Arment

BLACK CATS
Zodwa Maphumulo
476 mm diameter
Private Collection

PLATE WITH RED HEART
Zodwa Maphumulo
370 mm diameter
Collection of Trisha Wilson

RED, WHITE, AND BLUE SCHOOL GIRLS
Zodwa Maphumulo
388 mm diameter
Collection of Oprah Winfrey

following pages, right:
ZULU WOMEN
Zodwa Maphumulo
420 mm diameter
Private Collection

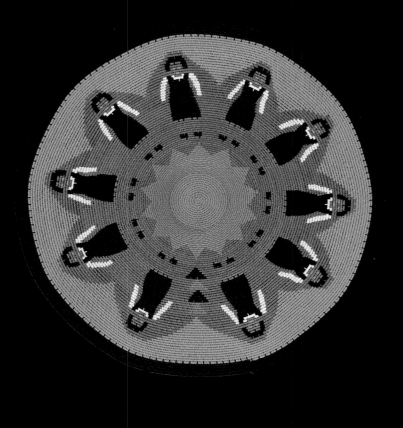

SIMON MAVUNDLA

Born 1970, Kranskop, KwaZulu-Natal

Simon left school after completing grade nine, to earn a living. He started by making woodcarvings to sell within the Kranskop community, but in 1996 he moved to Siyanda and started looking for work in Durban. Fortunately he never found work. He did, however, meet his future wife, Nomvuselela Msimang, who taught him how to weave, and who introduced him to the BAT Shop.

In 1998 he completed a training course and began to emerge as a respected telephone-wire weaver. His skill was immediately evident and he was invited to work on the Dirozulu project. On that project, Simon worked closely with Hervé Di Rosa and this two-year interaction had a significant influence on Simon's use of color and form.

Complex weaving patterns define Simon's work, which contains a free-flowing style of geometric design incorporating plant and animal motifs. With the inclusion of snakes and eagles, he references aspects of Zulu mythology. In 2000 he received the Masibambane Award at an exhibition of contemporary Zulu baskets in Johannesburg, sponsored by the French Institute and the Alliance Française. This was his first visit to Johannesburg and a trip to the zoo there proved to be inspirational. It was after that that Simon first started adding animals to his geometric designs.

Simon's improved financial situation has allowed him to buy a bicycle and now he travels around Durban on his mountain bike, dressed for the Tour de France. One can only imagine this sporty figure, a lone cyclist in a world of crammed taxis, weaving through the traffic and flying past the pedestrians and bus queues, with his latest creation safely tucked into his backpack. House proud, he has painted his tin home a royal blue that stands out from the other homes, and has a neat fenced garden in the front.

With demand for his baskets growing, Simon was eventually able to afford the last down payment of his *lobola,* the traditional price for a bride in Zulu culture. He and Nomvuselela were married at the end of 2003.

opposite page:
CROCODILES AND SNAKE
Simon Mavundla
440 mm diameter
Collection of David Arment

following pages, left:
CRABS AND EAGLES
Simon Mavundla
432 mm diameter
Private Collection

following pages, right:
SNAKES AND BIRDS
Simon Mavundla
425 mm diameter
Collection of David Arment

ELLIOT MKHIZE

Born 1945, Richmond, KwaZulu-Natal

Elliot was introduced to the world of weaving at a young age, when he went to school at Inhlazuka near Richmond. At school, children in the early grades were taught grass-weaving techniques in their art-and-craft classes. At the same time he was introduced to art and, one could say, to the economy of art at home, where both his grandfather and his father carved wooden spoons and utensils for trading. Using money he earned from his craftwork, his grandfather was even able to buy cattle for *lobola*. So in the 1960s, when Elliot had to choose a career path, it seemed natural that he chose to study at the reputable Ndaleni Art School in Richmond, which was then enjoying its heyday.

But, art being art and economic reality its often ugly self, Elliot went back to Sibonelo High School to finish his formal education. Thereafter, he found a job as a supervisor with Lever Brothers in Durban. In 1968 his daughter, the first of ten children, was born. From then on, his growing family necessitated steady employment and Elliot stayed on with Lever Brothers for several years. Then followed a brief stint as a machine operator at the *Natal Mercury* newspaper. A job at the Natal Playhouse theater as a night watchman was his brush with destiny. He was introduced to the "night watchman's art," the world of telephone-wire weaving.

After observing his fellow night watchmen use wire to decorate the handles of their sticks, Elliot began to experiment with telephone wire. He, however, worked with the more traditional bowl form and, in so doing, became one of the originators of the contemporary form of coiled-wire baskets. He wove his first basket in 1973, and took it to the African Art Centre in Durban. Jo Thorpe snapped it up and put it into the African Art Centre's collection, where it was displayed in the shop until it was stolen in a robbery. Elliot quickly became a sought-after weaver and in 1984 he began working full time as an artist. He is currently South Africa's most renowned and successful telephone-wire weaver, and the only master weaver with formal art school training.

opposite page:
ABSTRACT PLATE
Elliot Mkhize
360 mm diameter
Collection of David Arment

81

In one of his first works, Elliot used traditional designs, and included his name in prominent letters. Today he is known for his highly developed sense of color, weaving quality, and design detail. He typically uses abstract patterns, with occasional figures or letters, usually his initials, and he is a master at weaving intricate patterns in black and white. His trademark is an extremely tight weave, which gives his baskets a weight and density unlike any others.

Elliot was one of the first weavers to travel abroad, and has been to America, Denmark, France, Namibia, and Sweden. In 1995 he won a merit award in the FNB Vita Craft Now competition. He is also represented in major South African and international collections of contemporary Zulu arts. In the past he has been contracted to run workshops for weavers at the BAT Centre, and at the Durban Art Gallery he occasionally runs classes for hobby crafters.

opposite page, clockwise from top left:
ABSTRACT PLATE
Elliot Mkhize
255 mm diameter
Private Collection

ABSTRACT PLATE
Elliot Mkhize
273 mm diameter
Private Collection

ABSTRACT PLATE
Elliot Mkhize
290 mm diameter
Private Collection

ABSTRACT PLATE
Elliot Mkhize
280 mm diameter
Collection of the Phansi Museum, Durban

following pages, left:
ABSTRACT PLATE
Elliot Mkhize
280 mm diameter
Collection of Marisa Fick-Jordaan

following pages, right:
ABSTRACT PLATE
Elliot Mkhize
320 x 290 mm
Collection of the Phansi Museum, Durban

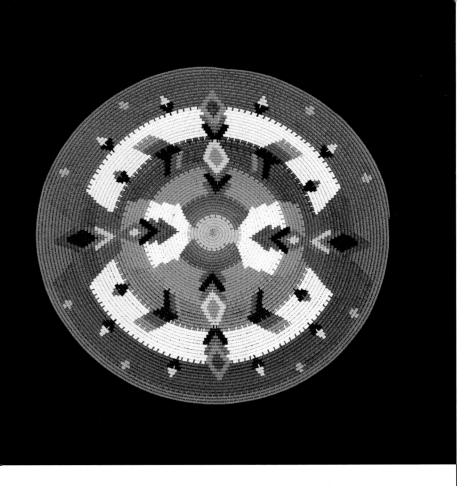
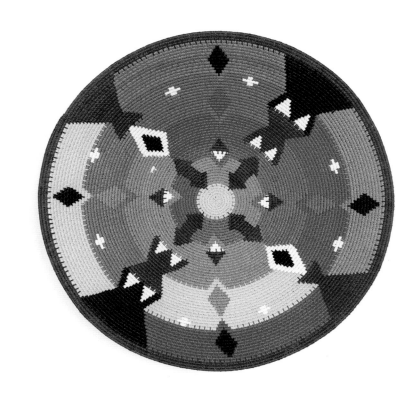

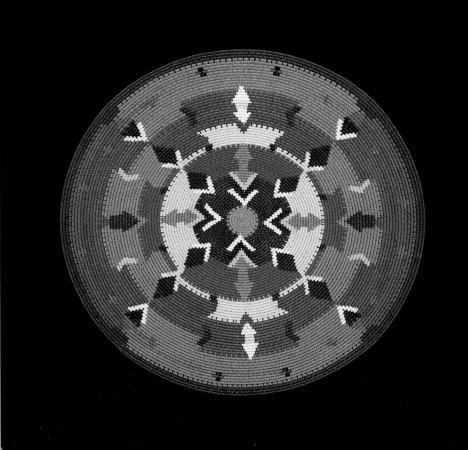

JAHENI MKHIZE

Born 1953, Greytown, KwaZulu-Natal

An accomplished weaver, Jaheni Mkhize is a consistent supplier to the BAT Shop. The quality of her work is exceptional and is frequently accepted for the FNB Vita Craft Now competitions

Jaheni uses the soft-wire technique that is the basis of much of the BAT Shop's zenzulu collection. Her weaving is done over a mold and on a scale that is unusually large. A perfectionist who weaves flawless baskets of outstanding quality, she loves working with vibrant colors. Yet she is also a natural minimalist, a quality that works well with soft-wire contemporary forms.

In Zulu culture a child's name always has a significant, and often literal, meaning. The Zulu word *jaha* means to chase, gallop, race, or be in a hurry. Her name refers to how quickly she was born and its meaning remains appropriate: she is a prolific weaver and learns, absorbs, and incorporates new ideas very quickly. She adapts and experiments frequently, and shows heaps of initiative, always seeking to take her craft and design forward.

Jaheni was first introduced to the world of wire weaving by her friend Mbopiseni Ngubani, one of the Waayhoek weavers. Mbopiseni used to visit Jaheni in Greytown, and taught her the craft during these visits. At that stage Jaheni pursued weaving as a hobby. In 1995 she moved to Siyanda in search of a place of her own. There she took further weaving lessons from Elliot Ndwandwe, the unofficial chief of the settlement. During that time she made four coiled baskets and sold them to the BAT Shop. Growing in confidence, she produced a soft-wire basket to sell. That single basket led to the later development of what became known as the Jaheni range of small bowls.

In addition to weaving, Jaheni was employed to teach the soft-wire technique at a BAT Shop workshop. Several members of her family attended the workshop, some coming all the way from Greytown. Her family remains the core group of zenzulu weavers.

opposite page:
RED-AND-PURPLE ZIGZAG BOWL
Jaheni Mkhize
380 mm diameter
Collection of David Arment

following pages, left:
LARGE, BRIGHT BOWL
Jaheni Mkhize
275 x 350 mm
Collection of David Arment

following pages, right:
ZIGZAG LAMPSHADE BOWL
Jaheni Mkhize
380 mm diameter
Private Collection

ALFRED NTULI

Born 1953, Maphumulo, KwaZulu-Natal

In 1985 Alfred moved to KwaMashu in Durban from the Maphumulo region of rural KwaZulu-Natal. A year later his family joined him and they moved to Siyanda, where they settled next door to Bheki Dlamini. This move was a turning point for Alfred as Bheki exposed him to the craft of telephone-wire weaving and he quickly set about weaving himself. Rather than weaving the same form as Bheki favored, Alfred wove vessels based on the shape of the *izinkhamba* (round beer pots), for which he later developed lids with an embedded top. Most of the weavers today still weave *izimbenge* (beer pot lids), and so Alfred's *izinkhamba* have become his trademark.

Alfred says that he learned the basics of weaving simply by watching Bheki work, but that Bheki actively taught him how to incorporate designs into the weaving process. In terms of design, he was originally inspired by the designs and colors used in traditional Maphumulo beadwork, but today he uses a wide palette of colors.

Between 1986 and 1987 he sold his work to other Siyanda residents who resold his work in Durban, but in 1987 Bheki introduced him to Paul Mikula and to the African Art Centre, where he started selling his creations more commercially. Paul became an active collector of Alfred's pots, is still Alfred's first sales stop today, and Paul's collection, housed at the Phansi Museum, includes a large collection of Alfred's work.

In 2000 Alfred and his family moved back to Maphumulo and into his original family homestead. His success today enables him to travel from there to Durban to sell his wares.

opposite page:
ABSTRACT LIDDED POT
Alfred Ntuli
215 x 254 mm
Collection of David Arment

following pages, left:
YELLOW LIDDED POT
Alfred Ntuli
190 x 230 mm
Collection of David Arment

following pages, right:
THREE LIDDED POTS
Alfred Ntuli
230 x 250, 225 x 240, and 215 x 240 mm
Collection of the Phansi Museum, Durban

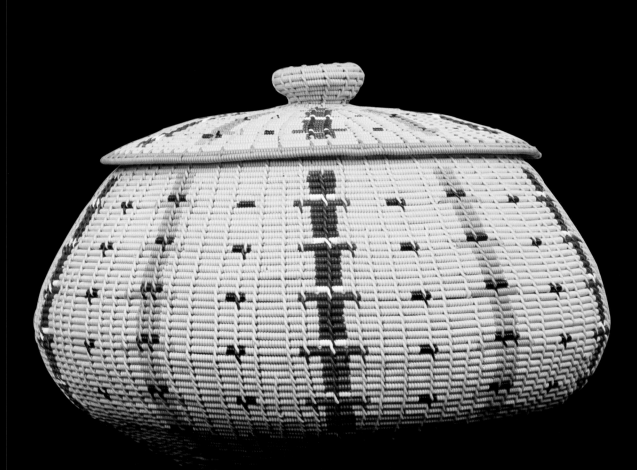

BHEKI SIBIYA

Born 1955, Hlabisa, KwaZulu-Natal

Bheki is married to Ntombifuthi Magwasa, who taught him how to weave. As a result of his and of his wife's success with their baskets, Bheki has recently stopped working at odd jobs and is focusing exclusively on his weaving.

He frequently collaborates with Ntombifuthi on design and pattern, and the influence is often apparent in their work. Yet the addition of stripes, diagonal patterns, and zigzags is what distinguishes his work. He identifies pink, red, purple, turquoise, and silver as his favorite colors. Bheki enjoys the challenge presented by the complexity of new design interpretations, but continues to find inspiration in traditional geometric Zulu beadwork patterns from the Nongoma and Hlabisa districts.

He comes from Hlabisa, a region that specializes in the making of traditional Zulu grass baskets. Although his mother made woven sleeping mats for practical use, there was no history of craft making in his immediate family. Perhaps this is why he lined his first wire *ukhamba* (clay beer pot) with thick glue, so that it would hold water and thus be more useful. Because the other weavers were producing *imbenge*, he initially produced a few *ukhamba* vessels with lids, hoping to corner a new market. Later he realized that large-scale *imbenge*-shaped baskets would have better financial returns as they appeal to collectors, a more lucrative market.

In 1973 Bheki arrived in Durban, where he managed to find odd jobs as a plumber and gardener. He relocated to Siyanda in 1988, where he met Ntombifuthi. Breaking with patriarchal tradition, Bheki supports Ntombifuthi's new-found fame and travels, and is happy to stay at home to look after the children and keep the home fires burning.

opposite page:
LARGE, OVAL ABSTRACT PLATE
Bheki Sibiya
460 x 380 mm
Collection of David Arment

VINCENT SITHOLE

Born 1970, Ilenge, Ladysmith,
KwaZulu-Natal

Tired of pushing wheelbarrows on construction sites in Ladysmith, Vincent Sithole moved temporarily to Siyanda in 1996 and lived with his sister while scouting for work. He failed to find any useful employment, but luckily discovered the vibrant Siyanda telephone-wire weaving community right under his nose.

First he noticed Bheki Dlamini weaving, and then others. He watched them and taught himself the technique. His first basket was monochromatic, but he soon produced work that showed a flair for pattern and color. Albert Dlamini, who helped him find materials, also introduced him to the BAT Shop. His early work showed his exceptional talent, and Marisa began buying his baskets immediately. Since establishing a name for himself, Vincent has moved back to his rural home outside Ladysmith, where he works and lives with his family.

Vincent's intricate geometric patterning and unusual combinations of color created designs reminiscent of stained-glass windows. He also references the natural environment, incorporating images of birds and plants into his designs. His interest in nature began, he says, as a child, when he used to herd his father's cattle and watching and interacting with the animals kept him occupied through the long hours. Vincent also enjoyed observing snakes, birds, and insects, the fish in the iThukela River and, more recently, the monkeys he saw while living in Siyanda. Incorporating these images in his work takes him back to his childhood.

In 1998 Vincent participated on the Dirozulu project. Hervé Di Rosa's designs called on him to weave in a free-flowing, figurative style, very different from the geometric patterns of his own work. The increased scale, bands of color, and organic shapes of Di Rosa's designs have had a lasting influence on Vincent's work. Large-scale pieces, such as *Zulu Wedding*, in the collection of the Mpumalanga Provincial Legislature, and *Bugs*, which is in David Arment's collection, express his increasing confidence and imaginative use of figurative and geometric designs.

opposite page:
CIRCLE OF LIFE
Vincent Sithole
560 mm diameter
Collection of David Arment

The story behind *Nature*, which is in Marisa Fick-Jordaan's collection, is quite beautiful. In 2002 Vincent's childhood home burned down and the family lost everything. After the fire they rebuilt the home and Vincent produced the basket titled *Nature*. The design is filled with images from nature and symbolically deals with the Creation and renewal.

In 1999 Vincent won first prize in the BAT Shop Masibambane Trust telephone-wire weaving competition. This prize led to his being invited to travel to Australia in 2000, one of the guest artists at the Durbs to *Freo Wire and Metal Act* exhibition, presented at the Perth International Arts Festival. Vincent's work has always been selected for the FNB Vita Craft Now Awards, and in 2003 he won the gold award. Most recently he was invited to exhibit his work at the inaugural Santa Fe International Folk Art Market in July 2004.

opposite page:

GARDEN

Vincent Sithole

600 mm diameter, Collection of Marisa Fick-Jordaan

following pages, left, clockwise from top left:

BROWN SNAKES AND WHITE DUCKS

Vincent Sithole

530 mm diameter, Collection of Trisha Wilson

BLACK MAMBA

Vincent Sithole

394 mm diameter, Private Collection

STAINED-GLASS PATTERN IN RINGS

Vincent Sithole

310 mm diameter, Private Collection

BUTTERFLIES

Vincent Sithole

390 mm diameter, Private Collection

following pages, right, clockwise from top left:

TWO LIONS

Vincent Sithole

340 mm diameter, Collection of David Arment

STAINED-GLASS PATTERN

Vincent Sithole

305 mm diameter, Collection of David Arment

RHINOS

Vincent Sithole

420 mm diameter, Private Collection

BUGS AND A SNAKE, PATTERNED AFTER A GIFT WRAP DESIGN

Vincent Sithole

650 mm diameter, Collection of David Arment

page 102:

BLACK CHAMELEONS WITH FLOWERS

Vincent Sithole

465 mm diameter, Collection of Margaret Daniel

page 103:

THREE ZULU DANCERS

Vincent Sithole

546 mm diameter, Collection of David Arment

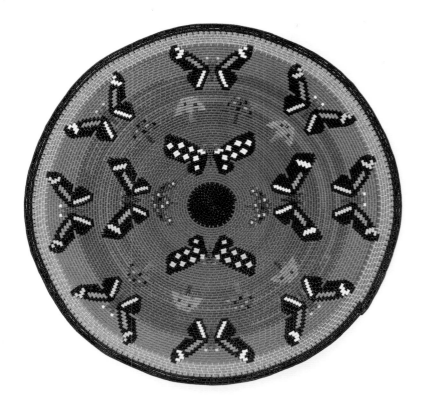

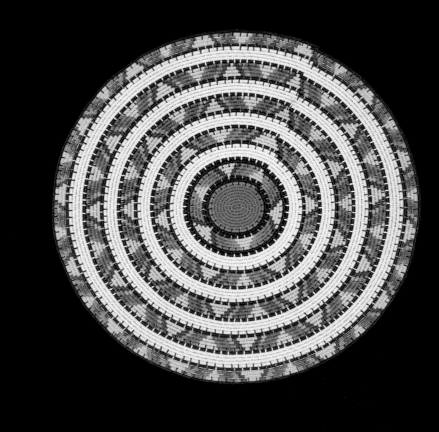

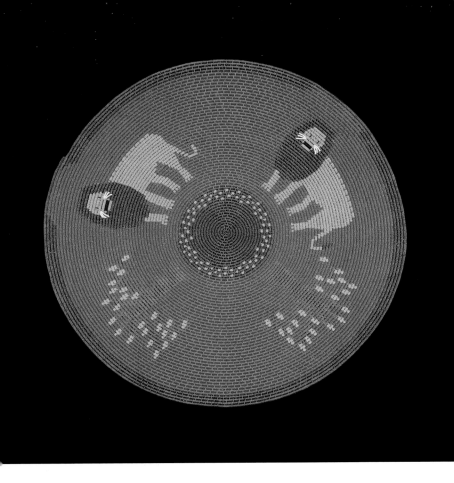

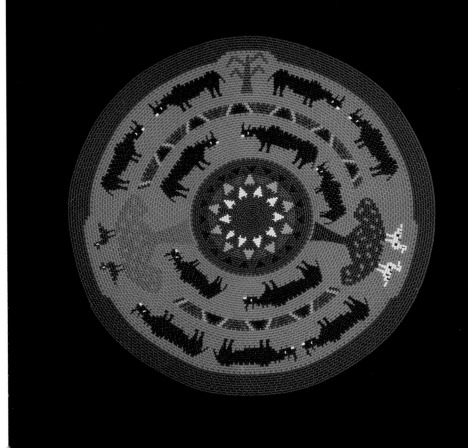

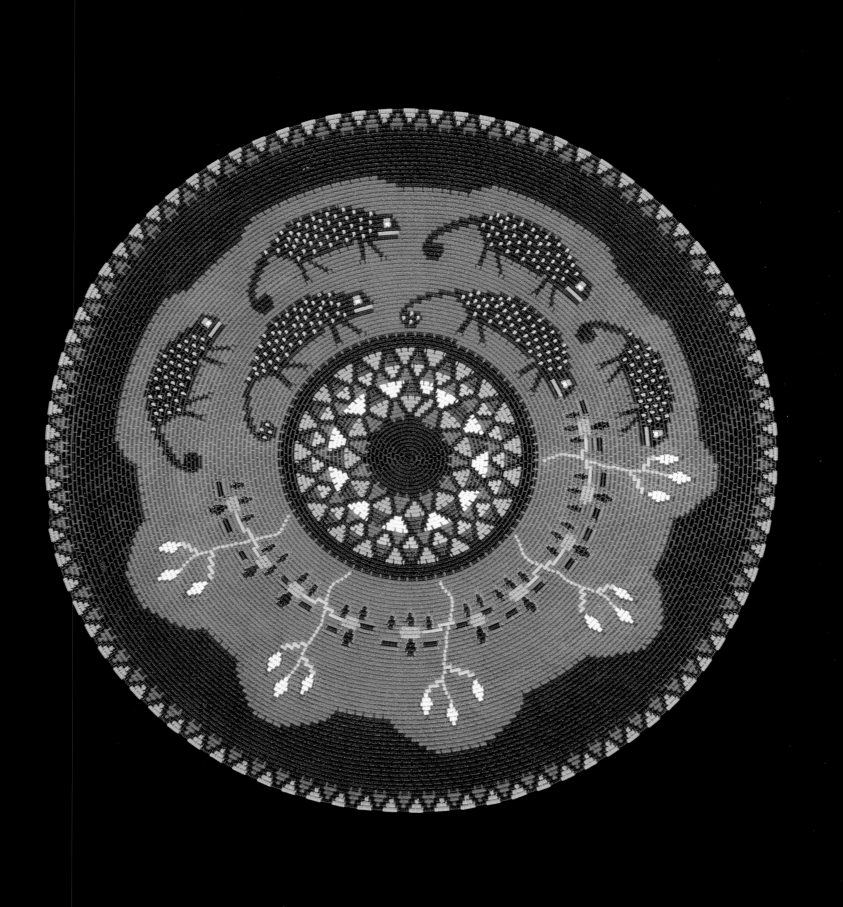

COLLECTIONS 3

The world has become a very small place. The early baskets traveled no further than to local collections in Durban; now the baskets are in collections all over the world. Through the marketing activities of the BAT Shop in Durban, stores in Paris, New York, Los Angeles, and London carry these baskets. International designers discovered in them an easy way to add an African touch to design projects. The Design Museum in London featured the baskets in an exhibit, and periodicals from *Elle Décor* to *Vogue* have included the baskets on covers as well as in their sections on hot trends.

Collectors have found the baskets irresistible, and collecting the wire plates can become addictive. A few collectors have become nothing short of passionate about them, citing, variously, the attraction of the colors, the artists, the designs, and the shapes. Dedicated collectors have found that one or two were simply not enough. What they wanted was to have baskets from all of the best weavers. Some collectors have focused on a specific style, a specific color palette (such as monochromatic or black-and-white baskets), a specific type of design (such the inclusion of figures or animals), a specific cultural motif (such as the AIDS epidemic); others are attracted to the contemporary styles of zenzulu; yet oth-

opposite page:
PRIVATE RESIDENCE
Santa Fe, New Mexico
Plate with copper wire over electrical wire
Artist unknown
Photograph by Peter Vitale

105

ers, and these are in the majority, have broader interests, and decline to limit the scope of their collections.

Telephone-wire baskets have a sophisticated aesthetic, contemporary yet very African, colorful, and distinctive. African art has long been a fundamental complement to contemporary art. The primitivism movement established the link between artifacts from Africa and contemporary art design. The baskets are entirely at home in a contemporary environment. That said, the baskets are not out of place elsewhere. The integration of craft into design can lend a more traditional aesthetic in a funky eclectic design; and these baskets can even become part of a collection of art in a traditional environment.

opposite page:
PRIVATE RESIDENCE
Durban, South Africa
Photograph by Sally Chance

following pages, left and right:
PRIVATE RESIDENCE
Dallas, Texas

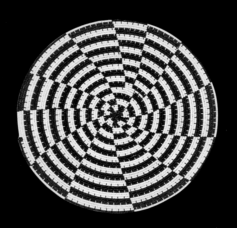

PLATES

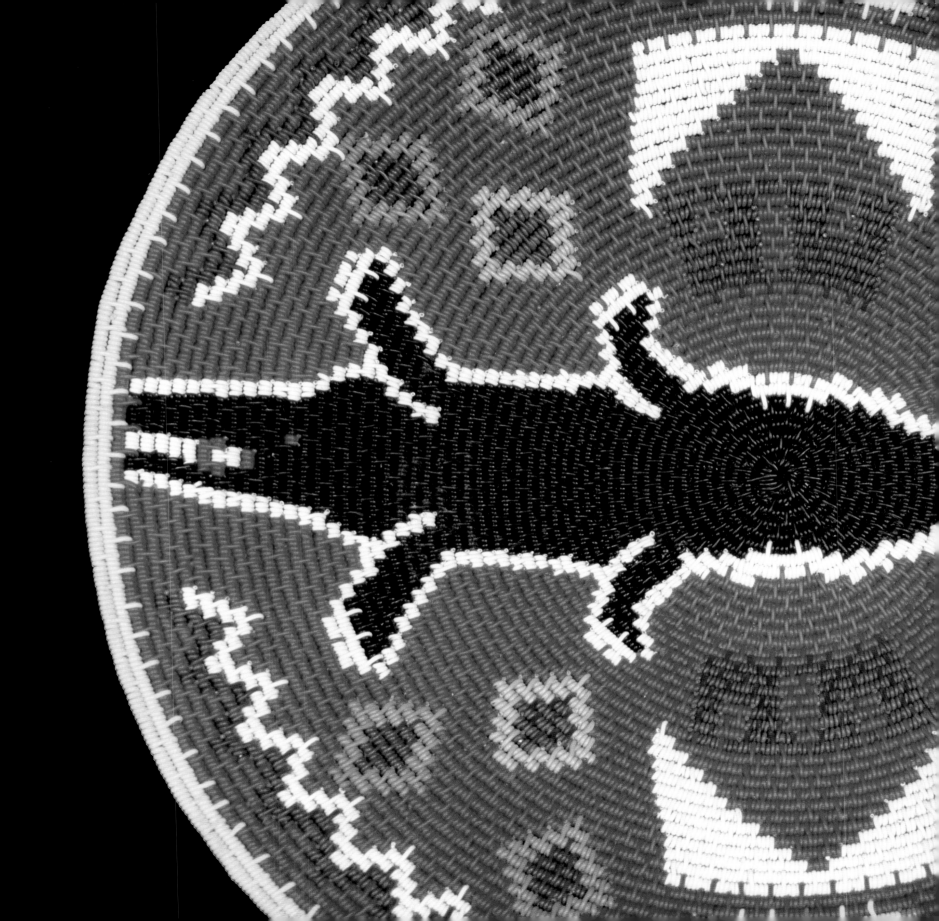

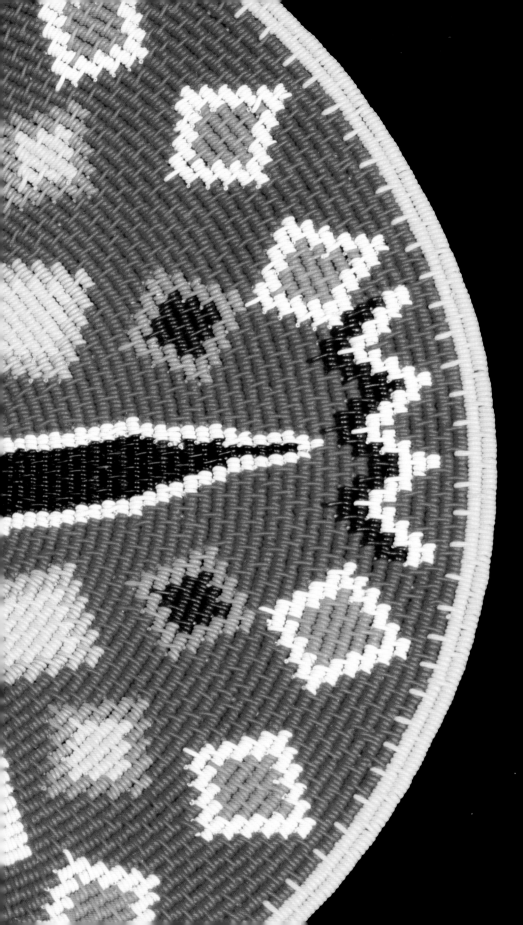

Basket weaving has a long tradition in African cultures. The transformation of available materials into useful objects is an art of utility. The introduction of telephone wire and, later, the availability of a stable supply of material in a wide range of colors, had a profound effect on the Zulu basket weavers. These colors immediately and dramatically opened the possibility of elevating this craft into art. Since the introduction of telephone wire, the colors have inspired many uses. The decoration of everyday objects, such as bottles, and ceremonial pieces, such as dancing sticks, has become more brilliant with the complex patterning that is possible with the colors that are now available.

Traditions and contemporary design fuse. From the traditional to the contemporary, telephone-wire baskets tell us stories and delight us with their complex and diverse pattern and detail. The sources of these contemporary patterns, clearly apparent in the baskets, include Zulu mythology, beadwork patterns, basketry designs, fabric and dress patterns, and houses of all shapes and sizes.

The objects illustrated here present an overview of the history and development of the use of wire. The designs often reflect an immediacy of personal experience, and are thus the stuff of life: people, celebrities, events, sports, nature, urban and rural landscapes, forms of transport, and traditional symbols.

opposite:
CROCODILE PLATE
Busi Ndlovu
280 mm diameter
Collection of David Arment

previous pages, left:
BLACK AND WHITE ABSTRACT PLATE
Joyce Mkhize
298 mm diameter
Private Collection

ZIGZAGS

One of the patterns evident in the earliest telephone-wire baskets is the zigzag. This pattern is also the most prevalent in the coverings on bottles and sticks and, since the 1980s, in the soft-wire bowls made first in the Waayhoek project and later developed into small nests of baskets in various color combinations by the BAT Shop. The zigzag also appears on early telephone-wire *izimbenge* and in the cladding, with telephone wire, of the traditional Zulu basket made from *ilala* palm—this is done to keep the rats out, a functional rather than a decorative application although the end result belies this.

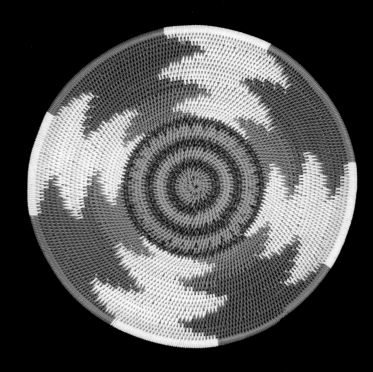

TELEPHONE-WIRE BOWL
Artist unknown
175 x 50 mm
Collection of Marisa Fick-Jordaan

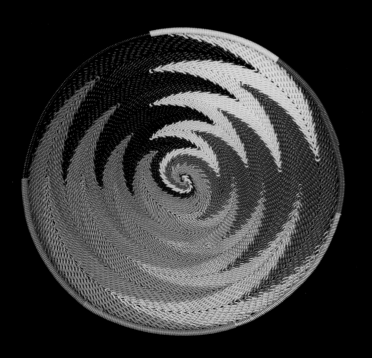

TELEPHONE-WIRE BOWL
Artist unknown
190 x 50 mm
Collection of Marisa Fick-Jordaan

opposite page:
THREE BRIGHT BOWLS
Robert Majola
180, 150, 100 mm diameter
Collection of Marisa Fick-Jordaan

121

TWO TELEPHONE-WIRE BAGS
190 x 120 x 50 mm
Collection of Marisa Fick-Jordaan

GLASS JAR COVERED IN TELEPHONE WIRE
Artist unknown
260 x 160 mm
Collection of Marisa Fick-Jordaan

opposite page:
ZIGZAG BOWL
Sipjo Khuzwop
280 mm diameter
Collection of David Arment

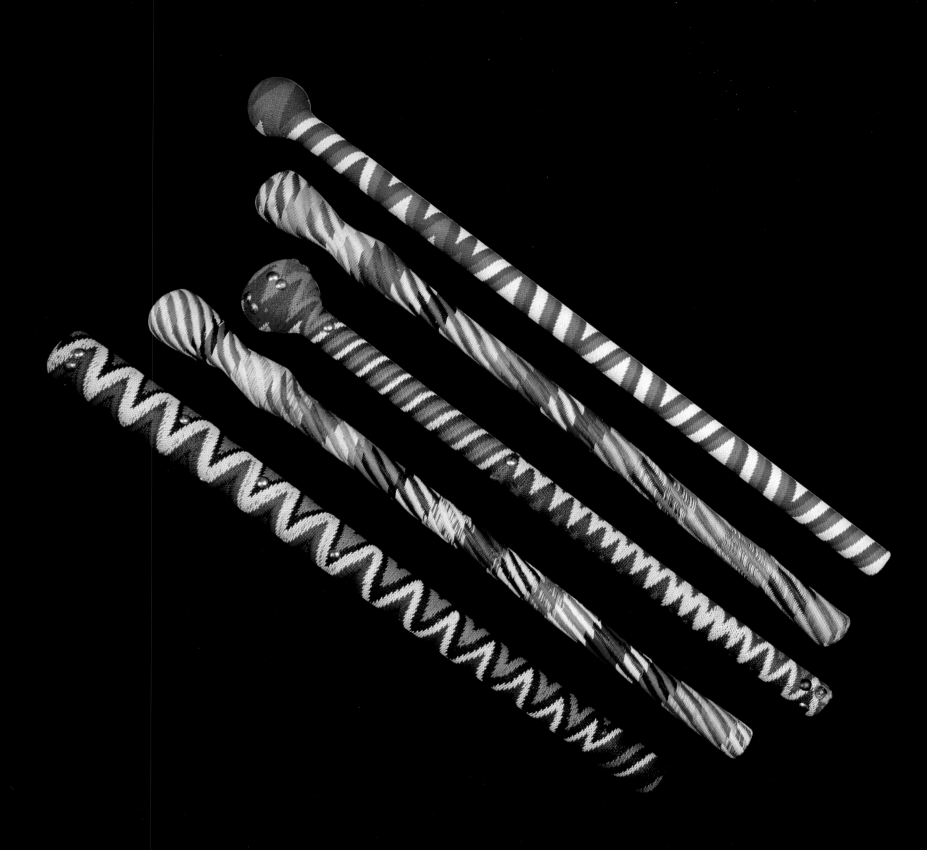

GLASS BOTTLES COVERED IN TELEPHONE WIRE
Artist unknown (left)
Sduduzi Gabela (center and right)
h: 320, 255, 285 mm
Private Collection

previous pages, left:
FIVE WOODEN STICKS COVERED IN TELEPHONE WIRE
Artists unknown, 20th century
top to bottom, h: 570, 530, 510, 530, 530 mm
Collection of David Arment

previous pages, right:
TWO WOODEN STICKS COVERED IN TELEPHONE WIRE WITH METAL STUDS
Artists unknown, 20th Century
h: 530, 510 mm
Collection of David Arment

GLASS BOTTLES COVERED IN TELEPHONE WIRE
Sduduzi Gabela
h: 320, 235 mm
Private Collection

opposite page:
GLASS BOTTLES COVERED IN TELEPHONE WIRE
Artists unknown
h: 265, 180, 460, 215, 265 mm
Private Collection

127

GLASS BOTTLE COVERED IN TELEPHONE WIRE
Artist unknown
h: 320 mm
Private Collection

GLASS BOTTLE COVERED IN TELEPHONE WIRE
Artist unknown
h: 220 mm
Collection of Marisa Fick-Jordaan

opposite page:
TELEPHONE-WIRE COFFEE POT
Alfred Ntuli
220 x 180 mm
Collection of the Phansi Museum, Durban

TELEPHONE-WIRE TEA SERVICE
Artist unknown
Campbell Collections, Durban

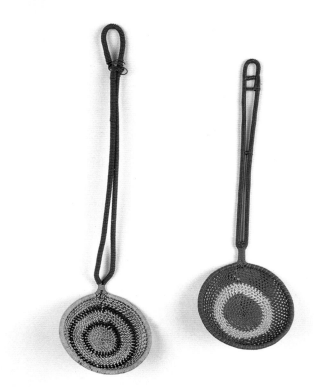

***ISIKHETHO* (BEER STRAINERS)**
Artists unknown
h: 320, 270 mm
Collection of the Phansi Museum, Durban

***ISIKHETHO* (BEER STRAINERS)**
Artists unknown
h: 330, 270, 350 mm
Collection of Marisa Fick-Jordaan

opposite page:
KITCHEN KNIVES WITH TELEPHONE-WIRE-COVERED HANDLES
Amos Khubisa
h: 170, 205, 170, 205, 260 mm
Private Collection

TELEPHONE-WIRE VASE
Alfred Ntuli
178 x 165 mm
Private Collection

TWO LIDDED POTS
Alfred Ntuli
205 x 205 and 190 x 190 mm
Private Collection

opposite page:
ORANGE LIDDED POT
Mr. B. W. Gcaba
152 x 228 mm
Collection of David Arment

TWO BOWLS
Artists unknown
270 x 105 and 220 x 60 mm
Collection of Marisa Fick-Jordaan

TWO PLASTIC SALAD BOWLS COVERED WITH TELEPHONE WIRE
Themba Ndlovu
255 x 210 x 100 and 350 x 210 x 100 mm
Collection of Marianne Fassler

opposite page:
TELEPHONE-WIRE POT AND BOWL
Pot by Siyanaphi Shangase
216 x 228 mm
Bowl by Gideon Nzuza
310 mm
Private Collection

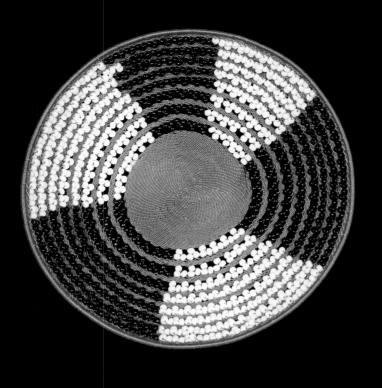

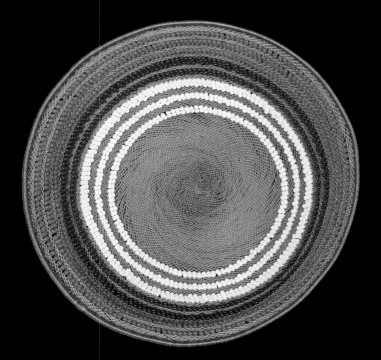
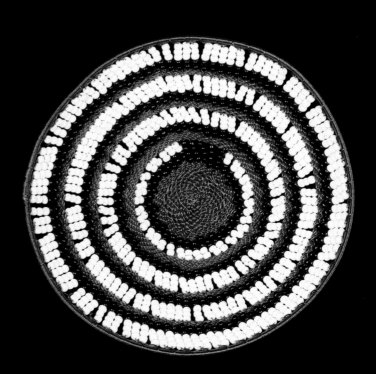

SWIRLS

Another pattern seen in early telephone-wire baskets is the swirl. This pattern is also found in soft-wire bowls, for which the shape is made over a form. Soft-wire baskets started showing up in the 1980s in funky color combinations that were the result of the limited availability of wire.

opposite page:
ZENZULU BOWLS
150, 150, and 190 mm diameter
Private Collection

previous pages, left, clockwise from top left:
COPPER BOWL WITH BLACK AND WHITE BEADS
Artist unknown
197 mm diameter
Private Collection

COPPER BOWL WITH GLASS BEADS
Artist unknown
210 mm diameter
Private Collection

COPPER BOWL WITH BLACK AND WHITE BEADS
Artist unknown
210 mm diameter
Private Collection

COPPER BOWL WITH BLUE AND WHITE GLASS BEADS
Artist unknown
203 mm diameter
Private Collection

previous pages, right:
**ZENZULU LAMPSHADE WITH COPPER-WIRE
AND GLASS-BEADED EGGS**
Artists unknown
380 mm diameter
Private Collection

140

ZENZULU BOWL
190 mm diameter
Private Collection

ZENZULU BOWL
190 mm diameter
Private Collection

opposite page:
THREE BLACK BOWLS WITH A WHITE SWIRL
Artist unknown
152, 195, and 254 mm diameter
Private Collection

opposite page, clockwise from top left:

PURPLE AND GREEN BOWL

Linus Ngube

178 mm

Private Collection

BLACK-AND-WHITE ZIGZAG BOWL

Artist unknown

190 mm

Private Collection

PURPLE AND BLUE BOWL

Linus Ngube

178 mm

Private Collection

BLACK-AND-WHITE ZIGZAG BOWL

Artist unknown

190 mm

Private Collection

following pages, left:

ZENZULU BOWL

190 mm

Private Collection

following pages, right:

STACKED ZENZULU BOWLS

190 mm each

Private Collection

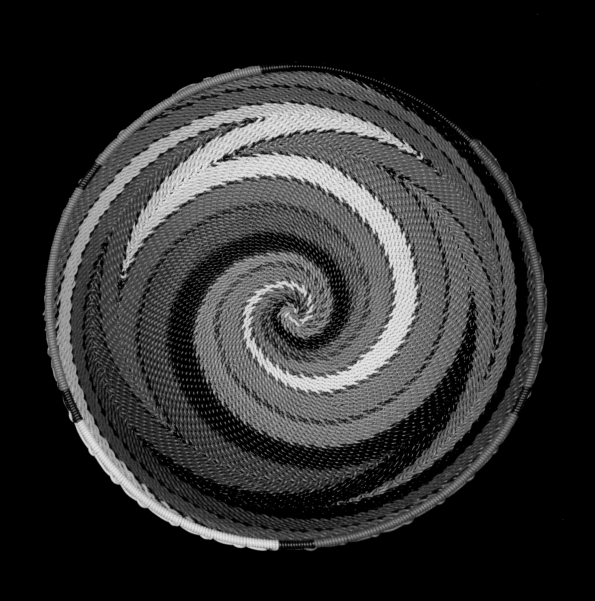

ZULU FLOWERS

What we call the Zulu Flower (*imbali*) is one of the original patterns used in telephone-wire baskets and is based on traditional patterns used for grass and palm *izimbenge*. This simple stylized design—a naïve rendition of a circle with petals radiating from the center—is, however, not confined to Zulu expression, and can be seen in coiled baskets of other regions of the world, including American Indians. The pattern lends itself to the circular form of basketry and appears in endless variations, sometimes quite elaborate. The first exhibitions at the BAT Centre were full of small-scale baskets decorated with variations of this pattern. With the growing confidence of the artists, this floral motif has become increasingly complex, a development that may be seen in a comparison of the earlier work of Bheki Dlamini with the later work of Ntombifuthi Magwasa and Simon Mavundla.

PLATES WITH ZULU FLOWER PATTERN
Various artists and sizes
Collection of Marisa Fick-Jordaan and
The Phansi Museum, Durban

following page left and right:
BLUE ZULU FLOWER PLATE
Artist unknown
250 x 225 mm, Collection of Marisa Fick-Jordaan

ZULU FLOWER PLATE
Artist unknown
250 mm diameter, Collection of Marisa Fick-Jordaan

GREEN ZULU FLOWER PLATE
Artist unknown
255 mm diameter, Collection of Marisa Fick-Jordaan

BOWL WITH ZULU FLOWER PATTERN
Bheki Dlamini
130 mm diameter, Collection of Marisa Fick-Jordaan

ZULU FLOWER ABSTRACTION
Nomthandazo Mtikitiki
406 mm diameter, Collection of David Arment

ZULU FLOWER PLATE
Busisiwe Makhanya
250 mm diameter, Private Collection

PLATE WITH ZULU FLOWER
Nomthandazo Mtikitiki
400 mm diameter, Collection of the Phansi Museum, Durban

ZULU FLOWER PLATE
Busisiwe Makhanya
260 mm diameter, Private Collection

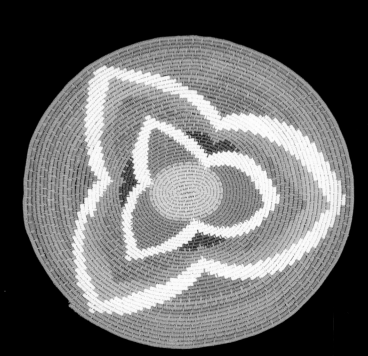

SPORTS

Sports have always been an important part of South African life and, since 1994, national soccer, rugby, and cricket events have brought many South Africans together. In 1995 South Africa hosted and won the Rugby World Cup, and in 1996 hosted and won the Africa Nations Cup for soccer. The excitement of these events inspired a series of baskets celebrating the national teams and events. "Bafana Bafana," the Zulu name for the South African soccer team, appears often on plates. Those baskets were the precursors to a series of rugby and soccer World Cup baskets that have honored the winners of these events, such as Australia and France.

BAFANA BAFANA WITH LOOPED CUT-OUT
Dudu Cele
315 mm diameter
Collection of Marisa Fick-Jordaan

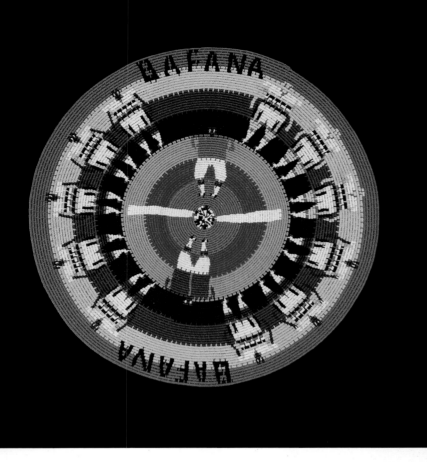

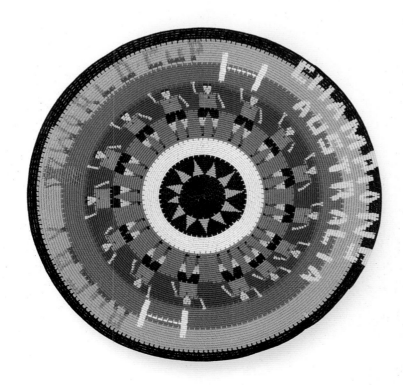
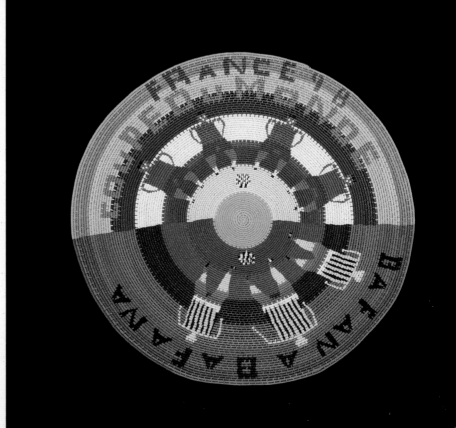

top left:

SPRINGBOK RUGBY W--- CUP

Bheki Dlamini

320 mm diameter

Collection of Marisa Fick-Jordaan

bottom left:

BAFANA BAFANA 1996

Bheki Dlamini

340 mm diameter

Collection of Marisa Fick-Jordaan

opposite page, clockwise from top left:

BAFANA BAFANA

Dudu Celi

394 mm diameter

Private Collection

BAFANA BAFANA WE LOVE YOU

Dudu Celi

370 mm diameter

Collection of David Arment

BAFANA BAFANA FRANCE 98

Bheki Dlamini

400 mm diameter

Collection of Marisa Fick-Jordaan

RUGBY WORLD CUP CHAMPIONS AUSTRALIA

Bheki Dlamini

432 mm diameter

Collection of David Arment

NEW SOUTH AFRICA

The formal end of the apartheid system of government in 1994 resulted in a wave of national pride.
Nelson Mandela and the new flag became important
themes for the telephone-wire artists. The six colors
of the flag, green, red, yellow, blue, white, and black,
became a frequently used color palette for the baskets, and the flag was represented on geometric as
well as on figurative baskets. Slogans such as "Bold
and Beautiful" appeared with the flag, and Nelson
Mandela's trips to Parliament and his wedding to
Graca Machel were honored by the weavers.

opposite page:
ANC AND AFRICAN ART CENTRE OVAL PLATE
Bheki Dlamini
320 x 340 mm
Campbell Collections, Durban

following pages, left:
BOLD AND BEAUTIFUL
Sibusiso Dhlodlo
260 mm diameter
Collection of Marianne Fassler

following pages, right:
THE NEW SOUTH AFRICA
Artist unknown
280 mm diameter
Collection of Marisa Fick-Jordaan

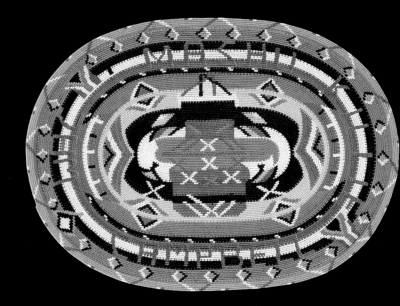

WORDS

Many of the weavers started incorporating script in the early 1990s. The first basket that Elliot Mkhize sold to Paul Mikula included the artist's first name as a mark of his work. Bheki Dlamini and Dudu Cele took up the challenge of adding messages to embellish their baskets. Dudu focused on greeting-card messages; Bheki wove traditional Zulu titles such as Udwendwe Lukakoto (attendants in a traditional Zulu wedding) into his work.

top right:
MERRY CHRISTMAS
Dudu Cele
285 mm diameter
Collection of Marisa Fick-Jordaan

bottom right:
KILLIE CAMPBELL PLATE
Artist unknown
400 x 530 mm
Campbell Collections, Durban

opposite page, clockwise from top left:
HAPPY YEAR 2001
Bheki Dlamini
450 mm diameter
Collection of Marisa Fick-Jordaan

BEWARE OF HIV AIDS
Muriel Ntuli
410 mm diameter
Collection of Marisa Fick-Jordaan

ONE TWO ONE
Aron Ngobo
260 mm diameter
Collection of Marisa Fick-Jordaan

BUS
Bheki Dlamini
360 mm diameter
Collection of the Phansi Museum, Durban

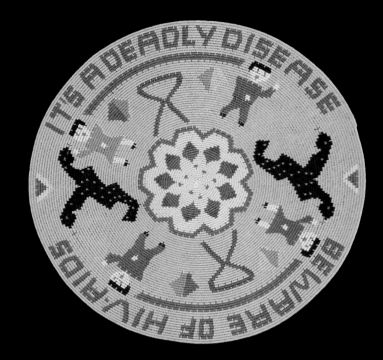

AIDS

AIDS has had a devastating effect on South Africa and particularly on the region of KwaZulu-Natal, which has the highest infection rate. In 2001 Durban hosted the thirteenth International AIDS Conference and, in support of this world event, the weavers created a whole series of AIDS baskets that were displayed at the Durban Art Gallery during the conference. Some of the most talented weavers, including Dudu Cele, have been lost to this pandemic.

opposite page:

AIDS IS THE NUMBER ONE KILLER IN OUR PROVINCE
Mboniseni Khanyile
395 mm diameter
Private Collection

FRILLY EDGES

The use of coiled wire as an edge or decorative detail was first introduced by Dudu Cele and later a more complex application of this innovation was developed by Rosalie Khanyile.

MOTOR CAR
Dudu Cele
270 mm diameter
Collection of Marisa Fick-Jordaan

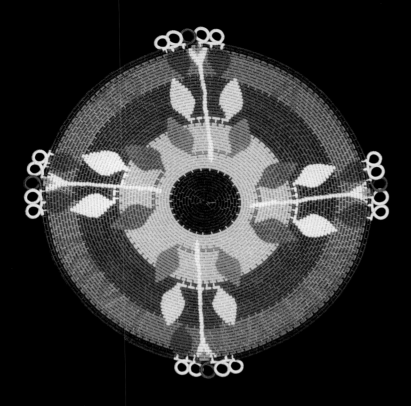

TO A SPECIAL LADY
Dudu Cele
280 mm diameter
Collection of Marisa Fick-Jordaan

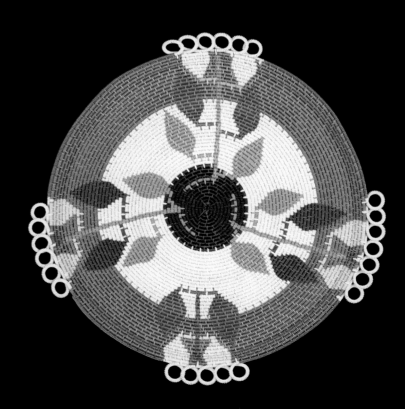

LOOPED FLOWERS
Dudu Cele
240 mm diameter
Collection of Marisa Fick-Jordaan

166

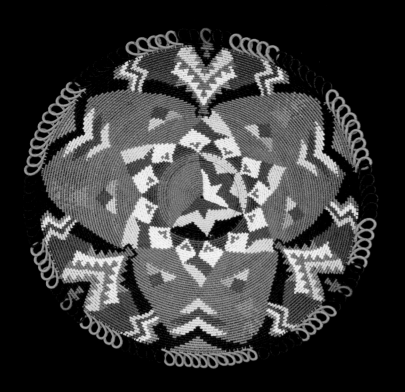

PLATE WITH A LOOPED EDGE
Artist unknown
355 mm diameter
Collection of Trisha Wilson

PLATE WITH A FANCY EDGE
Rosalie Khanyile
310 mm diameter
Collection of the Phansi Museum, Durban

ARCHITECTURE

The incorporation of traditional Zulu huts and modern *rondavels* (a traditional round African house) started early on. Over time, details including doors and windows were added and images of larger structures such as the Parliament buildings and high rises are depicted; see, for example, the work of Bheki Dlamini and Dudu Cele. A commission from the Cape Town Tourism Association introduced Cape Dutch architecture. In his more recent large-scale works, Vincent Sithole clusters rows of huts to create the image of a traditional rural family settlement. Although most of the weavers have built their own urban homes in a square form, they continue to reference the more traditional *rondavel*, often playfully contrasting the colors of the walls and roofs.

opposite page:
PLATE WITH HOUSE, JET, AND COW
Artist unknown
285 mm diameter
Collection of the Phansi Museum, Durban

following pages, left:
CAPE DUTCH HOUSES
Zithobile Khambule
292 mm diameter
Private Collection

following pages, right, clockwise from top left:
OVAL PLATE WITH HOUSES
Elliot Mkhize
390 x 320 mm
Private Collection

SWIRLED PLATE WITH HUTS
Octavia Gwala
440 mm diameter
Collection of Marianne Fassler

PLATE WITH FOUR HUTS
Nomthandazo Mtikitiki
286 mm diameter
Private Collection

TURQUOISE HOUSES
Sylvia Mhlamvu
290 mm diameter
Private Collection

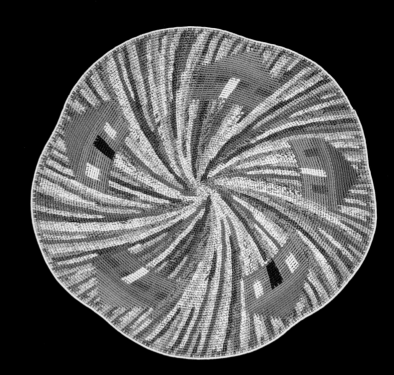

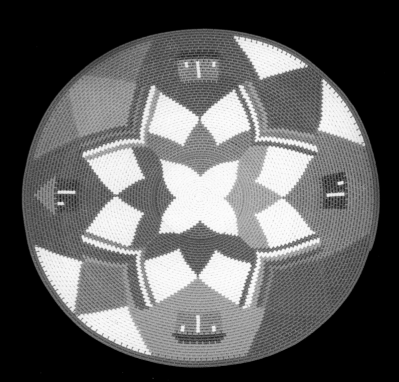

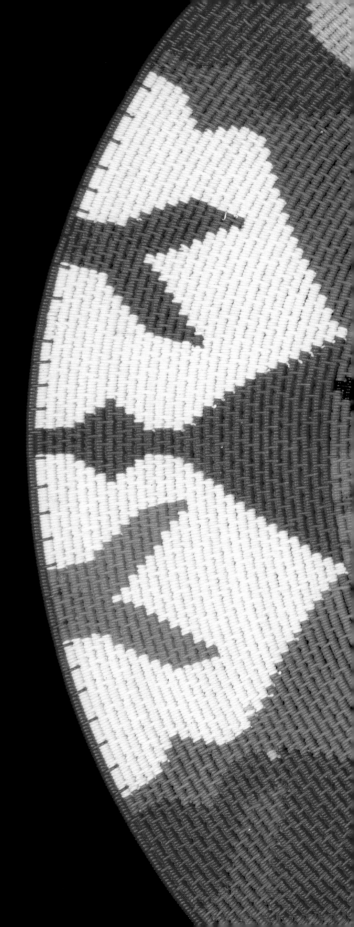

ABSTRACTIONS

Geometric patterns, initially inspired by Zulu beadwork, particularly the complex patterns from the Nongoma district and those of Zulu earplugs from Msinga, have become more complex and more abstract as a result of suggestions and examples from other sources. The annual BAT calendars celebrating traditional Zulu artifacts became a major source of inspiration. Exhibitions showcasing the best examples of traditional Zulu material culture from private collections encouraged a renewed pride in local design. When the colors were available, traditional combinations were used, but later weavers began to experiment with a wider color palette as new colors were developed. With the emphasis placed on the development of individuality, increasingly sophisticated and intricate abstract geometric designs have emerged and the weavers are pushing the boundaries of traditional Zulu patterning.

GEOMETRIC PLATE
Nomthandazo Mtikitiki
370 mm diameter
Private Collection

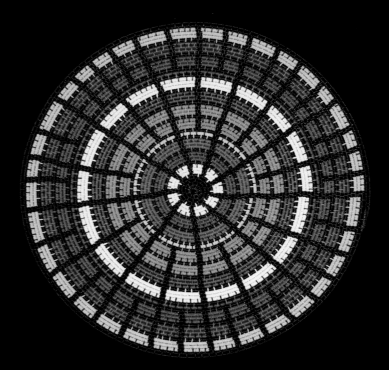

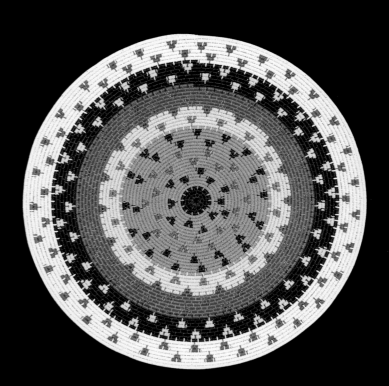

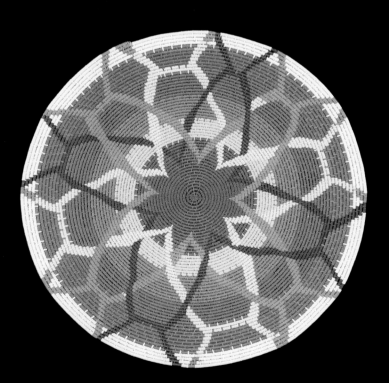

opposite page:

ABSTRACT PLATE
Khethayiphi Ndwandwe
273 mm diameter
Private Collection

previous pages, left, clockwise from top left:

ABSTRACT PLATE
Simon Mavundla
338 mm diameter
Private Collection

ABSTRACT PLATE
Joyce Mkhize
310 mm diameter
Private Collection

ABSTRACT PLATE
Joyce Mkhize
320 mm diameter
Private Collection

ABSTRACT PLATE
Joyce Mkhize
300 mm diameter
Collection of Margaret Daniel

previous pages, right, clockwise from top left:

ABSTRACT PLATE
Artist unknown
337 mm diameter
Private Collection

ABSTRACT PLATE
Nomthandazo Mtikitiki
335 mm diameter
Collection of Marisa Fick-Jordaan

STAINED-GLASS PATTERN
Vincent Sithole
318 mm diameter
Private Collection

ABSTRACT PLATE
Artist unknown
270 mm diameter
Collection of the Phansi Museum, Durban

NATURE

Initially the weavers did not incorporate even common African wild animals; instead, they referenced domestic animals. And these, like the early human figures, were very simple, two-dimensional forms. Suggestions and examples persuaded the weavers to consider wild animals as possible elements of design; images of crocodiles and snakes, leopards, insects, rhinos, and so on have become used much more frequently. Many of the weavers now also incorporate a variety of plants, from commonly seen wild plants to wildly imaginative, multicolored trees.

PLATE WITH GROUND HORNBILLS
Dudu Celi
280 mm diameter
Collection of the Phansi Museum, Durban

BLACK-AND-WHITE BOWL WITH FIGURES
Alice Gcaba
120 x 380 mm
Collection of David Arment

PLATE WITH TURTLE
Solomon Nzimande
350 mm diameter
Private Collection

opposite page:
TURQUOISE PLATE WITH FIGURES
Florence Maquvana
457 mm diameter
Collection of David Arment

PLATE WITH TREES WITH YELLOW FLOWERS
Khethayiphi Ndwandwe
292 mm diameter
Private Collection

CHAMELEON PLATE
Vincent Sithole
337 mm diameter
Private Collection

opposite page:
CHAMELEONS, BUGS, AND FLOWERS
Vincent Sithole
540 mm diameter
Collection of Margaret Daniel

BLACK AND WHITE

The weavers' inherent love of bright colors made them, initially, unreceptive to the possibility of producing monochromatic or even black-and-white baskets. The late Doris Mkhize and Bheki Dlamini were the first weavers to be persuaded, Doris creating a refreshing feather-and-arrow design radiating from a bold red dot in the center; Bheki creating a dramatic dartboard design. Then Ntombifuthi Magwasa began playing with positive and negative patterns. Soon a repertoire of designs emerged that have become classics. Repetitions of popular designs became the first attempts at mass production and the results have led to a substantial business from international craft-marketing enterprises.

opposite page:

**GLASS BOTTLES COVERED IN
BLACK AND WHITE TELEPHONE WIRE**
Artists unknown
h: 305, 195, 315 mm
Private Collection

BLACK-AND-WHITE PLATE WITH HUTS
Sandile Nzimande
300 mm diameter
Private Collection

BLACK-AND-WHITE PLATE WITH HUTS
Sandile Nzimande
300 mm diameter
Private Collection

opposite page:
BLACK-AND-WHITE PLATE
Nombuso Nkwanyana
286 mm diameter
Private Collection

top left:
BLACK-AND-WHITE PLATE
Vusi Khanyile
273 mm diameter
Private Collection

bottom left:
BLACK-AND-WHITE PLATE
Phumelele Dumakude
318 mm diameter
Private Collection

opposite page, clockwise from top left:
BLACK-AND-WHITE PLATE
Artist unknown
215 mm diameter
Collection of Marisa Fick-Jordaan

BLACK-AND-WHITE PLATE
Khangi Mngadi
286 mm diameter
Private Collection

BLACK-AND-WHITE PLATE
Ntombifuthi Magwasa
250 mm diameter
Collection of Marisa Fick-Jordaan

BLACK-AND-WHITE PLATE
Sandile Nzimande
337 mm diameter
Private Collection

ZENZULU

A commercial range of contemporary baskets, developed under the design direction of Marisa Fick-Jordaan, made by the weavers of Siyanda, and marketed under the trademarked name of zenzulu, is a fusion of contemporary design and the traditions of Zulu basket weaving. The range is being successfully marketed internationally, resulting in employment and development opportunities for the local community.

opposite page, clockwise from top left:

RED ZENZULU LAMPSHADE BOWL

380 mm diameter

Private Collection

BLACK ZENZULU LAMPSHADE BOWL

380 mm diameter

Private Collection

RED WITH BLACK DOT ZENZULU LAMPSHADE BOWL

380 mm diameter

Private Collection

BLACK WITH RED DOT ZENZULU LAMPSHADE BOWL

380 mm diameter

Private Collection

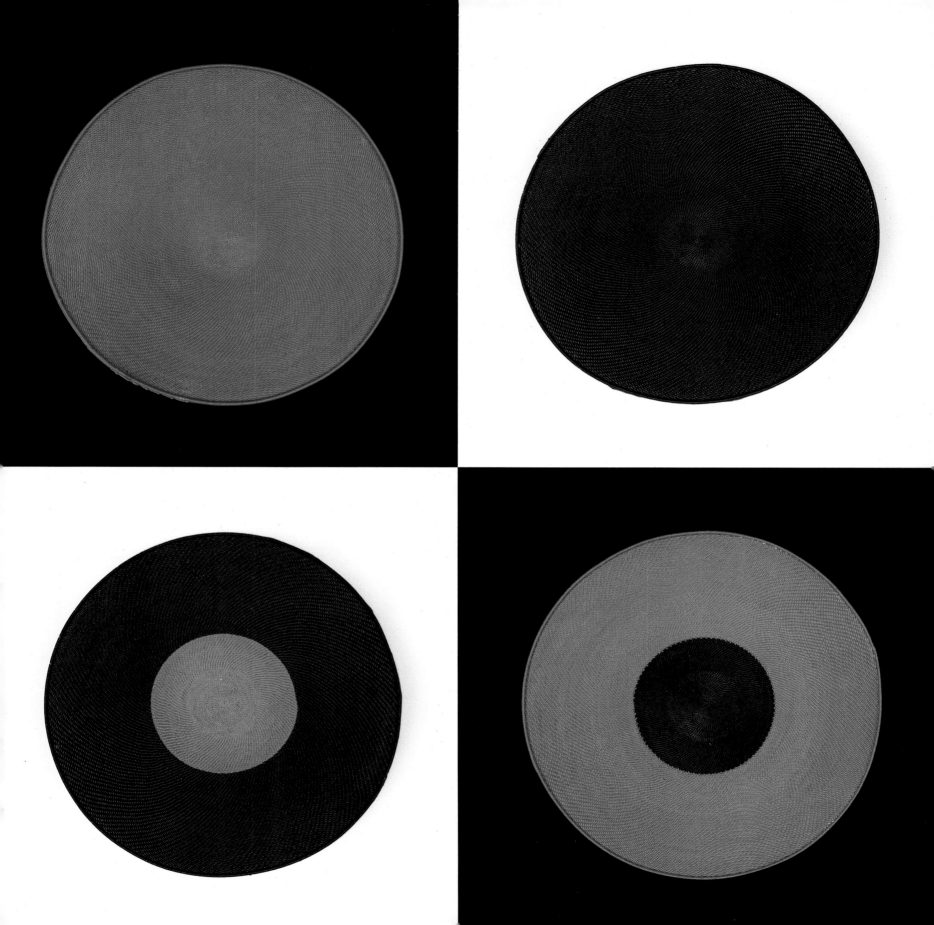

AQUA SWIRL ZENZULU LAMPSHADE BOWL
380 mm diameter
Private Collection

TANGERINE-AND-PINK ZENZULU LAMPSHADE BOWL
380 mm diameter
Private Collection

opposite page:
LARGE BLACK-AND-RED VESSEL
Jaheni Mkhize
275 x 350 mm
Private Collection

BLACK ZENZULU LAMPSHADE BOWL WITH
THREE TELEPHONE-WIRE-COVERED OSTRICH EGGS
Bowl 380 mm diameter, Eggs 140 x 180 mm
Private Collection

FIVE LIME GREEN BOWLS WITH COPPER SWIRL, ZENZULU
265, 222, 190, 152, 106 mm diameter
Private Collection

opposite page:
THREE SPICE ZENZULU BOWLS
200 x 180, 280 x 260, and 280 x 260 mm
Private Collection

194

LIME ZENZULU LAMPSHADE BOWL
380 mm diameter
Private Collection

BLACK-AND-WHITE ZENZULU BOWL
300 mm diameter
Private Collection

opposite page:
FOUR POLKA-DOT BOWLS, ZENZULU
180 x 160 mm
Private Collection

UNDER PLATES

Once weavers mastered the ability to reproduce designs to a standard size, a flat tray with a rim was presented to the interior designer Boyd Ferguson, in the hope that he might find a use for it in the innovative Singita Lodge in the Sabi Sand Reserve, adjacent to the Kruger National Park in South Africa, that he was working on. Ferguson seized on the tray immediately and, since then, trays with different designs and colors have been developed for other lodges he has worked on. Because the guests kept asking for them, these under plates are also offered for sale in the boutiques attached to each lodge. They now grace tables around the world and ensure a steady income for a core of weavers.

opposite page, clockwise from top left:

ZENZULU UNDER PLATE

designed for the Lebombo Lodge
320 mm diameter
Private Collection

ZENZULU UNDER PLATE

designed for the Ebony Lodge
320 mm diameter
Private Collection

ZENZULU UNDER PLATE

designed for the Tsweni Lodge
320 mm diameter
Private Collection

ZENZULU UNDER PLATE

designed for the Boulders Lodge
320 mm diameter
Private Collection

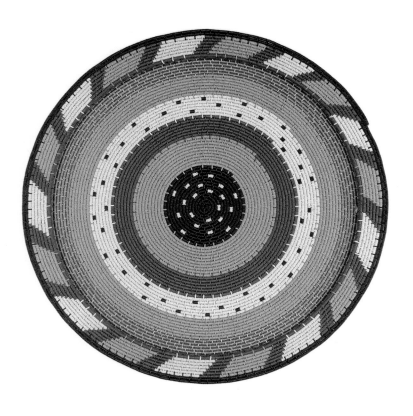

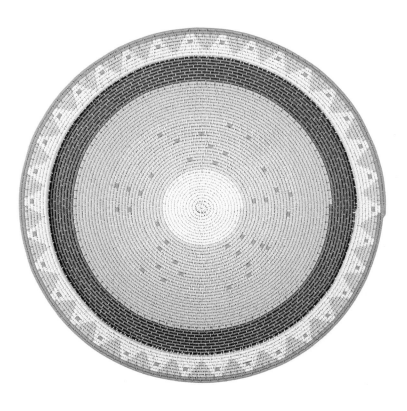

TELEPHONE-WIRE BOWL WITH PORCUPINE QUILLS AND BEADS
Artist unknown
130 x 330 mm
Collection of David Arment

CERAMIC BOWL COVERED WITH TELEPHONE WIRE
Joseph Msomi (wire) and Kim Sacks (ceramic)
100 x 140 mm
Private Collection

ZENZULU FLUTED-RIM BOWL
292 mm diameter
Private Collection

COPPER WITH GLASS BEADS
Artist unknown
216 mm diameter
Private Collection

DIROZULU

The collaboration between the BAT Shop weavers and Hervé Di Rosa on mandalas for the Dirozulu project had a profound influence on the weavers' own work. The technical challenges presented by Di Rosa's figurative designs and their large scale presented some difficulties at first, but the weavers managed to overcome them. Vincent Sithole, in particular, has continued to use this flat format and has applied what he learned from Di Rosa into his own designs.

opposite page:
EVOLUTION
1999
Design by Hervé Di Rosa
Woven by Vincent Sithole
800 mm diameter
Private Collection
Photograph by Pierre Schwatrz

GLOSSARY

ABAFUNDUKI: foreigners (Zulu)

ABAFUNDISI: teachers (Zulu)

ABALUNGU: white people (Zulu)

AMADLOZI: ancestors; ancestral spirits (Zulu)

AMASUMPA: a traditional decorative pattern used on Zulu clay pots

AMATHWASA: a trainee who is learning to become a traditional healer *(sangoma)*

BAFANA BAFANA: the Zulu name for the South African national soccer team

BAT: the Bartel Arts Trust, which funded the BAT Centre in Durban

BAT CENTRE: an arts-development center established by Bartel Arts Trust and located in Durban

BAT SHOP: an art and craft development and marketing enterprise located at the BAT Centre

CETSHWAYO: the monarch and ruler of the Zulu nation, who succeeded Shaka in the nineteenth century

DURBAN STATION: the original railway station in central Durban

FNB VITA CRAFT NOW: biannual craft awards sponsored by First National Bank

HARD-WIRE WEAVING: a coiled technique of weaving baskets, where telephone wire is coiled over a thicker base wire, typically made of aluminum

HLABISA: a rural district in northern KwaZulu-Natal

IGOLI: the city of Johannesburg, the largest in South Africa, a reflection of its gold production

ILALA PALM: an indigenous palm that grows mainly along the east coast of southern Africa and is traditionally used by the Zulu for weaving baskets

IMBALI: flower (Zulu)

IMBENGE (singular), **IZIMBENGE** (plural): a traditional Zulu beer-pot lid, the form that is the basis of contemporary Zulu telephone-wire plates and baskets

ISISHUNKA: an early Zulu beadwork pattern from the Msinga area

ISITHEMBU: an early Zulu beadwork pattern that came after the *isishunka*

ISANDLWANA: a famous battlefield; the site of a Zulu victory in 1879, during the Anglo-Zulu War

JAHA: to be in a hurry (Zulu)

JABULISA: a traveling exhibition of the art of KwaZulu-Natal, 1996, and a Zulu word for "to please"

KAISER CHIEFS: a well-known soccer team based in Johannesburg

KIST: a wooden storage chest

KNOBKERRIES: sticks used as weapons

KWAMASHU: a suburb of Durban, South Africa

KWAZULU-NATAL: a province of South Africa

LOBOLA: the traditional price for a bride in Zulu culture

MASIBAMBANE TRUST: a foundation established in 1994 by South African Breweries and Cosatu Affiliated Trade Unions to support economic development projects

NDEBELE: a northern Nguni tribe located in South Africa, the Ndebele people are well known for their artistic talent, especially with regard to their painted houses and colorful beadwork

NGUNI: a language group within southern Africa, the Nguni peoples are classified into three large subgroups: the Northern Nguni, the Southern Nguni, and the Ndebele, with the Zulu and the Swazi among the Northern Nguni

NONGOMA: a rural district in northern KwaZulu-Natal

PHALAFINI: a traditional Zulu beadwork pattern that came after the *umzansi*

PORTNET: the National Port Authority in South Africa

RONDAVEL: a traditional African house, a round structure with stone or mud walls covered by a thatched roof

SCOOBIE WIRE: colloquialism for PVC-coated copper telephone wire

SHAKA: a prominent nineteenth-century Zulu monarch

SIYANDA: an unincorporated settlement located outside Durban

SOFT-WIRE WEAVING: a technique of weaving, typically used for making bowls, without a base wire—instead the telephone wire is woven over a form, which is removed after the basket is completed

TOG WORKER: a casual laborer

TAXIS: privately run minibuses used as public transport in South Africa

UDWENDWE LUKAKOTO: attendants in a traditional Zulu wedding

UKHAMBA (singular); **IZINKHAMBA** (plural): traditional Zulu clay beer pot

UMTHAKATHI: to cast a bad spell or to bewitch

UMSAMO: a special place in the home set aside for conversation with the ancestors (domestic altar)

UMVOTI: a district of KwaZulu-Natal

UMZANSI: a traditional Zulu beadwork pattern that came after the *isithembu*

USUNGULU: a long needle used in Zulu basketry

WAAYHOEK: a resettlement community near Ladysmith developed for rural people who had been forcibly moved, by the apartheid regime, from areas designated for the exclusive use of whites, the Waayhoek project was one of the initial programs to build a commercial telephone wire basket market

opposite page:

DETAILS OF TRADITIONAL WEAVING TECHNIQUES
1. Typical basket construction, grass bundle spiral & *ilala* palm as binding
2. Detail of cable showing outer sheath and encased telephone wires
3. Plan of beginning of spiral, constructed with grass and palm
4. Grass spiral with telephone wire binding
5. Pattern making with grass and *ilala* palm using extended & dyed binding
6. Detail of spiral binding, showing how color stops and starts
7. Plan of beginning of spiral, constructed with galvanized wire and telephone wire
8. Galvanized wire spiral with telephone-wire binding
9. Detail of plaiting showing diagonal patterns generated by colored wires

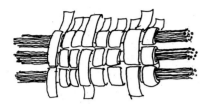

1

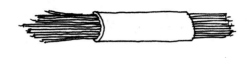

2

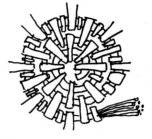

3

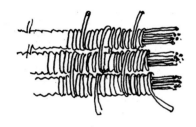

4

5

6

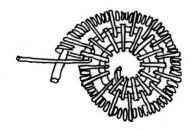

7

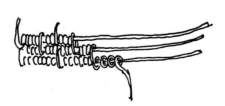

8

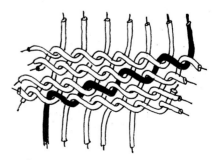

9

COLLECTORS

Phil Aarons
Africa Fair, Tenafly, New Jersey
Aid to Artisans, Hartford, Connecticut
Miss. Preston Arment & Mr. Jackson Arment
Ryan Arment
Carol Arment
Debra Arment
Terry Arment
Duane & Jean Arment
Snow Blackerby
Jean & John Berndt
Connie Campbell
Christmas at the Zoo, Portland, Oregon
Melanie & Leonard Cohen
Pat K. Culler
Tom & Pat DeGeorge
Marianne Fassler
Paul & Leo Fick
Marion, Angus, Duncan, & Megan Frew
John Fincher
Kim Sanders George
Harry Greiner
Susie Hart
Charlotte Hayes
David & Hope Jeffrey
Jill H. Kassis
Mr. & Mrs. Rich Kruszka
Roland Lee
Tryphina Malekoa
Marbry Purchasing International, Inc., Houston, Texas
Gayle Maxon
Steve Orr
Solveig Piper & Robert Hope
Nancy Reynolds
Jacqueline Reichert
Janet & Jerry Reichert
Jennifer & Jonathan Rimelspach
Pamela Robinson
Rock Resorts, Denver, Colorado
Caryn Smith
Val Taylor
Will Taylor
Kevin Twedt
Peter Vitale

opposite page:
BLACK-AND-WHITE BASKETS
Various artists
Private Collection

UNITED STATES

Casa Nova by Natalie
530 South Guadalupe Street
Santa Fe, NM 87501
Tel 505 983-8558 Fax 505 983-9670
casanova1@attglobal.net

Out of Africa Experience
47940 Via Opera
La Quinta, CA 92253
Tel 949 929 9399/949 929 9029
mail@africanriches.com

Africa & Beyond
1250 Prospect Street
La Jolla, CA 92037
Tel 858 454 9983
africaandbeyond@aol.com

UNITED KINGDOM

Witty Fish, Ltd.
4 Lyndhurst Square
London, England SE 15 5 AR
Tel/Fax 020 7701 9336
ameliathorpe@wittyfish.co.uk

NAMIBIA

Art Africa
10 Tobias Hainyeko Street
Swakopmund
Tel/Fax 264 64 404024 Mobile 081 127 0931
burns@namibnet.com

SOUTH AFRICA

African Art Centre
1st Floor Tourist Junction
160 Pine Street, Durban 4001
Tel 27 31 304 7915
anthea@afri-art.co.za

African Image
Corner Church and Burg Street
Cape Town 8001
Tel 27 21 423 8385 Fax 27 21 422 1575
contact@african-image.co.za

Africa Nova
Cape Quarter
72 Waterkant Street
Greenpoint, Cape Town
Tel 27 21 425 5123 Fax 021 789 1196
canova@iafrica.com

Art Africa
62 Tyrone Avenue
Parkview, Johannesburg
Tel 27 11 4863193 Fax 27 11 486 2052
artafrica@yebo.co.za

Art Africa
Lighthouse Mall, Chartwell Drive
Umhlanga Rocks
Tel/Fax 27 31 5611515
artafrica@yebo.co.za

African Attitude
Knysna Quays
Waterfront Drive, Knysna
Tel/Fax 27 44 382 1650
artafrica@yebo.co.za

BAT Shop
45 Maritime Place
Small Craft Harbour, Durban, 4001
Tel 27 31 3329951 Fax 27 31 3685062
batcraft@mweb.co.za

Delagoa African Arts & Crafts
delagoa@iafrica.com

4 locations:
Shop 002, Clock Tower
V & A Waterfront, Cape Town
Tel 27 21 425 3787 Fax 27 21 448 9689

Pretorius Street & Eastwood Street
Arcadia, Pretoria / Tshwane
Tel 27 12 342 8752 Fax 27 12 430 3945

Main Street & Louis Trichardt Street
Graskop, Mpumalanga
Tel 27 13 767 1081 Fax 27 13 767 1348

Hugenote Street & Gunning Street
Dullstroom, Mpumalanga
Tel 27 13 254 0672 Fax 27 13 254 0672

Heartworks
98 Kloof Street, Cape Town
Tel 27 21 424 8419 Fax 27 21465 3289
woermann@iafrica.com

Kim Sacks Gallery
153 Jan Smuts Avenue,
Parkwood, Johannesburg
Tel 27 11 447 5804 Fax 27 11 726 6420
Mobile 27 83 377 9076
kim@kimsacksgallery.com

Piece
Shop 82 The Firs
Cradock Avenue, Rosebank, Johannesburg
Mobile 27 083 400 5126
info@piece.co.za

Singita Trading Stores
Singita Private Game Reserve
Sabi Sands, Mpumalanga
Tel 27 13 7355 456 Fax 27 13 7355 746
Mobile 27 083 657 1554
atstore@mweb.co.za

opposite page:
TWO STRIPED SOFT-WIRE BOWLS
Artist unknown
100 x 155 and 95 x 130 mm
Private Collection

Published in the United States by S/C Editions
Distributed in the US & Europe by the Museum of New Mexico Press
Distributed in South Africa by David Krut Publishing

S/C Editions
1012 Marquez Place, #106A, Santa Fe, NM 87501
(505) 983-3121
Founding publishers: David Skolkin and David Chickey

Museum of New Mexico Press
725 Camino Lejo, Santa Fe, New Mexico 87505
(505) 476-1155   www.museumofnewmexico.org

David Krut Publishing
140 Jan Smuts Avenue, Parkwood, 2193 Johannesburg
Tel (011) 880-4242 Email: info@davidkrutpublishing.com

Design: David Chickey / Skolkin+Chickey
Editor: Frances Bowles
Proofreader: Laura Addison
Editorial Assistance: Donald Woodburn
Color separations: Wes Pittman
Printed and bound by SNP International, China

Library of Congress Cataloging-in-Publication Data available
from the publisher upon request.

frontispiece:
Zulu flower plate
Artist unknown
250 mm diameter
Collection of Marisa Fick-Jordaan